TURKISH GERMAN CINEMA IN THE NEW MILLENNIUM

Film Europa: German Cinema in an International Context
Series Editors: **Hans-Michael Bock** (CineGraph Hamburg); **Tim Bergfelder** (University of Southampton); **Sabine Hake** (University of Texas, Austin)

German cinema is normally seen as a distinct form, but this series emphasizes connections, influences, and exchanges of German cinema across national borders, as well as its links with other media and art forms. Individual titles present traditional historical research (archival work, industry studies) as well as new critical approaches in film and media studies (theories of the transnational), with a special emphasis on the continuities associated with popular traditions and local perspectives.

The Concise Cinegraph: An Encyclopedia of German Cinema
General Editor: Hans-Michael Bock
Associate Editor: Tim Bergfelder

International Adventures: German Popular Cinema and European Co-Productions in the 1960s
Tim Bergfelder

Between Two Worlds: The Jewish Presence in German and Austrian Film, 1910–1933
S.S. Prawer

Framing the Fifties: Cinema in a Divided Germany
Edited by John Davidson and Sabine Hake

A Foreign Affair: Billy Wilder's American Films
Gerd Gemünden

Destination London: German-speaking Emigrés and British Cinema, 1925–1950
Edited by Tim Bergfelder and Christian Cargnelli

Michael Haneke's Cinema: The Ethic of the Image
Catherine Wheatley

Willing Seduction: *The Blue Angel*, Marlene Dietrich, and Mass Culture
Barbara Kosta

Dismantling the Dream Factory: Gender, German Cinema, and the Postwar Quest for a New Film Language
Hester Baer

Belá Balázs: Early Film Theory.*Visible Man* and *The Spirit of Film*
Belá Balázs, edited by Erica Carter, translated by Rodney Livingstone

Screening the East: Heimat, Memory and Nostalgia in German Film since 1989
Nick Hodgin

Peter Lorre: Face Maker Stardom and Performance between Hollywood and Europe
Sarah Thomas

Turkish German Cinema in the New Millennium: Sites, Sounds, and Screens
Edited by Sabine Hake and Barbara Mennel

Postwall German Cinema: History, Film History and Cinephilia
Mattias Frey

Homemade Men in Postwar Austrian Cinema: Nationhood, Genre and Masculinity
Maria Fritsche

The Emergence of Film Culture: Knowledge Production, Institution Building, and the Fate of the Avant-Garde in Europe, 1919–1945
Malte Hagener

Turkish German Cinema in the New Millennium

Sites, Sounds, and Screens

Edited by

Sabine Hake and Barbara Mennel

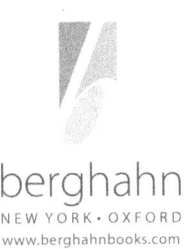

berghahn
NEW YORK · OXFORD
www.berghahnbooks.com

First edition published in 2012 by
Berghahn Books
www.berghahnbooks.com
©2012, 2014 Sabine Hake and Barbara Mennel
First paperback edition published in 2014

All rights reserved. Except for the quotation of short passages for the purposes of criticism and review, no part of this book may be reproduced in any form or by any means, electronic or mechanical, including photocopying, recording, or any information storage and retrieval system now known or to be invented, without written permission of the publisher.

Library of Congress Cataloging-in-Publication Data

Turkish German cinema in the new millennium : sites, sounds, and screens / edited by Sabine Hake and Barbara Mennel. -- 1st ed.
   p. cm. -- (Film Europa: German cinema in an international context ; 13)
Includes bibliographical references and index.
ISBN 978-0-85745-768-4 (hardback : alk. paper) -- ISBN 978-1-78238-665-0 (paperback : alk. paper) – ISBN 978-0-85745-769-1 (ebook)
  1. Motion pictures--Germany--History--21st century. 2. Motion pictures, Turkish--Germany--History--21st century. 3. Foreign language films--Germany--History--21st century. 4. Stereotypes (Social psychology) in motion pictures. 5. Culture in motion pictures. 6. Motion pictures and transnationalism. 7. Motion picture audiences--Germany. I. Hake, Sabine, 1956- II. Mennel, Barbara Caroline.
PN1993.5.G3T86 2012
791.43094309'05--dc23
                                              2012024973

British Library Cataloguing in Publication Data
A catalogue record for this book is available from the British Library

ISBN 978-0-85745-768-4 hardback
ISBN 978-1-78238-665-0 paperback
ISBN 978-0-85745-769-1 ebook

Contents

List of Illustrations   vii

Introduction   1

I. CONFIGURATIONS OF STEREOTYPES AND IDENTITIES: NEW METHODOLOGIES

1. My Big Fat Turkish Wedding: From Culture Clash to Romcom   19
   Daniela Berghahn

2. The Oblivion of Influence: Mythical Realism in Feo Aladağ's *When We Leave*   32
   David Gramling

3. The Minor Cinema of Thomas Arslan: A Prolegomenon   44
   Marco Abel

II. MULTIPLE SCREENS AND PLATFORMS: FROM DOCUMENTARY AND TELEVISION TO INSTALLATION ART

4. Roots and Routes of the Diasporic Documentarian: A Psychogeography of Fatih Akın's *We Forgot to Go Back*   59
   Angelica Fenner

5. Gendered Kicks: Buket Alakuş's and Aysun Bademsoy's Soccer Films   72
   Ingeborg Majer-O'Sickey

6. Location and Mobility in Kutluğ Ataman's Site-specific Video Installation *Küba*   84
   Nilgün Bayraktar

7. *Turkish for Beginners*: Teaching Cosmopolitanism to Germans   96
   Brent Peterson

8. "Only the Wounded Honor Fights": Züli Aladağ's *Rage* and the Drama of the Turkish German Perpetrator   109
   Brad Prager

III. INSTITUTIONAL CONTEXTS: STARS, THEATERS, AND RECEPTION

9. The German Turkish Spectator and Turkish Language Film Programming: Karli Kino, Maxximum Distribution, and the Interzone Cinema — 123
   Randall Halle

10. Mehmet Kurtuluş and Birol Ünel: Sexualized Masculinities, Normalized Ethnicities — 136
    Berna Gueneli

11. The Perception and Marketing of Fatih Akın in the German Press — 149
    Karolin Machtans

12. Hyphenated Identities: The Reception of Turkish German Cinema in the Turkish Daily Press — 161
    Ayça Tunç Cox

IV. THE CINEMA OF FATIH AKIN: AUTHORSHIP, IDENTITY, AND BEYOND

13. Cosmopolitan Filmmaking: Fatih Akın's *In July* and *Head-On* — 175
    Mine Eren

14. Remixing Hamburg: Transnationalism in Fatih Akın's *Soul Kitchen* — 186
    Roger Hillman and Vivien Silvey

15. World Cinema Goes Digital: Looking at Europe from the Other Shore — 198
    Deniz Göktürk

Notes on Contributors — 213
Works Cited — 218
Index of Names — 243
Index of Films — 247

List of Illustrations

1.1	Dirk's family visiting Özlem's home in *Evet, I Do!*	26
1.2	Ian Miller (John Corbett) is baptized in *My Big Fat Greek Wedding*	27
1.3	Dirk (Oliver Korittke) and Özlem (Lale Yavas) in *Evet, I Do!*	28
1.4	Berlin Cathedral and television tower in *Evet, I Do!*	29
2.1	Cem (Nizam Schiller) in *When We Leave*	35
2.2	Gül (Nursel Köse) and Umay (Sibel Kekilli) in *When We Leave*	41
3.1	Can (Tamer Yigit) in *Dealer*	51
3.2	Any-Spaces-Whatever in *Dealer*	51
4.1	Fatih Akın in *We Forgot to Go Back*	64
4.2	Mustafa and Hadiye Akın in *We Forgot to Go Back*	67
4.3	The Black Sea in *We Forgot to Go Back*	70
5.1	Hayat (Karoline Herfurth) and Toni (Ken Duken) in *Offside*	78
5.2	Turkish woman looking through fence in *Girls on the Pitch*	80
6.1	Installation view of Kutluğ Ataman's *Küba*, The Sorting Office, London, March–June 2005, commissioned and produced by Artangel, photo courtesy Artangel	87
6.2	Installation view of Kutluğ Ataman's *Küba*, The Sorting Office, London, March–June 2005, commissioned and produced by Artangel, photo courtesy Artangel	90
7.1	The Öztürk-Schneider blended family of *Turkish for Beginners*	100
7.2	Yagmur (Pegah Ferydoni) and Costa (Arnel Taci) in *Turkish for Beginners*	104
8.1	Simon (August Zirner) in *Rage*	114
8.2	Can (Oktay Özdemir) in *Rage*	117
9.1	Education Level of the Participants	132
9.2	How Frequently Do You Go to the Movie Theater?	133
10.1	Dylan (Mehmet Kurtuluş) and Charlotte (Nina Hoss) in *Naked*	141
10.2	Ali (El Hedi ben Salem) in *Ali: Fear Eats the Soul*	142

10.3	Fitzcarraldo (Klaus Kinski) and Molly (Claudia Cardinale) in *Fitzcarraldo*	145
10.4	Cahit (Birol Ünel) and Maren (Catrin Striebeck) in *Head-On*	146
12.1	Attitude toward EU Accession in the Turkish Press (above) and Nationalist Tone in the Turkish Press (below)	163
13.1	Daniel (Moritz Bleibtreu), Juli (Christiane Paul), and Fatih Akın (cameo) in *In July*	180
13.2	Sibel (Sibel Kekilli) in *Head-On*	183
14.1	Illias (Moritz Bleibtreu) in *Soul Kitchen*	187
14.2	Ali Davidson (Bülent Celebi) in *Soul Kitchen*	188
15.1	*I Passed Through with Songs: A Film for Kazım*, courtesy Kalan Müzik	200
15.2	Black Sea Files, 2007 installation, Peacock Visual Arts, Aberdeen, courtesy Ursula Biemann	208
15.3	Nejat (Baki Davrak) in *The Edge of Heaven*, courtesy corazón international	209

Introduction

Sabine Hake and Barbara Mennel

When Yasemin Samdereli's *Almanya–Willkommen in Deutschland* (*Almanya: Welcome in Germany*, 2011) premiered at the Berlin Film Festival 2011, with the German President and the Turkish Ambassador in attendance, it also served as a celebration of fifty years of labor migration from Turkey to Germany. This historical moment confirmed the status of culture, particularly film, as both object and subject in the history of labor migration and its aftereffects. The 1961 labor recruitment agreement between the Federal Republic of Germany and the Republic of Turkey had launched a migration flow that changed individual and familial lives and transformed the social and cultural landscapes of both nations in unforeseen ways. Fifty years later, as *Almanya* retells the story of labor migration in a comedic vein, the resulting social conflicts and cultural clashes and often heated debates about integration, multiculturalism, and ethnic and national identity have produced a diverse body of films, television series, and multi-screen installations that we evoke here under the heading of Turkish German cinema.

An integral part of the cinema's own history of defining peripheries and centers and constructing images of self and other, Turkish German cinema is often associated with a particular sensitivity toward national belonging and ethnic embodiment and an acute awareness of the politics of identity and place. However, this body of work has more recently been associated with attempts to complicate and destabilize discourses—of social realism and identity politics—no longer found adequate to the multiple affiliations and fluid attachments in a globalized world. The films made since the 1990s tell stories about the problems of dislocation and integration; yet they also open up new ways of thinking beyond fixed categories of identity and the binary logic of native and foreign, home and abroad, and tradition and modernity. Against this backdrop, the volume at hand maps the emerging field of Turkish German film studies in relation to contemporary German and European culture and society, the transformations of filmic conventions and audiovisual styles in the age of digital culture and multimedial platforms, and the authorial strategies and performative styles that at once mediate, resist, and illuminate the dynamic and fluid positions marked by the qualifiers "Turkish" and "German."[1]

The individual contributions presented here engage productively with the methodological approaches and theoretical inquiries on hyphenated identities, transnational cinemas, and new approaches to documentary, genre, and art film. As editors, we have consciously chosen not to gloss over the contradictions that situate this growing field of inquiry within specific discursive traditions, scholarly debates, and institutional contexts. On the contrary, our decision to leave out the hyphen signifies our unwillingness to reduce the remarkable productivity of Turkish German filmmakers to the easy logics of compatibility and commensurability implied by it. Thus it is the purpose of the introduction to demarcate the field in which the films circulate, beginning with a brief overview of the history of postwar migration and the politics of social, political, and legal integration that found expression in the first wave of films about Turkish Germans that continue to inform the filmic imagination in the new millennium.

A Brief History of Labor Migration: From Guestworker to Fellow Citizen with Migration Background

Labor migration has been central to West Germany's economic development, definition of citizenship, and self-understanding as a western nation and Judeo-Christian culture (Göktürk et al. 2007). Postwar labor migration began with the first recruitment treaty signed with Italy in 1955, six years before the treaty with Turkey. These treaties responded to the shortage of working-age men after World War II and played a key role in the Economic Miracle and, by extension, the geopolitics of the Cold War; the building of the Berlin Wall in 1961 and the resulting stop of refugees from the East only exacerbated the situation. The so-called *Gastarbeiter* (guestworker) program presumed that these largely manual workers constituted a temporary labor force without immigrant status. In fact, the very term reflects the assumption of temporariness and the reduction of human beings to their labor power (Chin 2007). Its legacy continues to haunt the critical reception of films thus reduced to unmediated reflections of ethnic identities and histories of migration. We revisit the history of labor migration here to open up lines of inquiry into the reconceptualization of filmmaking as artistic labor and of German cinema as a long tradition of creative exchanges, cultural contacts, international and transnational relations, with film professionals as the quintessential guestworkers and the cinema as the very model of cultural hybridity and cosmopolitanism.

The unexpected consequences of the early labor migration program found expression in a problematic discursive construction, the use of Turks as the embodiment of the guestworker and the immigrant. The doubling of their numbers during the early 1970s contributed to the rise of ethnic stereotyping and xenophobic rhetoric and resulted in growing public criticism of the guestworker program, including by leftist intellectuals. Initially the German government had stipulated a principle of rotation specifically in its treaty with Turkey, limiting residence permits to two years. However, because rotation was neither profitable nor practical, the government routinely granted extensions and, until the *Ausländergesetz* (Foreigner Act) of 1965, left the details to corporations employing most of the guestworkers. The global oil crisis in 1973 and ensuing high unemployment radically changed official policies and public debates, with the *Anwerbestopp* (cancellation of recruitment agreements) of November 1973 ushering in a new phase in the approach to migration and immigration.

The end of the active recruitment of laborers coincided with a shift toward integration as a new discourse based on the assumption that German society could absorb a certain number of foreigners. The emphasis on culture inherent in the concept of integration provided a context for migrants to assert agency through cultural production and to acquire an understanding of German identity, nation, and belonging in the absence of actual citizenship rights. The new term "foreign fellow citizen" recognized immigration as a fact, requiring "a complete reorientation of foreigner policy toward making guest workers and their families into full members of West German society" (Chin 2007: 104); but the phrase still implied an authoritative perspective at the center from which these new fellow citizens were to be defined and treated.

The emerging self-understanding since the mid-1980s of West Germany as a country of immigration coincided with the rise of multiculturalism as a critical concept that focused on ethnic (cultural, religious) diversity as constitutive of postfascist society and embraced it as a form of social and cultural enrichment rather than a mere economic necessity. Seen as a progressive, emancipatory concept at the time but since then often criticized as naive, flawed, or obsolete, multiculturalism facilitated not only differentiation among immigrant groups, but also within them. In regards to immigrants from Turkey, this meant greater public awareness of ethnic, religious, and political differences among Alevis, Sunnis, and Shiites or between Turks and Kurds. Along similar lines, multiculturalism provided a context for dialogues with other racialized and ethnicized groups, including Afro Germans and German Jews.

In the absence of full legal recognition, migrants' participation in the field of cultural production assumed particular relevance, with literature—that is, nonnative speakers writing in German—playing once again a privileged role as a substitute public sphere (Cheesman 2007; Chiellino 2007; Teraoka 1996). Confronted with their instrumentalization as native informants and exoticized others, migrant authors developed various strategies for engaging with those broader structures of reception, from outright defiance or denial to exaggerated performances of ethnicity and self-branding to an elaborate critique of the culture industry in their work. Comparable to the ethnographic gaze, these structures of reception often reduced artistic production and aesthetic imagination to a reproduction of social reality. These conditions continued throughout the conservative 1980s as political discourses shifted to a rhetoric of essential differences in line with Europe's new racisms and nationalisms. The same fault lines can be traced in the post-Wall debate on parallel societies and the shift from dreams of a unified Europe to the critique of a supposed Fortress Europe. Today politicians and the popular media increasingly look to Turkey—and by extension, Islam—to explain the problems of, and with, migrants in Germany, with the Turkish woman cast as the embodiment of deeper threats to western notions of gender, modernity, and democracy.

The difficulties of German unification in 1989 further undermined the public commitment to diversity and gave way to a period of unprecedented rightwing violence that began with attacks on asylum seekers and contract workers from Vietnam and Mozambique in the former East German towns of Hoyerswerda (1991) and Rostock-Lichtenhagen (1992) and culminated in two fire attacks killing Turkish women and children in the former West German towns of Mölln (1992) and Solingen (1993). A decade later, the violence of 9/11 and subsequent attacks in London and Madrid produced yet another tectonic shift from the appreciative engagement with national, religious, and ethnic differences to the often reductive and undifferentiated focus on Islam as absolute Other (Wohlrab-Sahr 2007). This global realignment occurred one year after the change of the citizenship law, from *ius sanguinis* to *ius soli*, which provided a legal framework for a new understanding of German citizenship and, by extension, national identity.

Against this backdrop the filmmakers discussed in this volume must be seen as actors on a national and transnational stage; they intervene in, and respond to, local and global frames of reference. Many are the children of labor migrants, grew up during the culturally innovative 1970s, witnessed the debate about belonging in the 1980s, and became adults when the Berlin Wall fell in 1989. By the time 9/11 occurred, Turkish German filmmakers had already been telling their stories for over half a decade, reason enough for us in the next section to revisit the beginnings of Turkish German cinema to define its significance and cultural contribution to the overlapping fields in which its films circulate.

The Making of Turkish German Cinema

Film professionals work within existing frameworks of culture and industry and present their artistic visions against prevailing political, economic, and discursive horizons. However, they also create new modes of production, develop innovative ways of seeing, and inspire new aesthetic styles and sensibilities. As an integral part of German and European cinema, Turkish German cinema has been identified with three distinct historical periods and critical paradigms. The first phase, roughly lasting from the 1970s through the 1980s, brought initial attention to the living and working conditions of guestworkers primarily by directors identified with New German Cinema. Drawing on a social realist tradition and relying on ethnic stereotypes, many used empathetic identification to promote social reform and political change. Critics today tend to associate these films with a social worker perspective and take issue with what they perceive as essentialized representations of Turks as mute victims.

The second phase, which has been described as a shift from "'the cinema of duty'" to the "'pleasures of hybridity'" (Göktürk 1999: 1; the terms are from Malik 1996), is associated with the self-reflexive appropriation of generic conventions by a new generation of younger German, Turkish, and second-generation Turkish German filmmakers. Inseparable from postmodernism and its antiessentialism, the emphasis in many films is on playfulness and performativity, and the affective habitus is one of empowerment and self-assertion. The third phase, which begins with the new millennium, has brought more critical engagement with questions of migration and immigration beyond Germany and greater interest in documentary and experimental modes. These three paradigms, in turn, can roughly be equated with three very different sets of narrative conventions and affective styles. First, the cinema of mute victims is predicated on a binary relationship that implies a paternalistic structure and exoticizing aesthetic. The embrace of multiculturalism and hybridity during the second phase resituates the films in a transnational context and responds to the performative quality of identity, thus moving beyond the earlier focus on topicality and social realism. Finally, in the contemporary configuration, the presumed link between filmmakers' biographies and filmic representation is further complicated, if not completely severed, in cosmopolitan productions made by Turkish Germans as well as ethnic Germans or Austrians, featuring Turkish actors cast as ethnic Germans, and involving multiscreen installations about migration within Turkey exhibited in Germany and elsewhere.

In order to understand this trajectory, we need to return to the first films thematizing "the problem" of the guestworker. From the beginning this process of inscription and projection involved the overdetermined figure of the suffering and entrapped Turkish woman, a key witness in both feminist critiques of patriarchy and liberal arguments for secular democracy. In three controversial films, Helma Sanders-Brahms's *Shirins Hochzeit* (*Shirin's Wedding*, 1976), Tevfik Başer's *40 qm Deutschland* (*Forty Square Meters of Germany*, 1986), and Hark Bohm's *Yasemin* (1988), Turkish women experience oppression at the hands of Turkish men. As many scholars have noted, using women's bodies as ciphers for oppression shifts the discursive framework from labor migration to gender and sexuality, connections that resonate in the headscarf debate today (Abu-Lughod 2002).

Rainer Werner Fassbinder's *Angst essen Seele auf* (*Ali: Fear Eats the Soul*, 1974), by contrast, must be seen as the prime example of an enlightened victimology. His film straddles the tension between criticizing postwar racism as a continuation of the Nazi past and reifying the mute stranger as an object of orientalist fascination. Fassbinder originally intended the film to tell the story of a Turkish labor migrant titled "All Turks Are Called Ali." Instead his film aestheticizes the nude body of the main character Ali, a Moroccan. Ali's spectatorial objectification falls in line with the central role that female characters have played for a liberal discourse of tolerance that pivots on the melodramatic staging of feminine victimization; to what degree an ethnicized masculinity serves similar purposes will be examined by Berna Gueneli in this volume.

The guestworker as a heuristic device in the negotiation of identities also appeared in Turkish films where migration has constituted an important trope in thematizing the movement from the country to the city in economic terms (Dönmez-Colin 2008). Framing transnational labor migration from a Marxist perspective, Yılmaz Güney's film *Baba* (*The Father*, 1971) features a poor fisherman who dreams of working in West Germany in order to be able to take care of his wife and two children, but he does not pass the medical exam required for a work permit. When his rich landlord murders a man, the main character, Baba, takes the fall for him, falsely confessing to the crime. The film suggests that his subsequent time in prison equals the life he would have spent abroad as a labor migrant. While Baba is in prison, the landlord destroys his family, forcing the daughter into prostitution and leading the son into a life of crime—an anticapitalist critique largely missing from the films made in Germany.

In the mid-1990s heretofore unseen images produced by Turkish Germans of the second generation brought a fundamental change in the modes of representation and enunciation. Several films launched new careers, with Seyhan Derin's *Ben Annemin Kızıyım–Ich bin die Tochter meiner Mutter* (*I Am My Mother's Daughter*, 1996), Aysun Bademsoy's *Nach dem Spiel* (*After the Game*, 1997), Thomas Arslan's *Geschwister—Kardesler* (*Brothers and Sisters*, 1997), Fatih Akın's *Kurz und schmerzlos* (*Short Sharp Shock*, 1998), Yüksel Yavuz's *Aprilkinder* (*April Children*, 1998), Hussi Kutlucan's *Ich Chef, Du Turnschuh* (*Me Boss, You Sneakers!*, 1998), Kutluğ Ataman's *Lola + Bilidikid* (*Lola and Billy the Kid*, 1999), and Ayşe Polat's *Auslandstournee* (*Tour Abroad*, 2000) all appearing over the course of four years. Gone were the exploited guestworkers and their suffering wives and oppressed daughters. The majority of these emerging filmmakers was born in Germany or Turkey and grew up with one or two parents with migration background. The films offer self-confident responses to lived experiences often in conflict with the parent generation and open to other minoritarian positionalities, be they other immigrant or refugee groups or gays and transgender people. In the process, they leave behind old dogmas of privileging politics over aesthetics, realism over fantasy, suffering over pleasure, and an aesthetic of estrangement over emotional engagement.

Today genre cinema has emerged as the dominant form of Turkish German cinema, a development examined explicitly in the contribution by Daniela Berghahn. However, proliferation across networks and platforms, including television and art installations, has also diversified forms and formats, addressing different audiences and modes of cultural consumption, a point confirmed in the essays by Brad Prager, Brent Peterson, and Nilgün Bayraktar. Market forces highlight mainstream genres, as evidenced by *Almanya* and its reworking of history as comedy in asserting the new normalcy of Turkish Germans and, by extension, German multicultural society. Feature-length films privilege genre conventions, some with ironic distance, and others with calculated conventionality. Ayşe Polat's youth drama *Luks Glück* (*Luk's Luck*, 2010), Feo Aladağ's melodrama *Die Fremde* (*When We Leave*, 2010), Fatih Akın's comedy *Soul Kitchen* (2009), and Thomas Arslan's Berlin neo-noir *Im Schatten* (*In the Shadows*, 2010) share a subtle sensitivity vis-à-vis assumed ethnic or national identities and an embrace of genre conventions, at times playful. They overcome the traditional split between genre cinema with its commitment to popular entertainment and the kind of auteur cinema or *cinema engagé* often aligned with ethnic or political minorities. The proliferation of new forms even extends to lowbrow comedies such as Anno Saul's *Kebab Connection* (2004) or films that do not focus on Turkish German characters such as Buket Alakuş's *Finnischer Tango* (*Finnish Tango*, 2008) and Thomas Arslan's *Ferien* (*Vacation*, 2007)—all powerful indications of the normalization of ethnic imaginaries and the possibility of moving beyond paradigms implied by ethnicity altogether.

Documentary forms, attractive to many filmmakers because of the lower production costs, do not enjoy the privileged status of feature films among the viewing public and generally receive little scholarly attention. Several recent documentaries explicitly engage with this new normalcy in more critical ways, thus paradoxically revealing its status as not-yet-taken-for-granted, a dynamic explored by Ingeborg Majer-O'Sickey and Angelica Fenner. The same tension can be found in first-time filmmaker Anna Hepp's documentary *Rotkohl und Blaukraut* (*Turkish Kraut*, 2011) and its endearing portrait of Turkish Germans in the industrial Ruhr region. Other documentaries such as Martina Priessner's *Wir sitzen im Süden* (*We Are Based Down South*, 2010) and Asli Özge's *Men on the Bridge–Köprüdekiler* (2009) move the scene of representation to Turkey, thus expanding the spatial imaginary toward a global south, in the former film through the story of Turks who grew up in Germany working at an outsourced German call center in Istanbul. Moreover, *Men on the Bridge* confirms the increasing difficulty of defining the boundaries of national cinema. Director Asli Özge and cameraman Emre Erkmen grew up in Turkey and now live and work in Germany. The film's production company is German-based with backing from German as well as Turkish and Dutch film and media funds, revealing connections also observable in the methodological and theoretical shift from binary and reductive scholarship to more dynamic, dialogic, and multidimensional models explored by Randall Halle in his contribution to this volume.

Turkish German (Film) Studies: Intersecting Fields, Emerging Paradigms

Scholarship on Turkish German cinema has changed greatly in response to the explosion of films since the mid-1990s; the resultant disagreements and contradictions are an integral part of this process. Thus one of the first German-language publications on the subject, the 1995 anthology *"Getürkte Bilder": Zur Inszenierung von Fremden im Film* (*"Fake* [related to: *'Turkish'*] *Pictures": About the Staging of Strangers in Film*), edited by Ernst Karpf et al., achieves a compelling deconstruction of the filmic representation of the figure of the foreign and the foreigner. But the criticism of the representation of migration and ethnic minorities in Germany remains within a limited theoretical frame that imagines the migrants on screen only in terms of their foreignness. In the late 1990s Deniz Göktürk observed a gradual shift in filmic sensibilities from the above-mentioned "cinema of duty" to the "pleasures of hybridity"; the implications of this shift have since been discussed extensively in numerous scholarly articles (Ezli 2009; Fenner 2003; Göktürk 1999; Rendi 2006).

In responding to new filmic and critical sensibilities, scholars on both sides of the Atlantic also make use of important theoretical interventions such as Homi Bhabha's theorization of the postcolonial location of culture, Arjun Appadurai's writings on the labor of the imagination under globalization, and Hamid Naficy's concept of accented cinema (Bhabha 1994; Appadurai 1996; Naficy 2001). Gender and sexuality emerged as an important nexus of analysis and a particularly salient marker of cultural and conceptual change (Eren 2003; Göktürk 2000; Kılıçbay 2006; Mennel 2002a and 2002b). On the level of formal analysis, cinematic spaces and soundscapes, too, have emerged as major sites for analyzing the films' political efficacies and aesthetic practices (Baer 2008; Gallagher 2006; Kosta 2010; Kraenzle 2009) and for utilizing the various spatial, visual, and affective turns in relation to Turkish German culture (Kaya 2007).

The theoretical apparatus developed over the last two decades, however, not only draws on methodologies from film studies and cultural theory. Literary scholars, in particular, have made critical interventions that force us to reconsider the larger theoretical framing of discussions of Turkish German culture in general. Leslie Adelson, Azade Seyhan, and B. Venkat

Mani have complicated the terms taken for granted in earlier debates on migration, ethnicity, and (national) identity. Adelson persuasively argues against reading cultural production about migration as a mimetic representation of social reality and rejects the view of migration as "in-between" two whole cultures incommensurable with each other (2001). Seyhan extends the context for Turkish German cultural production, focusing on narratives that are not "bound by national borders, languages, and literary and critical traditions" (2001: 4). Opposed to the terms ethnic and immigrant literature, she prefers the concept "transnational" as "a genre of writing that operates outside the national canon" (2001: 10). Continuing Adelson's and Seyhan's complication of the relationships of authors and texts bound by national imaginaries, B. Venkat Mani endows literary texts with the ability to "push the boundaries of the German language and transform its grammar and vocabulary both literally and figuratively" putting forth "cosmopolitical claims," based on multiple simultaneous affiliations that unsettle the links among "home, belonging, and cultural citizenship" (2007: 5 and 7). Analyzing a "literature of Turkish migration" that incorporates itself "into and beyond national archives," Adelson in fact observes a Turkish turn in German culture (2005: 12).

Nonetheless, these contributions confirm that ethnicity continues to be a valid, even if problematic, category of inquiry, enhanced by a set of recent scholarly works that enable us to theorize ethnicity beyond its reductive, normative, or exclusionary functions. Ruth Mandel has shown that the German state aspires to present itself as cosmopolitan by branding itself as "tolerant humanist, and universalist" precisely through its engagement with the question of ethnicity (2008: 14). Another way of rethinking ethnicity informs Katrin Sieg's concept of ethnic drag and its implications for the productivity of cultural performance, including forms of self-ethnicization (2002). Her model allows for a conception of identity not as biologically innate but a performative masquerade able to negotiate power in the field of culture. In film studies, the interpretative frameworks anchored in this new understanding of cosmopolitan and cosmopolitical claims also extend to economic relations in the New Europe and beyond. For instance, Randall Halle's study on *German Film after Germany: Toward a Transnational Aesthetic* grounds the theorization of transnational film aesthetics in an economic approach, emphasizing ensembles of production and funding (2008: 30–128). In Akın's films, the focus of the anthology's fourth part, he finds a transnational normalcy that moves beyond the model of cohabitation and opens up a space similar to Mani's vision of cosmopolitical claims.

Theoretical approaches to the transnational flows of culture have significantly shaped the discussion of Turkish German cinema since the mid-1990s and linked it to new research in critical geography, anthropology, and cultural studies. The growing interest in European cinema as a category of academic inquiry and cultural consumption has allowed scholars to examine Turkish German cinema in comparative contexts, from Deniz Göktürk's participation in early transnational diasporic cinema research to Daniela Berghahn's and Claudia Sternberg's coedited 2010 volume on *European Cinema in Motion: Migrant and Diasporic Film in Contemporary Europe*. Meanwhile Turkish German films are used to expand and complicate standard accounts of German film history (Bergfelder et al. 2008; Hake 2008; Brockmann 2010); this phenomenon can even be observed in the limited academic engagement with Turkish German cinema in Germany, as evidenced by Özkan Ezli's 2010 edited volume on Akın's *Auf der anderen Seite* (*The Edge of Heaven, 2007*). Last but not least, on both sides of the Atlantic, the growing interest in Turkish German cinema cannot be separated from the proliferation of film festivals such as the Nuremberg-based Filmfestival Türkei/Deutschland (Film Festival Turkey/Germany), the availability of many (subtitled) films on DVDs and their exhibition in noncommercial and commercial venues, the inclusion of representative films in German-culture courses offered at British and North American universities, and the active involvement of academic publishing houses in promoting scholarship on the subject.

Turkish German Cinema on Multiple Screens: Theoretical Interventions and Institutional Frameworks

In this volume, we propose to move beyond the traditional focus on representation and signification to approach Turkish German cinema as part of a long history of film professionals in German and European cinema with a migration background. The connection between the transnational as a function of film production and film aesthetics, and the movements of film workers and ethnic/national stereotypes across borders and media are an essential part of this long history. As argued earlier, the important, provocative, and innovative—but sometimes also mediocre and conventional—films subsumed under the category of Turkish German cinema cannot be reduced to the discourses of identity, as defined through a fixed number of narrative themes and motifs, the implicit equation of filmic representation and social reality, and specific assumptions about film authorship and (auto)biography. Instead of abandoning identity as a critical category altogether, we suggest expanding our definition of Turkish German cinema to include the perspective of filmmaking as a profession and of ethnicity as a function of self-branding. This enables us to theorize transnational cinema as part of Europe's new creative economies and its long history of film migration and cultural exchange. Turkish German cinema makes a rightful claim to occupying both sides of the divide marked by the absent hyphen: of being self and Other, at home and abroad, foreign and native—a unique position that explains the frequent enlistment of these films in larger theoretical debates about national cinema.

Even a cursory look at recent publications confirms the transnational as a key category in explaining the new cinema of hybridity that emerged in the Berlin Republic and the New Europe of the 1990s and that today finds privileged expression in Turkish German cinema. Central to most writings on these films is the search for critical tools adequate to the movements of peoples, ideas, and services in a globalized world and the filmic constructions of identity as fluid, contingent, and multiple (Bergfelder 2005; Hjort 2009). Scholars have recognized the limitations of the national as a category of film analysis (and do the same for the distinctions between art cinema and popular cinema) and begun to reassess the historical narratives and cultural topographies that place Germany within Europe and both in relation to Hollywood (Silberman 1996; Higson 2000). Furthermore scholars have rejected the critical binaries—captured in terms such as in-betweenness, interculturalism, and so forth—that still conceive of such artistic trajectories and aesthetic sensibilities primarily in one-directional terms (i.e., from the south to the north, from the periphery to the center) and hierarchical modes (i.e., through the dynamics of self and other, majority and minority, or the universal and the specific).

In the growing body of scholarship, the conflation of the economics and politics of transnational cinema and the filmic representation of the problems of ethnic, racial, and national identities has produced important new insights and critical blind spots. As we have shown above, the latter result from the discursive enlistment of, or self-presentation by, Turkish German filmmakers as native informants or typical immigrants and a reading of their films as allegories of multiculturalism and cosmopolitanism, that is, as either accurate reflections of social reality or utopian projections of the pleasures of hybridity. At the same time, the theoretical preoccupation with fluid subjectivities, contested identities, and negotiated meanings ignores well-established traditions that, in the form of genre conventions, type casting, and the star system, have made ethnic stereotypes and the actors who perform them an integral part of German cinema since the Wilhelmine era. More specifically, ahistorical approaches often elide the material conditions under which film professionals with migration background come to perform their various roles: as directors insisting on their status as unhyphenated filmmakers but willing to speak out on Turkish German issues; as actors both empowered and constrained by being cast in ethnic roles; as screenwriters at once resisting and relying on the demand for typical stories in typical settings with typical characters; as producers and distributors marketing Turkish Germanness as a commodity to different audiences (German, Turkish German, Turkish, European); and as creative individuals building on informal networks of family and friends to realize their film projects under the typical conditions of artisanal production and new local and regional funding schemes, points addressed in greater detail in the final section on Akın.

From its inception German cinema has been multicultural, accented, hybrid, and hyphenated; Turkish German cinema is only the latest manifestation of a model of cultural production and representation unique to cinema and other modern forms of entertainment. Notwithstanding the official discourse on national cinema, filmic production, distribution, and consumption have always been international as well as transnational, with film professionals (both native and foreign-born) as the quintessential skilled migrant worker. Examples include the Danish film professionals in Wilhelmine cinema, the Russian film as the first diasporic cinema in post-1918 European cinema, the contribution of German Jewish actors and directors to Weimar cinema, or the leading role of Austro Hungarians in the sound film of the late 1920s and early 1930s (Behn 1994; Diestelmeyer 2006; Schöning 1995 and 2005). German cinema after 1933 may be described as the model of a national/nationalistic cinema; but the Central European exiles and émigrés in Hollywood and elsewhere also became the best-known historical example of an accented or diasporic cinema. After the war, such transnational movements continued in the contribution of remigrants, political exiles, and avant-garde cosmopolitans (Peter Lilienthal, Jean-Marie Straub/Danièle Huillet) to New German Cinema, and the East German coproductions with Eastern Bloc and Third World socialist countries. In order to understand ethnicity as a representational, performative, discursive and historical category, we therefore need to untangle the various strands that define its contradictory functions in the making of national and transnational cinemas, beginning with the self-representation of directors and actors as ethnic or foreign in changing historical contexts.

Linking the mobilization of ethnic and national stereotypes in genre and art cinema to the professional and artistic choices of film directors and actors with migration background leads us to a better understanding of the significance of Turkish German cinema as a unique social, cultural, and artistic phenomenon. These film professionals stand in a long history of mobility and cultural contact made possible by the great disruptions of twentieth-century history: wars and revolutions, but also exile, diaspora, global capitalism, labor migration, and cultural modernity. Yet the filmmakers discussed here also differ fundamentally from most of their precursors in that most are German-born, second-generation immigrants, unlike the foreigners, migrants, and exiles who have performed ethnicity and projected otherness on German screens until now. In this sense Turkish German cinema resembles more closely early Hollywood cinema and its heavy reliance on immigrants and foreigners as the producers and consumers of popular constructions of nationhood and images of Otherness.

Nonetheless, filmmakers such as Fatih Akın, Thomas Arlsan, Kutluğ Ataman, Ayşe Polat, and Seyhan Derin, along with the actors regularly cast in their films, share with their predecessors—the Danes of the 1910s, the

Russians of the 1920s, and the Austrians and Hungarians of the 1930s—an acute awareness of the profitable, productive, and performative quality of ethnicity as a marker of difference and an essential part of the economics of signs and significations in national and transnational cinemas. In that sense, the central position of Turkish German cinema within a contemporary visual culture that encompasses film, television, live comedy, hip hop music, social networks, Internet culture, and installation art not only refers back to a longer history of media convergence and aesthetic hybridization but also opens up a perspective from which to rethink existing accounts of German film and film history beyond the national and beyond identity.

The volume at hand responds to this proliferation of new artistic and critical approaches by attempting a systematic but not comprehensive stocktaking of contemporary filmic practices of Turkish German cinema. Individual contributions access a range of disciplinary frameworks, including reception studies, television studies, star studies, feminist theory, and minority studies. Several take the opportunity to expand on themes that have emerged in the previous years such as Fatih Akın's representative role as auteur in a new global art cinema. Throughout we propose to make productive use of the disagreements and contradictions that, as outlined on the previous pages, define rather than confine this field of artistic production and critical engagement. In other words, the volume seeks to reproduce the centrifugal proliferation of methodologies that accompanies the prevalence of Turkish German visual culture, including film, television, installation art, actors and actresses, and the reception of films in Germany and Turkey. At the same time, the fifteen contributions resonate with each other and their geographically and materially constituted fields, with keywords such as identity, stereotype, hybridity, migration, globalization, cosmopolitanism, social realism, spectatorship, nostalgia, and performativity functioning like an invisible thread.

Accordingly the first three essays intervene in the status quo of scholarly debates about Turkish German cinema by revisiting the objects of study that have haunted its theorization from the outset: ethnic stereotypes. Daniela Berghahn's "My Big Fat Turkish Wedding: From Culture Clash to Romcom" opens the section by illustrating popular culture's contemporary self-aware employment of stereotypes in romantic comedies and their globally circulating spin-offs. Using Roland Barthes's notion of myth, David Gramling focuses on cinematic narratives that appear to adhere to well-known conventions. His "The Oblivion of Influence: Transmigration, Tropology, and Myth-Making in Feo Aladağ's *When We Leave*" invites us to read the film's seeming realism as a myth-making in which the actors' iconic presence overrides their roles and undermines the film's narrative legitimacy. The section concludes with Marco Abel's provocative intervention into scholarly debates overdetermined by the concern with identity. Building on Jacques Rancière's notion of the political, "The Minor Cinema of Thomas Arslan: A Prolegomenon" theorizes Arslan's films as minor cinema in the Deleuzian sense and entails a reconceptualization of the political through the film's formal and aesthetic choices.

The volume's second section foregrounds the diversity of genres and media that Turkish German visual culture inhabits today. In her piece "Roots and Routes of the Diasporic Documentarian: A Psychogeography of Fatih Akın's *We Forgot to Go Back*," Angelica Fenner resituates Akın's autobiographical documentary through his public self-presentation and the film's dynamic spatial designators, and examines its invocation of nostalgia as a symptom not of individual affection but of larger social and cultural phenomena. Ingeborg Majer-O'Sickey's "Gendered Kicks: Buket Alakuş's and Aysun Bademsoy's Soccer Films" also concerns documentary modes but shifts the focus to the ways in which these cinefeminists use filmic soccer narratives to imagine and advance women's presence in the public sphere. Nilgün Bayraktar's "Location and Mobility in Kutluğ Ataman's Site-specific Video Installation *Küba*" continues these lines of inquiry by focusing on recent shifts in the modes of exhibition from single-screen movie theaters to multiscreen installation art. As the first of two contributions on television, Brent Peterson's *"Turkish for Beginners*: Teaching Cosmopolitanism to Germans" argues that a popular television series can teach cosmopolitanism to Germans via its staging of interethnic romances. Similarly Brad Prager's "'Only the Wounded Honor Fights': Züli Alakuş's *Rage* and the Drama of the Turkish German Perpetrator" uses the political debates about violent Turkish German youth to shift attention to the portrayal of the emasculated liberal German father as a symptom of the fragile authority of the generation of 1968 and its surface habitus of social tolerance.

The undergirding question of how institutional contexts and practices shape Turkish German cinema comes to the fore in our third section, beginning with Randall Halle's reading of the institution of the motion-picture theater as an interzone, a term he proposes as an alternative to Arjun Appadurai's concept of the ethnoscape, and which he tests in his empirically based case study of Karli Kino in Berlin. Berna Gueneli continues this line of inquiry by focusing on two actors, Mehmet Kurtuluş and Birol Ünel, and the ways in which their casting reproduces orientalist strategies of sexualization and eroticization, not least through the continuities and discontinuities with New German Cinema. The final two contributions in this section survey the reception of Fatih Akın in the German and Turkish press, outlining two distinct but related sets of responses in which a desire for national identification and representation emerges as a central concern. Karolin Machtans traces the reactions to Akın's oeuvre and public persona in the German press, whereas Ayça Tunç Cox reads the Turkish reception of Akın in the larger context of Turkey's relationship to Europe and of individual newspapers' ideological positions within Turkish party politics. These last two essays prepare the ground for the fourth section, a case study on Fatih Akın and his contribution to what Rosalind Galt and

Karl Schoonover call global art cinema (2010). Accordingly Mine Eren's "Cosmopolitan Filmmaking: Fatih Akın's *In July* and *Head-On*" relates cosmopolitanism in Akın's films to the arabesque as a recurring aesthetic theme and affective mode, outlining a shift in Akın's hopes and attitudes toward Europe from *In July* to *Head-On*. The final two essays engage with music as an integral part of Akın's cinematic strategies. The practice of citing, riffing, referencing, and remixing within a global musical archive and the citational community that it seeks to create shapes Roger Hillman and Vivien Silvey's jointly authored argument in "Remixing Hamburg: Transnationalism in Fatih Akın's *Soul Kitchen*." Their observations on how global soundscapes contribute to the construction of a local place—in this case Hamburg—dialogues with the last contribution, Deniz Göktürk's "World Cinema Goes Digital: Looking at Europe from the Other Shore." Here Göktürk shows how contemporary global cinema constructs locality based on a close reading in *The Edge of Heaven* of the music of Kazım Koyuncu from the Black Sea region, negotiating the aural dimension of film that proliferates in the digital world of multiple textual platforms.

This project grew out of a workshop held at the University of Texas at Austin in March 2010. Not all participants were able to contribute, but several other contributors were added in order to include underrepresented areas of inquiry. From the beginning, our goal has been threefold: to offer an overview of contemporary practices and debates associated with Turkish German cinema, to outline the shifts in aesthetic and critical sensibilities since the 1970s, and to complicate the dominant terms of analysis by introducing intertextual, contextual, institutional, and transnational perspectives. The resulting contradictions remain an integral part of the contemporary discourse on Germany as a country of immigration and characterize the overall organization and purpose of this volume as well. We propose that this structural tension is integral to the richness and diversity of Turkish German cinema and the theoretical field that it has constituted and that continues to be constituted through it. The strategies with which filmmakers respond to those tensions speak to broader issues of social belonging and artistic expression in the globalized world; they also allow us to affirm the power of film and related audiovisual media in making sense of its actual and imaginary movements and places.

Note

We would like to acknowledge the generosity of the Department of Germanic Studies and the Texas Chair of German Literature and Culture at the University of Texas at Austin in funding the 2010 workshop that provided the impetus for this anthology. The Department of Languages, Literatures, and Cultures at the University of Florida provided a generous publication subsidy. At Berghahn Books, Mark Stanton has been an enthusiastic supporter from the start; the professionalism of the editorial staff, especially copyeditor Paula Clarke, made this project a very enjoyable experience. Last but not least, we are grateful to Katrin Sieg, Amy Abugo Ongiri, and Jeffrey S. Adler for feedback on the introduction, Tamar Ditzian for preparing the index, and thank all the contributors for their professionalism and good humor during the editing process.

1. A note on translations: All translations from German or Turkish are by the contributors unless noted otherwise. All films are quoted first in their original language and then by their English release title or translated title. We followed the correct spelling of Turkish names and quotes whenever possible, but did not correct incorrect spelling in original quotes and titles.

I

CONFIGURATIONS OF STEREOTYPES AND IDENTITIES: NEW METHODOLOGIES

Chapter 1

MY BIG FAT TURKISH WEDDING:
FROM CULTURE CLASH TO ROMCOM

Daniela Berghahn

From the destructive fantasy of a wedding that never takes place in *Shirins Hochzeit* (*Shirin's Wedding*, 1976) to the misery and even tragedy associated with arranged marriages in *Düğün—Die Heirat* (*Düğün—The Wedding*, 1991) and *Aprilkinder* (*April Children*, 1998), weddings and marriage practices occupy a prominent place in Turkish German cinema.[1] In particular the theme of arranged marriage throws the fissures and tensions between values and traditions of Turkish and German cultures into stark relief and functions as a contested site of difference. The choice of bride or groom and different ideas of what marriage is or should be typically give rise to intergenerational conflicts in the family. While the parents endeavor to preserve the family's ethnic identity through arranged marriage within the Turkish (diasporic) community, for their children these considerations are hardly relevant when falling in love with a partner from German majority culture. Whereas in the above-mentioned films the Turkish tradition of arranged marriage is portrayed as irreconcilable with Western notions of romantic love and individual self-determination, more recent productions such as the television comedy *Meine verrückte türkische Hochzeit* (*My Crazy Turkish Wedding*, 2006) and the feature film *Evet, ich will!* (*Evet, I Do!*, 2009) emphasize the convergence of Turkish and German cultures. They center on the paradox of similarity and difference and celebrate interethnic romance with the spectacle of a big wedding, allowing the romantic couple to cross ethnic divides.

This essay traces the paradigm shift from culture clash to cultural convergence and links it to a concomitant change in the representational strategies of Turkish German cinema. While *April Children* and *Düğün* as well as the earlier social problem film *Yasemin* (1988), made by the ethnic German director Hark Bohm, are in keeping with the conventions of social realist drama, *Evet, I Do!* and *My Crazy Turkish Wedding* follow and inflect the generic conventions of the romantic comedy. The essay situates Sinan Akkus's *Evet, I Do!* in the framework of genre criticism and aims to identify the distinctive features of the ethnic romantic comedy and wedding film. It adopts a transnational perspective, comparing this Turkish German romantic comedy with the similarly themed Hollywood and British Asian films *My Big Fat Greek Wedding* (2002) and *Bride & Prejudice* (2004). These wedding films can be regarded as a particular subgenre of the romantic comedy that gained prominence with the British box-office hit *Four Weddings and a Funeral* in 1994 and has been reworked many times since, in films such as *My Best Friend's Wedding* (1997), *The Wedding Singer* (1998), and *The Wedding Planner* (2001). Wedding films bill the dual attraction of a romantic happy ending coupled with the visual spectacle of one or even several wedding celebrations in the title (see Ingraham 1999). What wedding films set in an "ethnic" milieu add to this tried and tested formula is the exotic allure of non-Western wedding rituals, dress codes, music, and dance. Nowhere is this more apparent than in Bollywood-style wedding films of which *Monsoon Wedding* (2001) and *Bride & Prejudice* represent the most prominent examples in the West. This essay, then, proposes that *Evet, I Do!*, set in Berlin's sizeable Turkish diasporic community, inscribes itself into this popular generic trend and asks how the film negotiates cultural difference on the levels of narrative, aesthetics, and ideology.

The wedding practices of diasporic communities capture the popular imagination because they seem to crystallize the Otherness of diasporic culture. As Homi Bhabha has argued in relation to colonial discourse, Otherness is invariably charged with ambivalence, attempting to position the Other simultaneously inside and outside Western knowledge (1994: 94–131). The Other is split between contradictory positions with the negative pole connoting inferiority and the positive one fantasies of exotic allure. Stereotypes have the function of arresting the ambivalent sliding between the polarities of similarity and difference in a fixed image that is repeated over and over again.

Diasporic wedding films capitalize on these ambivalent connotations, capturing the interest of culturally diverse audiences and inviting different viewing positions. For diasporic audiences wedding films are often redolent with nostalgia. They provide the comforting reassurance that cultural traditions and family values of the homeland can and do live on despite displacement and dispersal. To Western majority audiences, Jigna Desai suggests, wedding films offer a "non-threatening spectacle of otherness that ... can be absorbed into the narrative of universal heterosexuality. [... At the same time, c]ross-cultural consumption of wedding films relies on the rejuvenation of an anthropological desire for knowledge of and intimacy with the other" (2004: 222).

Although Desai's observations hold true for the ethnic romantic comedies considered in this chapter, they need to be qualified for social problem films such as *Yasemin*, *Düğün*, and *April Children*. These films appeal to the "anthropological desire for knowledge of the other" but use the insights they convey into the lives of the Other and, in particular, the social practice of arranged marriage as evidence of an irreconcilable culture clash between liberal and enlightened German majority culture and Turkish or Kurdish tradition. Bohm's widely discussed *Yasemin* was instrumental in establishing the paradigm of young victimized Turkish German women, who get caught in the conflict between traditional Turkish patriarchy and German culture, imagined as enlightened, liberal, and based on gender equality (see Berghahn 2009; Burns 2007a and b; Göktürk 2000 and 2002a). When Yasemin's older sister Emine fails to produce the required bloodstained bridal sheet as evidence of her virginity after her wedding night, the girls' initially fairly liberal father transforms into a despotic patriarch, intent on protecting the family honor that Emine has supposedly violated. Yasemin's revelation that the groom's impotence rather than her sister's sexual transgression is at stake challenges the archaic principles accorded to Turkish patriarchy, which blames the woman for the man's shortcomings. The seventeen-year-old title heroine is put under house arrest to be deported to Turkey, but is rescued by her German boyfriend in the last minute.

Gegen die Wand (*Head-On*, Fatih Akın, 2004) and *Die Fremde* (*When We Leave*, Feo Aladağ, 2010) testify to the persistence of the stereotype of the victimized Turkish German woman. In these more recent films, however, the protagonists Sibel and Umay do not depend on men to be saved from patriarchal oppression. Moreover, the weddings featured in these two films represent unconventional updates of Turkish weddings and marriage practices: In *When We Leave*, the wedding of Rana, Umay's younger sister, may look like a traditional Turkish wedding but the marital union represents a hybrid between a modern love marriage with premarital sex and a baby on the way, jeopardized by an archaic honor code that almost prevents the groom from marrying into a family dishonored by Umay's perceived moral trespasses, and salvaged through a financial deal closed by the family patriarchs.

The wedding celebrations of Sibel and Cahit in *Head-On* mark the beginning of an alibi marriage by the beautiful and promiscuous Sibel in the hope to escape from her father and brothers' vigilant efforts to protect her modesty and family honor. The drop-out Cahit appears to be the ideal husband in such a set-up, since he has nothing to lose and is likely to give Sibel the freedom she desires, while his Turkish background makes him acceptable in the eyes of her parents.

Meanwhile, the Kurdish German films *Düğün* and *April Children* modulate the familiar theme of victimization by focusing on young men instead of women. In Ismet Elçi's *Düğün* Metin is lured from Germany, where he has a job and a German girlfriend, back to his native village in rural Anatolia under the pretext that his mother is dying. When Metin realizes that his father has arranged for him to get married to a local girl, Aygül, he rebels—but to no avail. The wedding with its numerous rituals is presented in considerable ethnographic detail. In contrast to South Asian diasporic wedding films, *Düğün* does not stage the wedding as an exotic spectacle but instead foregrounds the other-worldliness of these atavistic rituals. When Metin abandons the bride on the wedding night, without having consummated their marriage, he is evidently not aware of the consequences this will have for her. The dishonored bride knows all too well and commits suicide, unbeknownst to Metin, who is already on his way back to Germany.

Yüksel Yavuz's *April Children*, about the everyday life of a Kurdish German family in Hamburg, ends with the arranged marriage of the family's oldest son Cem to one of his cousins from the family's Anatolian natal village. Acting like a good Kurdish son at home while leading a westernized life outside the domestic space, Cem earns his living in a non-halal slaughterhouse and is in love with Kim, a German prostitute. Nevertheless, he bows to family pressure and marries the bride brought to Germany from "back home." The wedding ceremony does not hail the promise of a happy ending. Even after lifting the bride's veil and discovering a very beautiful young woman, Cem looks sad. Although Yavuz refrains from passing an explicit judgment, be it on Cem's parents or on Cem, the wedding scene conveys an overwhelming sense of resignation and claustrophobia. The newlyweds are at the center of a circle formed by their families who witness the unveiling of the bride, the kiss on her cheeks, and who clap to the rhythm of the music that accompanies the wedding ritual. But the approving smiles on their faces momentarily look like sarcastic grimaces—or so they may seem to Cem from whose point of view the scene is shot. As the couple begins to dance, the camera swirls and swirls round in ever more rapid circles. The faces of the onlookers get more and more blurred and eventually disappear completely, reduced to an abstract rapidly moving line that encircles the dancing couple until Cem is completely caught in the circle of his family—and there is no escape from it.

Both Elçi's and Yavuz's films illustrate what Rob Burns has theorized under the term "cinema of the affected," a particular type of social realist drama borne out of the authenticity of personal experience. These films inscribe a perspective testifying to filmmakers' alienation from their cultures of origin. "[T]he focus [of the cinema of the affected is] unremittingly on alterity as a seemingly insoluble problem, on conflict of either an intercultural or intracultural variety" (Burns 2006: 133). Although this Manichaean world view has not been rendered entirely obsolete but continues to inform in a more nuanced form recent productions such as Aladağ's award-winning film about an honor killing, *When We Leave*, on the whole, these gloomy images of alterity have given way to more favorable portrayals over the past fifteen years or so. The reappraisal of predominantly negative stereotypes went hand in hand with the attempt of second-generation filmmakers to move Turkish German cinema out of the ethnic niche into the mainstream. Some Turkish German filmmakers have liberated themselves completely from the "burden of representation," eschewing the identity politics in which migrant and diasporic filmmakers are expected to partake (Mercer 1990). Others have abandoned the social realist approach in favor of popular generic templates, notably gangster films, road movies, comedies, and romantic comedies.

Turkish German romantic comedies culminating in a wedding take their inspiration from the surge of mainstream romcoms made in the wake of *Four Weddings and a Funeral*. What distinguishes the ethnic romantic comedy set in a Turkish German or any other diasporic milieu from that set in a white middle-class milieu is the centrality of the family. This points toward the generic affinity between romcom and family melodrama.[2] In order for the couple, typically configured as a minority culture bride and a majority culture groom, to get together in the final minutes, they need to obtain the consent of the bride's parents whose ethnic minority background automatically implies that they are the last bastion of traditional family values.

According to the narrative formula "boy meets, loses, regains girl" of the romcom, the couple has to overcome a major obstacle in order to get together. Since the happy ending and the formation of the couple constitute the moment when desire is satisfied and when romance turns into marriage, romcoms delay this moment, thereby heightening desire through a series of obstructions that need to be overcome (Shumway 2003: 400). Typical obstacles in romcoms set in a white, middle-class milieu are a romantic rival (whose unsuitability serves to prove the rightness of the central couple's romance), fear of commitment, intrigues, misunderstandings, false consciousness and differences of social class and education. In romantic comedies in which the couple has to overcome racial or ethnic divides, such as *My Big Fat Greek Wedding* and *Evet, I Do!*, the chief obstacle is the parents' anticipated or actual disapproval. The parents perceive outmarriage as a threat to the ethnic homogeneity and lineage of the diasporic family. They also worry that a partner from Western majority culture will fall short of the superior family values on which diasporic families pride themselves.

Ethnic romantic comedies are "unlikely couple films," as defined by Thomas E. Wartenberg. They trace "the difficult course of a romance between two individuals" whose different ethnicities make "their involvement problematic. The source of this difficulty is the couple's transgressive makeup, its violation of a hierarchic social norm regulating the composition of romantic couples" (1999: 7). Unlikely couple films such as *It Happened One Night* (1934) and *Pretty Woman* (1990) offer criticism of existing social norms and power structures by mobilizing sympathy for the transgressive couple, whose love represents a human value that transcends the sociocultural differences and prejudices that the couple overcomes.

In this way the unlikely couple film potentially challenges social hierarchies and ethnic or class stereotypes.

Although there are quite a few unlikely couple films in which the lovers negotiate their future together along racial and ethnic divides, including *Guess Who's Coming to Dinner* (1967), *Angst essen Seele auf* (*Ali: Fear Eats the Soul*, 1974), *Jungle Fever* (1991), *Mississippi Masala* (1991), and *Ae Fond Kiss ...* (2004), by no means all of them are romcoms. The paradigmatic ethnic romcom to cast the lovers as an unlikely couple is *My Big Fat Greek Wedding*. The unexpected box-office success of this American "indie," with a modest production budget and a skilful marketing and release strategy (Perren 2004), partly stems from its effective use of ethnic stereotypes and a clever reworking of familiar generic conventions. The film centers on Toula Portokalos, a second-generation Greek American woman in her early thirties, and Ian Miller, a WASP high-school teacher. The Portokalos embody a nostalgic dream of family life of a bygone era that supposedly still exists in American immigrant culture but has become extinct almost everywhere else in Western societies. They are emotionally very close, live in each other's pockets, and maintain an extended kinship network. The Millers, by contrast, are emotionally reserved, only have one son and, ostensibly, no other relatives at all.

Family structure and food habits are deployed as the chief markers of difference: when the Millers are invited to one of the Portokalos's family feasts, they bring a modestly sized, dry Bundt cake as a gift, whilst the Portokalos family provides an abundance of Greek culinary delights, including a whole spit-roasted pig; the Millers try to abstain from alcohol, whereas the Portokalos family drink gallons of ouzu and spontaneously break into Zorba-the-Greek style bouzouki dance. Although the patriarchal family structure and the emphasis placed on communal family values restrict Toula's personal freedom, the film leaves us in no doubt whose family has more fun and more love and whose family we would rather belong to. Thus, not surprisingly, Ian and even his parents "go Greek" in the end.

Evet, I Do! borrows a number of plot elements from Joel Zwick's Greek wedding film and combines these with the multi-stranded narrative structure of *Four Weddings and a Funeral*, an international box-office hit about extravagant white weddings in a predominantly upper middle-class British milieu. Akkus's wedding film intertwines four narrative strands about Turkish German, Kurdish German, Turkish, gay, and heterosexual couples.[3] The central couple are the Turkish German Özlem and her German boyfriend Dirk, both university students in their early twenties. He is shy and under his mother's thumb (an inversion of the stereotype of the oppressive Turkish patriarch), she is beautiful, confident, and a far cry from the stereotype of the victimized Turkish woman. Dirk and Özlem are an unlikely couple in the above sense, whose romantic fulfillment is potentially thwarted by social expectations and norms, were it not for the fact that the generic conventions of the romantic comedy open up a utopian space for the realization of romantic love. "Particular films may toy with the progress towards a 'happy ending', but it remains a firm structural expectation, which the path of courtship leads towards" (Neale and Krutnik 1990: 139). The couple in romantic comedies can scoff at social decorum and social conventions and find happiness in "a self-sufficient marital unit distinct from their social milieu"—a path not open to couples in family melodrama, who have to resign themselves to the "strictures of social and familial tradition" or else suffer exclusion (Schatz 1981: 222). Ethnic romantic comedies conjoin the narrative conventions of romcom and family melodrama in as much as a happy ending *without* the family's approval would be inconceivable. The transgressive couple cannot find happiness in isolation but needs to be reconciled with and reintegrated into their families (or at the very least the diasporic family with its superior family values). The ethnic romcom achieves this through reappraising cultural traditions and norms hitherto regarded as incontestable truth.[4]

Romcoms typically narrate and visualize this process of negotiation as the crossing of borders. "Validating love as a traversing of borders, romantic comedy moves each partner from the territory of the known to the sexual and emotional space of the other. On occasions, the motif of boundary crossing is directly visualized. The *locus classicus* is found in *It Happened One Night* (1934) where the unmarried protagonists, forced to share a bedroom, erect a rope-and-blanket partition to demarcate their respective spaces" (Krutnik 1998: 26). In order to overcome what they refer to as the "Walls of Jericho," at least one partner has to undergo a fundamental transformation. More often than not, it is the woman who needs to be taught the correct values and demeanor by the man.[5] By contrast, in the ethnic romcoms under consideration here, the majority culture male needs to be educated in the customs and traditions of the minority culture bride before he can marry her.

Evet, I Do! imagines the crossing of borders both in spatial and ritualistic terms. Turkish tradition prescribes that a proper marriage proposal does not just require for the man to elicit the magical words, "Evet, I do" from the woman he loves, but that the father of the bride also gives his consent. Therefore, the film's most important scene, repeated with variations in all four narrative strands, is the meeting between the bride's and groom's families.[6] Dirk and his parents are required to enter "alien territory," a high-rise building inhabited almost exclusively by Muslims, as Dirk's father notes when he reads the foreign-sounding names next to the doorbells.

The décor of the living room marks Özlem's home as equally alien territory: the settee in shades of beige and brown is old-fashioned, the wallpaper dazzlingly patterned, the room stuffed with laced table mats and quaint objects, the most peculiar item being a mosque-shaped alarm clock that goes off to remind the parents to roll out their carpets, turn toward Mecca and say their prayers. The scene makes much of the two families'

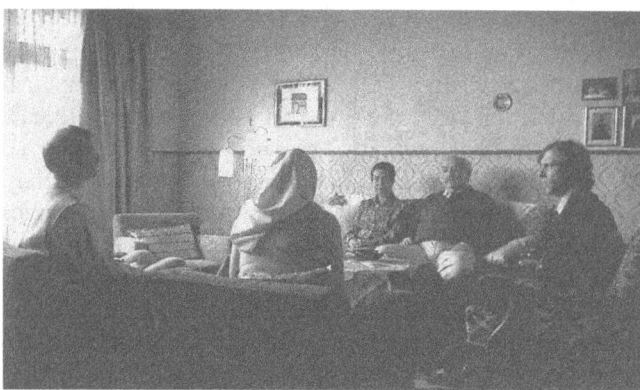

Figure 1.1 Dirk's family visiting Özlem's home in *Evet, I Do!*, DVD capture

inability to understand each other without the help of Özlem and her sister who happily translate or mistranslate as they see fit. Dirk's parents bend over backward to demonstrate their open-mindedness regarding Turkish customs and traditions. Dirk's mother has donned a headscarf since she assumes that this is the appropriate dress code for such an important occasion but Özlem's mother seems puzzled by Helga's strange attire. Dirk's father has learned a few words from the Koran but mispronounces them so that Özlem's parents are unable to understand him. He has also carefully considered whether he should begin proceedings by saying, "In the name of Allah and *our* Prophet," or "*your* prophet," and eventually stutters "In the name of Allah and *a* Prophet."

Evet, I Do! translates inverse class snobbery, a plot device common in screwball comedy and still to be found in postclassical romcoms, into inverse ethnic snobbery, whereby the ethnic minority family considers the majority culture groom unacceptable. Dirk's amorous pursuit of Özlem can only be accomplished if he is prepared to assimilate to Turkish culture. Turkish identity post-9/11 is defined first and foremost in terms of religion. The shift in conceptualizations of Turkish identity from exploited guestworkers over oppressed Turkish women, through drug-pushing and otherwise delinquent young men to Muslims indicates that religion has become central to discussions about identity, difference, and belonging. Yet in the popular imagination, Islam has all too readily become associated with Islamic fundamentalism, which explains its negative image.[7] Both *Evet, I Do!* and the thematically similar television comedy *My Crazy Turkish Wedding* explicitly address this form of negative ethnic stereotyping, thereby voicing fears prevalent in German majority culture.

The generic conventions of comedy allow for the containment and domestication of ethnic and religious difference by incorporating "alien" elements within normal, everyday life (see Neale and Krutnick 1990: 244).[8] In *My Crazy Turkish Wedding*, for example, the groom's friend and business partner wears a T-shirt with the slogan "Bin im Laden" (literally "I'm in the shop"), an obvious pun on Osama bin Laden.[9] Similarly the formation of the couple deflates the perceived threat of Muslim Otherness and its exaggeration in the specter of Islamic fundamentalism by incorporating difference into the family unit through the conjugal bond between a German man and a Turkish German woman and through the groom's conversion to Islam. In an attempt to subvert the demonization of Islam, the film stages Dirk's conversion as the performance of its allegedly most alien or embarrassing ritual practice—circumcision. Dirk, who is terribly scared of the surgical procedure, initially provides fake photographic evidence of a circumcised penis (though not his own). When he finally succumbs to the operation, his father joins him—but for all the wrong reasons, since he believes that circumcised men make better lovers. An Islamic cultural and religious practice is translated into a secular Western system of values by associating it with improved sexual performance. In this way the supposedly irreconcilable differences between the Islamic world and Western secularism as delineated by Samuel Huntington in his controversial study about "the clash of civilizations" are literally reduced to the existence or non-existence of a tiny piece of skin (1996).[10] For this German male, the removal of the foreskin is loaded with fear as unjustified, the film seems to suggest, as the fear of Islam and its association with Islamic fundamentalism and the threat of terrorism. *Evet, I Do!* uses humor to trivialize ethnic difference and, thereby, make a case for the rapprochement of Turkish Muslim and German secular cultures.

My Big Fat Greek Wedding also uses sexual innuendo in order to secularize and normalize "alien" cultural and religious practices. In this ethnic romcom, the white Anglo-Saxon Protestant groom Ian Miller needs to be baptized and become a member of the Greek Orthodox Church before he can marry Toula. His sexy and voluptuous sister-in-law sensuously anoints Ian's muscular body, whereupon the priest dunks Ian three times into an inflatable paddling pool, which serves as the supersize baptismal font required for the christening of a fully-grown man.

This rather grotesque rite of passage integrates the majority culture groom into the ethnic minority community and even transforms him from an unsuccessfully dating high-school teacher to a desirable Greek

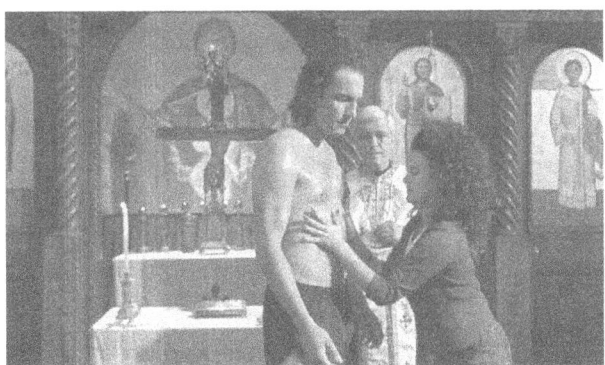

Figure 1.2 Ian Miller (John Corbett) is baptized in *My Big Fat Greek Wedding*, DVD capture

man, as testified by Ian's proud proclamation, "I am Greek now!" But interethnic romance has not only hybridized Ian's identity; Toula, too, has been transformed from an ugly duckling, waitressing in her father's restaurant, to a beautiful and confident bride who has finally learnt to accept her Greek American identity with its emphasis on a vast kinship network, consisting of Toula's twenty-seven first cousins, uncles and aunts, parents and brothers, and all-embracing family love.

In *Evet, I Do!* the groom's integration into the Turkish German family fulfills a similar function in that it facilitates a return to traditional family life and marriage. Whereas Dirk's parents, both members of the so-called '68-generation, rejected marriage as a capitalist bourgeois institution, their son's choice of a Turkish German bride and big Turkish wedding signifies an act of rebellion and a return to a more traditional family life, and one supposedly rapidly disappearing in Western society.

The trope of inverse cultural assimilation hints at a nostalgic longing for more traditional forms of family life (typically imagined as an extended multigenerational family of a preindustrial and preurban era) and the invigorating encounter with the exotic Other. After initial reluctance, Dirk's parents embrace Turkish culture with proverbial German thoroughness. At her son's wedding, Helga performs a Turkish belly dance in which everything moves except for her belly, while her husband Lüder happily mingles with his new in-laws. These well-meaning German parents, at whom the film pokes as much fun as it does at the Turkish German families, do not get it quite right. Nor would they have to try so hard to demonstrate their acceptance of Turkish culture, for Germany is already "Turkified," as the film's playful engagement with notions of cultural hybridity suggests.

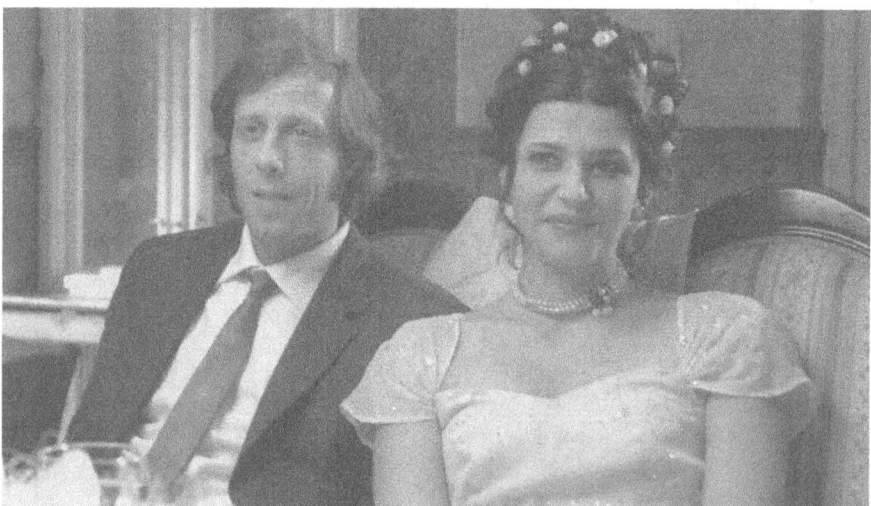

Figure 1.3 Dirk (Oliver Korittke) and Özlem (Lale Yavas) in *Evet, I Do!*

Figure 1.4 Berlin Cathedral and television tower in *Evet, I Do!*, DVD capture

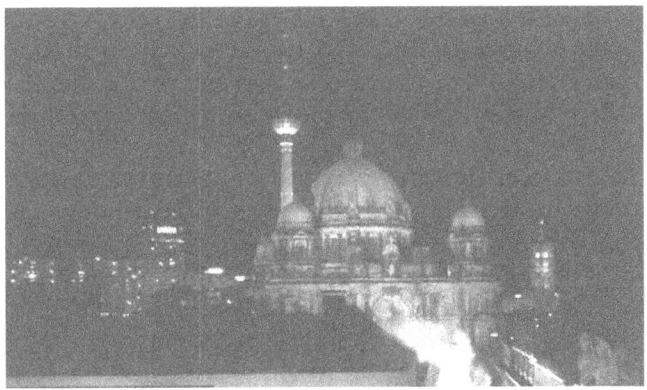

Evet, I Do!'s final frame captures the Berlin Cathedral and the television tower at night. The juxtaposition of these two architectural landmarks of Berlin's cityscape creates a vista that looks like a mosque with a minaret. The Orientalized architecture epitomizes what Doreen Massey has theorized as "a global sense of place," which reflects the time-space-compression of the postmodern era, a progressive sense of place characterized by the continuous crossing of social and ethnic boundaries and a positive integration of the local and the global (1994: 146–56). The fusion of the Berlin Cathedral and the television tower in the image of a mosque and a minaret translates the notion of hybridity from the domestic sphere of the family into the public sphere, thereby reinforcing the symbolic function of the family as a microcosm of society.

However, Ella Shohat and Robert Stam remind us that any celebration of hybridity needs to be attentive to the asymmetrical power relations implied (1994: 43). As I have argued above, *Evet, I Do!* valorizes Turkish Muslim identity only up to a point. While at face value endorsing the assimilation of Germans to Turkish Muslim culture, ultimately the film promotes assimilation to a moral universe in which Western values of romantic love, premarital sex, gender equality, and individual self-determination are prioritized over a Turkish Muslim value and belief systems.

Just as the unlikely couple does not mount challenges to the social norms and hierarchies of dominant culture, the film's aesthetics conform to mainstream Western generic templates rather than embracing a diasporic optic, defined by Sujata Moorti as a particular "visual grammar that seeks to capture the dislocation, disruption and ambivalence" of diasporic subjects and that taps into a "warehouse of cultural images," generic conventions, narrative and musical traditions, languages, and performance styles from more than one (film) culture (2003: 359). We can observe the "sideways look ... that does not reside in one place, but in several locales simultaneously" and that Moorti identifies as characteristic of the diasporic optic, at work in another ethnic romcom, the Asian British *Bride & Prejudice* (2003: 359). Gurinder Chadha's film translates European high culture via its popular inflections in the shape of screen adaptations of Jane Austen's canonical novel *Pride and Prejudice* (1813) into the idiom of Indian popular culture, notably Bollywood cinema. It Bollywoodizes stylistic conventions of European heritage cinema and mainstream romantic comedy, as programmatically announced in the film's tagline "Bollywood meets Hollywood ... and it's a perfect match." The film's hybrid aesthetics and playful use of pastiche disavow hierarchies of high and low cultural forms, of ostensibly sophisticated Western art and allegedly lowbrow Indian entertainment. *Bride and Prejudice* is based on the premise that in today's globalized world the commonalities between cultures outweigh their differences and that matchmaking and marriage follow the same rules the world over—and have done so since Jane Austen's times. *Evet, I Do!* also articulates difference by emphasizing similarity but does so by relying on a homogenizing rather than a hybridizing aesthetics to convey its message.

In contrast to the Turkish German social realist dramas, briefly considered at the outset, which identify the practice of arranged endogamous marriage as a key signifier of cultural difference that marks the Turkish diaspora as premodern and out of synch with the Western world, the ethnic romcom *Evet, I Do!* portrays marriage and the spectacle of a Turkish German wedding in unambiguously positive terms. It thereby aligns itself with the celebratory stance that other contemporary ethnic romcoms—notably *My Big Fat Greek Wedding* and *Bride and Prejudice*—have taken to ethnically mixed couples. Differences between Turkish minority and German majority cultures provide a rich source of humor and determine the obstacle course that the couple has to negotiate on their path to romantic fulfillment and heterosexual coupledom in marriage. By ostensibly inverting gender and ethno-racial hierarchies— only to ultimately reaffirm Western notions of love and marriage—these ethnic romcoms revolve around the dramatic and narrative tensions between similarity and difference. Nobody expresses this paradox of similarity in difference more memorably than the father of the bride at the end of *My Big Fat Greek Wedding*. Having welcomed both the Portokalos family and the Miller family, who have come together for Toula's and Ian's big day, Mr. Portokalos invents yet another one of his funny, far-fetched etymologies. He explains in broken, heavily accented English, "the root of the word Miller is a Greek word. Miller come from the Greek word milo, which is apple," and Portokalos "come from the Greek word portokali, which is orange," which leads him to conclude triumphantly: "So here tonight we have apple and orange. We all different, but in the end, we all fruit."

Notes

This essay is part of a Research Fellowship on "The Diasporic Family in Cinema," generously funded by the Arts and Humanities Research Council of Great Britain.

1. I use the term "Turkish German cinema" here to refer to films about Turkish diasporic subjects in Germany regardless of whether the films are scripted and directed by filmmakers of Turkish descent or by German majority filmmakers.
2. According to Kathleen Rowe (1995: 191–212) postclassical romantic comedies are heavily infused with melodrama, expressed in emotional pathos, a feminization of men, gender inversion and, especially with regard to the minority culture couple, the family. *Moonstruck* (1987), set in an Italian American milieu, is paradigmatic in this respect.
3. The inclusion of gay characters or gay couples has become *de rigueur* since *Four Weddings and a Funeral*. The film's main gay characters, Gareth and Matthew, invalidate common prejudices against gay promiscuity, embodying deep love and commitment to each other that becomes thwarted by Gareth's sudden death. Yet in spite of validating gay love, the film at the same time denies its vitality and long-term future by linking it with a funeral rather than a wedding.
4. The widely held belief that marriage outside one's own ethno-religious community or social class involves high risk, jeopardizing family lineage, cultural traditions and the prospect of a long happy marriage exemplifies such an "incontestable truth."
5. George Bernard Shaw's *Pygmalion* (1916) is the archetypal text, which has been modified countless times, e.g., in *My Fair Lady* (1964), *Educating Rita* (1983), and *Pretty Woman* (1990).
6. In the case of the gay couple, Tim and Emrah, the family's official marriage proposal involves a Turkish German woman and results in the disclosure of Emrah's homosexuality.
7. This conflation of Islam with Islamism, a form of religious absolutism and particular variety of religious fundamentalism characterized by a rightwing totalitarian ideology, explains why Islam has been associated with terrorism in western societies (Tibi 2008).
8. This also holds true of the ethnic comedy *The Infidel* (2010), which downplays the differences between Jewish and Muslim identity.
9. *My Crazy Turkish Wedding* spins out this narrative thread, adding further trials such as the halal slaughter of a sheep, fasting, and sexual abstinence during Ramadan, which the German groom has to master before he can elope with the Turkish German bride, who is about to marry a Turkish German man, and even obtain his father-in-law's approval.
10. In the British Asian comedy *East is East* (1999) the circumcision of eleven-year-old Sajid constitutes an important aspect of the film's ethnic humor. It is also secularized in the sense that Sajid's Muslim-Pakistani father decides to "bloody fix him," a term one would use for the neutering of a cat or a dog (see Mather 2006: 67–117 on ethnic humor).

Chapter 2

THE OBLIVION OF INFLUENCE: MYTHICAL REALISM IN FEO ALADAĞ'S *WHEN WE LEAVE*

David Gramling

> I love silence because it creates space for an audience to interpret for itself.
> (Feo Aladağ in Jenkins 2011)
>
> I don't know any Turkish families who talk that little at the dinner table.
> (Incredulous spectator [Hikmet Kocamaner] of *When We Leave*)

Hatun Sürücü, age twenty-three, died on 7 February 2005 at the hands of her brothers Mehmet and Alpaslan, near a bus stop in Berlin-Tempelhof. Two days afterward, the *Berliner Kurier* newspaper's editorial staff saw fit to refer to the murdered woman in its headlines by first name, with the intimate paternalism of a state-appointed guardian: "Did Hatun have to die just for leaving her husband?" (2005). The *Berliner Zeitung* saw and raised the *Kurier's* rhetorical bid, nominalizing what was alleged about that one winter Monday with the front-page declaration "Execution in Broad Daylight" (2005). Even before her funeral, Ms. Sürücü had been claimed, repurposed, and narrativized into a proprietary social fable about postmulticultural Germany, one that seemed predestined to find its way into the annals of mythical realism. Nearly five years prior to the January 2010 release of Feo Aladağ's Kreuzkölln milieu tragedy *Die Fremde* (*When We Leave*), the public narrative about Ms. Sürücü had already unhinged itself from the historical and forensic record, and become the property of myth.[1] The compulsory message those first headlines conveyed about this young German citizen's death was thus no longer assessable in terms of accuracy or inaccuracy, truth or equivocation; the signifying structure of myth had put both Sürücü and the crime she sustained "at a distance, and ... at one's disposal" (Barthes 1973: 118).

In the half-decade between the Sürücü murder and the Aladağ film, a tectonic shift took place in the German-speaking debate on Islam and multiculturalism, as commentators from Henryk Broder to Monika Maron zealously converted to a rigid Enlightenment fundamentalism (see Göktürk et al. 2011: 349–54). Concurrently racialist diagnostic treatises (Sarrazin 2010) and ex-Muslim coming-out testimonies (Kelek 2005, 2010) flew off the shelves of German train station bookstores, while the belletristic "literature of migration" in domestic trade publishing sold only sluggishly. The genre of applied social romanticism, which had sustained such vigorous critique and carnivalesque ridicule in mid-1990s Germany, seemed to have proven its automaton-like staying power on the market in Germanophone narratives about Islam and Turkishness (Göktürk 1994; Kanak Attak 1998; Terkessidis and Holert 1996). In the same period, Turkish, and particularly Turkish-speaking Islamic, mass media have invested in strategies of governing the family through television and film, through a kind of Huxtablization of Islam.[2] Private cable and satellite channels have shifted programming away from Qu'ran-based, didactic broadcasts and toward neoliberal edutainment that foregrounds pious yet modernist depictions of Muslim Turkish family lifeworlds.[3]

When We Leave is a revelatory moment in German film history because it offers a crystallization of all of these concurrent sociopolitical developments, without critiquing any of them. Its German original title, *Die Fremde*, conveys a telos of transhistorical foreignness—whether as gendered subject, alien territory, or both, i.e. "the (female) foreigner" or "foreign domains"—and by way of this ambiguity is able to lay out a flexible alibi for the dysphoric postmulticultural discourses that flourished in Germany between 2005 and the film's high-profile international release on the festival circuit in 2010.

In this essay, I propose that an understanding of the signifying operations at work in this film requires an approach that goes beyond a concern with stereotypes and depictions at the level of the signified. Such a corrective criticism would be insufficient because the cunning, interpellary realism of the film preempts the critiques that would emerge from such an intervention. Instead, I turn to Roland Barthes's post-World War II essay "Myth Today," translated in the collection *Mythologies*, in which he claims that myth is something profoundly different than a mere origin story of dubious heuristic value, shared throughout the generations among an imagined collectivity (1973). Rather for Barthes, "myth is a type of speech"—i.e., a kind of utterance structure, an applied syntagm of a particular pragmatic sort, independent of and indifferent to truth-value. In what follows I suggest not only that *When We Leave* epitomizes and builds on the semiotic logic of myth as Barthes describes it, but also that Turkish German cinema has always—since Helma Sanders-Brahms's *Shirins Hochzeit* (*Shirin's Wedding*, 1976) at least—been a primary contestatory threshold upon which mythologization and demythologization have been negotiated. At the close of the essay, I suggest how the high-profile stars cast in *When We Leave* strain onscreen against its myth, creating an uncanny iconographic surplus that is steadily becoming a regular feature of Turkish German film and literature.

Realism in the Service of Myth

In his essay, originally published in 1957, Barthes strongly objected to the reductionist characterization of myth as either an inherited, strategic inaccuracy or an originary genre that helps a society recognize itself in periods of turmoil. Barthes tells a contravening anecdote about "myth today," one based on his early confrontation with a Latin grammar textbook, where he encounters the sentence *"quia ego nominor leo"* (because my name is lion), borrowed from Aesop or Phaedrus. He realizes this clause has very little to do with its first-order signifieds, but rather that the sentence is "a grammatical example meant to illustrate the rule about the agreement of the predicate." Barthes observed: "I am even forced to realize that the sentence in no way signifies its meaning to me, that it tries very little to tell me something about the lion and what sort of name he has; its true and fundamental signification is to impose itself on me as the presence of a certain agreement of the predicate" (1973: 115). For Barthes there is nothing necessarily duplicitous or pernicious in the "true and fundamental" illocutionary force that *quia ego nominor leo* bears, as a grammatical example for a Latin pupil. Still its force of meaning is necessarily of a second order; it "leaves its contingency behind; it empties itself, it becomes impoverished, history evaporates, only the letter remains" (1973: 115). Such an evacuation of history, and of first-order signification, is indeed also the meaning-making principle of Aladağ's *When We Leave*. In lieu of, say, a story about Hatun Sürücü's life and murder, Aladağ's film instead compels the "presence of a certain agreement of the predicate"—a predicate whose subject is the collectively imagined, young Muslim German Turkish woman. The predicate to which this subject is made to agree is the inevitability and omnipresence of patriarchal violence toward each and every Muslim woman—regardless of whether she is in Turkey or Europe, whether she wears a headscarf or does not, or whether the perpetrator of that violence appears integrated into, or hostile toward, proper Northwest European secular liberalism. *When We Leave* is the strategic rehearsal of this absolute subject-predicate agreement.

If myth is indeed a motivated, syntagmatic, and performative arrangement of ordinary signs, the primary connective term for myth's utterance in *When We Leave* is the cuddly, messianic figure of Cem. The film's establishing shot, or rather sound, is the dying voice of this oracular child, calling out "Anneciğim?" (mommy?) to the protagonist Umay Aslan, who has not yet appeared on screen. With his simple declarations in both Turkish and German, Cem is established early in the film as the embodiment of unsentimental, universalist justice, beyond any cultural disposition or pretense. With unprompted questions like "Where were you, Mommy?" and "Why can we not go to Rana's wedding?" as well as his epic, unstudied judgments about the Aslan family's emotional toxicity, Cem quickly becomes the film's delivery-device for moral universalism.

Like any good element of mythic signification, the boy Cem appears ageless, transcendent, and impervious to the influence of context. In a workplace face-off with his mother's boss Gül, while the latter is babysitting for Umay in a pinch, the four-year-old Cem staunchly refuses any sort of childish diversion—whether in the form of coloring, games, jokes, or small talk. While Cem's obstinacy forces Gül to ignore her paperwork and raise the politeness of her tone, in order to convince him to busy himself with something childlike, Cem expresses very little resembling childhood affect, functioning rather as a kind of moral punctuation for the violent episodes that fuel the narrative. It is this absence of anything disorderly, unreasonable, inexplicable, or juvenile in the character of the child— except when provoked by an adult's own unbecoming child's play—that allows him to function as a kind of syntagm of rational causality, an *ergo* that connects and arranges a string of mythic speech elements. His accidental murder, at the beginning and end of the film, both dissolves and memorializes his conjunctive role in the "sentence" that *When We Leave* issues.

Just as there is nothing tangential or unmotivated about Cem's Christ-like presence in *When We Leave*, silence functions in the film not as an empty space (*Leerstelle*) for heterodox viewer responses, as Feo Aladağ herself proposes above, but rather as a kind of mythic hygiene, constituting the foreignness of Turkish Germans. While Aladağ expresses a preference for silence, on the basis that her audiences can then better pursue their own interpretations, interpersonal talk in the film proceeds according to a rigid thematic economy—not primarily a diegetic economy of intrafamilial, social power on the level of the signified, but one of strict topical relevance vis-à-vis signs. What at first appears to be the silence of patriarchal

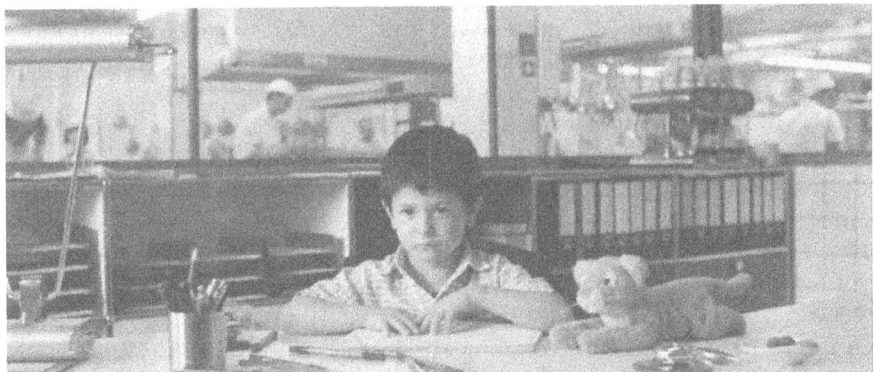

Figure 2.1 Cem (Nizam Schiller) in *When We Leave*, DVD capture

repression and enforcement turns out to be the silence of the narrative design of the film. What is being suppressed by the film's silences is not any given character's social inability to assert his or her right to speak when the Aslan family assembles. Rather, it is the film's overarching mythic bearing that requires and regulates a strict economy of relevant topics among the characters' spoken exchanges. The mythical realism of the film is thus one that sanitizes or excludes impurities. In stunning contrast to the aesthetic and ideological bearing of most Turkish German films of the 2000s, *When We Leave* is an orthodox regime of signifiers rather than an illustration of orthodox signifieds.

Not only is there little in the way of uncompelled spoken discourse among the characters, the meager volume of casual talk, unmotivated banter, and lighthearted gossip only serves to emphasize the coerced restraint on the part of the film's foreign, i.e., nonethnic-German characters. In this film foreignness is a territorial or characterological constant; it is not contingent upon one's current subjective position, as in films such as Akın's *Auf der anderen Seite* (*The Edge of Heaven*, 2007), where Nejat's or Ayten's foreignness is critically contextualized. In *When We Leave*, Turks are foreignized through silence, both in Germany and Turkey; the speech of Turkish-marked characters, whether speaking German or Turkish, is always characterized by restraint, apoplexy, extreme emotion, or despair. Meanwhile German-marked characters speak freely, casually, affectionately, and independent of coercion.

This tone is set during Umay's abortion procedure early in the film, in an Istanbul doctor's office on the European side of Istanbul's Bosphorus Strait. The practicing physician is not seen on the screen, and he has only one word to exchange with Umay, "Tamam mı?" (ok?). In shaping the scene in this particular way, the film places Umay in the position of verbally enacting the abortion procedure, as if the male physician were a passive bystander with no procedural instructions to convey. The fading sound of the fetus's heartbeat is then selectively emphasized among the ambient sounds, in juxtaposition to the arpeggiated, minor-key neoromantic piano accompaniment that serves as nearly the only nondiegetic musical motif throughout the film. Turkish music only rarely appears, and in such cases it conveys coerced communitarian atmospherics.

The film's practice of image doubling serves as the other pole of this exoticized, austere topicality. Intrafamilial hierarchies are established through two dining tables, one belonging to Umay's in-laws in suburban Anatolian Istanbul, and one belonging to Umay's own parents in Berlin's East Kreuzberg. These dining-room tables, of roughly the same shape and configuration, are shot from the same camera angle in both settings. There is no narrative explanation for the fact that Umay and Cem are seated in the same positions at both tables in both Istanbul and Berlin and are positioned in the same quadrant of the long shots. The two shots set up an absolute equivalence between Turkish family life in suburban Turkey and

Turkish German family life in urban Berlin; these two modern patriarchal Muslim families are aestheticized identically, regardless of their current country of residence. Rather than underwriting the familiar dichotomy between a progressive, secular Germany and a patriarchal, pious Turkey, this doubling enframes Umay and Cem within a dystopic house-of-mirrors, in which Turkish Turkey and Turkish Germany are indistinguishable. Migration and its feted hybridities are no match for the irredentism of the patriarchal dinner table.

Further instances of doubling ensue. Both the Turkish husband Kemal and the elder Turkish German brother Mehmet strike nearly identical blows to Umay for her immodest speech, such that she ricochets off her right shoulder against a piece of furniture and cries out with a nearly identical loud grunt. Hostile Turkish male figures repeatedly kidnap Cem by snatching the boy up over their left shoulders such that his chest faces into the men's left arm. In a further, fascinating instance of neo-baroque recitation, Umay slashes her own left wrist in precisely the same cross-body gesture as Kekilli's character Sibel in Fatih Akın's *Gegen die Wand* (*Head-On*, 2004). Whereas in *When We Leave*, Kekilli as Umay performs this suicidal rite to protest her father's unwillingness to release her from an arranged marriage, as Sibel in *Head-On* she does so to protest Cihat's unwillingness to enter into a show-marriage with her, in order that her parents might relent in insisting she find a nice Turkish husband. Meanwhile, the municipal bus driver who kicks Sibel and Cahit off his bus for fighting, after her initial suicidal attempt, reappears in *When We Leave* at her younger sister Rana's wedding in the role of her future father-in-law.

This mythic plentitude of iconographic repetition suggests that, while most press discussions have focused on the film's explicit ideological claims as a realist milieu drama, *When We Leave* is equally rife with semiotic tutelage and dramaturgical doubling—meaning-making operations that may be best understood within the traditions of baroque, or perhaps neo-baroque, mannerism. And yet the film gained political praise for its iconoclastic, closeup portrayal of Turkish identities, generational differences, and migration itineraries. Surely it would be imprecise to say that the film invents unrealistic portrayals of quotidian Berlin—whether a Berlin that is autochthonous, transnational, German, Muslim, Turkish, or a combination of these. *When We Leave*'s strategic myth lies not in antirealism, but in how it parasitically appropriates a certain species of local, semiotic capital—whether that of the successful, dauntless Turkish-speaking business woman, the ethnically non-Turkish Berliner who speaks Turkish as an occasional lingua franca, the moderate Muslim woman who wears a piously styled headscarf according to situational needs rather than personal conviction, the nationally indifferent German man who appears uninterested in perceiving Umay as Turkish, or the elderly heterosexual Turkish couple who make private decisions collaboratively, even if they appear to subscribe to patriarchal regularities in the presence of their children and friends. Each of these emblems results from an intricate tradition of semiotic precedent and refinement within Turkish German film since the 1970s. Nonetheless these emblems recede, reluctantly, behind the second-order signification of the film. In proper didactic style, the film pronounces the mythic narrative at its outset, then spells it out letter by letter in the intervening 110 minutes, and then reiterates the violence, in a modulated intonation, at its close.

The *trompe l'oeil* in *When We Leave* is one that harvests local realism for the purposes of myth, i.e., it appropriates three-dimensional figures that are familiar to many viewers and transmogrifies them into flat conveyers of fable. Its mythology lies in how these realistic images, poached from familiar Berlin sites such as Hermannplatz and the Landwehrkanal are set for a very specific mythical signification. The multidimensionality of the figures is conscribed and enthralled to the myth for the duration of the film. It is revealing that Hatun Sürücü's father's name is changed for the film from Kerem (virtue) to Kader (fate) and, correspondingly, that his profession is changed from a garden assistant to a floor worker at the local newspaper *Berliner Woche*—Berlin's premier distributer of localized, neighborhood news narrative. A vocation (taking care of plants) that would have been difficult to embed into the film's myth is thus transformed into a hyperlocal means of narrative dissemination. Each day the *Berliner Woche* distributes specific street-by-street content for thirty-one Berlin districts. As the accidental mastermind of a now legendary Neukölln crime, Kader is implicated in the productive forces enabling the distribution of local, urban news, including the honor killing of his own daughter, which in turn reinforces Kreuzkölln's notoriety throughout the Federal Republic.

The Poverty of Mythic Realism

Through a procedure of semiotic attenuation, the data that organize the film's realism are prevented from signifying anything else than that Muslim women are never and nowhere safe from violence, with or without headscarf or other expressions of piety, with or without German institutional aid or personal companionship. Furthermore the condensed effect of the myth is to insist that cultural pluralism itself is always exposed to the same degree of bare, mortal fragility as Hatun Sürücü embodied one day in 2005 at a bus stop in Berlin-Tempelhof. Ines Kappert puts it succinctly in her 2010 review: "Ultimately, the film gets entangled in clichés of the dark, eternally incomprehensible Turk, who looks friendly to be sure, but is a *de facto* time bomb for the enlightened German parallel society."

Rather than considering such "entanglements" of cliché as a flaw, equivocation, or immoderation in the film, I read them as the internally coherent, underlying structure of its narrative design. Almost no sonic, verbal or visual data appear on screen that do not underwrite this imposed syntactic agreement between young Muslim women and inevitable violence. Despite the camera's relatively wide social and aesthetic aperture upon cosmopolitan Berlin, there is no extra signifying material that is not made relevant to the myth. Contemporary Berlin and its cultural plurality are incidentally depicted—whether in the form of Keith Haring posters or beer drinkers on the Admiralbrücke—but their potential to signify is suffocated by the exhaustive seamlessness of the film's one mythic statement. Rather than providing nuanced contextualization, these details are mobilized and subsumed. As Barthes claims, myth has no particular difficulty appropriating and subduing dissident impulses.

Because of its realist depictions and opportunistic attempt to portray an ambivalent, three-dimensional Muslim woman, Aladağ's *verité* has met with admiration in a gamut of press reviews. The director's well-publicized creative magnanimity in inviting her Turkish-speaking actors to improvise their dialogues and shape their characters autonomously, initially exempted her from charges of ideological heavy-handedness (see Helmcke 2010). Despite the aura of a democratized representational project that admits authorial and authoritative plurality, this naturalistic effect is in the end a *trompe l'oeil*, which nourishes itself on, and then disposes of, any Berlin or Istanbul milieu data that do not pertain syntactically to *When We Leave*'s overall mythic utterance.

Barthes continues his account of myth by insisting that one, "any material can arbitrarily be endowed with [mythic] meaning," two, that no phenomenon is more naturally or transhistorically prone to mythologization than any other, three, that myth "points out and it notifies, it makes us understand something and it imposes it on us," four, that it appears neutral and authentic, and five, that it is "speech (*parole*) stolen and restored; ... a brief act of larceny" (1973: 110–25). The critical reception of *When We Leave* thus far in Germany and elsewhere, whether admiring, faint, or damning, has generally been captivated—and I choose this word carefully—by what transpires on the level of the signified. The historical accuracy of the narrative, the plausibility of the dialogue, the authority with which the film's director animates a particular vision of Turkish German families and their private realms—each of these patently contestable arenas of critical judgment have left the structure of the film's significations largely unaddressed in journalistic reception. Kappert's doorknob confession, for example, "Great—but somehow also cliché" (2010) or *Der Spiegel*'s praise—that the film forgoes the "folklore of veiling" by exploring the lifeworlds of so-called "integrated" Turkish Germans (Buß 2010)—each of these assessments nods briefly to the power of symbolic systems, and then flees back to pro-and-contra arguments about accuracy and authenticity in socioromantic realism. In Buß's review in *Der Spiegel*, the film wins the designation "uncompromising" because it refrains from dispatching incorrigible Islamist fanatics, as in *The Edge of Heaven*, or affectless agoraphobic homemakers, as in Kutluğ Ataman's

Lola + Bilidikid (*Lola and Billy the Kid*, 1999) to propel the narrative pathos along, instead opting to feature female entrepreneurs of Turkish descent and male Muslims of moderate, unspectacular, and complex piety.

That Umay's journey of return is not from Germany to an ancestral Turkey, but rather from a coerced marital resettlement in suburban (Anatolian) Istanbul to her preferred childhood home in central Berlin, also nourishes the film's political aura of iconoclasm, innovation, and commitment to debunking stereotypes through radical authenticity. The film goes so far as to display an ethnic German actor speaking Turkish with her Turkish German supervisor. Beyond the diegetic realm, public attention to Aladağ's own background—as a blonde, white Viennese with the Turkish surname of her Turkish German husband, filmmaker Züli Aladağ—tends to lead would-be detractors to the notion that *When We Leave* is no less than the logical result of all the hybridity critics and politicians during the 1990s had been appealing for. And yet it is not. Buß is certainly on stable footing in describing the film as an "absolute" or "unconditional" (*bedingungslos*) cultural statement. While this commendation clearly issues in a spirit of admiration for the director's commitment to an unequivocal narrative program—of, say, telling the story of Hatun Sürücü, once and for all, without pandering to institutional euphemizations of any sort—the unconditionalness of this film lies elsewhere, in its myth-making structure: imperious, arresting, and interpellative.

The Iconography of Witness

The mythic form of Aladağ's film is nourished, and troubled, by an iconographic peculiarity that has persisted in Turkish German film since the 1990s and found its most crystalline expression in Fatih Akın's 2009 film *Soul Kitchen*, namely the performative blending of actors with their roles (a point also explored by Berna Gueneli in this collection). Elsewhere I have argued that the actors in *Soul Kitchen* are playing themselves: the main character Adam Bousdoukos (who had played Costa in *Short Sharp Shock* twelve years prior) suffers back pain throughout the movie, indexing how the tropes and personnel of Turkish German film are themselves aging (Gramling 2010). This productive matrix of iconic Turkish German film stars tactically or unwittingly blending their own public personae into the narrative world of the film takes a fascinating turn in *When We Leave*, a film in which no fewer than four primary roles are occupied by actors whose signifying valence in other films overdetermine, and at points subsume, their current roles. Simultaneously, however, those actors' (and their previous roles') iconic presence stand in critical witness to *When We Leave*'s narrative legitimacy. Sibel Kekilli (Umay) and Nursel Köse (Gül Hanım, Umay's boss at the catering company) have both played major roles in the canon of German Turkish film—Kekilli as Sibel in *Head-On* and Köse as Jessie/Yeter in *Auf der anderen Seite* (*The Edge of Heaven*, 2007). Meanwhile Settar Tanrıöğen (Kader, Umay's father) and Derya Alabora (Halyme, Umay's mother) have taken major film roles in Turkey as well. The way in which this cast is constructed, and particularly the way each of the actors appears visually before the camera, produces a collective signature of witness beneath the mythic narrative of the film.

This is however a semiotic rather than ideological signature. Kekilli's choice to take the role of Umay has met with rancorous, perplexed responses. In lieu of evaluating whether it is appropriate for her to pursue the right to "criticize Muslims" (Helmcke 2010), I consider Kekilli's (and especially Köse's) presence in this film from a purely iconographic point of view, regardless of their stated feelings about the role or the film as a whole. The surplus value of Kekilli's media presence—from her tactical inversion of wedlock for the sake of polyamory and hedonism in *Head-On* to her public vilification for having acted in pornographic films—implicitly intrude on the hermetic fable of *When We Leave*. The *Hürriyet* newspaper, for instance, hailed the arrival of the film in Turkey on 21 March 2010 with the derisive headline "Sibel Kekilli türbana girdi!" (Sibel Kekilli puts on a turban!)[4]

Similarly Nursel Köse's sudden materteral appearance in *When We Leave* resurrects the slain prostitute Jessie/Yeter from *The Edge of Heaven* in an iconographic bid to redress the fatal domestic violence that her character in that film suffered, and consequentially to chaperone and vouchsafe the cinematic representation of Hatun Sürücü's life. Clearly to pursue critically this ongoing, iconographic problem of personal signature in Turkish German film is not the same as asking: "Why would these artists want to be involved in such a film?" Rather, it is again a question of the mythical, second-order signification that those artists bear when they are situated within a particular arrangement of signifiers.

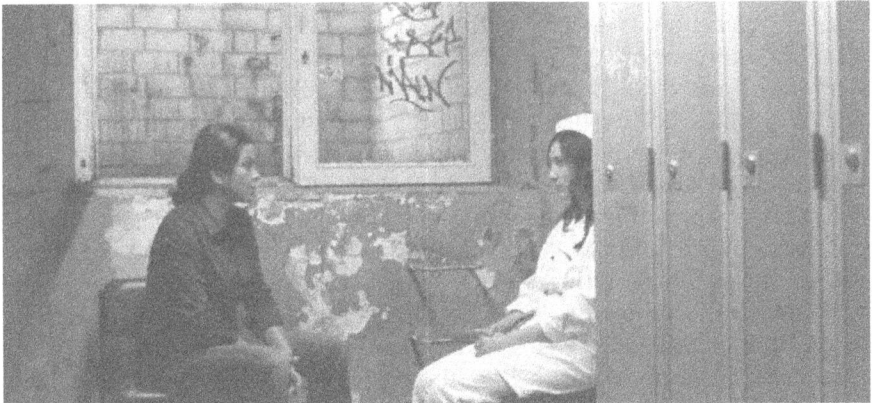

Figure 2.2 Gül (Nursel Köse) and Umay (Sibel Kekilli) in *When We Leave*, DVD capture

Perhaps Kekilli's most poignant gesture toward the tactical inversion of myth occurs when her blond male German coworker Stipe invites her to a certain spot in Berlin-Friedrichshain, on the Oberbaumbrücke. Stipe, the unassuming, gentle, accidental savior of this Turkish German woman-in-crisis (see Ewing 2006), had wanted to share with Umay one particular panoramic view of Berlin that he holds dear. When they arrive at the spot, Umay asks Stipe, "What did you want to show me?" to which he answers, "This here." Umay makes no further response, nor seeks further clarification, I propose, because she is the iconic Turkish German actor Sibel Kekilli and has *seen it all before*.

As noted above, Aladağ reports that she encouraged her actors to improvise broadly upon their dialogue scripts (Jenkins 2011), and this particular moment, as the two lovers gaze (or do not gaze, as it were) upon the mythic ciphers of the city, offers a laconic, yet crucial instance of the unwitting critique of myth in the film. The composite persona(e) of Umay Aslan and Sibel Kekilli, together, ask the prototype liberal middle-class ethnic German interlocutor, what exactly it was that he sought to show her. What he wants to show, particularly to her, and from a standpoint literally bridging East and West, is the diorama of reunified Berlin—an historiographic myth-unity that compulsorily signifies the struggle for emancipation—from monarchy, fascism, American hegemony, Soviet rule, and by extension any other forms of self-imposed immaturity or entrapment. And yet, Kekilli/Aslan registers perplexity at having been shown it; they already know it, they do not need it to be shown. This is perhaps one of the few moments that express incredulity toward the surface grammar of the film's myth.

This leads to a broader question: what mood or political temporality has made such a film as *When We Leave* possible or compulsory, such that an impressive showing from among the small cadre of celebrated Turkish German (and Turkish) film stars both gravitate toward and tacitly, tactically resist it? One may wonder whether something fundamental has shifted since the moment of Ataman's *Lola and Billy the Kid*, Hussi Kutlucan's *Ich Chef, Du Turnschuh* (*Me Boss, You Sneakers!*, 1998), or even Fatih Akın's *Im Juli* (*In July*, 2000), such that self-referentiality, anti-essentialism, and speaking-back have been defrocked of their critical viability. To a great extent, many of the same actors, though older and suffering back pain as in *Soul Kitchen*, are both critiquing and partaking in this transformation from anti-identarian rupture to neo-baroque cultural fetishism. And yet in *Soul Kitchen* it was the monolingual Turkish naturopath, Bone Cruncher Kemal who solved the problems of the aging cast of German migration film by wrenching its momentary ringleader's spine back into place, in a way that no neoliberal German health care institution would have permitted. Such a mood of renunciation and correctivity seems to be currently holding sway over this arena of filmmaking. One wants to undo the ideological entanglements of previous decades; one wants to seek a sober alternative.

Of course, this mood corresponds very well to a broader disciplinary ritual—and here I mean disciplinary in the Foucauldian sense—of issuing judgment on the stylistic, rhetorical, and ideological excesses of the 1990s, an endeavor I think of as a "very new sobriety". This mood, or stance, seems to have made its way quite potently into film production, where both Michael Haneke and Turkish German filmmakers (here represented by Feo Aladağ) have made an aggressive, peripetetic break with their predecessor films, in a bid to render a newly sober, newly authentic portrayal of social phenomena that had previously been fodder for shrill dispute and deconstructive reinscription (see also Daniela Berghahn in this volume).

The ambient discursive field surrounding *When We Leave*, as well as the academic reception and public discourse poised to greet it, exhibit the aesthetics of a postironic mood, one which soberly delights in taming the (ludic or tropic) negativity of preceding decades' filmic and literary interventions. Whether this moment might enter the critical history of Turkish German film as a labor of strategic essentialism—or, perhaps, as strategic mythology—is not yet clear. What *When We Leave* demonstrates most profoundly is that the pleasures and displeasures of hybridity (Göktürk 2001; Malik 1996; Ewing 2006) are just as susceptible to mythological expropriation as any other semiotic domain. The current decade of Turkish German filmmaking will be a crucial proving ground for this struggle between hybridities and mythologies, a struggle in which *When We Leave* has staked an unequivocal claim.

Notes

I am particularly grateful to Jessica Nicholl, Sabine Köhler-Curry, Hikmet Kocamaner, and Patrick Carlson for sharing their insights on the film.

1. Kreuzkölln has come to denote the cultural milieu encompassing East Kreuzberg and North Neukölln in central southeastern Berlin.
2. In reference to the NBC's *The Cosby Show* of the mid-1980s (for a discussion of genre and family imagery in the American television show, see Taylor 1989: 13–28).
3. I thank Hikmet Kocamaner for this observation.
4. Directly below this headline, the *Hürriyetport.com* Arts and Culture editorial staff gruesomely underscored their announcement by placing two still photographs in immediate juxtaposition to one another: on the left, a closeup headshot of Kekilli in *When We Leave*, grinning slightly, wearing a tight headscarf traditionally associated with pious Sunni Islam and, on the right, a slightly blurry, low-quality shot of her in the midst of sexual intercourse with an unnamed male porn actor.

Chapter 3

THE MINOR CINEMA OF THOMAS ARSLAN: A PROLEGOMENON

Marco Abel

Prologue

Whenever the work of Thomas Arslan is mentioned in a discussion of contemporary German cinema, it is almost always framed through the lens of identity—specifically the identity of people of Turkish descent living in Germany. The problem I have with this approach to his work is not that I think it is "wrong." Yet, this reduction (no matter how productive in some regards) of what his films *do* to what they *are* blocks investigations into his oeuvre that might open conversations about both his films and, possibly, those of other so-called Turkish German filmmakers to contexts that cannot readily be reduced to an identitarian, or representational, framework and its (un)stated assumptions about Germans as a people. To make my case for the need to reframe Arslan's work, however, I purposefully want to abstain from primarily focusing on those films that do not explicitly deal with characters of Turkish descent, such as *Mach die Musik leiser* (*Turn Down the Music*, 1994) or *Ferien* (*Vacation*, 2007). Merely to foreground that Arslan also made films—both before and after his so-called Berlin trilogy—that show no overt concern for the question of Turks in Germany would simply skirt the real issue at hand. My point is that even in *Geschwister—Kardeşler* (*Brothers and Sisters*, 1997), *Dealer* (1999), and *Der schöne Tag* (*One Fine Day*, 2001) Arslan's primary concern does not lie with the question of identity; or, rather, if it does then only insofar as he puts its underlying assumptions at stake. If we can agree that the political quality of films is frequently assessed in relation to how they represent identities, then I want to make the point that Arslan's cinema calls for a reconceptualization of this very understanding of the political.

In this sense I offer the following as a prolegomenon—remarks that seek to define a project and the conditions that make it both possible and necessary. A prolegomenon does, however, not try to be comprehensive and instead hopes to function as a provocation for others to help develop this project further. The aim, thus, is decidedly not to insist that what follows constitutes a better or more correct interpretation of Arslan's work; a prolegomenon is simply not in the business of engaging in hermeneutical questions and playing their attendant truth games. Rather, the goal is to proffer an experimental sensibility with which to revisit Arslan's oeuvre, "in order to make a picture for oneself (*sich ein Bild zu machen*)," to quote Arslan's rationale for making his filmic travelogue *Aus der Ferne* (*From Far Away*, 2006) about Turkey (Arslan 2004: 16). To make—rather than take—a picture: this formula not only encapsulates Arslan's cinematic attitude towards his parents' home country to which he had not returned since attending school there (1967–71) but arguably also serves as the creative algorithm at the heart of his films. With this formula the director articulates his cinematic attitude toward profilmic reality, which insists that the cinema's job is less to represent (to take a picture) than to construct it in singular fashion in order to effect what French philosopher Jacques Rancière calls a "redistribution of the sensible"—that is, of "the system of self-evident facts of sense perception that simultaneously discloses the existence of something in common and the delimitations that define the respective parts and positions with it" (2004: 12).

Differences

Arslan's oeuvre, from his student films to *Im Schatten* (*In the Shadows*, 2010), is primarily concerned with the question of change. It so happens that the same question preoccupies critical responses to his work as well. It is, however, precisely how change is conceived differently by, on one hand, scholarly responses to his films and, on the other, by and in his films—by the films themselves and by the protagonists in these films—that renders both possible and necessary this prolegomenal project.

The main thread traversing scholarly accounts of Arslan's work spins around the question of whether his films offer new ways of depicting Turkish identities in Germany. For example, Barbara Mennel ends her lucid discussion of transnational auteurism and ghettocentrism in Fatih Akın's *Kurz und schmerzlos* (*Short Sharp Shock*, 1998) as well as Arslan's *Brothers and Sisters* and *Dealer* with the question of whether "the spatial politics of these films *depart* from earlier portrayals of Turkish identity and suffering in Germany" (2002a: 155, my emphasis). Rob Burns perceives Arslan's cinema to mark a *"shift* from a 'cinema of the affected' to a 'cinema of hybridity'" (2007a: 375, my emphasis). And Deniz Göktürk argues that *Brothers and Sisters* "signals a *new* mode of depicting immigrants and their hybrid offspring" and that this *"shift* in the representation of migrants corresponds with recent trends" in how theoretical accounts of migration "have come to appreciate the migrant as the 'modern metropolitan figure'" (2000: 65, my emphases). Jessica Gallagher, however, disagrees with what she takes to be Göktürk's overly optimistic assessment of Arslan's representation of immigrants. To her, a closer analysis of at least the first two films of his trilogy reveals how the protagonists *"continue* to struggle with the same or similar problems as their predecessors in the *Gastarbeiterkino"* (2006: 339, my emphasis) such as Helma Sanders-Brahms's *Shirins Hochzeit (Shirin's Wedding*, 1976) and Tevfik Başer's *40 qm Deutschland (Forty Square Meters of Germany*, 1986)—a "'cinema of duty'" (Göktürk 2002a: 250) that many consider less progressive than what critics variously theorize as "le cinéma de métissage" (Seeßlen 2000), an "accented cinema" (Naficy 2001), or a "cinema of double occupancy" (Elsaesser 2005). These approaches share an understanding of difference as constituting a difference from a prior (representation of) identity. Conceptually speaking, difference functions here as something posited as secondary in relation to a presumed primary moment of (self-)identity. That is, difference or change, as operative in these responses to Arslan's work, is conceived dialectically.

Difference as dialectics, dialectics as the engine for change: this Hegelian configuration of difference and change effectively territorializes material processes of transformation—of becoming—onto the plane of representation and its governing (idealist) logic. It is this habitual representational deployment of change—change or difference measured against a prior moment of self-identical identity—that Arslan's films self-reflexively question. They do so not to denounce the representationalist account of change as false but, rather, to ask whether this dialectical conception of difference is in fact capable of accounting for the material sociopolitical processes that obviously concern the critical discourse on his work. This putting at stake of representationalism is thus not so much a matter of insisting on a different "truth" than those offered by identitarian approaches to these issues as it is a matter of cost: Arslan's films prompt us to ask whether the discursive dominance of a deployment of change that frames difference through a logic of representational identity might not cost us too much in terms of our ability to theorize not only the issue of identity but also issues closely related to it such as those of the nation, the people, and, finally, what counts as political.

In contrast to the conception of change operative in the critical discourse responding to his work, Arslan's films posit difference immanently, in terms of (affective) intensity rather than dialectics. We can observe this intensive rather than dialectical conception of transformation in each of his films. For the purposes of brevity, however, two examples must suffice: the first from Arslan's student film, *Im Sommer—Die sichtbare Welt* (*During Summertime—the Visible World*, 1992) and the second from the middle installment of his Berlin trilogy.

Change

During Summertime is a black and white film in which, as is typical for Arslan's style, no one scene assumes paramount importance. For my purposes, however, the moment is crucial when the unnamed male protagonist, who is "bored with everything, so [he tries] to do less and less," reads aloud from the German translation of Paul Valéry's *Cahiers*: "There is nothing extraordinary to my life. But it is being transformed by *how* I think about it" (my translation and emphasis). Reflecting on Arslan's career, I cannot help but consider this brief moment—cinematically rendered in the same nonchalant style as all of the protagonist's activities—the experimental algorithm that programmatically permeates his entire oeuvre, not least because this early film explicitly raises the issue of transformation, of change, in the context of an aesthetic concern with the question of visibility (note the film's subtitle), including the crucial questions of what is and is not visible and how something becomes visible or not. Yet instead of dramatizing these occurrences of visibility, of becoming visible, and thus of transformation as extraordinary, this and the director's other films render sensible (rather than represent) the ongoing process of change by intensely observing the utterly mundane, ordinary lives of his protagonists to whom nothing much happens. The intensity with which Arslan's filmic gaze observes his characters results from both the visual staging of the mise en scène and his use of sound, as well as the fact that his characters are predominantly examples of what Deleuze describes as "seers" (1989: xi), characters who relate to their environment as observers rather than agents. The effect is that Arslan's films do not merely represent the ordinariness of his protagonists' lives but render it sensible for the viewer. Rather than exteriorizing—representing—change on the narrative level, Arslan subjects viewers to the sensation of change that occurs immanently, from within the very ordinariness of the mise en scènes and the "boring" lives traversing them. Consequently, change, in these films, is not measured against a prior moment of self-identity but, rather, is brought about by modulating the same moment, by intensifying it to a point at which the change immanent to that moment becomes sensible, not by being represented for us but by being affectively impressed on the presubjective level of our nervous system.

The very notion of transformation that *During Summertime* explicitly posits as the outcome of a particular way of thinking—indeed, as the outcome of a specific attitude manifesting itself in how rather than what one thinks about (the ordinariness of) one's life—ends up being affectively instilled in the viewer's nervous system in analogous fashion, that is, not because of what is represented but because of the intensity with which what is staged is being staged. Arslan uses a number of different cinematic means to accomplish this, including his repeated deployment of the long take, which forces viewers to linger on the image well beyond the point at which they have understood its meaning. Frequently spending an inordinate amount of time imaging something that could have been depicted more briefly, Arslan's cinema thus foregrounds not only that his images are made but also that his point is less to inform us of something than to test what happens beyond the moment at which their informational content has been comprehended by their addressees: the becoming-sensible of the force of change in the absence of any representation of change on screen.

During Summertime and Arslan's oeuvre at large explicitly configure change as resulting from a style, or particular intensity, of thinking ("how") and, by implication, of filming. Thus, in his films change is always a matter of aesthetics. While such an aesthetic conceptualization of change runs the risk of being judged apolitical, I suggest that it affirms the affective force that ontologically inheres in the political—at least if we are willing to follow Rancière in positing politics as a matter of (re)distributing the sensible, i.e., that which can and cannot be seen, perceived, and sensed. The political is for Rancière the result of a process of partitioning the realm of the sensible, a process that assumes different outcomes at different historical junctures. This desire to engender such a redistribution of the sensible in and for us makes Arslan's cinema function as a counter cinema or what Deleuze theorizes in *Cinema 2—The Time-Image* as "minor" cinema precisely because it ends up demanding of us that we theorize, which is to say: see, politics as something that operates on a level that lies beyond or below, and is thus incommensurable with, the logic of identity—incommensurable, that is, with an act executed "in the name of" this or that already existing identity (the people, the nation, this or that ethnicity, etc.).

Politics, as per Rancière, is "a matter of subjects or, rather, modes of subjectification." By subjectification he means "the production through a series of actions of a body and a capacity for enunciation *not previously identifiable* within a given field of experience, whose identification is thus part of the reconfiguration of the field of experience" (1999: 35, my emphasis). Politics names those acts of subjectification that drive a wedge into society, separating it from itself through issuing a challenge to the existing partitioning of the sensible, that is, of an allegedly natural order of bodies, structures, and relations. Revolving around "what is seen and what can be said about it, around who has the ability to see and the talent to speak, around the properties of spaces and the properties of time," politics is thus a matter of "aesthetic practices" (Rancière 2004: 13); in fact, politics has its own aesthetics insofar as aesthetics is "a mode of articulation between ways of doing and making, their corresponding forms of visibility, and possible ways of thinking about their relationships" (2004: 10). "Aesthetic politics," Rancière holds, "always defines itself by a certain recasting of the distribution of the sensible, a reconfiguration of the given perceptual forms" (2004: 63). Hence, aesthetics is precisely not reducible to, or even a matter of, content (and therefore not of identification and representation, the logic of which always necessarily presupposes a self-identical content that subsequently can be represented). In contrast, so Rancière says, "the dream of suitable political work of art is in fact the dream of disrupting the relationship between the visible, the sayable, and the thinkable without having to use the terms of a message as a vehicle" (2004: 63).

From this conception of politics follows that what Rancière calls "dissensus"—an act that performatively effects a transformation in the world of the sensible—is an operation that cannot be reduced to a dialectical conception of change with which we are all too familiar. *Au contraire*: dissensus is "a supplement to the simple consensual game of domination and rebellion" (2009: 9). It is an expression of an immanent logic that, in accordance with Rancière, I want to insist on calling aesthetics: an expression of affective modulation that occurs on the micro, presubjective level because it directly acts upon and intervenes in the realm of the sensible—without any recourse to the detour of mediation (signification, representation). Aesthetics is thus not the Other to politics; it does not lie outside its realm but rather names the force that immanently actualizes politics' virtual potential. Consequently one cannot presume to be familiar with such an intervention's result precisely because the result of such a modulation is an event—something that can be neither anticipated nor ignored, and that comes into being and has existence only through and in its effects. Its occurrence and presence manifest and thus gain existence only as effects that have no prior existence. An event occurs only performatively, as effects to which one cannot *not* respond because they affect a subject before there is a subject *qua* subject that might be able to choose whether or not to respond to them. The responding subject comes into being through the process of subjectification engendered by actions and the creation of capacities that are not identifiable within a subject's prior framework of experience. Differently put, dissensus, the bringing about of transformation or change, is a matter of force, of becoming, and as such is the strangest (but paradoxically also most common) phenomenon. It is just this phenomenon with which Arslan's cinema is preoccupied and in response to which he finds time and again cinematic means in order to confront his viewers with the sensation of the strangeness that constitutes change.

The Strangeness of Change

One of the most complex examples of Arslan's career-long experimentation with the material processes of transformation occurs at the end of *Dealer*, when we are made to listen to its drug-dealing protagonist, Can, played by Tamer Yigit, declaring that it is "strange how everything changes" at the very moment when, presumably, he finds himself offscreen behind bars, facing possible expulsion from Germany. Rather than following both

Gallagher and Burns in asserting that "in reality nothing has changed" (Gallagher 2006: 348) for Can because "his freedom of action was essentially no less restricted in his urban environment than it is now in this real prison" (Burns 2007a: 373), I propose we take Can by his word and think through the strangeness of how everything changes. What strikes me as crucial about Can's remark is the not-altogether-unimportant qualifier "strange" prefacing what is primarily an observation rather than a declaration: "strange, how everything changes." Analogous to *During Summertime*, this moment marks once more Arslan's career-long effort to conceptualize transformation as a matter of rendering sensible rather than representing, not least because change itself and the process of how it comes about—"how everything changes"—is inherently strange. Change is not actually knowable and thus representable as such because it is effected on the micro, presubjective level; it performatively actualizes at a moment when an affective threshold is being crossed, that is, when a body is affected so that its capacity for action increases or decreases.

Indeed, not only is Can's voice-over remark about change prefaced by an expression of strangeness, but the exact phrasing also foregrounds that what is strange is precisely not that everything changes but how everything changes. Strangeness is attributed not to the potentially verifiable, representable content that change might assume but to the process of change. The form taken by inquiries such as, "did or did not everything change for Can?" or "does Arslan's trilogy change how German cinema depicts Turkish people or not?" posits terms of identity as an a priori in relation to which any subsequent attempt at addressing these questions necessarily remains beholden, thus inevitably reducing the strangeness of change to its overly familiar dialectical logic. In contrast, insisting with Can— and by proxy Arslan—on the strangeness of change, on the strangeness of both its process and any sensation thereof, that is, on strangeness as the proper, ontologically immanent condition of transformation, I submit that what is at stake in Arslan's cinema, including his trilogy, is less the issue of identity or that of an identifiable (read: measurable and verifiable) representational result than how one conceptualizes change in the first place. What is at stake is how change, or pure difference, can be imaged or rendered sensible.

How, then, does Arslan's work engage the issue of change, if not by trying to represent it, if not as a matter of representation and thus through the dialectical logic of identity? Let us return to *Dealer*. Toward the end of its final sequence's nearly one-minute long opening shot, Jale, played by Idil Üner, the mother of Can's child, leaves after she tells Can that he should not expect her to wait for him. As she gets up, Arslan cuts across the 180-degree axis to shot two, thus undoing the spatial orientation established by the first shot's perspective. Jale walks around the table and caresses Can's face, which is framed in a tight profile shot. Then a subdued piano score, which we first hear in the film's opening moments, commences before this static

The Minor Cinema of Thomas Arslan   51

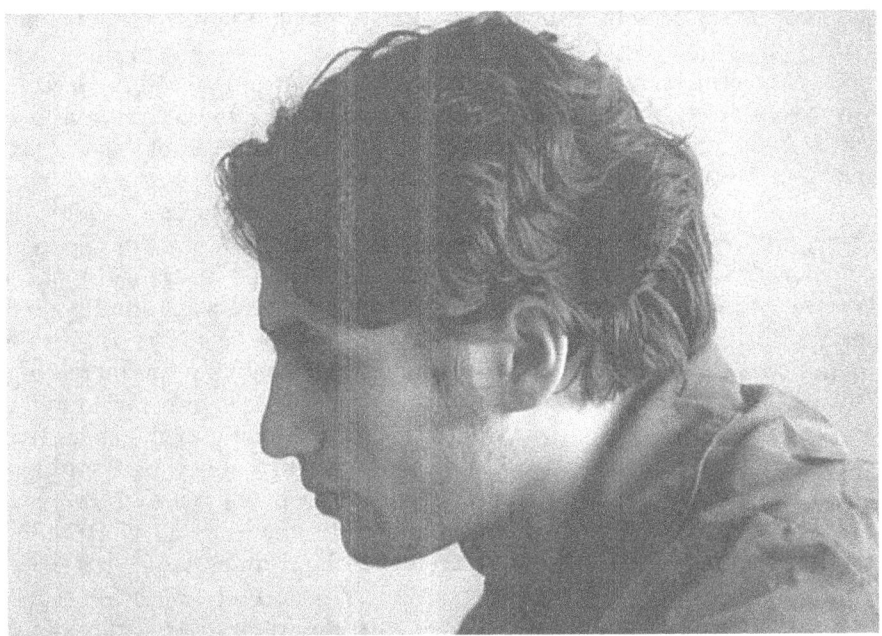

Figure 3.1 Can (Tamer Yigit) in *Dealer*, DVD capture

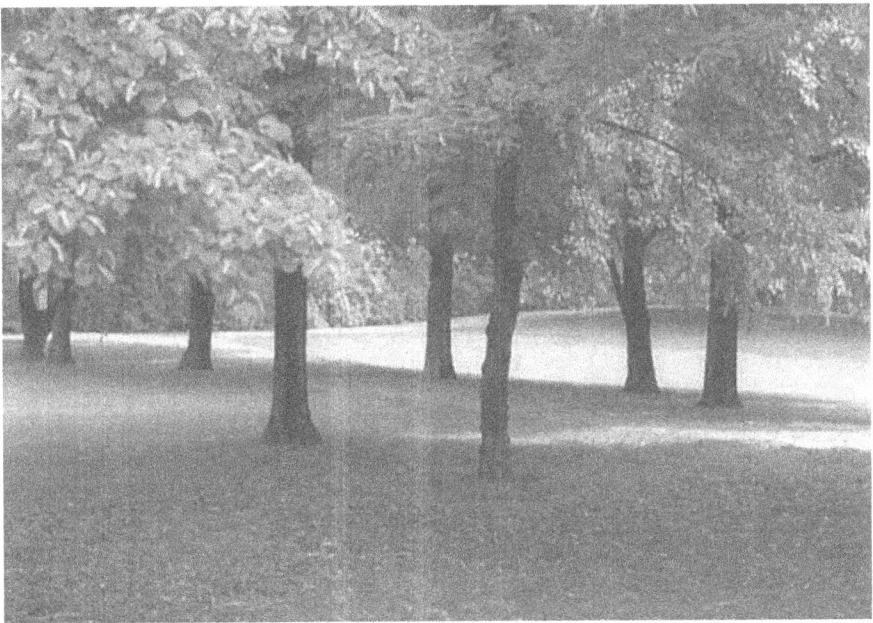

Figure 3.2 Any-Spaces-Whatever in *Dealer*, DVD capture

long take is replaced by a shot of a park in bright sunlight. With the piano score still audible, we now hear Can's voice-over as the camera slowly yet briefly travels to screen right. Unlike in the shots from within the prison, we are no longer given any diegetic sound from here on out; the final five static shots construct a slow montage of what are now empty spaces we may recall from earlier scenes in the film.

This roughly two-and-a-half-minutes-long concluding sequence stages what we might call with Deleuze and Guattari Can's "incorporeal transformation" through purely cinematic means: a transformation precipitated by Jale's speech act—"I'm supposed to wait [four years] for you? ... Are you serious?"—which cements the fact that he can no longer consider himself in a relationship, thus finalizing his increasing isolation. The instantaneousness of Can's incorporeal transformation—something that is "recognizable ... by the simultaneity of the statement expressing the transformation [such as Jale's rhetorical question] and the effect the transformation produces" (Deleuze and Guattari 2007: 81) on a real body such as Can's—is further marked by the camera's violation of the 180-degree rule, isolating his face in profile through which his body assumes the definitive contours of an imprisoned body. With the piano score linking shot two and three, thus creating an impossible continuity insofar as the spaces it links are incommensurable, the film cuts to a series of what Deleuze calls "any-space[s]-whatever" (1989: 5), which in this case are marked by both an evacuation of human, and thus social, life and the absence of any sounds properly belonging to them. In other words, these are abstract, rather than representational, spaces. Although they do evoke spaces we have seen earlier, they are no longer the same spaces. In fact, it is impossible to determine their temporal relation to the narrative and discern whether they mark an earlier or later moment. We can neither decide how much earlier or later these shots occur in relation to the prison scene nor determine why these spaces are so empty and are exposed to a redistribution of the sensible—of what can and cannot be sensed and perceived—as we behold the same spaces, but differently so.

Though we may be inclined to read these spaces as metaphors that comment on the narrative, the nature of such commentary is aesthetically marked as literally impossible by the spatiotemporal incommensurability between this montage and the voice-over spoken off screen. Arslan thus impresses upon us the sensation of hearing a voice that is not anchored in a real time and space—that does not belong to an already constituted body or identity. The voice-over is disembodied insofar as it hovers above the images as much as the images hover above the prior narrative. This voice is given a body only through or as its sonority, in and as the affective force of the materiality of sound as such, that is as a potential rather than representational body. Unlike, say, the piano score that begins in shot two and continues to the end, the voice-over occurs only in shot three, a shot emptied of any human presence, including Can's. Thus instead of simply ascribing the space and time of this utterance to Can's represented prison body, we have to suspend such referentialization and instead recall the film's prior moments of voice-over (intermittently used throughout the film), which now also begs the question of their spatiotemporal specificity, that is, their ontological indeterminacy.

The film's overall strangeness is thus brought to a concluding climax in what we might call a moment of transcendental empiricism. As is typical for all of Arslan's work, the film relentlessly foregrounds the physicality of the bodies and spaces through which they move, or, rather, the other way around: the physicality of the spaces and the bodies that are moved through them. This strategy configures them as these and not those bodies and investigates these bodies in terms of their *potenza* rather than their *potere*, to use Antonio Negri's terms from his discussion of biopolitics, which "turns into biopower [*biopotenza*; in original] intended as the potentiality of constituent Power" instead of "bio-Power [*biopotere*; in original] intended as the institution of a domination over life" (Casarino and Negri 2008: 148). In the latter articulation of biopolitics, *bios* creates power, whereas in the former *bios* is subjected to constituted Power, the goal of which is to dominate what Negri argues is the a-priori-constituent power of the multitude. (The relation between *potenza* and *potere* is, however, asymmetrical rather than dialectical.) Arslan's cinema is thus a materialist cinema, and affect—that is, transformation or potential—is the constitutive force of matter. Can's nonspatializable and nontemporalizable observation of the strangeness of the process of total change—an utterance that expresses a transcendental quality precisely to the degree that it is a purely material description—instills in us this very strangeness immanent to the ontological condition of matter performatively, which is a matter of affect: that is, in and as our sensation, in and as the condition for our transformed capacity to sense and perceive. Throughout his work Arslan is invested in affirming this materiality as something that is always already constitutive of the process of transformation. And he aims to heed this inherent strangeness of change, its potential, as the experimental engine for discovering what its becomings produce: states, themselves always merely in transition, in-between, that are necessarily of the future, in potential, and thus not beholden to the logic of representation, that is, identity.

Materialist Cinema

Arslan's oeuvre conceptualizes as well as renders change through the logic of a-dialectical intensification, that is, through how his cinema attends to the strangeness inhering in the processes of transformation. To become sensitive to this process, we have to suspend a metaphoric, representational, dialectical approach to images and sounds and instead heed the affective, a-signifying logic expressed in Arslan's insistence to make, rather than take, pictures. The notion of "taking a picture" presupposes the stable existence of something that can then be represented and that on some level is seen to exist for representation. The desire to "make a picture," in contrast, begins from a position of radical wonder, perhaps even disagreement with the very assumptions of the former, which have resulted in a particular partitioning of the social that cannot be contested unless that which can and cannot be sensed and perceived is altered first. Such a diagnostic move posits the question of bodies in immanent rather than identitarian terms. Doing so enables a consideration of how Arslan's cinema constitutes an attempt at imaging postunification Germany without presuming to know already who the Germans and its Others are. And this may well be the most important task for filmmakers in the post-Wall era—an era marked by the political refusal to constitute Germany anew, as a new people, an era in which the people, un-constituted as they are, remain quite literally to-come.

Lest I be misunderstood: I am not arguing that it is irrelevant to attend to the specificity of the bodies that are in front of Arslan's camera; but in my view accounting for these bodies in terms of ethnicity or nationality is precisely not materialist enough. Long ago, the great materialist philosopher Baruch Spinoza argued that categories of species and genus—and Deleuze's thought compels us to say identity in general—are confused ideas precisely because they do not account for a body's capacity to affect and be affected. This is why a draft horse has in fact more in common with an ox than a racehorse, even though it is part of the same species as the latter (Deleuze 1978). "Identity" reduces actions to states, verbs to nouns, what a body can do to what it is. The question to ask is thus precisely not the identitarian question of, "what are you: Turkish, German, Turkish German, trans- or hybrid?" but the materialist question of, "what is this body capable of doing?" That is, categories of species, genus, and, indeed, identity are imprecise, confused ideas precisely because they presuppose that we already know what a body—this body over here, that body over there—can do, when in fact, as Spinoza suggests, we do not even know what its capacities are. Spinoza is convinced that the notion of identity precludes us from even trying to find out. For Spinoza, as for Deleuze—and I think for Arslan as well—discovering what a body, any body, is capable of is above all an affective, that is material and materialist question, not an ideational, identitarian one.

In the end, therefore, Arslan's cinema is a radically materialist cinema, one first and foremost invested in "ein Bild *machen*" (to make a picture). Conceptually speaking, Arslan's emphasis on this *machen* (to make)—on the primacy of cinema's affective materialism, on the fact that we never respond to the level of represented content prior to being affected by how its production works—suggests that we have to consider his cinema as a "minor cinema," a cinema invested in imaging change intensively, indeed in rendering sensible the yet-to-come in what "is." His is a cinema invested in the question of how to render a becoming-sensible in ways that do not posit difference as difference from a prior identity. Instead, his interest lies in rendering change or difference, *as such*, as immanent material, affective modulations of what is always already in variation. Change in Arslan's films is rendered sensible as the crossing of a threshold that cannot be said to exist prior to the modulation that lends this threshold its affective expression and effectivity; change obtains this affective force precisely through and at the time of the event of modulation itself. And this event manifests itself only on the level of its effects, that is, through its becoming-sensible as an increase or decrease in its *potenza*, in one's capacity to affect and be affected: to sense, to perceive, to act.

So whereas the scholarship on Arslan has thus far primarily focused on his Berlin trilogy and on whether it differs from the "cinema of duty," my prolegomenal suggestion is to change the terms of the debate altogether, as they are beholden to the very identitarian logic that Arslan's films simply refuse to accept as their a priori condition of production. Performatively hailing a people that is still missing and thus yet-to-come, his supremely cinematic films constitute a minor cinema insofar as the category of the minor is expressive of the capacity to directly intervene on the political level by virtue of redistributing the sensible, rather than of a notion of representationalist identity. The political quality of Arslan's films is thus less defined by what they are about, by what they depict, than by how they work and what, as a result, they are capable of doing.

II

MULTIPLE SCREENS AND PLATFORMS: FROM DOCUMENTARY AND TELEVISION TO INSTALLATION ART

Chapter 4

ROOTS AND ROUTES OF THE DIASPORIC DOCUMENTARIAN: A PSYCHOGEOGRAPHY OF FATIH AKIN'S *WE FORGOT TO GO BACK*

Angelica Fenner

Since the mid-1990s, several autobiographical documentaries have emerged in the German media, shot by filmmakers of Turkish or Kurdish descent utilizing the camera as an experiential device for exploring their relationship to their bicultural heritage. As an increasingly global film practice, first-person filmmaking displays myriad stylistic variations: on the one hand, avant-garde abstraction from the indexical image, lyricism, and poetic qualities, and, on the other, an investment in referentiality and history. In some films, the evidentiary status of the self is visibly verifiable and retraces a personal chronology also encompassing family members, while in others authorial self-inscription may only be discernible in the voice-over commentary. Paul John Eakin's notion of relational identity remains salient in all instances, such that experiences of different individuals are "nested one within the other—self, family, community, set in a physical and cultural geography, in an unfolding history" (1999: 85). What makes the autobiographical stance such a powerful mode of intervention is the use of reflexivity "not to necessarily eradicate the real as much as to complicate referential claims" regarding the self and others (Lane 2002: 18). There is a powerful spatial dimension to this endeavor, one captured in the German term *Selbstverortung*, implying as it does the localization of self, of getting one's bearings in space and time, somewhere between past and present, between here and there (Curtis 2006: 7). In negotiating between the subjective intimacies of personal experience, i.e., the world within, and the quasi-objective public nature of historical circumstance, i.e., the world without, this mode also correlates with other scales of spatial negotiation especially pertinent to the interstitial position of the Turkish German filmmaker of dual heritage, the "diasporic documentarian." Ensconced in the German cultural realm but also possessing internal cultural and linguistic access to Turkish communities in both Germany and Turkey, they are able to shift optics to view both countries and cultures "from afar," to quote Thomas Arslan's essay film *Aus der Ferne* (*From Far Away*, 2006).

Their geographical traversals of national borders constitute metaphors of heightened mobility that render ambiguous the distinction between points of origin and of return. There is a sustained tension between "routes" and "roots," as the second generation reverses the path of global capital and flexible labor practices that first lured their parents to Germany, enacting journeys of return that may verge on revalorizing a bounded sense of primordial place in the maternal or paternal village of origin. The ambiguity about which sphere—territorial, cultural, linguistic, discursive—ultimately constitutes the inside and which the outside becomes itself an important source of inspiration as well as friction. To acknowledge the spatial ambiguities that haunt these cultural explorations, however, is by no means to relegate their human subjects to that "imaginary bridge 'between two worlds'" Leslie Adelson (2001) maintains has haunted sociologically inflected public discourse and scholarly discussion of cultural production by foreign nationals and by variously "hyphenated" Germans. That locus, she suggests, "is designed to keep discrete worlds apart as much as it is pretends to bring them together" (2001: 246). She describes her own object of study, Turco-German literature, as "a threshold that beckons, not a tired bridge 'between two worlds'" and adds: "Entering this threshold space is an imaginative challenge that has yet to be widely met" (2001: 248).

Homi Bhabha's notion of third space has also gained popularity among postcolonial scholars. The term has assumed different meanings in his writings, at once describing a cultural locus produced by "wandering peoples who ... are themselves the marks of a shifting boundary that alienates the frontiers of the modern nation" (1990: 315), but also the "general conditions of language" (1994: 36), in which the ongoing performance of cultural discourses always produces an excess or non-coincidence of a given culture with itself that enables "third spaces." Pointing out the potentialities and pitfalls of the concept, Deniz Göktürk has maintained, "the experience of migration can be understood as a productive provocation which creates a transnational 'third space' of travel and translation where our traditional patterns of classifying culture are put into question. While celebrating this 'third space' however, we ought to be cautious not to forget about local specificities and differences as we create a third box for 'mixed pickles'" (2001: 133). Having come to mean too many things in too many contexts, I believe the term's gestural invocation in otherwise cogent scholarly discussions of the Turkish German cultural nexus enacts an ultimately illusory Hegelian *Aufhebung* (sublation), an unsatisfying resolution of negotiations of perhaps irreconcilable discursive complexity. When such readings produce a valorized third space out of a facile amalgam of purportedly homogeneous German and

Turkish realms, they verge on perpetuating precisely those binaries they seek to deconstruct. Although often attributed an emancipatory valence in relation to dominant cultures, the hybridization processes that underpin notions of third space are, moreover, equally at work in the operations of hegemony, and indeed, of capitalism (Mitchell 1997).

My ensuing analysis tries to circumvent static spatial designators, instead working off the dynamic and performative notion of "spatial practices" advanced by Michel de Certeau (1984). The latter theorist employs the term in his exegesis on the practice of everyday life to refer to the ways we variously use, appropriate, and define specific locales or places, and hereby instantiate socially inscribed spaces. In asserting that "space is a practiced place" (1984: 117), de Certeau acknowledges his intellectual debt to Maurice Merleau-Ponty, who first maintained that "space is existential" and "existence is spatial" (Merleau-Ponty 1989: 342). The tension between place and space, i.e., between concrete geographical locations and the spatial operations of historical subjects that produce a space and imbue it with cultural, ideological, and political associations, is salient to the human experience. But it is also inherent to storytelling, "carrying out a labor that constantly transforms places into spaces or spaces into places," for stories "organize the play of changing relationship between places and spaces" (de Certeau 1984: 118). This assumes a certain medium specificity in cinematic narration, where several layers of spatial organization are operative, from the protagonists who occupy the mise en scène in strategic ways, to cinematographic considerations involving camera placement and movement, to the specific spatiotemporal logic charted by the editing itself.

The type of first-person filmmaking under examination here, in particular, can be understood to function as what Adelson elsewhere has coined *Orte des Umdenkens* (Sites of Reorientation), defined as "imaginative sites where cultural orientation is being radically rethought" (2001: 247). Via the camera, these filmmakers work through their affinity for, and affiliation with, the respective geographical locales of Germany and Turkey, physically traversing these sites and bringing forth the topological dimensions of the Greek word for recounted or narrated story, *diegesis*. Functioning at once as author, narrator, and protagonist, they literally enact an itinerary that variously redraws boundaries, charts new vectors between people and places, and expands frontiers.

Fatih Akın's *Wir haben vergessen zurückzukehren* (*We Forgot to Go Back*, 2001) is richly exemplary for these spatial practices. Akın was inspired to make his film after viewing Seyhan Derin's *Ich bin die Tochter meiner Mutter* (*I Am My Mother's Daughter*, 1996), which constituted her final project in fulfillment of the degree requirements at the Munich School of Film and Television (HFF München). Coincidentally both films trace journeys to the same region of northern Anatolia bordering the Black Sea where their respective families originate. Their production circumstances, however, are quite distinct. Derin's biographical circumstances, like those of Kurdish German filmmaker Yüksel Yavuz (*Mein Vater, der Gastarbeiter/ My Father, the Guestworker,* 1995), conform to those Jim Lane (2002), writing in the American context, has maintained characterize a genre in which the authors "are not artists with a large body of established work that may engender wide recognition or viewership. The autobiographical documentarist is more often a filmmaker working in anonymity, at a very local level, under low-budget constraints. We enter the film or video with little preconception of the author's history, a situation akin to such nontraditional written autobiographies as slave narratives, captivity narratives, diaries, and memoirs" (2002: 4). The artist may thereupon gain public recognition, even acclaim, but their initial autobiographical authority depends "less on who they are as public figures and more on their existential interaction with historical events" (2002: 4).

By contrast, Akın had yet to achieve auteur status but had received enough critical acclaim for his first feature-length film *Kurz und schmerzlos* (*Short Sharp Shock*, 1998) and the ensuing light-hearted road movie *Im Juli* (*In July,* 2000) to induce a heightened awareness of his public self-presentation. This emerging investment in the status of one's image—a perhaps inevitable liability of international success—arguably makes it more difficult to take the emotional risks that otherwise lend the autobiographical genre its depth of emotion, originality, and discursive complexity. Akın had already drawn media attention for his Turkish heritage, and thus his journey to explore his family background risks overdetermination. The challenge becomes that of not surrendering to pre-existing clichés generated by the popular press about oneself or one's ethnicity, or alternately, of appropriating them through acts of postmodern citation that defer authorial identity along a string of pre-existing popular culture associations and thereby also deflect any intimate confrontation with the self. This latter approach appears operative in Akın's film, whether self-consciously fashioned or simply an extension of his general inclination, as a self-identified member of the hip hop generation, to "sample" or borrow from other filmmakers, most particularly American independent cinema.[1]

Richly evident is, for example, the influence of Martin Scorsese's family documentary, *Italianamerican* (1974), also shot before he became an acclaimed auteur but had established himself with three feature films, including *Mean Streets* (1973). The clumsy, inadvertently humorous, and richly insightful family portrait of Scorsese's working-class parents and their Sicilian heritage reveals the personal motivation for his early and continuing directorial preoccupation with Italian American street life in New York. Akın's film takes up techniques and themes from Scorsese's film and struggles in analogous manner with how much to incorporate the authorial self within the unfolding domestic scene. Scorsese's relationship to his historically and geographically removed Sicilian heritage is mediated entirely through the oral narratives of his native New Yorker parents. Their description of living standards of an earlier era acquires visual and historical veracity by intercutting still portraits of familial ancestors and stock photos of back alleys of typical New York tenements draped with the laundry of multiple families. References to the "old country," in turn, posit a romanticized ancestral homeland as structural antinomy to the trope of cultural integration, and, ultimately, of assimilation within multicultural America exemplified in his mother's self-conscious efforts to appear tolerant of other ethnic groups (e.g., the Irish) in the same neighborhood.

Akın's project explicitly takes up this multi-culturalist trope, whose prevalence in American popular culture already in his earlier films functions, in the words of Gerd Gemünden, as "a model for social and ethnic integration, cultural hybridity, and progressive notions of immigration and citizenship" (2004: 189). Yet in contrast to Scorsese, whose film was shot entirely in his family's living room, Akın and other Turkish/Kurdish German documentarists display a more mobile relationship to space. Indeed, their literal border crossings between Turkey and Germany exemplify the more historically immediate nature of their family's integration into a nation that has emerged only recently as "a land of immigration." If there is a positive effect to be found in the globalization of American popular culture and of Hollywood in particular, Gemünden maintains it resides in "the fostering of supranational imagined communities that displace those of the nation state. For minorities living in a nation such as Germany ... this is an attractive position" (2004: 188). Yet that popular culture, as Fredric Jameson has pointed forth, also "represses social anxieties and concerns by the narrative construction of imaginary resolutions and by the projection of an optical illusion of social harmony" (2000: 138). In participating in this "cultural dominant" involving a postmodern repetition of mass cultural forms, Akın's documentary treads an uneasy path between utopian longing and reification.

The film was co-commissioned by the Bavarian and West German Public Broadcasting Companies as part of the series, "Denk ich an Deutschland ... Filmemacher über das eigene Land" ("When I Think of Germany ... Filmmakers Focus On Their Homeland"), whose title draws inspiration from the first verse of a Heinrich Heine poem "Nachtgedanken" (Night Thoughts), which begins with the phrase "Denk ich an Deutschland in der Nacht, dann bin ich um den Schlaf gebracht" (If I think of Germany at night, I am robbed of all sleep). Also featured are documentaries by Doris Dörrie, Andreas Dresen, Andreas Kleinert, Peter Lilienthal, Katja Riemann, and others, which take stock of the increasingly complex social, political, and economic landscape of post-Wall Germany. It is perhaps in this funding framework that Akın dwells more explicitly than other compatriot directors of bicultural heritage engaged in first-person endeavors, on questions of local, national, and cultural affiliation, with consequences for how the biographical, narrational, and profilmic self is articulated and, perhaps, reified relative to different scales of space.

If the initial forty to ninety seconds of a film are among the most self-conscious (Bordwell et al. 1985: 25), this is particularly true for first-person films, which often seal what Philippe Lejeune has coined "the autobiographical pact" by confirming that author, narrator, and protagonist are one and the same (1989: 4). By introducing his film with a photographic portrait of his parents early in their marriage, taken probably in the late 1960s, Fatih Akın appears to displace attention to them as the actual object of his investigation. Yet his accompanying voice-over recollection of being raised with their recurring reminder that "someday we will return [to Turkey], we are not here to stay" underscores not only the young Turkish couple's initial ambivalence about settling in a foreign country, but also the point of intergenerational tension in the film itself, against which their son Fatih arguably shapes his own identity as that of a native Hamburger, at home within the ensuing referential setting of the film but also fully secure in the role he occupies as its narrator and protagonist.

The pop tune "Family Affair" (Sly and The Family Stone, 1971) initiates the cut to a photo studio portrait from the later 1970s, panning across the faces of individual family members as the title, *We Forgot to Go Back* is superimposed on the scene. Voice-over, musical lyrics, image, and print text converge to convey that transience and impermanence dwell at the core of this particular version of what Sigmund Freud once coined the "family romance" (1975: 9). The Viennese psychoanalyst and family father of six adopted the term to identify a fantasy the adolescent psyche commonly invokes to aid in the process of parental separation and individuation: that of being freed from the family of birth and becoming associated with one of higher, or otherwise idealized or normative social standing. This desire fundamentally originates out of questions of identity, not relative to the

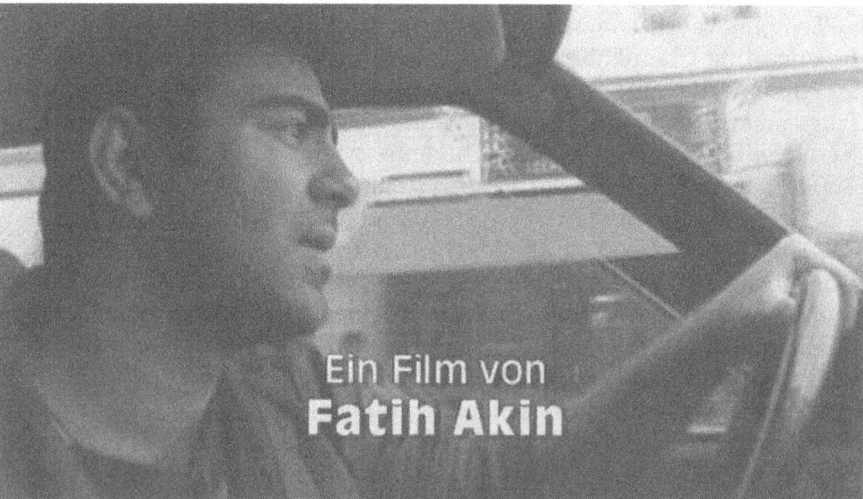

Figure 4.1 Fatih Akın in *We Forgot to Go Back*, DVD capture

ego or the agency of the mind, but as an effort to locate oneself within a personally viable and meaningful relational history and to use this as the basis for making sense of and in the world. In Akın's case, the path to individuation involves casting the terms of his origins in such a way as to establish a geographically and culturally secure standing, i.e., of indigeneity and unconditional belonging in relation to a bounded place and socio-cultural context—here, Altona in Hamburg, Germany. Through use of African American pop music from the 1970s as a sound bridge between key scenes, however, he also connotatively aligns this identity with the cosmopolitan consumerism of global youth culture and its tendency to engage in "nostalgia without memory" (Appadurai 1996: 30).

Those musical lyrics trail off precisely on the phrase "One child grows up to be …" and a match edit from his toddler face to Akın in close profile within a car interior, so as to link the trope of "local boy makes good" to a man that had already garnered a degree of celebrity status. The opening voice-over now anchors itself in the diegesis as Akın goes on explain to the unseen passenger beside him—the camera operator and stand-in for the spectator—why he is making this film. The dramaturgical conceit of filming him while driving literally and figuratively underscores that he is in the driver's seat, in control of the narrative journey on which he is embarking. In contrast to scenes shot in a moving train, which often connote passive contemplation and travel via regulated timetables and along predetermined routes, the automobile has long served in different cultural and historical contexts as a symbol of social mobility lending the driver an aura of bourgeois propriety, and evincing his or her autonomous and individualized mastery of space. Akın's staging is thus charged with a degree of performativity in which the car becomes a "bionic prosthesis" (Lackey 1997: 32) for his expanded identity, enabling him to display what Mark Osteen, discussing the role of the automobile in American film noir, refers to as "upward mobility through automobility" (2008: 187). Given Akın's cathected relationship to American cinema, where traveling shots within car interiors have long occupied an iconic role, it is little wonder he would choose an analogous maneuver to refute his parents' long-standing assumption that they would return for good to Turkey and abnegate anything but a transient cultural and social claim to live in Germany. Instead, the scene affirms Akın's affinity for his home district and his sense of social belonging, as he confidently surveys the neighborhood through the windshield and nods in recognition at the occasional passerby.

As in other diasporic documentaries, movement through time and space becomes the anamnestic vehicle for stream-of-consciousness recollections. Yet, whereas the psychoanalytical regression in, for example, Seyhan Derin's visual dreamscape in a moving train is enacted entirely at the nonlinguistic level, Akın's bears echoes of the Freudian talking cure. The intimate setting mimics the therapeutic encounter in which the analysand (driver) voices his associative thoughts while facing away from the analyst (i.e., camera operator). The Oedipal anxieties about Akın's origins and about the role of the totemic paternal signifier against which he has variously shaped his own gendered identity are intercut with recorded footage of another quasi-therapeutic confessional encounter—that of his parents on their living room couch responding to Akın's off-camera queries about their arrival in Germany back in the 1960s and about their early married life. The film's discourse is thus generated from the point of view of a son caught up in object relations, expressing his fascination with past anecdotes his parents have shared about their individual lives in Turkey, about their hopes and struggles upon arriving in Hamburg, and about early married life. This engagement with his parents as individuals whose history precedes his own entry into the world represents a site of universal fascination and anxiety for all (adult) children. It destabilizes the prevalent narcissistic assumption that our parents' lives essentially commenced to have meaning only upon our arrival in the world. The relocation of Mustafa and Hadiye Akın to Germany assumes an almost exotic dimension when their son speculates that the cultural adjustments had to have been as dramatic "as if I were to up and move to Russia or something." But Akın's pride in them is also closely linked to the agency of the ego-ideal, which Freud (1914) suggests gradually emerges out of the ego's original narcissism as it is repeatedly "disturbed by the admonitions of others and his own critical judgment is awakened" (1959: 51). Lacan, in turn, has read Freud's ego ideal as that agency for whose gaze the individual subject or ego seeks to actualize itself in the most idealized light (1981: 257).

Ever the storyteller, Akın begins subconsciously to frame not only his parents but also himself in the nostalgic discourse of classic American immigration and upward mobility. Following his visit to his parents, where he had posed questions as once did Martin Scorsese, from off camera, while they sat on the living room coach, he explains: "I wanted to make a film about my *family*. I wanted to show, 'Hey, these guys came here and didn't even have a toilet and now their kids are working at the German consulate and making films.'" His recourse (within the original German dialogue) to specifically the English word "family" implies that the German cognate would be inadequate to the trope he conjures from American multicultural identity politics. Having inserted himself into this idealized integrationist narrative of the American dream, he projects an extended genealogy that also includes the next generation, his (yet to be conceived) children, whom he anticipates one day regarding him with the same degree of historical distance and, perhaps, fascination as he has his own parents: "That's why I'm making this film. So that someday I can show my kids, 'Hey, those are your grandparents.' My kids will probably be more German than I am, assuming they have a German mother. So 'This is where they're from, this is how they spoke German, this is what they were like.'" Embedded in the narrative of his parental heritage is thus also a narrative of the self as projected from the place of the big Other, here, his future children, similarly bearing witness to their father's habitus and speech.

If the film's editing deftly enunciates "the peculiar chronicities of late capitalism" (Appadurai 1996: 30) in temporal registers of past, present, and future perfect, from a spatial point of view, it also evokes the Freudian topological division of reality into an interior world—here, the automobile as prosthetic extension of Akın's psyche—and an exterior world of object relations that include his parents but also the urban landscape and its ethnically diverse inhabitants. The car windshield herein substitutes for the camera lens itself as the technology enabling distanciation between observer and observed, with the open window evincing the semi-permeability of this simultaneously psychical and cinematic membrane. The visual style of urban flanerie is very reminiscent of that of Raoul Coutard, cameraman for Jean-Luc Godard's *À bout de souffle* (*Breathless*, 1960) and soon after, for Jean Rouch's *Chronique d'un été* (*Chronicle of a Summer*, 1960). The striking glimpses of Paris in late summer captured by Coutard's camera while filming Jean-Paul Belmondo driving in his stolen Thunderbird convertible were enabled by, and participated in, the French cinéma verité movement. That approach to documentary emerged as a result of the lightweight 16 mm Arriflex cameras used with the portable Nagra sound recorders, which allowed a reduced crew to accompany subjects in everyday routines such as riding a car or walking in the street. Proponents of the American direct cinema movement (Robert Drew, Richard Leacock, D. A. Pennebaker) sought to replicate "being there" under the assumption that the less obtrusive technology exercised no discernible influence upon the scene at hand. French ethnographer Jean Rouch and

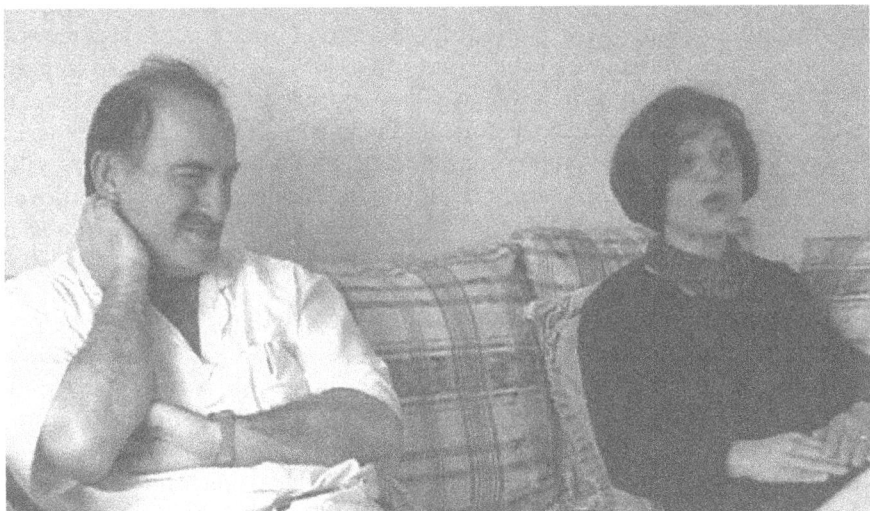

Figure 4.2 Mustafa and Hadiye Akın in *We Forgot to Go Back*, DVD capture

sociologist Edgar Morin, however, used the camera as a "psychoanalytic stimulant" they maintained triggered truths from the individuals filmed that would not have emerged were a camera not running (Levin 1971: 136). Certainly, the famous scene in *Chronicle of a Summer* of Holocaust survivor Marceline Loridan recalling her father's deportation to Birkenau in 1943 as she perambulates through Les Halles exemplifies the way the mobile camera could be deployed to trigger stream-of-consciousness ruminations rich with psychological revelation even when that testimony was later revealed to be historically inaccurate.

The same ideological contradictions that inhere in *Chronicle of a Summer* also characterize Akın's automobile sequence: the camera's presence has a provocative effect on its participant but remains itself curiously invisible. Viewers are thereby subject to a naturalization of the profilmic event that entails repression of the work of signification on many levels: that of camerawork, editing, and even the speaking subject's own censorial interventions. Effectively, this is a tension between film as evidence, as reflecting meaning, on the one hand, and acknowledgment of film as text, as semiotic activity, on the other. This correlates with a sense of reality "out there" beyond the windshield, and of Akın as part of a cognitive apparatus "inside" the vehicle. Both realms are subject to interpretation even if Freud has maintained, "internal objects are less unknowable than the external world" (1975, 14: 171). Freud's later writings indicate he had begun to rethink this topology and view the "psychical apparatus extended into space" (1975, 23: 196), and space, in turn, as "the projection of the extension of the psychical apparatus" (1975, 23: 300). If Akın's running monologue expresses his desire to locate himself within a genealogy that is relational, i.e., pertaining to his social place among family and friends, the camerawork and editing in turn spatialize those relations by topologically mapping his desire onto his everyday surroundings. Shown in profile in the car interior as he remarks that his own children will likely be even more German than he is, the depth of field created through his side window enacts an extended tracking along the historical housing facades of Altona. Later in that sequence he speaks more emphatically about his identification with this milieu: "I'm from Hamburg. Altona is my home. This is where I was born. People from fifty-five different countries live here." As if on cue, he pulls up beside an Afro German friend on his bike to shake his hand as the man breaks into an enthusiastic street rap.

The film thereupon cuts to Akın on foot, explaining that they are now going to his friend Adam Bousdoukous, who invested his earnings from acting in *Short Sharp Shock* to open a tavern in Altona and "now it's our restaurant." Greek accordion music provides a sound bridge into the festive locale, which is filled to capacity. The camerawork becomes immersive, moving fluidly around tables of patrons and cutting to closeups as they talk animatedly amidst open bottles of wine and plates of food. The ethnic entrepreneur's remark, "I bring Greece to Germany, that is my job," capitalizes on national affiliations, but when later pressed as to where his personal identifications lie, he reverts to the local or even cosmopolitan: "I don't really think of myself as German. I'm a Hamburger." Ensuing footage of Akın's mother teaching a classroom of Turkish-speaking children in Hamburg similarly underscores the way that diasporic communities build upon "imagined worlds," which "are constituted by the historically situated imagination of persons and groups spread around the world" (Appadurai 1996: 33). Against the backdrop of a map of Turkey, they sing lyrics translated as, "Far away there is a village. This village is our village. Even when we are not there, even when we don't go to visit. This is our village."

Those lines initiate the shift in geographical setting, cutting directly to the Istanbul airport where a film clapboard snaps shut on a glimpse of jetlagged travelers pushing along luggage carts. The ensuing visual montage continues the theme of urban flanerie first initiated in Altona, with traveling shots of Istanbul at night from a moving automobile, an establishing shot of the city against the backdrop of the rising sun, and pedestrian footage of the dense throngs moving in broad daylight through city streets whose topography of donkeys and automobiles offers evidence of the nonsynchronicity within Turkey's modernity. This viewpoint is no longer explicitly aligned with Akın's persona as it was in the car interior; it diffuses into an anonymous touristic gaze whose primary function is to establish locality. The accompanying American soul tune, Johnny Mathis's "I'm Coming Home," creates an affective overlay for the testimonials Akın will gather in that city: "Going back where I come from. I've had more than I can stand of watchin' men destroy my dreams. They picked my brain till it was clean. When I was up, they knocked me down. I ain't goin' to hang around, I'm goin' home." His father's sister, Türkan, and her husband Fikret resided in Germany for many years and their daughter Vildan ("Villi") and son Hikmet were born and raised there; when the couple eventually chose to return home, their adult children followed them. Their comments are inevitably more nuanced than Mathis's lyrics, recounting the challenges of acculturation in Germany, but also of reintegration in Turkey. What binds their individual narratives is a wistfulness about what is lost and what is gained in both countries through the choice to be anchored in a particular locale.

Svetlana Boym defines nostalgia as "a longing for a home that no longer exists or has never existed" in her masterful study of its relationship to global modernity since the dissolution of the Cold War (2001: xii). If it is a sentiment of loss and displacement, it is also "a romance with one's own fantasy," one that "can only survive in a long distance relationship" (2001: xii). This is richly underscored when Akın's film signals its next shift in geographical setting via a faded touristic postcard offering an aerial view of undeveloped coastline—that of Filyos, a former fishing village on the Black Sea, and the primordial home of the Akın clan. The transitional montage begins with a closeup of a road map tracing the route Akın and his crew will take, and then shifts to traveling shots of villages their van passes along the way. The accompanying aural citation of global popular culture, Odyssey's "Going Back to My Roots," renders Turkey the projected site of a phantasmal homecoming for Akın as much as for his father's brother, Nejat Akın, who returned there after a short stay in Germany during the 1970s. Yet the lyrics "Zippin' up my boots, goin' back to my roots yeah, to the place of my birth, back down to the earth" contradict the affiliations the filmmaker previously articulated and will again assert in the final minutes of the film, as a native-born Hamburger. The acoustic fantasy fades amidst the diegetic sound of tides lapping on an empty beach behind Akın, who gazes around him, disoriented and incredulous. He explains that there used to be thirty or forty fishing boats moored along the shoreline, which he found wonderful; yonder they always played football in the fields between old rusting wagons. The camera pans 360 degrees, as if to register his vertigo about the changes wrought upon the former village of "about ten homes, no more" now peppered with low-rise apartment buildings and single family dwellings. In the ensuing encounter with Nejat Akın at his home, the uncle seems ill at ease, first reluctant to talk and then rambling in an elliptical fashion that evidently defied editorial assimilation. Nejat indicates that he never regretted returning to Turkey and would otherwise not have the children and the life he has today, which enables him to go out fishing on the sea in summer, away from people and problems.

As Boym suggests, "homecoming—return to the imagined community—is a way of patching up the gap of alienation, turning intimate longing into belonging" (2001: 255). Certainly, the desire for belonging powerfully

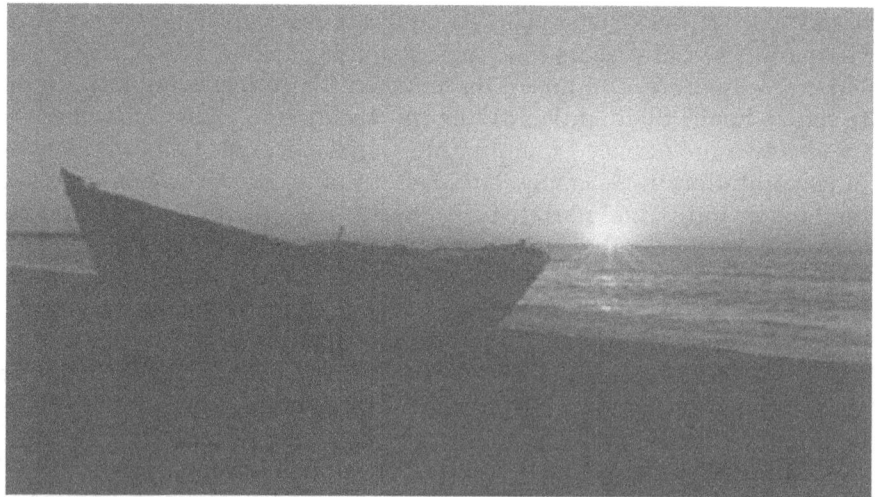

Figure 4.3 The Black Sea in *We Forgot to Go Back*, DVD capture

informs both Akın's approach to his project, and the testimonials of his wider circle of relatives—cousins, uncles, and aunts— who have traversed continents in the search for an elusive sense of entitlement within either Germany or Turkey and eventually settled in Turkey for good. Operating as "a defense mechanism in a time of accelerated rhythms of life and historical upheavals" (2001: xiv), nostalgia can be discerned in their sentimental recollections of either a seemingly prelapsarian era prior to emigration or, alternatively, an idealized life left behind in Germany. Even as the ambivalences expressed most especially among the second generation, i.e., Akın's cousins, bear an immediate historical and cultural specificity, they will also resonate with a multitude of film viewers, since, as Boym suggests, "the mourning of displacement and temporal irreversibility is at the very core of the modern condition" (2001: xvi).

As a psychical defense mechanism, then, nostalgia need not be solely regressive but can also be understood as "a symptom of our age, a historical emotion" (Boym 2001: 225). The archival value of *We Forgot to Go Back* rests in how the documentary bears witness to this emotion at the level of both discourse and diegesis, navigating a tenuous path between what Boym has identified as restorative nostalgia, i.e., local longing preoccupied with a return to origins, and reflective nostalgia, which dwells in ambivalence, embraces contradictions, and, as such, represents precisely "a new understanding of time and space that made the division into 'local' and 'universal' possible" (2001: xvi). Akın's use of the participatory mode of visual anthropologists blends with elements of autoethnography to map these conflictual psychical processes onto the topographies of both Germany and Turkey. The final two shots of the film evoke the disjunctures that underpin such an endeavor. On her living room couch in Hamburg, Hadiye Akın pragmatically points out that Turkey today is only a three-hour flight away, herein underscoring spatiotemporal continuity between two countries and cultures. However, the ensuing final image of a small rowboat resting on the shores of Filyos against the backdrop of the sun setting into the sea situates us once more in the temporally remote phantasm of Akın's childhood recollections of an unchanged Turkey. If this recourse to poetic closure accords all too easily with the clichés of the touristic imagination, it may also point forth a liability: that of the exhaustion of representational signs that haunts certain postmodern constructions of diasporic subjectivity.

Note

1. "When my ideas come, they all come at the same time and they come from a lot of different sources. I even recycle, like sampling in hip hop music, which I love." Interview with Fatih Akın. "It's easier to hate than to love," 19 September 2007, website of the Kaunaus International Film Festival. www.kinofestivalis.lt/en/news/easier-to-hate-than-to-love/.

Chapter 5

GENDERED KICKS: BUKET ALAKUŞ'S AND AYSUN BADEMSOY'S SOCCER FILMS

Ingeborg Majer-O'Sickey

The globally televised 2010 World Cup in South Africa once again highlighted the similarities between the performances in and around the games as expressions of attitudes by players and spectators. Promoters of soccer claim that the sport connects people across social, ethnic, national, political, sexual, and generational divides on and off the field.[1] While one might be optimistic about soccer's socially transformative potential in a general sort of way, for people concerned with sexist representations of women's bodies, the news is not so good. In the aftermath of the World Cup, websites attempted to lure viewers with provocative photos and videos of scantily clad female soccer fans. They used alliterative titles ("Sexy Soccer Superfans"), promised "soccer models in body paint," and previewed events such as "Body Paint Soccer Cup" and "Pornobol Germany vs. Australia" to rope in customers. The days are gone when spectators were simply treated to men exhibiting crazed fan behavior, wild rivalries, and other hyperbolic celebrations of masculinity. We thus have to view soccer through a theoretical grid that takes into account the sexualized and gendered conventions of the sport as spectacle.

It is therefore reasonable to conjecture that filmmakers who desire to make socially transformative films about girls and women playing soccer would be mindful of the hypersexual gaze constructed by these websites. In my discussion of Buket Alakuş's 2005 fiction film *Eine andere Liga* (*Offside*) and Aysun Bademsoy's documentary trilogy *Mädchen am Ball* (*Girls on the Pitch*, 1995), *Nach dem Spiel* (*After the Game*, 1997), and *Ich gehe jetzt rein* (*In the Game*, 2008), I argue that their soccer films work against the grain of popular consumption of female bodies that I mention above. Further, in that they thematize generational and class struggles as well as problematize profilmic intersections between generations, sexualities, social classes, ethnic groups, and religious practices, they represent important political interventions into discourses that concern second- and third-generation Turkish Germans.

Although the films under discussion are grounded in specific neighborhoods of Hamburg and Berlin respectively, Alakuş's and Bademsoy's cinefeminist works should be seen in the context of global cinematic depictions of female soccer.[2] In the following, I demonstrate that Alakuş's *Offside* and Bademsoy's three documentary films put pressure on received orthodoxies regarding spectatorship. To this end, I put into circulation issues related to the "cinematic gaze" (Alakuş) and the "look" (Bademsoy), because these are intricately connected to the directors' minority status as Turkish German women filmmakers and because their reconstruction of visual address is consonant with the genres they rework.

Transformative Film Praxis

The feature-length narrative film *Offside* is the coming-of-age story of a twenty-year-old soccer player (Hayat) who, in the midst of an inspired exhibition of playing, is struck down with what turns out to be breast cancer, the same disease that had killed her mother some years before. Hayat's cancer is stopped with a partial mastectomy and drugs. When Hayat's father forbids her to play soccer and her coach agrees with him, Hayat finds a new team and practices secretly. Except for her friend Ali, who has a secret crush on her, the young women from Hayat's original soccer team, Elbe SC, shun Hayat after her surgery. Her new team is undisciplined and disorganized, and trained by an initially lazy and indifferent coach named Toni. Under Hayat's influence the team gains the discipline and skills to compete and win against Hayat's former elite team, Hamburg's SC Elbe.

Even though soccer films about girls and women are a relatively new phenomenon, they have established a formula that uses the conventions of generic sports films. These include the topos of the underdog who overcomes a variety of challenges, be they social pressures (generally of economic, political, or psychological origin) or physical limitations (often caused by sports injuries). Indeed, a number of similarities exist between *Offside*'s Hayat Rudolph and Jesminder "Jess" Kaur Bhamra, the heroine of Gurinder Chadha's successful film *Bend It Like Beckham* (2002). Both Hayat and Jess are determined and talented soccer players; they train some of the time in secret; and their inspired playing propels their respective underdog teams to a higher standing in the league. The two films also share class-based and ethnic clashes between teams; the protagonists' initial dislike of the male coach that turns into a crush; the potential for lesbian romance; moments of jealousy; and a kind of happy ending for the girl-boy couple. For all these similarities, Alakuş's tragicomedy subverts the so-called cinematic gaze that holds together Chadha's film.

Aysun Bademsoy's documentary trilogy forges new territory in cinematic history.[3] Most documentaries on women playing soccer are feel-good movies that do not concern themselves with power relations in their subjects' social and political milieus or treat their subjects' lives diachronically over time.[4] The trilogy depicts important moments during thirteen years in the lives of five passionate and talented Turkish German soccer players, beginning in 1995 with *Girls on the Pitch*, followed in 1997 by *After the Game* and ending in 2008 with *In the Game*. After the completion of the first film, Bademsoy remained in contact with five players in the all-girl Berlin club Agrispor: the striker Safiye Kok, the left fullback Arzu Calkilic, and three midfielders, the Celic sisters Nalan, Nazan, and Türkan. In the first film, the young women's intense love for soccer dominates their thoughts and actions. By 1997, their soccer passion is tempered with worries about their professional chances and whether they will be able to live independently even if they choose not to marry. They soberly assess their professional and personal prospects as complicated by their status as the daughters of migrant parents from Turkey.

That second-generation Turkish German women are Bademsoy's main subjects is unmistakable from the very beginning. Most films about first-generation migrant women show them shut away in apartments or in other circumscribed spaces. By contrast, the subjects of the trilogy represent a new generation of Turkish German women; they circulate freely in and around Berlin-Kreuzberg; they play soccer, stroll, or picnic in Berlin's parks; shop for the latest trendy shoes; shoot pool in their neighborhood bar; and drive around Kreuzberg. Though traditionalists focus negatively on the women's bodies in their opposition to female soccer playing, the films capture the players as less self-conscious about their bodies. They accept that they are looked at, but seem more focused on their playing skills than on their appearance. Though the five young women have the same desires as other girls without migration background—they want to be independent of their parents and are eager to get good jobs—we also learn that they are different from their non-Turkish German peers in significant ways. Even though Bademsoy presses them for information about their attitude about their parents and whether they have boyfriends, their answers show a protective attitude toward their parents and a quiet reserve about topics such as dating. Furthermore, they exhibit a deep affinity for their heritage. In the first film, *Girls on the Pitch*, most of the seventeen- to nineteen-year-old players in the team introduce themselves as Turkish. By the last film (*In the Game*), the five players—now in their late twenties—discuss the pros and cons of marrying a non-Turkish German. By this time, features of being Turkish German have become a complex sociopolitical reality for most of them. One has to do with being typecast: "I have a German passport," declares one player, "I don't see myself as a Turkish woman, but I am a Turkish woman because I am treated as one by the Germans."

By the time the final film was shot in 2008, many of the dreams of the five players had been shattered. Intercuts from the preceding films into *In the Game* sharpen the contrast between the girls' earlier dreams and present-day reality. Most had to let go of their soccer passions. Only Safiye, who had founded the original team Agrispor, still remained in the game; she started a new club (Al Dersin Spor) that she and fellow trainer Mehtap are building for competition on a national level.

The Back Story

It is significant that the status of Alakuş's and Bademsoy's protagonists as soccer players is mirrored in their own status as transgressive film artists. Female Turkish German filmmakers are often overshadowed by the disproportionate attention newspaper critics and academic scholars give their male colleagues. As Barbara Mennel writes: "The success of filmmakers Thomas Arslan, Yüksel Yavuz, Fatih Akın, and Kutluğ Ataman has contributed to defining contemporary minority cinema in Germany as Turkish and male" (2002b: 53–54). Not so surprising, then, is this tag at the end of the promotional for Alakuş's *Offside*: "From Wüste Film, the producers of Fatih Akın's *Head-On* (winner of the 2004 *Golden Bear* in Berlin as well as the German & European Film Awards), comes another drama by a Turkish German director, Buket Alakuş. Her first feature *Anam* (*My Mother*, 2000) won the Prix Europa and numerous other awards. In *Offside* she proves a sure hand in treating a sensitive subject matter with liberating lightness" (http://www.german-films.de).

Several recent publications concern themselves with the conditions of production for, and media reception of films by, women filmmakers. Mennel's article "Local Funding and Global Movement: Minority Women's Filmmaking and the German Film Landscape of the Late 1990s" uses production conditions as a heuristic category for analyzing minority women filmmakers' cinematic representation. In the article, Mennel takes up B. Ruby Rich's challenge for cinefeminists to return to multiple film-theoretical approaches that Rich sees as having gotten lost in the wake of Laura Mulvey and others' focus on psychoanalytical models. Mennel analyzes Seyhan Derin's 1996 *Ich bin die Tochter meiner Mutter* (*I Am My Mother's Daughter*) and Angelina Maccarone's and Fatima El-Tayeb's 1997 *Alles wird gut* (*Everything Will Be Fine*), theorizing a link between "conditions of production, distribution, and reception," on the one hand, and "cinematic representation," on the other. She shows that this link "often serves as a linchpin for women filmmakers, specifically for minority women filmmakers, because funding and distribution are tied in implicit and explicit ways to identity politics, and thus to cinematic representation" (2002: 47). Likewise Seyhan Derin's article "No Money, No Movie" makes a strong case for the interdependence between cinepolitics and cinematic representation. Derin explains that regional film subsidies are tied to restrictions on the director that have an impact on shooting location, choice of crew and actors, and on a host of other important directorial decisions (2010: 27–29).

These and other accounts of the asymmetrically structured film-industrial environment refute the very nomenclature and claims of postfeminism. Fair to say, the situation for women filmmakers has improved since the early days of feminist film praxis. In their 2009 dialogical autobiography *Fantasie und Arbeit* (*Imagination and Work*), Iris Gusner and Helke Sander, two of the first German postwar feminist filmmakers, explain that their struggles with making films in the 1970s and 1980s had to do with bureaucratic hurdles (Gusner in the GDR) and with sexual politics and limited access to funding sources (Sander in the FRG). As Sander relates, many projects ended up in the desk drawer, and hiring women in film jobs (from camera women to assistant directors) was nearly unheard of in West Germany (Gusner and Sander 2009: 175). Furthermore feminist filmmakers, who were active in the SDS (Socialist German Student Association), as Sander was, had to be concerned about being blacklisted. Sander's sharp critical stance led to the cancellation of a series on soccer spectatorship commissioned by the WDR (West German Broadcasting) and became the pretext for Sander's and Gesine Strempel's founding of the first German feminist film journal—*Frauen und Film* (*Women and Film*)—in 1974. Radical feminist film praxis in the 1970s—with Sander at the forefront—smoothed the way for the next generation of women filmmakers. However, at the same time that the funding structure for the second generation of Turkish German and non-Turkish German filmmakers has changed radically, asymmetrical media attention in popular outlets as well as in academic journals still marginalize women by canonizing male Turkish German filmmakers (Mennel 2002b: 53–54).

Questions about the conditions of production and distribution and issues of "the cinematic gaze" and "the look" that were raised in Germany by *Frauen und Film* in the early 1970s are still relevant today, especially for minority women filmmakers. Alakuş's and Bademsoy's coming-of-age stories set in the world of soccer problematize them at times overtly. *Offside* interpellates its spectators via a recalibrated version of what has been theorized as the cinematic gaze, while Bademsoy's documentary trilogy creates new ways of looking that I shall call the "deep look of documentary."

The Cinematic Gaze

"The look" has always had a central place in the history of discourses about cinema. In the mid-1970s, it was joined by "the gaze" in major cinema journals that concerned themselves with questions of spectatorship.

Instrumental was British filmmaker and critic Laura Mulvey when she put the debate about the cinematic (male) gaze squarely into the field of psychoanalysis with her path-breaking essay "Visual Pleasure and Narrative Cinema" that first appeared in 1975 in the influential British film journal *Screen*. Mulvey's essay interrogates classical Hollywood film through "a political use of psychoanalysis" and proposes that woman's *"to-be-looked-at-ness"* is part of the voyeuristic regime that is specific to narrative film (1988: 57 and 62). She demonstrates that the objectification of woman "is what makes cinema quite different in its voyeuristic potential form" because it partakes of the "tension between film as controlling the dimension of time (editing, narrative) and film as the controlling dimension of space (changes in distance, editing), cinematic codes create a gaze, a world and an object, thereby producing an illusion cut to the measure of desire" (1988: 67).

Making scopophilic (erotic) pleasure a central concern, Mulvey argues that classical Hollywood film interpellates the male gaze in ways that structure power asymmetrically. Mulvey differentiates between three distinct cinematic looks that comprise the masculinist structure of the gaze: the one of the camera in the pro-filmic event; the one of the spectator in the cinema, and the one between the characters. From a standpoint theory of the "male gaze" Mulvey posits two modalities that constitute the look/gaze, the fetishistic scopophilic modality and the narcissistic one (1988: 61–64).[5] Women's "to-be-looked-atness" is complicated further by the new media that I mention at the outset. It increasingly reflects (and constitutes) spectators' scopophilic habits. The tradition that poses women as "appearing" rather than "acting" (to use John Berger's formulation) has, in the case of soccer, found new outlets on the web with "Soccer Babes" and all the rest (arguably begun by *Sports Illustrated*). Contemporary audiences, who are passionate about women playing soccer, and oppositional filmmakers such as Alakuş and Bademsoy, find it increasingly difficult to construct counterdiscourses.

The Recalibrated Gaze in *Offside*

For all that, Alakuş's *Offside* refocuses the spectator's conventional gaze, as theorized by Mulvey and prestructured in mainstream soccer discourses. Alakuş achieves this with two different moves in two key sequences. First, she frames the spectatorial understanding of gender as socially constructed—as performative—when she portrays Hayat and Toni crossdressing for a costume party: Hayat appears as a Chaplinesque character and Toni as a sexy woman. This performance of gender signals the characters' ability to imagine a hybrid and fluid sexual identity. Such a reading is supported with the second key sequence that depicts Hayat's and Toni's first intimate encounter. If Toni were represented in the scopophilic regimes of classical narrative cinema as described by Mulvey, Toni's desire to look at Hayat's "absent" breast would be constructed in terms of the Freudian explanation of male psychosexual development, which posits that the male child's understanding of sexual difference occurs when he sees that the female is missing a penis. This moment of gazing at that which is absent would install the male's castration anxiety. In such a case, Toni would be shown to disavow what he has (not) seen, and he would devise a fetish to alleviate his fear. The spectator of classical narrative films with such a scopophilic trajectory would be interpellated to partake of Toni's fetishistic gaze.

Alakuş intervenes brilliantly into this classical spectatorial economy by constructing a male protagonist who, because he does not have a rigid investment in sexual difference, overcomes the cultural taboo of the imperfect female body. Toni's unraveling of Hayat's bandaged chest serves as a metaphor for the sequence's unraveling of the economy of desire as based on fetishism, scopophilia, and narcissism. The sequence's establishing shot is of Toni undressing with his back to the camera. He frontally presents his sex to Hayat. This configuration installs the woman as a desiring subject. In an earlier scene at the football locker room, Hayat had gazed at Toni's naked body from the back; it is from this perspective that the spectator is invited to gaze at Toni in the love scene. When Hayat kisses Toni passionately and moves him to the bed, the assignment of passive/active gender roles within the traditional female/male dichotomy is reversed. Once Hayat and Toni face each other on the bed in the middle of the room, the camera frames Toni's unraveling of Hayat's partially removed breast.

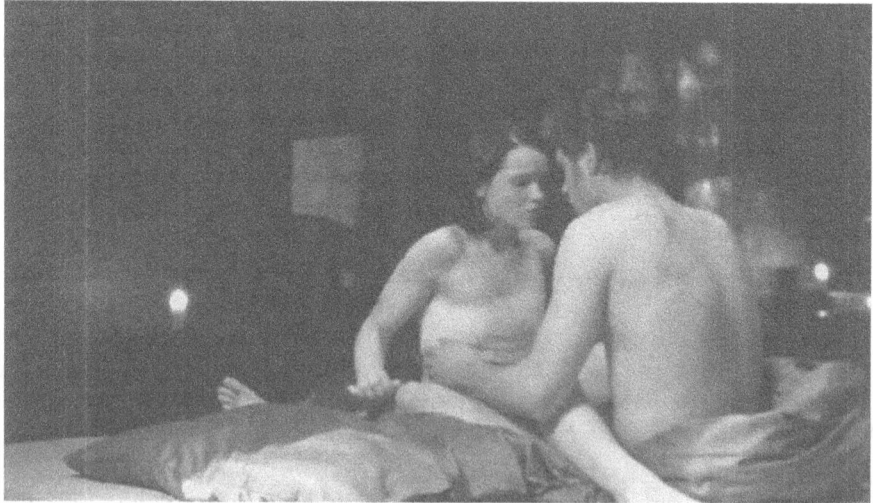

Figure 5.1 Hayat (Karoline Herfurth) and Toni (Ken Duken) in *Offside*, DVD capture

From a slightly canted angle, the camera circles half way around the couple on the bed, then zooms in tightly on their faces. At one point, Toni's intense gaze is juxtaposed to Hayat's as her eyes briefly drift away, signifying the female character's oblique relationship to the scene. Indeed, the sequence of Hayat's first intimate encounter with Toni is structured in a way that shows her struggle for subjectivity as both the desiring subject and the desired object, seeking to escape from the objectification she had previously internalized. This deliberate recalibration of the Oedipal drama, I suggest, depicts the possibility of fluid sexuality and a proposal for split subjects that are outside of phallogocentric image production.[6]

The Deep Look of Documentary: Committed Filmmaking

Bademsoy's feminist soccer films enter documentary film history at an oblique angle. In as much as women playing soccer is still regarded as a subversive activity, and in as much as a film about Turkish German women playing soccer puts pressure on media scripts of the "oppressed" Muslim woman versus the "liberated" Western woman, Bademsoy's films oppose institutionalized discourses that "record" men playing soccer. Both onscreen and offscreen, Bademsoy's social actors (to borrow Bill Nichols's term) circulate in a dialogic relationship to the majority culture in Germany: their moments in time are refracted through discourses of gender and ethnicity as well as those of sexuality, generation, religious affiliation, and social class. To my mind, Bademsoy's major achievement with the trilogy is that she reveals the operations of governmentality—in Foucault's sense of governments' production of citizens to fit its needs.

John Grierson's oft repeated definition of documentary in the 1930s as the "creative treatment of actuality," however useful as a starting point generally, is inadequate in explaining Bademsoy's address to the spectator (for theories of documentaries, see Alter 2002; Nichols 2010; Waldman and Walker 1999; Winston 1995). Indeed, Bademsoy's films best fit Thomas Waugh's concept of "committed documentary," the goals of which Julianne Burton explains to be "to expose and combat the culture of invisibility and inaudibility" (qtd. in Waldman and Walker 1999: 18). Bademsoy proposes her documentary method with an intercut image into *Girls on the Pitch*. The image is of a traditionally dressed Turkish woman—perhaps in her mid or late twenties—who stands outside the soccer field, behind a fence that marks off one side of the field. She has raised her arms and linked her fingers into the chain links, as she looks intently at the Agrispor players who are kicking near the goal. Bademsoy's camera shoots her image through the netting of the goal.

Thus the female Turkish spectator in the diegesis watches the game through the fence, while the film's spectator watches her through two grids: the fence she looks through and the mesh of the net goal. The image encapsulates the complexity that Bademsoy's film presents to spectators. It suggests that any understanding of the lives of the Turkish German soccer players necessitates looking through a number of grids that require historical awareness and knowledge about government policies, especially as these relate to migrant children's education and laws that regulate access to citizenship. The discourses are tied to both social and cultural practices of Turkish Germans and non-Turkish Germans. These discursive strands are not separate, but intertwined in complex ways. Bademsoy's deep look into the young women's lives invites spectators to discern certain strands of rational governmentality as these are intertwined in the women's micropolitical realities of their everyday lives (for a discussion of governmentality in anthology films, see Deshpande 2010: 81–82; see also Ewing 2006: 267). Bademsoy takes great care to show the specificities of the women's interactions with certain German institutions: the soccer commission, a hospital, a career counseling center, a social worker's office, and so on.

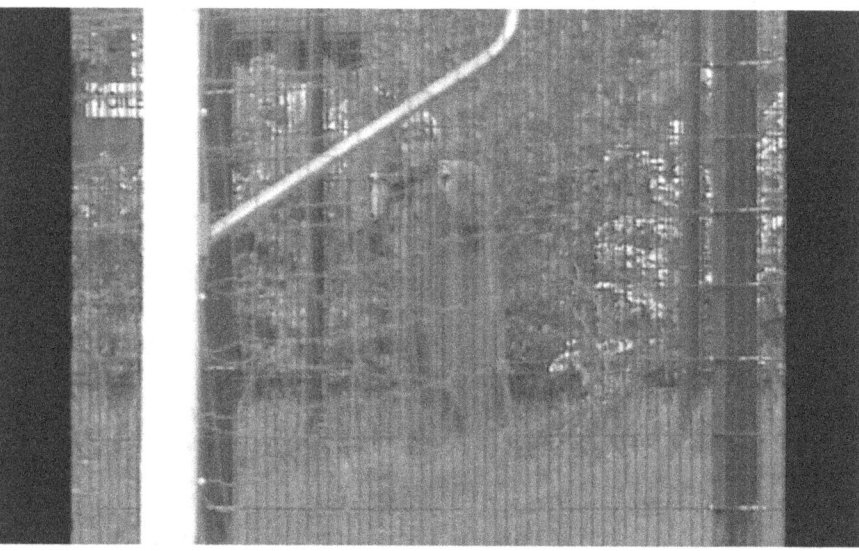

Figure 5.2 Turkish woman looking through fence in *Girls on the Pitch*, DVD capture

A long sequence that depicts Nazan seeking job counseling helps to illuminate Bademsoy's thus defined deep look at the intertwining of bureaucracy that impacts the young Turkish German women in the trilogy. Nazan is looking to sign up for a banking or hospitality apprenticeship; to find out how she must proceed, she visits a career counselor. The sequence in question begins at the moment when the counselor asks Nazan about her school grades. Both are seated at a glass table in his office. The counselor is framed by professional accoutrements (computer, telephone), and his status is signaled by a large window and upscale furniture. Nazan is clearly an interloper into this space: except for the bottom part of a framed picture, the wall behind her is blank. While he leans back in the chair, his legs crossed comfortably, Nazan is shown sitting forward in her chair, initially leaning slightly toward him. The camera moves in tightly on Nazan's facial expression when the counselor tells her that it is too late to apply for an internship. No such intimate camera work captures the social worker; the distance he creates with his dismissive tone of voice and superior demeanor is mirrored in the distance the camera keeps.

Two points are crucial to the way Bademsoy frames Nazan's relationship to the situation. One lies in a durational past (Nazan's schooling, her academic record) and the other lies in the "fact" that it is "too late" to apply for either of the career tracks that interest her. Bademsoy's camera zooms in on Nazan's face, documenting the polarizing effect of the counselor's enactment of bureaucratic rules and social policy, and appeals to the spectator to pay attention to the nearly hidden aspects of the policies that have brought Nazan to this demoralizing encounter with the social service's destructive force. It is up to the spectator to understand the hopelessness Nazan feels about the outcome of such job counseling. Bademsoy's shock cut to two of Nazan's soccer friends (Safiye and Arzu) playing pool facilitates this understanding, as does a later sequence that shows Nazan working in the hotel business as a room cleaner. The film invites non-Turkish German spectators to shift to another aspect of the grid through which to look at the micropolitics of the everyday lives of the five young Turkish German women. If nothing else, the shock cut from the social worker's office to Safiye and Arzu playing pool reminds spectators not to reduce the film's subjects to victims of the broken social system.

Conclusion

The fluid status of minority women's soccer as compared to the privileged (and firmly institutionalized) status of men's competitive soccer finds a correlative in the positionality of Turkish German women filmmakers to male minority filmmakers in Germany. Images and videos circulated via the new media that frame discourses of female soccer on and off the field make it clear that pressure must be put on the myth of soccer as the great equalizer on a global scale. The films discussed in my essay productively intervene into both realms in different ways. Alakuş recalibrates the cinematic gaze at the female body and attempts to call attention to the habits of gazing at the female body, while Bademsoy's cinefeminist documentaries offer a deep way of looking at the micropolitical realities that her subjects face in contemporary Germany.

Notes

1. The organization "Football Unites, Racism Divides" responds to the racism on and off the field with "an anti-racist, football-based community project, working in the areas of social inclusion and community cohesion." http://www.furd.org/.
2. Other notable films with overtly socially transformative intent are Ginger Gentile's and Gabriel Balanovsky's *Goals for Girls* (2010), a documentary that portrays a group of avid soccer players from the Buenos Aires shantytown, Villa 31. *Goals for Girls* highlights the teens' inspired playing in an inter-slum championship, their remarkable team spirit and discipline, establishing a sharp contrast between the young women's perception of and goals for themselves and their parents' and the media's opinion that they will end up as teenage mothers, or that they are at best suited for work as maids, or at worst, as petty criminals. David Assmann's and Ayat Najafi's *Anstoß in Teheran* (*Football Under Cover*, 2008) is a documentary that depicts a women's soccer team's trip from Berlin-Kreuzberg to Iran where the team members play against the Iranian national team. The film depicts the problematic political climate that nearly scuttles the match between BSV AL-Dersimpor and the Iranian women soccer players. Bahareh Hosseini's *Afghan Girls Can Kick* (2008) follows the story of Roya Noori, who grew up in the middle of Kabul's slums, where she helped her family's economic survival by collecting waste paper. Sponsored by an Afghan charity organization, Roya was able to go to school and learn how to play soccer. The film includes dramatic depictions of her as center forward for the Afghan national women's team, her work as a teacher, and sponsor of children who are pressed into service as child laborers. Probably the most advertised of these films is Jafar Panahi's film *Offside* (2006), showcased at the 2011 Berlinale. The film thematizes soccer's connection as a spectator sport to soccer films as spectacle. It portrays several young Iranian women who, disguised as boys, smuggle themselves into the soccer stadium so that they can watch the game.
3. Other films by Bademsoy include *Deutsche Polizisten* (*German Police*, 1999), which thematizes Turkish German policemen's social and ethical conflicts in their contact with largely migrant communities. *Ein Mädchen im Ring* (*Boxing Girl*, 1996) shows the vicissitudes Fikriye Selen faces when her plans to study and box in an all-male boxing club collide with those of her parents. *Am Rande der Städte* (*On the Edge of the Cities*, 2006) reveals that Turkish migrants' dreams to live in comfort in their former *Heimat* is a chimera.
4. Exceptions are the CBC-TV documentary *The Girls of Summer* (2008) that depicts the team members on and off the field for one year during which they prepare for FIFA's U-17 World Cup in New Zealand; the HBO special *Dare to Dream: The Story of the US Women's Soccer Team* (2005); and the independent production, Jenny Mackenzie's *Kick Like a Girl* (2008) that follows each game during the nine-match season.
5. In this essay, Mulvey uses the terms "look" and "gaze" interchangeably, though by the end, she has all but replaced "look" with "gaze." Mulvey's theory of spectatorship was debated vigorously for a decade or so. My readings are also informed by Teresa de Lauretis's intervention into the largely heterosexual discourse about spectatorship in her book *Technologies of Gender* (1987) that critically engages Althusser's notion of ideological interpellation. In conjunction with her other book, *Alice Doesn't: Feminism, Semiotics, Cinema* (1984), *Technologies of Gender* prepared the ground for much of the subversive feminist theory to follow, including Judith Butler's influential *Gender Trouble* (1990), which argues for a coalitional feminism that puts into question notions of essential gender identity, theorizing in its stead the performative nature of gender. These early struggles with masculinist representations of female subjects still inform feminist film studies in significant ways. At the same time, and important for minority cinema in Germany, the methodological limitations of white Eurocentric discourse

in feminist film criticism began to be critiqued. Important accents were set by Robert Stam's and Louise Spence's introductory essay in *Screen*, titled "Colonialism, Racism and Representation" (1983: 2–20), and Donald Bogle's critique of stereotypical black roles and representations in Hollywood film (1989). bell hooks's (1992) call to rethink black female spectatorship as necessarily oppositional to black male spectators (115–31) was answered by film theorists such as Jane Gaines (1988) and E. Ann Kaplan (1997) who also highlighted the ethnocentrisms of much early cinefeminism.

6. Importantly, other references to Hayat's body function to counter myths of multicultural harmony. Hayat's former teammate, the blonde Germanic Amazon Silke is a foil for ethnic differences (and animosities). When the two later run into each other in a Victoria's Secret store after Hayat had her breast partially removed, Silke taunts Hayat with Toni's chances with "real" women and snidely asks Hayat about how she intends to fill the bra Hayat looks at. Silke's Germanic looks reference historical images of who was worthy as a full member of society. The specter of Nazi body politics rises in the two women's encounter at the lingerie shop. If this reading seems reductive, it is so because Silke's character (indeed, most of the characters that comprise the football team SC Elbe) functions in the film in instrumental ways to show difference as socially and historically contingent and constructed. Significantly the final sound track, "Ofsayt" (offside) by Aziza A., is Turkish hip hop.

Chapter 6

LOCATION AND MOBILITY IN KUTLUĞ ATAMAN'S SITE-SPECIFIC VIDEO INSTALLATION *KÜBA*

Nilgün Bayraktar

Kutluğ Ataman's award winning feature film *Lola + Bilidikid* (*Lola and Billy the Kid*, 1999) introduces most of its characters in a sequence in which we see a drag cabaret show of a performance group called *Die Gastarbeiterinnen* (the female guestworkers) in a dark and smoky bar.[1] On stage, the performers Scheherazade, Calypso, and Lola ironically perform the stereotypical role of the victimized female guestworker with a headscarf (Göktürk 2000). In so doing, they subvert the stereotype of the submissive Turkish woman in Germany by reenacting that identity in the form of a stage performance: as hyperfeminine belly dancers, they sing, dance, and interact with the audience very comfortably. The handheld camera places us first on stage with the dancers and then with the audience watching them, which evokes a sense of intimate but also claustrophobic space shared with the characters. As the first film to explore queer Turkish German subjects openly in cinema, *Lola and Billy the Kid* foregrounds the sexual and ethnic diversity of migrants in Germany as well as the multiplicity of the experience of migrancy (for a more detailed discussion, see Mennel 2004 and Clark 2006). Thus the film transgresses essentialist identity politics that assign fixed roles to migrants and natives.

Even though Ataman did not personally experience migration to Germany, his film has been discussed within the frame of a new wave of Turkish German filmmaking that has flourished since the mid-1990s.[2] The significant role assigned to *Lola and Billy the Kid* in this context encourages us to formulate new ways to approach migrant and diasporic cinema, moving beyond ethno-racial or territorial definitions that fail to account for multidimensional mobilities and moorings of our global age (see Hannam et al. 2006). *Lola and Billy the Kid* aptly illustrates Ataman's artistic and political concerns that pervade his cinematic and video works: the issue of mobility and marginality, performative and constructed identities, and idiosyncratic senses of places. Ataman's multichannel, sculptural installations expand these issues to include experimentation with different forms of presentation and exhibition as well as incorporation of the viewer and the site as integral parts of the artwork. In this essay, I focus on Ataman's forty-channel video installation *Küba* (2004) in relation to issues of migration, displacement, and urban marginality as well as embodied spectatorship and site specificity. In *Küba*, as in *Lola and Billy the Kid*, Ataman underscores both particular individuals and the collective. He subverts essentialist notions of identity politics through embodied spectatorship and the extended duration of the installation, challenging conventional forms of passive observation. Furthermore, he offers countermodels to the stereotypical representation of Others by incorporating traditional forms of political cinema such as documentary and social-realist filmmaking.

As *Lola and Billy the Kid*'s reception in the festival circuit testifies, Ataman has started a successful career as a filmmaker, but following his first video installation *semiha b. unplugged* (1997), which was a hit at the Istanbul Biennial of the same year, he has begun to produce works in the domain of contemporary art and since then become one of the best-known Turkish artists in the international art world.[3] His works have been presented at prestigious art exhibitions and galleries in the United States and Europe.[4] The single-screen projection *semiha b. unplugged* is an eight-hour video that features an interview with Semiha Berksoy, an octogenarian Turkish opera singer whose life story was enmeshed with modern Turkish history, which the video reconstructs from her own personal perspective. Following his first video work, extended duration and open-ended monologues with no clear beginning or ending have become Ataman's signature in his installations. For example, *semiha b. unplugged*'s 465 minutes of almost uninterrupted monologue deliberately subverts the standards of conventional narrative cinema despite its allusions to documentary. Like most of Ataman's video works, *semiha b. unplugged* offers multivalent expressions of experience and narrative of a self that expand the notion of documentary into fiction through storytelling. And Berksoy's monumental tale, staged in the intimacy of the diva's Istanbul bedroom, allows viewers to create their own versions of the piece based on fragments they watch in the exhibition site for, in Ataman's words, "it is impossible to watch" the piece in its totality.[5]

With his four-screen installation, *Women Who Wear Wigs* (1999) that premiered at the Venice Biennale, Ataman has started using multiple screens in different scales and positions, simultaneously featuring several stories in sculptural forms (Baykal 2008: 49). In *Women Who Wear Wigs*, Ataman uses the wig as a link holding together the stories of four different women: a revolutionary who spent several years in hiding, a journalist who lost her hair following chemotherapy, an activist in the Turkish transvestite and transsexual community, and an unnamed university student who wore a wig to cover her headscarf to be able to circumvent its ban at institutions of higher education. In *Women Who Wear Wigs*, Ataman juxtaposes four screens next to each other to allow viewers to be able to experience the different stories simultaneously. Indeed, in his later work, Ataman has experimented with the spatialization of narratives using the particular spatial characteristics of a chosen site, the physical and psychological involvement of the viewer, as well as the practice of montage in space. While Ataman's earlier works center on eccentric individuals such as an aging opera diva or an English woman who devoted her life to her passion for the flower amaryllis, his more recent works *Küba* (2004) and *Paradise* (2006) are multicharacter installations that evoke notions of collective identity and belonging.

Ataman's award winning video installation *Küba*, commissioned by the London-based arts organization Artangel, is a forty-channel video installation based on interviews in a *gecekondu* (shantytown) neighborhood of Istanbul populated primarily by migrants from southeastern Turkey.[6] The installation addresses issues of forced migration and the spatial construction of displacement and confinement in Istanbul's urban space. For his video installation, Ataman spent two years filming interviews with residents of the shantytown of the same name in Istanbul. Ataman convinced Küba residents to take part in his work and gained access to their private spaces through the mediation of an ex-Küba resident who spoke of Ataman as a trustworthy person (Horrigan 2004: 3). Ataman promised his subjects not to show the piece in Turkey because many of the stories refer to conflicts in the neighborhood, state violence, criminal activities, and sexual and domestic violence that might cause trouble for the interviewees if the content became public knowledge. Thus the subjects presented in *Küba* were not the intended audience of the piece.

In the installation, Ataman incorporates video-based images into a sculptural mise en scène and creates a virtual neighborhood that consists of forty talking heads, articulating their own descriptions of alternative community. Ataman presents these interviews on forty secondhand TV monitors that are placed on used tables with forty mismatched armchairs. The installation allows viewers to move among the monitors, piecing together the videos according to their own choices in the exhibition site. Elizabeth Cowie points out that the multiscreen format renders the piece "inherently unstable, unavailable as identically repeatable," as each viewer's experience is personal and unique (2009: 127). Indeed, *Küba* calls for an engagement with the extended duration of the work, proposing an active and participatory form of spectatorship that demands constitutive relations from viewers. In so doing, it makes the viewer and the experience of viewing central to the work.

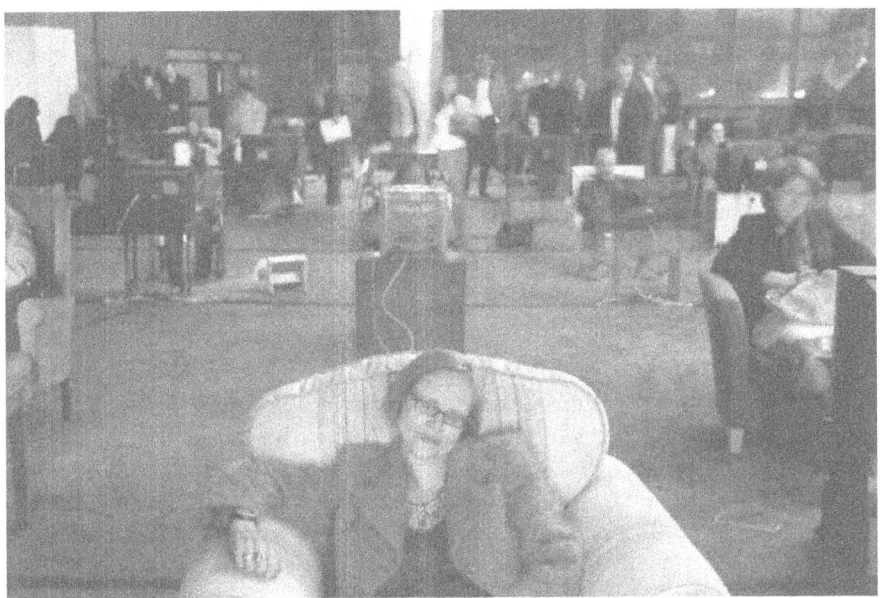

Figure 6.1 Installation view of Kutluğ Ataman's *Küba*, The Sorting Office, London, March–June 2005, commissioned and produced by Artangel, photo courtesy Artangel

Küba has been presented in various sites, each time producing a new mode of experiencing the work: in museums, in a derelict postal sorting office in London, in a courtroom in Southampton, in a passenger ferry terminal in Sydney, and on a container barge traveling along the Danube River. The spatial articulation and meaning of *Küba* has changed in relation to the architectural, historical, and cultural specificity of each location that housed the virtual neighborhood, and the work has taken on the memories of the sites of its display. For instance, Stuttgart's Central Station where *Küba* was exhibited in old railway cars was a place where many of Germany's "migrant laborers from Turkey first arrived on their long journey" (Halle 2009: 46). In this particular site-specific constellation, Istanbul's *gecekondu* neighborhood Küba expanded to encompass the history of guestworkers who migrated to Germany in the 1960s and 1970s—guestworkers whose descendants make up a large number of European citizens today. In the Central Station, the sign *Küba*, showing the way to the old railway cars placed on Track 1A, brought the viewer to an unfamiliar yet very intimate zone of Kurdish stories mainly told in broken Turkish with English subtitles. The installation does not mark its subjects ethnically but most of the stories provide various references to the subjects' Kurdish identity and their experience of migrancy. In the railway cars, viewers could sit on a seat to watch a story unfolding on a TV monitor also placed on a passenger seat; they could enter into a cloistered compartment in which the movement of other passing trains on nearby tracks was highly felt. Indeed, the installation invited not only art audiences who enter the station to see the work but also travelers and other people who use the space for various purposes. In the Stuttgart exhibition, in particular, the installation underscored the ways in which migrant experiences are conditioned by travel networks, infrastructures, and transport technologies, and produced a palimpsestic spatiotemporality marked by various migratory routes.

In London, *Küba* was presented on the enormous upper floor of a derelict postal sorting office with additional electric heaters due to the cold weather. The worn-out, wooden floor and broken windows of the postal office provided a stage for the tales of Küba residents, further emphasizing their vulnerable condition in urban space. To see the exhibition, the viewer went through seemingly unsafe staircases, following arrows that led to the exhibition site; "the circuitous journey echoe[d] the journey to the obscure, out-of-the-way, Istanbul slum that is Küba" (Lebow 2007–8: 61). As Randall Halle points out, each installation of *Küba* "took on a different quality, mirroring differently various aspects of ghettoization/community building" (2009: 47). Thus *Küba* as a site-oriented artwork navigating various spaces not only indicates a shift from static notions of time and space toward a coexistence of multiple spaces and histories, but also relates to a notion of site specificity that indicates "a shift in visual art toward the conceptual and performative contexts in which the *idea* of the work is defined" (Kaye 2000: 183, emphasis in the original). Constructing a dialogic relationship between the artwork and its site, *Küba* blurs the boundaries between material and cinematic spaces and calls into question what Nick Kaye defines as "the art object's material integrity and the very possibility of establishing a work's proper location" (2000: 183). While remaining integrally linked to its place of origin, the shantytown, *Küba* has undergone a process of reconstruction in each installation, persistently rearticulating the relationship between moving images and the site of their display.

Catherine Fowler's notion of "gallery films" helps to articulate the altered relationship of "in-frame" and "out-of-frame" in video installations. Fowler explores "the continuum between the in-frame (the content of the image and issues of film style) and the out-of-frame (the space within which that image is placed to be viewed)" in order to understand "how context might affect both the content of the images and the viewing experience" (2004: 326). As Fowler suggests, the migration of moving images from theaters to galleries has produced new forms of spectatorship that alter the viewing experience and meaning of images by allowing the viewer to "perambulate, choose when to enter or exit, where to stand, sit or walk, and even (with multiscreen work) where to look" (2004: 329). To take these arguments a step further, I suggest that an engagement with the specificity (historical, cultural, geographical, or architectural) of the site of display and how it informs the viewer's experience of images is crucial in understanding embodied spectatorship in a particular context rather than framing it through an abstract notion of spectating or site. The installation *Küba* is able to evoke specificity of time and space through its geographical, social, and personal context as well as through "[its] architectural space, organizing the spectator's access to mobility and stillness" (Cowie 2009: 124). The sites temporarily occupied by *Küba* become its constitutive parts with their architectural and sociohistorical specificity, conjuring up unique forms of engagement with the work. Hence, *Küba* attests to Jonathan Crary's statement that "contemporary installation art involves the creation of unanticipated spaces and environments in which our visual and intellectual habits are challenged and disrupted" (2003: 7).

The stories told by the residents of Küba present their neighborhood as an exclusive island in the city—a politically charged environment of displacement, poverty, and alternative community formation. In that sense, the installation belongs to a growing body of site-specific art practices that can help to "provide support for greater visibility of marginalized groups, and initiate the re(dis)covery of 'minor' places so far ignored by the dominant culture" (Kwon 1997: 105). In the installation, the medium closeup images of various people telling their stories in their living rooms produce the sense of place and of location. The staged domestic environment of the installation—the mismatched, secondhand TV monitors and chairs—foreground the authenticity of Ataman's subjects because these secondhand objects seem to possess an indexical relation to the sites and subjects presented in the work. In fact, one might find them in the houses of individuals portrayed in *Küba*. As documentary filmmaker Alisa Lebow observes, "Ataman recreates the atmosphere of a neighborhood, not by faithfully reconstructing its streets and structures, but by inviting us into the residents' living rooms for a *sohbet*, an informal chat" (2007–8: 60). Art historian and critic Miwon Kwon argues that site specificity and ethnographic methods in this context can be mobilized to provide "distinction of place and uniqueness of locational identity, highly seductive qualities in the promotion of towns and cities within the competitive restructuring of the global economic hierarchy" (1997: 106). Indeed, in contemporary art, there has been a strongly pronounced interest in ethnographic methods that involve marginal or peripheral places and subjects, an interest that often turns the Other or the hybrid into assets of cultural economy.

In his 1996 essay "The Artist as Ethnographer," art historian Hal Foster has identified an "ethnographic turn" in contemporary art—a system of artistic production based on investigations of the cultural Other. Focusing mainly on site-specific art practices, he outlined a variety of problems that arise when artists try to follow the ethnographic methods without any ethnographic training or clear ethical framework. According to Foster, such quasi-ethnographic practices might reify cultural and ethnic

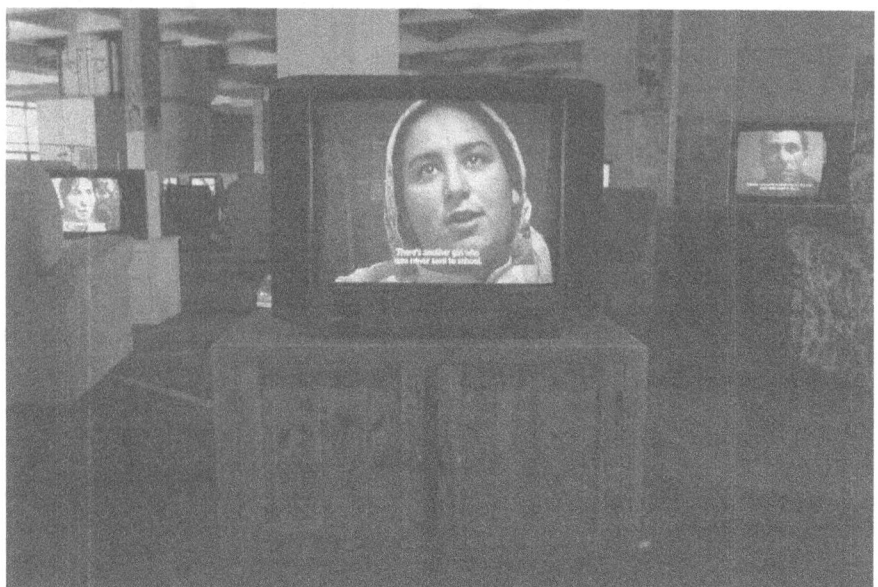

Figure 6.2 Installation view of Kutluğ Ataman's *Küba*, The Sorting Office, London, March–June 2005, commissioned and produced by Artangel, photo courtesy Artangel

differences, colonizing these marginal spaces and turning them into global commodities.

Küba might be considered a quasi-ethnographic artwork, for Ataman has used interviews with sociopolitically and economically disenfranchised subjects as the basis of his installation. Additionally Lebow sees the extended duration of Ataman's installation as an obstacle in conveying the politically charged issues raised by the interviews. She argues that "the dehistoricized context of Western exhibition sites" might reduce *Küba*'s stories into "mini-soap opera[s] of the poor and dispossessed" (2007–8: 64). In *Küba*, however, the ethnographic gaze, initially foregrounded by the interview format, and the sculptural component's impression of authenticity are undermined by the extended duration of the interviews. It would be impossible to view *Küba* in its totality because the forty screens show more than thirty hours of interviews. Unlike many ethnographic documentaries or commercial films that tend to present "authentic" or "exotic" Others to First World audiences, *Küba* constantly reminds us that visual access is not a given. The work demands an embodied durational engagement from viewers who have to take their time to grasp the work, to explore the multidimensional nature of the persons portrayed as well as the work's relationship to its particular site. In so doing, *Küba* refuses its viewers the satisfaction offered by mainstream news images of disenfranchised people from a Third World city. Furthermore, with its open-ended stories running in loops, *Küba* offers a circular structure in which the linear time loses its meaning. Hence, the structural framing of this video installation prevents viewers from treating the residents of Küba as fully accessible or consumable subjects. In that frame, Ataman's *Küba* subverts the essentialist and homogenizing aspects of identity politics.

Irit Rogoff insists that *Küba* "is not a body of information about a place, or a demographic, it is not social or cultural history ... If we were to leave *Küba* with some notion that we knew something about Kurdish migrants into Istanbul or about ghettoized ethnic communities—we would have failed it" (2006: 35). *Küba*, as most of Ataman's work, alludes to documentary and social-realist filmmaking (which has been prevalent in migrant and diasporic cinema) by depicting authentic characters in their original locations and filming unscripted and improvised narration of the characters with minimum direction of the filmmaker whose presence is felt through the sudden and small movements of the handheld camera (see also Baykal 2008: 9). Hence, *Küba* incorporates some elements of what might be seen as conventional documentary methods such as location shooting and interviews. Sometimes we hear Ataman's voice asking very brief questions from behind the camera but we also see characters addressing him directly by asking a question or even threatening him.

In an interview, Bozo, a middle-aged Küba resident, tells Ataman: "Tomorrow I'll say, 'Kutluğ, let's send Hakan [Bozo's son] to school.' You won't send him to school? I will take out a gun and shoot you. You think I wouldn't? I would. Someone is going to make it out of Küba. No one has, but he will." And in the video, we do not hear Ataman's reaction to Bozo's threat. Bill Horrigan defines Ataman's method as an "ethic of self-effacement" (2003: 25) and points out elsewhere: "Ataman is an artist whose medium is people's lives that, for him and for us, take form in the words they produce. As that artist, he accords them respect by submitting to the time it takes to listen to them speak. The contract he extends to his viewers requests that they do no less" (2004: 1). Ataman's handheld camera, like Ataman himself, does not react to its surroundings—it stays focused on the character and never zooms out or provides an establishing shot that would help the viewer locate the person within a larger picture. There is no voice-over narration that addresses the viewer directly or renders the images mere illustrations of what the authoritative commentary describes. Thus Ataman's videos defy notions of objectivity and truth foregrounded by conventional documentary filmmaking that claims to be presenting first-hand experience and reality.

Ataman's approach suggests that the artist is not interested in replicating or reproducing the experience of the everyday as lived in a socioeconomically and culturally marginal site of Istanbul. Rather, he is intrigued by the representation and remaking of place in the act of storytelling and narration. The aesthetic and political efficacy of *Küba* lies in the ways in which it generates countermodels to the dehumanizing representations of the so-called Others and offers a strong political comment on the nature of documentation and information. It utilizes storytelling and narrative to refer to very concrete personal and social matters and takes the viewer to an unfamiliar zone of ignored or silenced communal memory of poverty and violence. Hence, the composition of the installation emphasizes the contact with disenfranchised subjects that are neither victimized nor idealized by the artist. Furthermore, by foregrounding storytelling, *Küba* defamiliarizes the banal activity of TV viewing—one of the most dominant cultural experiences, which effects viewing conditions and expectations for today's viewers. And the installation demands an engagement with the slowness and introspection of the activity of storytelling and listening.

Most stories of Küba's residents concern issues of immigration and mobility as well as social and economic marginalization in Istanbul's urban space. They invoke cultural conflicts concerning the rights of ethnic and religious minorities as well as the rifts between the urban population and the new migrants to the big city. *Küba* portrays Istanbul as a "heavily trafficked intersection … instead of a circumscribed territory," and evokes the city as a place "crisscrossed by the movement and multiple migrations of people, sometimes voluntary, but often economically propelled and politically coerced" (Conquergood 2002: 145). The representation of Istanbul as a city of migration is not unfamiliar to viewers of Turkish cinema, which has addressed internal (rural to urban) mass migrations, urban decay, and class conflicts since the 1950s.[7] As Ipek Türeli aptly explains: "Migration was formative in the rapid growth of Istanbul in the second half of the twentieth century so much so that contemporary Istanbul can be considered a 'city of migrants' with most of its adult population born elsewhere in Turkey. Although no longer the driving force of the city's population growth, migration remains central to cultural imagination" (2010: 144).

The second half of the century witnessed economically driven, massive rural-to-urban migration in Turkey, followed by concentration of migrants on the outskirts of major cities who built their own houses and villages known as *gecekondu* areas or squatter settlements. These rural-to-urban migrants expanded the city geographically and created a more polarized class structure. Internal migration movements have changed in the 1990s. Since the mid-1980s, the civil war between Kurdish militants and the Turkish army in the southeastern region of Turkey caused displacement of rural people from their regular places of residence. Kurds constituted the majority of internally displaced people whose villages had been burned down or evacuated due to armed conflict (Yıldız 2005). The forced migration has had a profound effect on urban areas, developing various subcultures and changing the urban texture of Istanbul.

Significantly most residents of Küba are Kurdish and have migrated from eastern and southeastern Turkey since the early 1960s. Küba has become a shantytown of nearly three hundred households on the outskirts of Istanbul. We learn from the interviews presented in the installation that the city authorities destroyed parts of Küba several times because of the illegal status of households that accommodate the poor, unemployed, criminals, and drug addicts. But each time, the community replaced the demolished houses overnight. A Küba resident, Arife, recounts: "When they wrecked houses, we'd get together and built it again in one night. People gave cement, bricks, and other materials. By morning, we'd have it done" (*gecekondu* literally means "built over night"). After 1984, when the Turkish government declared a state of emergency in the southeast, thousands of Kurds fled to the cities. In the installation *Küba*, Dilşah talks about the difficulty of life for Kurdish people in Istanbul and not knowing much Turkish when she married her uncle's son. Fevzi remembers his village in the southeast: "When I was in the village ... the soldiers were pursuing the PKK [Kurdistan Workers' Party], the PKK passed through our village. The soldiers came into the village too. With the intention of protecting the animals, the villagers fired a few shots, fearing that there might be a wolf. Then the soldiers start shooting at them, left and right, at the tents and so forth." Makbule tells about her longing for her land in the southeast, and how she wrote a petition in Kurdish, in her native language and got arrested for "terrorism." "I want my language. I want education. I want to read," she says, articulating her rights in the idioms available to her. Muzaffer complains about not having proper education in the east. He says that the people who come to his coffeehouse speak in broken Turkish: "We have a coffeehouse. Ninety percent of the customers are unemployed Kurds. And we always speak Turkish. Poor and broken Turkish. If we spoke Kurdish we'd be more at ease, we could communicate more ... We are afraid to speak Kurdish. There are constant raids, constant complaints, constant prohibition."

The stories in Ataman's installation suggest that what unites Küba residents is the shared experience of discrimination, poverty, and urban segregation—not their ethnicity, religious beliefs or political views. Ataman states, "Living in Küba—above all else—defines their sense of identity, unique in the sense that it has no political, ethnic, gender, religious or national determination. If you are from Küba then that's enough ... Küba is first and foremost a state of mind. This consciousness etched in childhood and constructed through adult life is more important than religion, or origin" (qtd. in Horrigan 2004: 3). The installation evokes the shantytown Küba as an urban myth (no one really knows where it is), an illegal settlement located somewhere on the outskirts of Istanbul. Küba exists not in official records but in the imagination of people who do not occupy the secure place of citizenship. Bahri informs us in the installation: "They named this place Küba. To tell the truth, I don't know this name. Who named it, why? How? I really don't know." Yet Zübeyde provides another explanation: "I don't know why they call it Küba. There was a film once on television, I remember. Wasn't there? There was a film. A film about Cuba. A poor place where there were a lot of fights. Because of that film, the young people, they spread that name around and it stuck." A very young Küba resident Arafat says: "It's a nice neighborhood. When you are from Küba, you look and act bigger. When you go places, people don't dare to bother you. 'I'll beat you up,' he says, 'I'm from Küba. If you mess with me, I have a lot of people behind me.'" The stories of *Küba* propose a postnational basis of collective identification, one based upon the construction of a culture of non-belonging, exclusion, and resistance to authority within common experiences of displacement, violence, and poverty.

In his interviews, Ataman insists that *Küba* is not an overtly political artwork about the Kurdish minority or urban poverty in Turkey. Rather than reconstructing the specific suburban area in Istanbul, Ataman attempts to create an imaginary place that could be anywhere in the world, that could be defined not as a real, territorially bounded geographical location but as a metaphor, as a state of mind. Bill Horrigan suggests, "what matters to Ataman are 'alien narratives coming into an alien city and mixing with it.' Village by village, legally and illegally, Turkey is absorbed into the European union" (2004: 4). Hence, for Ataman, *Küba* is about various articulations of a precarious collective identity and resistance to authority that could be found on the edges of any major city. Ataman highlights the creation of a defiant collective identity rather than the historical and sociocultural context of the stories. But this attempt to downplay the specificity of *Küba* becomes difficult when the weight of the individual stories that involve civil war, the state of emergency, or military coups as well as poverty and domestic and sexual violence exert their own pressure on the work. When we think of the Küba residents in the larger context of European mobilities and the question of the borders of the European Union, we realize that *Küba*'s story is not new. Ataman brings *Küba*'s stories into an interpretive arrangement with the long tradition of labor migration but also with the current dynamics of undocumented migration and urban segregation (Küba residents might be seen as potential "illegal" migrants by the European Union). The intertwined stories of a mobility that stretches toward Europe include Turkish German labor migration and the increasing anti-immigration sentiments both in Turkey and Europe, and do not only belong to the private lives of a group of shantytown people. The stories of *Küba* and the installation placed in specific sites in Europe questions what it means to belong to a European space and who has access to its collective. As a site-specific video installation, *Küba* performs material and symbolic interventions into various public and private spaces, and it locates the metropolitan city as a place where belonging, the right to be in the world, is negotiated.

Notes

I would like to thank Deniz Göktürk, Barbara Mennel, and William Weprin for reading and commenting on earlier versions of this text.

1. *Lola and Billy the Kid* won the Teddy Special Jury Award at the Berlin Film Festival and the Best Film Award at New Festival, New York in 1999.
2. Many scholars have noted the shift from the earlier stereotypical representations of the victimized migrant to a new cinematic language that involves transnational and transcultural encounters and multiple border crossings. Ayşe Polat, Fatih Akın, Aysun Bademsoy, Yüksel Yavuz, Seyhan Derin, Thomas Arslan, among others, belong to this new wave of filmmaking that fosters a hybrid and plural Turkish German cultural identity (Göktürk 2002a; Mennel 2002a).
3. Ataman received the Turkish Film Critics Association Best Director, Best Film, and Best Screenplay Awards with his first feature film *Karanlık Sular* (*Serpent's Tale*, 1993). *Iki Genç Kız* (*2 Girls*, 2005) won the Best Director Award at the Antalya International Film Festival and Istanbul International Film Festival.
4. Alisa Lebow documents Ataman's professional trajectory: "His work has been included in some of the best known and arguably most important international exhibitions of the past decade, including *Documenta XI* (2002), the *Berlin Biennale* (2001), the forty-eighth *Venice Biennale* (1999), *Manifesta 2* (1998), and many more. In New York City, he is represented by Lehmann-Maupin, a well-placed Chelsea gallery, where he has had nearly one major show every year, each involving multi-channel video projections of his documentary images. He is also represented by high-profile galleries in Chicago, Sydney, and Istanbul" (2007–8: 58).
5. To explain the extended duration of the piece, Ataman states that *semiha b. unplugged* "is about life, it could be as long as one wishes. I very well remember thinking this: Make it impossible to watch. Because in eight hours, you at least have to pee or you get hungry, it's impossible to watch it in one go. Like a metaphor for life. You come and go, and continue watching from another bit" (qtd. in Baykal 2008: 25).
6. *Küba* won the prestigious Carnegie Prize in 2004.
7. Ipek Türeli refers to Halit Refig's *Gurbet Kuşları* (*Birds of Exile*, 1964) and Nuri Bilge Ceylan's *Uzak* (*Distant*, 2002) as "the earliest and latest most well-known examples of internal (rural-to-urban) migration films" (2010: 144).

Chapter 7

TURKISH FOR BEGINNERS:
TEACHING COSMOPOLITANISM TO GERMANS

Brent Peterson

The title of the award-winning German television series *Türkisch für Anfänger* (*Turkish for Beginners*) might remind older viewers of the 1982 program *Englisch für Anfänger* (*English for Beginners*). Aided by two British actors, that show's host presented a series of skits designed to teach English to a German audience. *Turkish for Beginners* (*TfB*) is not as overtly pedagogical, and its ambitions do not include teaching the Turkish language. Instead, the show's fifty-two episodes, broadcast over the course of three seasons (2006–8) on ARD, German television's premier network, use the tested formula of the family drama to depict life in multicultural Germany. *TfB* combines a blended family, the Öztürk-Schneiders, with another sitcom staple, romance. Indeed, the show's protagonists, a widowed Turkish German policeman with two teenage children and a German psychologist with a similarly aged daughter and son, provide enough characters for three interethnic romantic relationships. While there are certainly lessons that Turks living in Germany can learn from the program, not the least of which is seeing themselves depicted positively, I contend that *TfB* functions mainly to teach cosmopolitanism to Germans. After all, who are the beginners in the title if not the Germans and German-speaking members of other minority communities who can experience vicariously what it means to be Turkish in contemporary Germany?

TfB might also remind viewers of textbooks and online offerings that teach German to immigrants, even though elementary language instruction in Germany involves more than linguistic competence. The ability to speak German has become a prerequisite for work and residency permits, the reunification of migrant families, and the acquisition of German citizenship. Federally mandated language courses are called

Integrationskurse (integration courses), and the term "integration" dominates the discourse surrounding migrants and migration, even though "assimilation" is a more accurate description of what is demanded. Particularly since Thilo Sarrazin's 2010 book *Deutschland schafft sich ab: Wie wir unser Land aufs Spiel setzten* (*Germany is Doing Away with Itself: How We Risk Our Country*), public discussions of integration have centered upon the unfortunate binary of "us" versus "them": They have not learned our language; have not succeeded in our school system; have not taken on our norms, values, customs, and habits; and, most visibly, have neither emancipated their women nor left the neighborhoods where they congregate. Conversely, as this argument so clearly implies, Germans are fine just the way they are, except, as Sarrazin's numbing statistics demonstrate, German women are not having enough children. For all practical purposes, the concept of integration has been turned into a one-way street that begins with learning German and ends with migrants melting into the dominant culture (*Leitkultur*). Nowadays it no longer seems necessary to ask, as a group of guerrilla journalists once did, what are Germans doing to integrate themselves into the vibrant and varied culture that Germany has become (Kanak TV 2002).

In a 2011 book entitled *Deutschsein: Eine Aufklärungsschrift* (*Being German: An Enlightenment Treatise*) Zafer Şenocak makes the case for a different mode of dealing with migrants, namely, cosmopolitanism. His understanding of the concept is rooted in an ethos of tolerance, which requires knowledge and presumes acceptance within certain boundaries implied by the book's question: "How much diversity can we sustain or endure (*ertragen*)?" (36). The answer seems to be more than we now think, and it is worth noting that Şenocak, who was born in Ankara, migrated to Germany with his parents as an eight-year-old in 1970 and acquired German citizenship in 1994, includes himself in this "we." Şenocak begins with the Enlightenment, a period when people like Moses Mendelssohn aspired to be simultaneously something else, in his case Jewish, and German, just as in an ideal, cosmopolitan Germany, in which Turks could be German while retaining an otherness that their fellow citizens accept and value. However, according to Şenocak, Germans have been so buffeted by wars, division, and the longing for a homogeneity that never existed that their identities are fragile (*brüchig*) (2011: 27). They cannot imagine others assimilating into a culture where they scarcely feel at home themselves (2011: 89). His conclusion is that Germans will only feel comfortable in their own skins when they can welcome others not just into German society but into their homes (*bei sich unterbringen*) (2011: 55).

If we accept Şenocak's argument, it is precisely by locating Turks and Germans in the same household that *TfB* intervenes in the discussion of what it means to be German in the twenty-first century, which is necessarily a cosmopolitan identity. Among other things, the show's mainly adolescent target audience learns that the culture in which they live does not divide neatly along ethnic, linguistic, or religious lines. Even if the show is not high art, and shows slotted in the late afternoon and aimed at an adolescent audience seldom are, *TfB* warrants our attention, because it interrogates barriers built on ignorance and explores imaginary solutions to real social problems. In addition to depicting what it might be like to live in an ethnically blended family or to have a romantic relationship with someone who is *fremd* (foreign or unfamiliar), *TfB* lets its viewers see that many of the traits and habits that garner so much negative attention in the media are actually exaggerated, trivial, or surmountable. For example, the Turkish members of the Öztürk-Schneider family all speak flawless German; they are also German citizens and, despite a few hiccups, productive members of German society. In fact, my subtitle, "teaching cosmopolitanism to Germans," suggests that both ethnic and "other" Germans can gain something from the show's cosmopolitan sensibilities. In that sense it is worth mentioning that the terms "German" and "Turkish" as I use them here are constructed categories, a necessary shorthand, but also words whose content remains contested, and is, in fact, called into question by *TfB*.

There are, of course, other frameworks that might prove useful for thinking about the issues that *TfB* raises. The model of intercultural communication helped to legitimate the study of literature and film produced by minority authors in Germany (Ackermann and Weinrich 1986; Chiellino 2007), and the instruction paradigm that frames my analysis is certainly communicative. Unfortunately, the intercultural argument locates foreign or minority authors and filmmakers on a metaphorical bridge between two intact, separate, and distinct cultures, each contributing to the other. Intercultural suggests transience embodied in the concept of *Gastarbeiter* (guestworkers) who regularly return home, eventually to settle there permanently. Calling guestworkers migrants shifts the terms of the debate and acknowledges that Germans have relied on laborers from elsewhere for centuries, even if they have only recently begun admitting to themselves that these workers are immigrants who live in Germany and intend to remain there. So too are migrant authors and filmmakers not between anywhere, but rather both in Germany, often for generations, and legitimate participants in the discussion of what it means to be German in the twenty-first century (Adelson 2005; Şenocak 2011; Sezgin 2011).

Shifting to a model of cosmopolitanism suggests the existence in Germany of sensibilities that are neither strictly German nor any other national designator connected to German by a hyphen. Cosmopolitanism implies an extension of the concept of Germanness "in light of migration, mobility, nomadism, and hybridity" (Cheesman 2007: 52). If one considers the upper reaches of the German workforce, where technicians and managers may commute between their offices in Düsseldorf and the company headquarters in New York and then spend vacations at their second home in Spain, it is difficult to deny that transnational identities already characterize some sectors of German society, especially when the characters in this example could as easily be expatriates as Germans, citizens of the world rather than of a particular nation state (Terkessidis 2010: 18–27). Unfortunately, scholarly inquiries into cosmopolitan texts still tend to focus on works by migrant authors and directors who are, with some notable exceptions, concerned with the lives of their fellow migrants. As a result, the cosmopolitans who emerge from these studies are mainly migrants, and their cosmopolitanism is associated with high culture (Adelson 2005; Mani 2007; and, less so, Fachinger 2001). One could, however, as the sociologist Ruth Mandel proposes, examine "demotic cosmopolitanism," a category that includes the practices of anonymous "translocals" and, I would argue, texts such as *TfB* (2008: 50). Furthermore, while expanding the location of cosmopolitanism beyond the characters in aesthetically elite texts, one could again ask how Germans can become more cosmopolitan.

Despite a number of problems, which will come into focus toward the end of this essay, *TfB* performs the cultural labor of exposing its German viewers to the practice of cosmopolitanism. In the same way as the bourgeois tragedy of the eighteenth century brought the issue of middle-class emancipation to the public sphere, television has the power to encourage discussion of some of the most difficult problems facing Germany and Europe today for a larger audience than was possible in an earlier age. Of course, television's texts and audiences are thoroughly middlebrow, but that probably makes them more rather than less powerful (Hess 2010; Radway 1997). Such texts certainly warrant scholarly concern (see Brad Prager's essay in this volume), and, despite their presumed lack of artistic merit, it would be a mistake to question their theoretical sophistication. Not only does *TfB* move beyond the one-way street paradigm implicit in the discourse of integration, but even the most Turkish of its characters are also so rooted in German culture that notions of intercultural communication fail to explain the show's dynamic. Like the novel, where the narrative strategies of the family drama were developed, television encourages identification with its characters; anyone who sticks with the Öztürk-Schneider family for fifty-two episodes over the course of three years probably cares about what happens to one or more of its members and is therefore all the more likely to take seriously the show's negotiation of cosmopolitanism through private romance.

Romance remains a key device in building audience involvement (Radway 1984), and relationships across lines of region, class, religion, and nationality have long been used to test the plausibility of new sorts of families and new kinds of identities (see Daniela Berghahn's essay in this volume). For example, nineteenth-century historical fiction often explored new versions of what it meant to be German by fictionally marrying Prussians and Austrians, Catholics and Protestants, or noblemen and commoners (Peterson 2005: 199–265). Similarly if Turks can date or even marry Germans in *TfB*, the cosmopolitanism that undergirds such unions may well become possible in the wider culture; these ideas are also much more likely to gain traction, consciously and unconsciously, when they are linked to sympathetic characters instead of being the grist of idealistic appeals.

As *TfB* begins, viewers encounter a Turkish German couple, Metin Öztürk and Doris Schneider, who are about to tell their children of plans to blend their families. Since the show's primary audience is adolescents, *TfB* pays comparatively little attention to the parents' relationship, but it is worth noting the degree to which Metin confounds stereotypes about Turks in Germany. Judging by his command of German, one has to assume that he was born or educated in Germany. Although he also speaks Turkish, Metin's position in the upper-middle ranks of the Berlin police force indicates that he has obtained German citizenship, and he presumably did so before the 2000 law made that change in status easier. Moreover, despite his frequently being the butt of comic situations, a topic with its own set of tropes that would be worth examining (see Boran 2005), *Kommissar* Öztürk embodies the possibility of Turkish success in Germany, and he, rather than the family's flighty German mother, forms the bedrock of their blended family. In the economy of the show's narrative, Metin's eventual marriage to Doris sets a high standard for the two adolescent relationships that anchor *TfB*'s central plot developments. After introducing the two romances in outline form, a more detailed examination will show how and why the series both succeeds and fails in its attempt at renegotiating the integration debate by teaching cosmopolitanism to Germans.

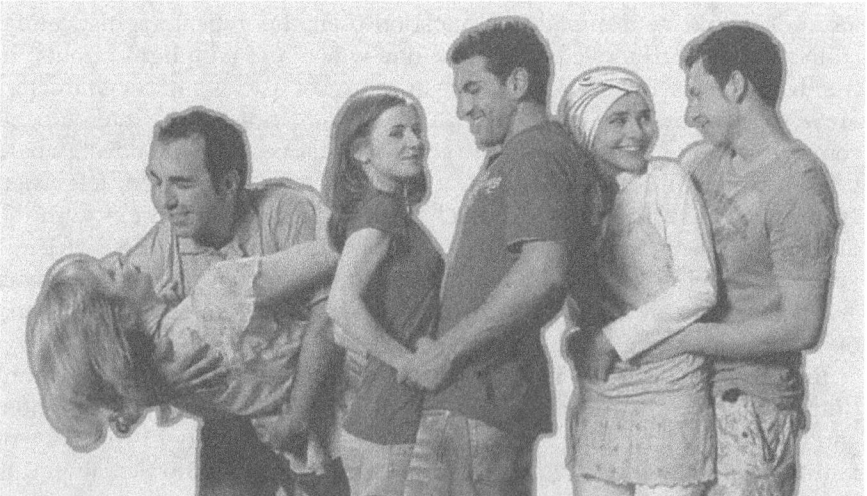

Figure 7.1 The Öztürk-Schneider blended family of *Turkish for Beginners*, DVD capture

First, the policeman's pious Muslim daughter Yagmur struggles with her attachment to Costa, her brother Cem's Greek best friend. Here the series examines the problems faced by a likeable young woman who proudly wears a headscarf, but who, contrary to the stereotype of arranged marriages in the Turkish community, also chooses her own mate, opting for someone from a different culture and religion. Already in this one narrative arc *TfB* lets viewers see a sympathetic character caught between the demands of her faith—to cover her hair, remain chaste, and marry another Muslim—and the dreams and desires of a German adolescent with hormones and access to a computer. If nothing else, Yagmur realizes that dating while still wearing a headscarf will be difficult, and because viewers get to know her quite well over the course of three seasons, they too come to care about her problems. Without offering solutions, or at least by putting them off for dozens of episodes, the series humanizes and complicates issues that are both intensely personal and highly charged politically. Simply by presenting information about others in their midst, *TfB* promotes the understanding and acceptance of otherness, that is, tolerance, and, to the degree that German viewers come to regard Yagmur as being like them as well as different, the show promotes cosmopolitanism.

Second, the series' other narrative arc traces a romance between two of the couple's children: Cem, the macho, not very successful Turkish male—he fails to graduate from high school and cannot find a real job—is both drawn to and repelled by his German stepsister Lena. She is liberal and liberated, and not yet worried that having a profession will impinge on her relationships with men. These two characters correspond to widely held stereotypes, but by providing names and faces to problems that Germans and migrants might otherwise view from afar, Cem and Lena involve viewers emotionally in real issues. Cem eventually settles into a respectable job, while Lena does well at high school and ultimately falls into a dream career; but she cannot resolve the competing demands of domesticity and independence posed by the relationship with her stepbrother. As *TfB* approaches the end of its final season, both the genre conventions of romance and the narrative logic of the show's cosmopolitan message require a happy ending, but in order to start their own blended family Cem and Lena not only have to overcome the personal problems that every fictional couple in romantic drama faces; they also have to reconcile differences that are implicitly coded as German or Turkish.

Comedies thrive on misunderstandings, but it is worth paying particular attention to the mistaken assumptions that propel *TfB*'s plot because they frequently arise from the same ignorance and prejudice that cause strife between Germans and migrants in the larger context of German society. For example, as the series begins, Lena calls Metin an Albanian terrorist, lumping an accomplished, Turkish German civil servant into the undifferentiated category of dangerous, dark-skinned Others. Her mistake occurs just before she meets Cem and Yagmur, and viewers learn that they are no better informed than their soon-to-be stepsister. Cem claims that Chinese restaurants serve dog meat, while Yagmur assumes that the waitress has never heard of Islam. Not an auspicious start, but by episode two the new blended family moves in together, and the stage is set for the confrontations, complications, and compromises that make up the program's plot.

The newly blended family moves to Neukölln, an ethnically mixed Berlin neighborhood that has a reputation for gang violence, thematized in films such as *Knallhart* (*Tough Enough*, 2006), and dysfunctional schools. *TfB* contests these clichés with some fact (Neukölln has recently become fashionable), some fiction (the actual *TfB* house, whose exterior can be seen in almost every episode, is located in Friedenau, a solidly middle-class section of the city, not in Neukölln), and a bit of wishful thinking: The school that the children attend is clean, modern, and well run. Starting in the second season, Doris's sister teaches there, apparently without difficulty. In accordance with educational policy in Berlin, the school is a *Gesamtschule* (integrated comprehensive school); it not only serves students of all abilities, but, like so much of what happens in *TfB*, the school also questions received wisdom, models cosmopolitanism, and implicitly joins the debate over the place of migrants in German society. Of course, even at good schools not every student succeeds, and Yagmur's character seems designed to put the integration paradigm to the test.

Viewers first see Yagmur as she enters the Chinese restaurant, looking somber, walking a pace or two behind her father and clad entirely in black, including her tightly wrapped headscarf. The image forces viewers to think about the symbolism of Yagmur's clothing, especially the presumption that no rational woman would choose such restrictive garb. As Rita Chin argues, the headscarf debate in Germany began in the 1970s, as liberal feminists tried to foster the emancipation of Turkish women, in part by encouraging them to reject the headscarf as a symbol of patriarchal oppression. By the 1980s conservatives co-opted the discussion by claiming that the headscarf and the victimization of women it implied "served as evidence for an unbridgeable chasm separating guest workers and Germans" (Chin 2007: 143). It is therefore an important revelation when viewers hear Yagmur explaining to Doris that neither her father nor her older brother forced her to cover her hair. Instead, her mother asked if she wanted to wear a headscarf when she was twelve years old (Episode 27). Yagmur insists, while wearing a looser, pink headscarf and smiling, that she made the decision herself, on religious grounds. She continues to cover her head even though she believes that headscarves make her look "hässlich" (ugly). Yagmur's explanation, during which she takes over the adult role while Doris is fretting about menopause, is not just that values trump appearance, but also that the valorization of certain forms of beauty, including clothing, damages women across the age spectrum. In addition to arguing that she and Doris are both beautiful despite social conventions,

Yagmur hints that a headscarf could actually be a sign of freedom in Germany, a choice that until recently was much easier to make outside the confines of a rigorously secular Turkey (see Toprak 2010: 19–36).

If *TfB* did nothing more than complicate viewers' perceptions of what it means to wear a headscarf, it would have performed a considerable service, but the program probes deeper by exploring at considerable length the consequences of Yagmur's preadolescent choice as a fifteen-year-old who falls in love for the first time. Since her beliefs forbid unsupervised contact with young men, Yagmur begins a chat-room relationship with someone who identifies himself as "verknallt in Neukölln" (smitten in Neukölln). In the days before Facebook and Skype, chatting was only words, so when the boy she mistakenly takes for her online boyfriend fails to appear for their first date, Yagmur wonders if the problem is her appearance. Lena tries to comfort her, but stumbles into an uncomfortable question about males who might be put off by what the traditional look implies. Yagmur explodes with a mixture of resentment and self-doubt, asking if Lena is saying that "kein gesunder Junge" (no healthy or normal boy) would want to meet a girl with a headscarf and "Werte" (values, Episode 26). Lena can only respond that Germany is not yet that progressive. The prospective boyfriend might have been afraid, and she suggests that Yagmur tie her headscarves a bit looser.

Since she is at home, Yagmur is wearing a hoodie rather than a headscarf, and viewers get a glimpse of the hair that remains covered in public. Of course, they have already seen it in other scenes that take place in the privacy of the bedroom that the two young women share, because the show has invited them into the family. By putting familiar, believable faces on behaviors that have been politicized across Europe, *TfB* gives viewers an emotional stake in concerns that would otherwise be abstract; it also lets them see the private ramifications of issues in the public sphere. In short, viewers begin to learn the lessons of cosmopolitanism.

Yagmur's role is far from over at this point, in part because the narrative conventions of romance demand a happy ending, even when achieving a satisfactory closure bumps into the difficult reality of multicultural Germany. The third season's narrative jumps ahead two years and opens with Yagmur still struggling to stay true to her religion while maintaining a relationship with Costa, the real "smitten in Neukölln." Although she is aware that her reluctance to allow any form of sexual advance may drive him away, Yagmur believes that her value system is essential to Muslim women, especially in Germany. But Yagmur is also a product of her German adolescence; she understands and even shares Costa's frustrations. Things come to a head when he threatens to end the relationship unless Yagmur stops wearing a headscarf. Metin supports the demand, going so far as to warn his daughter that, if she decides to study something technical, in this post-9/11 world, people might think she is part of a sleeper cell, intent on building bombs. In other words, Metin demonstrates his adherence to

German values rather than those of the stereotypical Turkish patriarch. He never expresses religious sentiments, nor does he worry that the family's honor is at stake in Yagmur's actions. Metin stands in sharp contrast to the father of one of Yagmur's previously pious friends whose daughter returns from Turkey and ostentatiously sheds her headscarf when the father is not looking, declaring that she is in a foreign country, where it is her duty to show Germans that she is normal (Episode 42). In this context normal is a synonym for German, and Yagmur uses the argument to transgress what had been an inviolate boundary. She arranges to meet Costa that evening in front of the Brandenburg Gate, the prototypical symbol of contemporary Germany. In the previous sequence Lena decided to sleep with Cem for the first time, and the musical backdrop, Christine Aguilera's "Hurt," a song that expresses regret over missed opportunities, continues as Yagmur, with the Brandenburg Gate gleaming behind and between her and Costa, and warmly backlighting the couple, removes her headscarf and lets Costa touch her hair.

The narrative might have ended at this point with the triumph of Western values, but the series refuses to take quite such a conventional path. When viewers return for the next episode, they find Yagmur, with her hair uncovered but piled up nearly as high as Marge Simpson's, again plagued by doubt. Her dilemma is how to live in Germany while remaining true to her religion. There seems to be no answer to the question until Costa emerges as a cosmopolitan role model. He notices Yagmur's struggle and declares, in front of her extended family, that he fell in love with her the way she was rather than the way he wanted her to be. Costa goes so far as to fetch the headscarf that Yagmur so recently took off, and to put it on

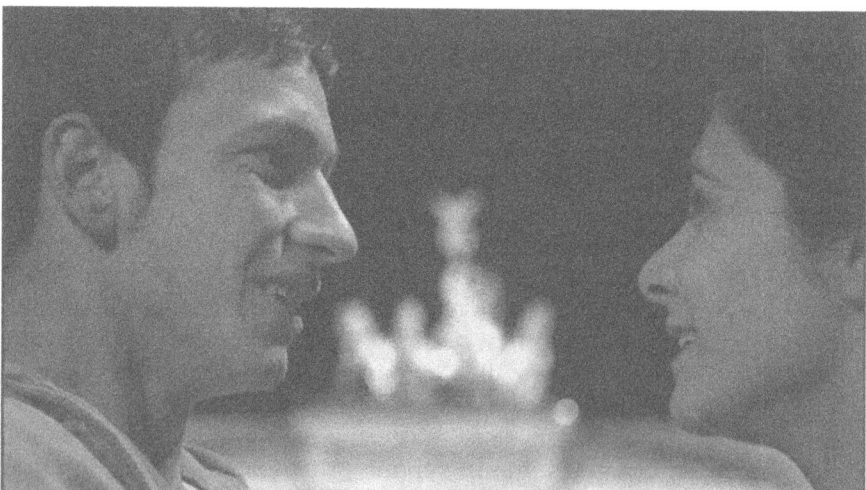

Figure 7.2 Yagmur (Pegah Ferydoni) and Costa (Arnel Taci) in *Turkish for Beginners*, DVD capture

her head before he falls on one knee and proposes. This change of heart signals not only Costa's acceptance of values that are coded as Turkish but also, and more important, his willingness to live with difference. With that shift, the curtain can finally come down on a happy ending for one of the two young couples.

Meanwhile, the narrative arc involving Cem and Lena has been exploring the same cultural issues, but with far less convincing results. Although the genre conventions of the screwball comedy and Lena's physical attraction to Cem probably lead viewers to suspect from the outset that the couple's bantering camouflages mutual attraction, the differences that separate Cem from Lena make it difficult to imagine a plausible resolution to their relationship. Had Cem and Lena both been either German or Turkish, or, like Costa and Yagmur, both from migrant backgrounds, standard-issue human foibles or gender stereotypes might have explained their problems, but the impetus behind *TfB* means that these two characters have to overcome the cultural norms and values that define them. The series therefore restages and intensifies the parents' ethnically charged struggles as it simultaneously increases their impact by locating those tensions in the same generation as *TfB*'s primary audience. Whatever one thinks of the results, the compromises forced upon the characters prove instructive for what they say about the lives of both Germans and migrants in contemporary Germany. It is, in other words, one thing to demand German language proficiency and quite another for Germans to be able to invite others into their homes.

Not only is there far more at stake in a Turkish German relationship, but Lena also functions formally as *TfB*'s central consciousness. The diegetic camera that opens most episodes shows her speaking to an absent friend or her biological father, as she comments on other characters' foibles or reflects on her own trajectory. Lena serves by turn as the show's authoritative voice or the primary recipient of its pedagogy. The other camera angles are omniscient, because no one else in the series, particularly not Cem, seems as strong or successful as Lena. Once her brother has been bundled off to boarding school, Lena also remains as the sole German adolescent coming to terms with life in a blended family. If she cannot integrate herself into multicultural Germany, if she cannot become cosmopolitan, then there is little hope for viewers who do not have the experience of living with Yagmur, Cem, and Metin on a daily basis. Both the task of teaching cosmopolitanism and the narrative logic of romance demand that something propel Lena and Cem into each other's arms; the challenge is to resolve the Cem-Lena narrative without resorting to implausible plot tricks while also treating their relationship, like the society it addresses, as a two-way street for both Germans and Turks. To judge by the results, the task even seems to have baffled the show's writers and producers.

In contrast to television production in the United States, the creators of *TfB* apparently did not have to present a draft narrative for the entire series before the show was commissioned. Reruns play a small role in the finances of German television, and the show ran on a public network where it must have been particularly isolated from such considerations. The first season comprised only twelve episodes, but there was considerable support for a television program with *TfB*'s ambitions, especially when it won the German equivalent of an Emmy, the Adolf-Grimme Award, for that first year (Grimme-Preis 2007). The second season was increased to twenty-four episodes, followed by only sixteen in the third, when the air had apparently gone out of the creative balloon. The third season was also delayed twice, and, in another indication of difficulties, its narrative started up again two years after the events that closed season two. One place to read both the problems and the potential that the series presented to viewers and critics alike is in the jury's justification for the Adolf-Grimme Award. The commendation begins by praising the network's decision to renew the series even though, in light of its relatively small viewership, that support was anything but self-evident. As the jury explains, *TfB* is "derart keck, witzig und politisch unkorrekt" (so bold, witty, and politically incorrect) that reaching a large audience was simply impossible. While praising the Turkish German author, Bora Dagetin, for his light touch with potentially difficult material, to say that he managed "die Botschaft trotzdem nicht bis zur Unkenntlichkeit zu verbergen" (to convey a message without making it completely unintelligible, Grimme-Preis 2007) sounds like the very least that viewers can expect. In effect the jury praises *TfB*'s intentions more than its accomplishments, as if the main point were to encourage similar shows in the future. Yet, someone still had to end *TfB*.

Lena's unexpected pregnancy is the complication that leads to a resolution. She and Cem have been sleeping together since early in the third season, but the plot development only works when this feisty young German on the verge of an implausibly successful career in journalism—she moves from intern to editor in a single step—is transformed into a Yagmur-like figure, but without the religion that motivates her stepsister's choices. The only alternative would have been an equally sudden reinvention of Cem, making him not only more intelligent but also more middle class. However, since bourgeois values have been virtually synonymous with being German since the late-eighteenth century, that change would have been character surgery in the service of Germany's dominant culture rather than cosmopolitanism. So when Lena's best friend says that abortion is her only realistic option, Lena announces, quite out of character—at least out of her previous character—that abortion is murder. Cem, who does not yet know that the baby is his, responds by saying that keeping the child would be suicide, but he makes the observation in the context of dismay and envy at Lena's success, having previously accused her of becoming a career woman (Episode 48). Cem, who did not finish high school, seems particularly afraid that Lena will be dissatisfied with his meager prospects and not stay at home as the ideal Turkish wife should.

Uncharacteristically but, in view of the narrative demands, necessarily Lena decides to perform her editorial work from the family couch, proclaiming, as the cliché would have it, "home is where the heart is" (Episode 51, as are the following quotations in this paragraph). With Cem scurrying to give Lena tea and a foot massage, itself a strange role reversal, Lena vetoes her friend's idea for the next edition's lead story, "Frauen stehen ihren Mann" (women stand their ground). She calls the idea idiotic and asks what sort of woman finds happiness in a profession. She even confesses that, although she has nothing against emancipation, at the moment "I just don't feel like it." It is as though Lena rejects the entire Enlightenment project that undergirds modern Germany, including, if Şenocak is correct, a much more nuanced cosmopolitanism. Sitting on the sofa in her slippers, Lena has become unrecognizable, and it seems far from accidental that her new outlook corresponds to norms and values that are coded as Turkish rather than German. All that is missing is a headscarf.

To his credit, Cem looks dubious at the prospect of getting what he wanted. Since he and Lena are only twenty years old, an age at which marriage would be an unlikely choice for today's Germans, viewers might wonder if Lena pays too high a price for what is supposed to be a happy ending. She could wake up at some point and realize that she has saddled herself with an underachieving husband, thrown away a unique career opportunity, and landed in the nineteenth century. Although it is difficult to imagine an alternative happy ending, the end of the Cem-Lena narrative scarcely satisfies. It does, however, simultaneously suggest that integration and especially cosmopolitanism demand a much more thorough rethinking of German culture and society than is to be found in contemporary political discourse.

In the larger scheme of things, *TfB* presents a very mixed message. On the one hand, by portraying the difficulties faced by a pious Turkish girl sympathetically, while simultaneously giving her the chance to move much further into German society than she had initially contemplated, the series performs a genuine service to its adolescent viewers. Both Costa and Yagmur make it seem possible that members of Germany's migrant communities can develop cosmopolitan identities and that there is more to them than German viewers might have assumed before watching the series. Indeed, after watching their story, and the one involving Metin and Doris, viewers probably have become more cosmopolitan, that is, much better, to paraphrase Şenocak, at imagining a multicultural Germany. On the other hand, it seems unlikely that Lena's choices resonated with the German adolescents who were *TfB*'s target audience. The question is whether the Cem-Lena narrative represents a failure of imagination or if it reflects a social reality in which it is difficult to envision the contours of a cosmopolitanism that Germans and migrants can share. Of course, the characters could have been made less stereotypical and their relationship more plausible, but if Cem and Lena had not conformed to the expectations of ordinary viewers, if they had both been working class or academic overachievers, then *TfB* would not have explored the social and cultural tensions that were the reason for the program's existence. However much we would like to believe in the possibility of a happy ending, particularly when the genre demands one, some social problems are genuinely intractable: in the Cem-Lena story *TfB* simply reached beyond society's grasp. But what I regard as an instructive failure in one of the show's three main narrative arcs should not detract from its success in teaching cosmopolitanism in the other two.

Chapter 8

"ONLY THE WOUNDED HONOR FIGHTS": ZÜLI ALADAĞ'S *RAGE* AND THE DRAMA OF THE TURKISH GERMAN PERPETRATOR

Brad Prager

The television film *Wut* (*Rage*, 2006) was first scheduled to air at 8:15 pm on Wednesday evening, 27 September 2006 on the public broadcast station ARD. Following the initial announcement, however, the schedule was amended. ARD had postponed the film's airing until a later slot on Friday 29 September at 10:00 pm, where it would attract a smaller audience and probably fewer young viewers. The station's decision ignited a controversy that drew a number of politicians into its fray. The change in the screening time was taken seriously by Edmund Stoiber, the Bavarian Minister President, who argued, "the truth has a right to be shown without any ifs and buts" (*Spiegel Online* 2006). The station's decision was described as "incomprehensible" by CDU politician Armin Laschet, who maintained that the film "is not xenophobic. It describes something that happens in this country, namely violence in the schools." He then added, "Moreover, there are many other films in which foreigners appear as criminals" (WDR 2006). Finally Fritz Pleitgen, the chairman of West German Broadcasting (WDR), the company that produced the film, claimed: "There is obviously a fear of critical headlines. ... The film shows reality as it is encountered by many children and youths, but it is a reality that we adults don't want to perceive. ... This film should prompt an engaged, controversial, and wide-ranging discussion. ... To conduct a socially important conversation at midnight is of course a waste of an opportunity" (*faz.net* 2006).

Examining the public discussion provides insight into the political expectations viewers had of the film, and into viewers' expectations of public television programming in general. However, when one watches the film itself, it becomes apparent that *Rage* is centrally concerned with the threat posed to the film's ethnic German patriarch's masculinity, which reveals itself to be so unstable that a lone teenage antagonist can swiftly throw it into disarray. Little of the public discussion dealt with that emasculation. Initially the film's action seems to pivot entirely around Felix Laub, the teenage son of Simon, a liberal university professor, and his wife Christa. Felix is bullied in the streets of Berlin by Can, a Turkish German drug dealer who also sells pot to Felix, which adds a supplementary layer of complexity to their relationship. Felix is pushed around, has his sneakers stolen, and also loses his spending money to Can's posse in a rigged street game. Simon attempts to intervene, believing that he can take care of the problem through careful intervention and dialogue. He is presented as a product of the German student movement, someone who would be a so-called "68er" because, owing to his age and apparent political leanings, it would be a natural assumption that the character participated in or was at least affected by the revolutionary activities associated with his generation. It should not go unnoticed that the roles of Simon and Christa are played by August Zirner and Corinna Harfouch, who also played lovers in Margarethe von Trotta's *Das Versprechen* (*The Promise*, 1994). This part of their history is relevant insofar as the two, as a couple, represent a particular era; they can be associated with a generational moment in German history, as it was memorialized in von Trotta's widely seen film, as well as in cinema history itself insofar as von Trotta still carries with her the auteurist cachet of New German Cinema, even into the 1990s. Simon's attempts to negotiate with Can fail, the situation escalates, and the film concludes with a crescendo of violence that echoes Michael Haneke's *Funny Games* (1997), in which a bourgeois family of three is held prisoner in their own home and on their own living room couch.[1] Distinct from Haneke's film, however, the intruder in this case meets with a grim end: Simon angrily struggles with Can and beats him to death in the family swimming pool.

Despite the many dimensions of the film, the major subject of public debate was that which was falsely perceived as extraordinary and taboo breaking: the depiction of a Turkish German antagonist. In this respect Laschet's assessment was correct: many other films featured nonethnic Germans as antagonists, and it was unusual to single out *Rage*. There had already been films with Turkish German criminals such as *Geschwister—Kardeşler* (*Brothers and Sisters*, 1997) and *Kurz und schmerzlos* (*Short Sharp Shock*, 1998)—films that self-consciously "appropriate and rework genre conventions of the ghetto action film" (Mennel 2002a: 155)—and those films were later followed by more exploitative ones, including *Knallhart* (*Tough Enough*, 2006) and *Chiko* (2008). Although much of the press coverage seemed to suggest otherwise, *Rage* hardly stood alone in exploring its themes. In the case of *Tough Enough*, which opened in theaters several months before *Rage* was televised, a Turkish German bully, played by the same actor who plays *Rage*'s antagonist, Oktay Özdemir, is again menacing a neighborhood. That film, directed by Detlev Buck and based on a young adult novel by Gregor Tessnow, features Özdemir as Erol, an overconfident tormenter who feels more or less secure in his position as the schoolyard's alpha male. Ultimately German law, in the form of a helpful and apparently ethnic German police officer, is introduced in order to assist the narrative's apparently ethnic German protagonist out of the lawless corner in which his dealings with Erol and other nonethnic Germans have placed him.[2] The film, which takes place in Berlin's Neukölln neighborhood, presents Erol's character as having concerns about family and masculinity that marginally mitigate his behavior, yet its depictions largely remain within the realm of stereotypes. *Rage* was distinguished from *Tough Enough* because it was made for television rather than for theaters and was therefore to be broadcast directly into German homes. It may be for that reason that it was said to be "playing with fire" (Festenberg 2006: 122). As Brent Petersen points out when discussing the television series *Türkisch für Anfänger* (*Turkish for Beginners*, 2006–8), programs on public television are typically expected to adopt a straightforwardly pedagogical function. More likely, however, *Rage* was a subject of disputation because its difficult conclusion was less digestible and reassuring than the one offered by Buck and Tessnow.

Züli Aladağ, the director of *Rage*, was born in Turkey but grew up in Stuttgart and studied in Munich and Cologne. He aimed to provoke with his film and was quoted as saying, "In talking with left liberals, I have noticed that there is bias when it comes to the issue of migrant criminality ... Many are frustrated that some immigrants transgress certain values—whether it has to do with honor killings or with brutality in secondary schools. There is uneasiness one would like to talk about without being exposed to the accusation of racism. To call things by name and formulate displeasure about certain situations is something very liberating for a particular class of Germans" (Aust 2006).[3] Owing to this type of expectation and reception, the character of Can was treated as exemplary, and the film thus provided license to speak in general terms about brutality perpetrated by nonethnic German students. Schoolchildren were interviewed to authenticate the film's alleged contentions. It was screened at the Kepler-Schule in Berlin-Neukölln, and one student was quoted as saying, "a couple of hundred of those types [like Can] run around here in Neukölln. Alone, most of the Turkish youths are harmless, but in their posse (*Clique*), a chance look in the wrong direction can provoke a beating." Another student added, "A short time ago, we had a Can in our school" (Serrao 2006: 31).

Newspaper articles asserted that the film had a symbolic meaning; that it was, for better or worse, a warning about the dangers presented by lawless Turkish Germans. The discussion centered on the representation as if a television film could function straightforwardly as a manifesto or party platform. The film is, however, more unruly than that. Although one may argue that the film's meaning is defined by its reception, it is also hardly as unambiguous as the debate suggests. Each of Simon's decisions—choices that escalate rather than defuse the film's violence—is rendered questionable. Daniela Berghahn points out that the film "does not just point the finger at the problems inherent in traditional Turkish patriarchy," but is also critical of the ethnic German family at its center, one that serves as "a microcosm of German hegemonic society" (2009: 67). As indicated, however, the film's meaning is not wholly contained by the anti-politically correct cachet that made it attractive to politicians such as Stoiber and Laschet. As much as Can's troublesome and lawless inclinations determine the course of events, the film also challenges Simon's paternal position—and that of much of the film's likely audience—as predicated on fantasies about themselves, as well as about the basis and limits of their tolerance.

More significant than its answer to the question of who is to blame for the cycle of violence unfolding in the film are *Rage*'s formal choices, which either consciously or unconsciously correspond to positions the film takes concerning the delegation and exercise of power. It is very concerned with the levels its characters occupy relative to one another, often literally, and it conspicuously frames its visual compositions to indicate that the film's tall German patriarch is more equal, so to speak, to his shorter Turkish German rival than he had assumed. To draw on Deniz Göktürk's terms, the film undermines Simon's apparent benevolent paternalism, which mirrors the kindly positions toward nonethnic Germans found in those films cited by Göktürk as indicative of the politics of the New German Cinema, including films by writer-directors such as Hark Bohm and even Rainer Werner Fassbinder, whose works were sometimes built around "good clichés" (Göktürk 2002a: 249–51). The central question in this case may not be so much one of whether a Turkish German story has been told by a Turkish German director—although in this case the film's director was born in Turkey[4]—but rather how the protagonist's paternalism is undermined by an equaling or leveling of positions throughout the film. The paternal relationship *Rage* seeks to thematize and reject conveys itself through Simon's condescending attitude, through his belief that he understands Can, and that his benevolent handling of the difficult situation ultimately serves Can's own interests. These beliefs are thrown into disorder, and the film in this way undercuts Simon's paternalistic framework.

The teleplay, written by Max Eipp, suggests a knowledgeable reflexivity when it comes to the structure of its narrative. Initially we see Simon in his capacity as a professor of literature elucidating literary principles to students in a university lecture hall. He explains to them that stories are a game, and that we can even be made to identify with a murderer. Simon explains, "however grim and sad the theme of a novel may be, the story itself—the process of writing—is play." He then foreshadows narrative turns to come, noting that where literature is concerned, "we can identify with the murderer, die with the victim and, the next morning, head back to the office." The metaphor of a game—of fiction as a playful masquerade—is central insofar as the film concerns itself with a string of gambits dictated by conflicts over terrain. The various acts of bullying in the film are based on the demarcation of various locales: playgrounds, homes, and lecture halls. On his way home Felix traverses the recreational space that appears as Can's domain, and the motif recalls one of *Rage*'s major intertexts, Heinrich von Kleist's *Michael Kohlhaas* (1811). Kleist's novella is not named, but is likely alluded to later in the film during one of Simon's lectures. *Michael Kohlhaas* begins with its protagonist passing through the territory of a greedy *Junker* (member of the landed nobility) who unjustly appropriates Kohlhaas's horses from him as a type of toll. With this relatively small theft a spiral of increasing violence begins. In *Rage* Can and Simon each have their territories, and the film's assertion is that balancing their domains is, as in Kleist's story, a more unwieldy task than Simon expected, perhaps even an impossible one.

In order to right the lawless situation—Can's shoe stealing infraction—from its onset, Simon indicates that he will "undertake something," which is how he expresses the notion to Christa. The German word for "undertake" (*unternehmen*) suggests the enterprising, even optimistic, spirit of an entrepreneur. Simon's first step is to initiate a reasonable dialogue, which involves paying a visit to Can in his territory, defined in this case as the streets and playgrounds where he hangs out with his posse. In this sequence, the director makes it apparent that Simon has no sense of what he is up against. Introducing himself to Can, he stands level with him in the belief that dialogue is to be had. The varying frame of the handheld camera underscores Simon's loss of balance, and the sequence also makes use of its music to highlight the shifting ground. Simon and Felix have just come from Felix's music class, and Aladağ deliberately transitions from a sequence in which Simon is expressing pride about his son's command of Schubert to one accompanied by diegetic hip-hop music, which is alien to Simon, yet so familiar to Can that he is able to seamlessly integrate its lyrics into his virtually ceaseless onslaught of verbal abuse. Simon tries to play the disciplining father, but loses control over the situation. The film suggests as much through its employment of the handheld camera, but also in Can's mean-spirited imitations. After Simon initiates a dialogue, Can accuses him: "What're you blathering about?" Simon responds: "I'm not blathering, we can speak normally with one another," and Can then parodically repeats Simon's line "speak normally." Can plays a game of repeating what Simon says, indicating the sentiment, "I can be like you," demonstrating that he has enough control over the exchange to engage in parody.

This first confrontation, only seven minutes into the film, presages the film's violence with its rapid cutting. Simon's nearly Habermasian belief in the positive potential of rational speech acts is—as far as he sees it—advanced as generosity offered to a perpetrator who, owing to his criminality, his status as a Turkish German, or both, apparently deserves a chance to correct himself. Can, however, mocks the idea of speaking "normally" with one another because the screenplay wants us to know that a reasoned enlightened dialogue is exactly what will not be achieved. The parodic response makes clear that Simon is not going to get anywhere with Can and his posse. Their discussion concludes with Simon's feminization—at the moment Can sticks a pair of hamburger buns atop Simon's chest as ersatz breasts—and with Simon calling Can an "asshole." The name calling appears as an invalidation of communicative rationality. The epithet is less a contribution to rational discussion than a forceful shove.

Simon's efforts to communicate are stymied at every turn. Much remains unsaid in his marriage, insofar as Christa is carrying on an affair with a close friend of theirs, and he also fails in most of his efforts to see eye-to-eye with Felix.[5] In the film's Oedipal struggles Felix and Can seem to have a stronger filial dynamic. Although Can's motives for ingratiating himself with Felix might be cynical, the two appear to have a genuinely good time smoking pot in Felix's room. The closeness between them recalls the relationship that develops between Robert De Niro's Max Cady and Juliette Lewis's Danielle Bowden in *Cape Fear* (1991). In that film as well, injudicious actions on the part of the film's ostensibly good patriarch, a lawyer played by Nick Nolte, are shown to be mainly responsible for threats to his family.[6] Felix is at times charmed by Can, but when he sits and has a beer with his father, their conversation takes wrong turns. Attempting to elicit information, Simon asks whether Felix came into contact with Can because he was purchasing "marijuana" from him. Felix then educates his

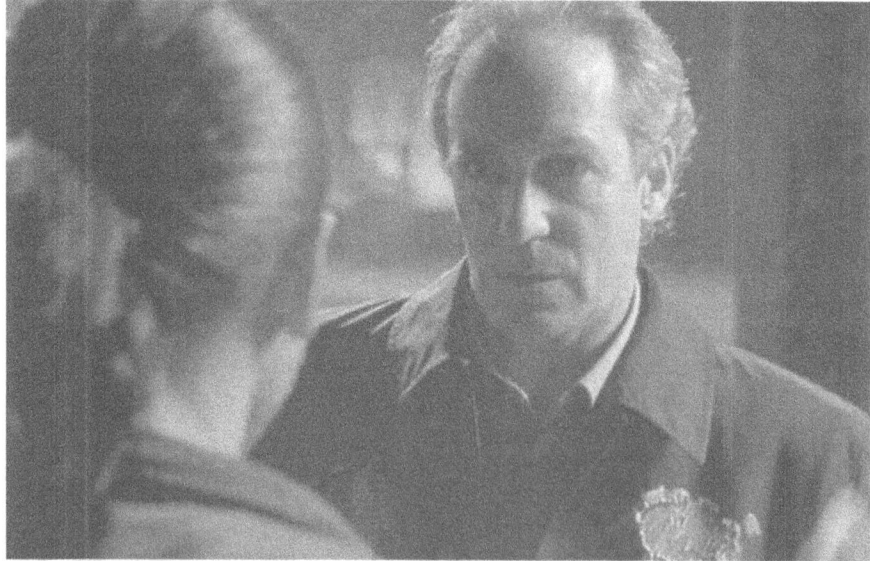

Figure 8.1 Simon (August Zirner) in *Rage*, DVD capture

father indignantly: "It's called dope." Felix also seems largely aware of the inconsistencies in his father's application of moral principles, especially where marriage and fidelity are concerned.

Simon escalates the conflict by visiting Can's home, operating again under the false assumption that power relations might still be determined vertically. Simon intends to speak to Can's father directly with the idea that the two of them will paternalistically and reasonably decide what is best for their sons. Can's father seems sensible, but he is more aware than Simon that his clout with Can is limited. Can, however, views the visit as a challenge to his authority and is clever enough to turn the tables by returning the gesture. Either consciously or intuitively, Can competently maneuvers around the film's figurative chessboard and, exploiting Felix, works his way into the house while Simon and Christa are away. The movement into their terrain—the violation of their "phat" residence complete with souvenirs from their travels and a large art photograph of what appears to be a woman of color overlooking the living room—literalizes his breach of their milieu. When the couple arrives home, Can indifferently breaks a valuable vase, which he half-heartedly stages as an accident, and slyly pockets a "tasteful" black and white nude portrait of Christa. After facetiously accusing the couple of poor hospitality, Can finally leaves, but he has made clear that one cannot simply go over his head; he does not expect to have to yield to Simon's or any other paternal authority.

Two subsequent sequences, also in systematic parallels, advance the conflict. When out on a date in a chic bar, Can notices Simon is similarly appointed with an attractive student. He boasts to his girlfriend, "I know that guy," and takes the opportunity to show that he sees their relationship as one between peers. As a paradigmatic indication of Simon's belief that their interaction can be overseen and controlled, he locates the maître d' and has Can thrown out. Can is embarrassed and retaliates by slashing Simon's tires. He then makes what appears to be a winning move. Through his close relationship with Felix, who is at this point less a protagonist than a pawn, Can comes upon the knowledge that the inaugural lecture connected with Simon's professorship, his *Antrittsvorlesung* at the university, is coming up. Can does not recognize exactly what this entails (he bungles the name of the event, referring to it as a *Vortrittsanlesung*) but is again sharp enough to recognize an opportunity. He decides to intrude into Simon's space at this public event, when he will be most vulnerable. The lecture hall is in general Simon's territory, and Aladağ indicates as much in the earlier sequence, where the camera takes note of the approbation the students offer following Simon's lecture (they rap affirmatively on their desks) as well as the erotically charged gaze of his particularly seductive young student. This is the professor's province, but Can upends everything. The camera presents him entering the hall from a low angle, which connects our gaze with Simon's but also makes the diminutive Can seem more foreboding. He then descends to Simon's level—which is, with respect to the amphitheater-style lecture hall, a metaphorical ascent to the podium—in order to present his opponent with the nude photograph of his wife, now defaced with the ballpoint sketch of a phallus, and thereby challenge in multiple ways Simon's erotic and patriarchal control.

At the podium Simon is in the process of introducing the second of two stories he means to interpret. The reference here may be to *Michael Kohlhaas* insofar as Simon makes a glancing allusion to brains having been bashed in, which is a feature of that story (a *Junker*, Hans von Tronka, has his brains spattered against the stones of a castle wall). Simon stands before his students and colleagues and begins to read from his notes: "Poverty suffers; it does not fight." The sentence is borrowed from the popular philosopher Rüdiger Safranski. The film does not establish clearly whether these are meant to be treated as Simon's own words, or if he is simply citing Safranski, whose book *Wieviel Globalisierung verträgt der Mensch?* (*How Much Globalization Can We Bear?*, 2005) was published in German in 2003, three years before *Rage* was released. Simon continues with Safranski's words: "Only wounded honor, or the desire for glory and recognition fight" (2005: 19). At that point Can enters, throwing the already nervous professor off his game. The intrusion reveals that power relations in the lecture hall are predicated on informal agreements: the students respect the professor's authority, but the relations that hold those norms intact can be undermined at any moment.

Standing eye-to-eye with Simon, Can ostentatiously gives him permission to continue. Initially Simon patiently appeals, "please leave this lecture." Knowing precisely what he is doing insofar as he is exposing not so much Simon's hypocrisy as the tenuousness of social power relations, Can approaches the student with whom Simon is carrying on his romantic relationship and asks whether the romance is ongoing or whether he is now having sex with a different student. Simon then escalates his response, performing his anger. He attempts to give his declaration force—again trying to shove Can with words—and adds an inflated remark: "You are sullying literature and academic study with your presence." Pointing at the door in a futile and hapless gesture that would serve as the centerpiece of any of Kleist's ironic stories, Simon adds: "Immediately leave my lecture!" The image is composed as an extreme high-angle shot, one that flattens the lecture hall's dimensions owing to its remoteness from its subjects. The distance diminishes Simon, underscoring his impotence and his inability to retain control. More significant, the extreme height of the shot flattens the space, placing the two of them at the bottom of the same deep well.

Although Can has at this point taken some distance from the podium, he has managed to throw all things out of balance. He provokes Simon further: "Fuck your literature!" Then, in an echo of their initial interaction, he asks, "what are you blathering about?," to which he adds, "fascist asshole." Simon becomes enraged. Switching to the informal—and in this case aggressively paternal and disciplinary—mode of address and adding an epithet, he says: "get your Turkish ass going and leave this room." Here Can has finally succeeded in exposing Simon, both to himself and to those around him. The slur reveals that even he is prone to racism when the chips are down. Can is aware of the specter he has raised and, before he exits, he hits below the belt, calling Simon a "rightwing loser."

In Kleist's *Michael Kohlhaas* the protagonist goes to great lengths—setting towns ablaze, for example—in order to exact retribution upon his adversary. The escalation of bloodshed in that story is the most likely reason it was chosen as an intertext. It may also be the case that, as Seán Allan points out, there is a "moral achievement" to Kleist's story (1997: 631), which is that Kohlhaas ultimately overcomes his desire for revenge and admits that his effort to extract justice from the world had been all too rash. Had Simon been allowed to continue, he may have been headed toward a similarly humanist conclusion. Many readings of Kleist present themselves, and a humanist one is surely possible. However, the question remains: why do Eipp and Aladağ draw on Safranski? Safranski's *How Much Globalization Can We Bear?* is an attempt to provide an account of the contemporary culture of integration as well as an alibi for those who believe that real cultural integration cannot be achieved. It underscores the role of the thymotic (from the Greek *Thumos*) in human history. Passion, which here sounds more like pride or vanity, is treated as the most significant historical motor. Reassuring readers that conflicts are eternal, Safranski asserts

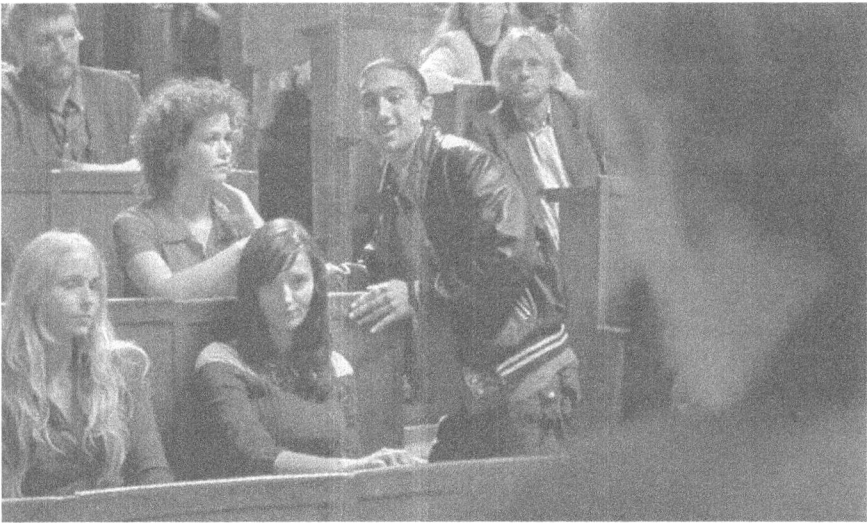

Figure 8.2 Can (Oktay Özdemir) in *Rage*, DVD capture

that, "[there] are the two great ideas of universality: one God and one humanity. But, in reality, the idols are many and humanity is torn apart by different families, tribes, peoples, nations, and kingdoms—and this remains the case in the age of globalization. The political world is still not a universe but a 'multiverse' ... Multiplicity ... inevitably mean[s] struggle and war" (2005: 21). Safranski is responding to a naive belief—a straw man he has constructed—that proponents of globalization would expect to build a world entirely free from distinctions. In response he repeatedly emphasizes that humanity exists only in the plural; that is, that there are many types of humans and a collective noun is, in this case, a fiction. Here he adopts Carl Schmitt's point that anyone who says "humanity" is already misleading; there is no humanity, but instead only an aggregation of interests (Schmitt 2007: 54).

With the words "poverty suffers; it does not fight" (2005: 19) Safranski puts forward an argument against what he describes as a "vulgar materialism," which "discovers purely economic motives everywhere" (19). It is, in his opinion, honor and dignity—specifically the passionate craving for difference (18)—that defines human struggle. Individual aggression of this sort is transferred to borders between nations and is thus responsible for wars. This latter conclusion, it should be emphasized, is best set aside as pseudo-Nietzschean fantasy, yet the question where Aladağ's film is concerned is whether Simon is at this point meant to be asserting with Safranski (as though Safranski's words were his own) that conflicts come down to individual pride rather than social causes, or is he supposed to be arguing against him and in favor of "vulgar materialism"? Kohlhaas's search for justice was certainly driven by vanity and pride, but where is Simon meant to be coming down on this? Is it possible that he is suggesting that we were not made to live harmoniously and that the idea of a collective humanity is a fiction? Given what we know about Simon one might more likely suspect that he is proposing *contra* Safranski that globalism is possible and that Kohlhaas, unlike an unrepentant Cain (cited as an example by Safranski 2005: 20), rightly seeks absolution where he attempts to overcome his egoism. This could surely be what Simon, the 68er, wants to believe he believes.

But all of that remains conjectural. Simon's lecture is interrupted, which underlines the superfluity of his literary speculations. His conflict with Can has put him in a position where he is forced to revise his thinking. When Simon first lectured, he explained that within the sphere of literature we watch things transpire, identify with the protagonists—even with murderers—and then return to the office. Aladağ's film, however, aims to place Simon beyond the simple game of understanding and into a position where he has to experience first hand what motivates Can's rage; he cannot go back to the office, and he cannot view the unfolding dynamic from outside, because it is one in which he is implicated. The film is depicting a literature professor who has been hauled beyond the game of literature, and it contends that his work has been heretofore limited as a vehicle for empathy and understanding.

In its denouement *Rage* confirms that Simon knows himself falsely; that is, when push comes to shove he is no longer committed to his principles. After involving the police fails to remove Can from his radar, Simon has a muscular pal of his, the same one who is conducting an affair with Christa, beat the daylights out of him. At home, Simon, who is by now revealed as a hypocrite, a deceitful father, and a cuckold, prepares an appetizing dinner for his family, and the film makes clear that the achievement of domestic peace is predicated on a violent and extralegal act of enforcement. The film at this point undercuts Simon's humanism; he is left concluding that he cannot do otherwise than exercise power; all there is, in the end, is force, and the struggle to maintain his domain. Can, now enraged and exiled from his father's household, returns to the Laub home and holds the family prisoner in their living room at gunpoint. Playing a Hanekesque funny game, Can offers Simon a deal: if he finds the courage to shoot himself or his wife then Felix will be allowed to live. Out of options, Simon puts the gun to his head and pulls the trigger, revealing that he would have been willing to end his life, possibly as a bold act of self-sacrifice, but more likely because he at this moment feels deeply debased. In still another comment on Simon's impotency, it turns out that the gun in his hands was unloaded. Can starts to make his exit, believing the point has been made, but a final struggle ensues in which Simon, now quietly enraged and attempting to salvage the masculinity of which he has been stripped, pursues Can. The two grapple with one another and fall intertwined into the pool. The camera descends beneath the surface of the water highlighting that the two have reached a new depth. During the fight Can's head is whacked against the pool's side, and the blow kills him. As Berghahn notes, Simon has now "betrayed the values on which his whole existence was founded" (2009: 64). He weeps, Turkish-language music plays over the end credits, and the drama closes.

For Simon, overcoming ire would be a trying if not impossible act, and here, as in *Michael Kohlhaas*, heads roll before there is repentance. His tears at the film's finale suggest an avowal that he has approached his dilemma too idealistically, and that he may not have drawn enough from his study of literature to prepare him for his life. In the public discussion about the film, which centered regrettably on the question of whether bullies such as Can indeed exist and on whether persons of a certain class feel liberated when given the chance to express that fact, Aladağ and Eipp's thematization of Simon's crisis and his emasculation remained largely unaddressed. There is a Turkish German perpetrator in the film, yet its narrative fully implicates Simon in its battle of egos. It is less Simon's family that Can assails than Simon's self-image and his fragile authority. In exploring his patriarchic anxiety the film examines the scope of this symbolic dislocation; it asks what precisely would be so threatening about a perpetrator such as Can. *Rage* surely trades on stereotypes, yet when it is understood in the context of other films, especially paternalizing ones of the past, the positions of which are here rendered naive, it can be seen to suggest that honor—that which fights—can be wounded in more ways than one.

Notes

1. Berghahn also notes the similarity to *Funny Games* (2009: 64).
2. The name of the protagonist of *Tough Enough*, Michael Polischka, suggests that his background might possibly include European migration, but the film does not explicitly address this point.
3. *Turkish for Beginners* was also lauded for being "politically incorrect." See Peterson's contribution to this volume.
4. Aladağ, the director, was born in 1968 in Van, in eastern Turkey, and came to Germany in 1973.
5. Berghahn adds more on the extramarital affair, noting how both Christa's behavior, as well as the fact that she seems to have provided capital to purchase the family home, constitute evidence of Simon's emasculation (2009: 65).
6. At the German Turkish Cinema Workshop in 2010, where this paper was initially presented, Marco Abel suggested the film's similarity to Martin Scorsese's *Cape Fear*.

III

INSTITUTIONAL CONTEXTS: STARS, THEATERS, AND RECEPTION

Chapter 9

THE GERMAN TURKISH SPECTATOR AND TURKISH LANGUAGE FILM PROGRAMMING: KARLI KINO, MAXXIMUM DISTRIBUTION, AND THE INTERZONE CINEMA

Randall Halle

Much research has been done on the Turkish German image projected onto the screen, or about the background of the auteurs who produce such images. Little work has been done on the institution of Turkish German cinema, its conditions of production, distribution, and display. Although Martin Hagemann, a producer from Zero Films, once complained that "Turks" do not go to these films, analysis of the audiences for Turkish German films is all but nonexistent (Hagemann 1999: 227). Moreover, if Turkish German film indeed did not draw the interest of German Turks, we still know relatively little about the actual viewing interests of and spectator statistics for this population because until recently the cinema had not been a primary mode for German Turks to consume culture. When we consider Turkish German films solely as produced in a network of German institutions and as media for a minority, then we ignore the interweaving of that industry with production in Turkey and disregard the fact that Turkish German productions are not the main forms of film consumed by German Turks. Indeed, German Turks appear to share with the general population in Germany a similarly limited interest in German films and a distinct preference for popular entertainment from Hollywood.

One aspect that distinguishes German Turks is their access to Turkish language productions. In this regard the multilingualism opens up an orientation toward entertainment possibilities not available to the general population. (Although most residents of Germany speak more than one language, limited Turkish instruction in the schools means that most people who speak Turkish do have a migrant background.) Media and entertainment consumption of Turkish-language offerings, however, has historically taken place elsewhere, through television, newspapers, radio, and Internet. In Germany it was not until 2003 that a cinema, the Karli Kino in Berlin Neukölln, began first offering regular Turkish-language offerings. What Turkish or Turkish German programming had made its way onto the German screens up to that point had been sporadic in appearance, often art house in nature, or had offered scenes of Turkish German suffering that Turkish audiences in Germany seem to have largely rejected.

This absence of opportunities has changed in the last years, to a great extent because of Karli Kino and other cinemas now following its model. It allows us to consider a German Turkish cinema as including films beyond representations of Turkish German problems as we might find famously in Fatih Akın's *Gegen die Wand* (*Head-On*, 2004). The spectators for the Turkish programming at Karli Kino do not represent an audience based only on local and particular interests, and, as this essay will explore, Karli Kino could not present its offerings if it were not for the presence of a larger apparatus of cinema.

Thus what interests me in this essay is how these developments are signs of cinema's ability to establish new political, economic, and cultural spaces. I want to insist from the start that this is not a simple Turkish *space* in spite of its largely Turkish-speaking audience nor is it an easy German *place* in spite of its immediate location in German multiplexes. This cinema derives from transformations in Germany and Turkey that are not simply simultaneous or mutual but rather convergent and interdependent. A thorough examination reveals that they belong to the dynamic of "deracination" in Germany that Ruth Mandel has identified as a way of refashioning discourses about ethnicity, specifically discourses of ethnic essentialism that serve as a basis for monoculturalist politics (2008: 1). Mandel observes in the relationship of what is typically determined by oppositions of native and foreign, or indigenous and migrant, that "a process of reciprocal transformation and social differentiation has taken place in German society to such an extent that in many realms it already is impossible to distinguish two distant, bounded totalities" (2008: 18). I would modify this observation to add that the process takes place not just in German but in Turkish society as well.

This dynamic of convergent and interdependent spaces is, on the one hand, an increasingly common experience and yet, on the other hand, an emergent quality of globalized space; approaches to interzonal dynamics typically misrecognize them because they rely on national frameworks or presume monoculturalism. In such an approach, Turks in Germany attending Turkish-language films would exemplify a willful ghettoization from Germany's dominant culture. The model of film production under discussion here would appear as a matter of simple import of one national film into the cultural realm of another. This approach misses the interconnected, indeed integrated quality of the cinematic space.

To obviate national discourses and to apprehend the specific quality of contemporary convergent and interdependent spaces, I identify such spaces as interzones, by which I mean that geographical and cultural space that develops as a space of transit, interaction, transformation, and vibrant diversity. It develops through border crossing in its broadest sense, not just geographically abutting borders, but also psychological boundaries. Border crossing in this sense is an act of montage that brings together two categories into a new relationship to produce a meaning that transforms them both. An interzone is in effect the opposite of Appadurai's ethnoscape; it is a conflictual dialogic space in which filiative terms such as ethnicity are in flux (Appadurai 1996). This essay will first offer a discussion of the Turkish German interzone established by and through cinema as a process of multidirectional and polyvalent cultural production. It will consider how the small space of exhibition and viewing in Berlin's migrant neighborhoods is a concrete site of the Turkish German interzone, which in turn has opened up a not-yet-fully realized public sphere. It will then present an initial evaluation of a survey conducted on audience members for Karli Kino's Turkish programming with the goal of providing some insight into the interests of the audience inhabiting this space.

Brussels in Beyoğlu

Neukölln, the district that houses the Karli Kino, is the most densely settled part of Berlin with 300,000 inhabitants. Further, it has always been a site of migratory labor; already in the nineteenth century, the district was one of the primary quarters in which the new urban proletarians settled on their way from the countryside. Starting in the 1960s, it became the home to many of the new immigrant workers from Turkey. Demographically Neukölln is a young area, having the highest birth rate in Berlin, well above the national average. Neukölln is experiencing an ongoing influx of residents with more than just an ethnic German background and simultaneously a form of what in the United States would be called "white flight." The collapse of long-term historic industries such as the Kindl brewery has fostered this transformation. The demographic shift, largely in the north of the district, is ostensibly an exchange of one working population for another, a multicultural immigrant precariat replacing a middle European migrant industrial proletariat (Beck 1986).

To understand the developments in Neukölln's Karli Kino though, we have to look well beyond that district. This is not a simple one-way migration, a cultural transfer from a sending to a receiving country. Neukölln is not an isolated locality. Just as with the travel and orientation of the district's residents, the production, distribution, and exhibition of Turkish films in its cinema arise out of a complex set of connections between Turkey and Germany. Neukölln as a locale proves in contact with reference points in the United States, India, throughout the Middle East, North Africa, and of course multiple countries in the European Union (EU).

Cinema as interzone here means we consider a space in which policy decisions taken in Brussels have a direct influence on films produced in the Beyoğlu neighborhood in Istanbul. To a large extent this interzone arose because the Mediterranean region has been a site of intense investment of EU-based resources, second only to Eastern Europe during the period prior to EU expansion. Through such programs as the European Neighbor Policy, the EUROMED Partnership, MEDIA Mundus, or the expansion of the Europa Cinemas network, the EU has sought to develop a Mediterranean sphere of influence. These initiatives started in the mid-1990s with the goal of "restoring" coherence to north and south, understood as inherent to the region since at least the Romans (Moulakis 2005). Clearly though the goal is not to reference the Roman Empire but rather to unblock national restrictions on a region that had been a crossroads of trade and communication.

Through the most successful of these initiatives, the EU has extensively fostered audiovisual production as a means to accomplish the stated goals of Mediterranean cultural unity. At this point for most of the non-EU EUROMED member countries—Morocco, Algeria, Tunisia, Egypt, Israel, Jordan, Palestine, Lebanon, Syria, and Turkey—the majority of film production takes place as coproductions with EU partners. To narrow the focus for the sake of this essay, we can note that of the non-EU Mediterranean partners, Turkey has received the second most support from the EU after Israel. And on various points of comparison Turkey has received more support than a number of Mediterranean EU member countries: more so than Malta, Cyprus, and even Greece.

As with the other EUROMED countries, this assistance has had an important effect on Turkey, imbricating it ever more fully into EU structures—in spite of anti-Turkish sentiment complicating its application for ascension. Since 1988 sixty Turkish coproductions have been arranged with European partners through the Eurimages program alone (Demirhan 2008). With a rate of film production in Turkey during the 1990s below twenty films per year, we recognize that this number has been about 10 percent of annual production. Such support has helped revitalize the industry. Indeed we can note successes such as the various film festival prizes for Nuri Bilge Ceylan, Yeşim Ustaoğlu, and Tayfun Perisemboğlu bringing international attention. However, these celebrated representatives of an auteurist Turkish cinema frequently if not exclusively produce their works as coproductions with European partners.

Along with art film, popular film has also experienced a boom. This productivity could be described as deriving from an indigenous development: the Turkish economy has been flourishing in the new millennium, expanding at rates in line with Brazil and India. However, in the era of globalized economies the boom should not be understood as a national phenomenon, but as in the case of Brazil and India deriving from external investments of finance capital. And in the case of Turkey, much of that capital comes from Europe and especially from Germany; Turkey may not be part of the EU free trade zone, but it is a preferred site of investment.

Thus EU economic and political investments are not simply benevolent mechanisms of support for local culture and indigenous peoples. As interzone it is not European or specifically German society that has changed; Turkish society has undergone dynamic changes as well. This investment transforms and reshapes Turkish culture. Mine Gencel Bek astutely argues that the relationship to the EU has had a bifurcated effect on the Turkish media in general (2009: 79). On a political level, the EU has pushed forward a democratizing agenda, which Bek sees positively. On the economic level, the entry into the European free market has brought new market pressures to bear on the industry. The EU forced competition and opened Turkish media to outside ownership, as with the presence in Turkey of the Axel Springer AG and its investment in the Doğan group, publisher of the *Hürriyet* daily newspaper. In film production we can note similar investments. Turkish popular film is profitable for European media funds, and production companies such as Geopoly or Plato Film Production bring European monies to Turkish popular film projects. Considering print and broadcast media Bek assesses that in this process "commercialization is being favored over communication" (2009: 79). We can extend this to film. The Turkish public sphere is being recreated as a consumer society of products from a culture industry financed in part by a Europe to which Turkey nevertheless remains outside. There is much more that could and should be said about these developments, but the key point here is that as part of this interzone, the revitalization of production in Turkey's film industry interconnects with the development of a new cinematic space in Germany.

Beyoğlu in Berlin

Shifting our perspective to the spatial coordinates of the Turkish German interzone, we can now consider cultural flows from Turkey to Europe and specifically Germany. As with the investments in Turkey, these relationships also transform Germany. We can focus on the approximately three million plus residents of Germany with historic ethnic and political connections to Turkey about whom relatively little is actually known—

especially in comparison to the number of presumptions expressed by politicians and disseminated in the media about this population. In conjunction with this essay, we can note that there are, for instance, relatively few studies of media consumption and viewing habits, although the popular press in Germany frequently uses the satellite dish on a balcony as a prejudicial symbol of Turkish culture.

Beginning in the mid-1990s a few studies were carried out that began to explore the community and its interests. Most research on German Turkish media usage has been focused on television and print media, showing for instance that the relationship to the media depends on linguistic abilities and not active distancing from the dominant society (Schatz 2000). This research has disproved a polarization of media usage: individuals rely equally on German and Turkish newspapers, dependent on their linguistic abilities, not as a result of *a priori* ethnic determinations (Butterwegge 2006).

In 2002 Lab One Medien und Kommunikation and GIM, two market research firms, for the first time undertook a general survey of patterns of media consumption in Germany (see Sinan 2004). The survey drew certain conclusions that are significant for the discussion here. First, existing Turkish media do not appeal well to the younger generation. But at the same time, especially Turkish German youth see themselves as represented largely negatively in the German media. Second, German Turks do not want to be reduced to being perceived only as Turks. They want their German self-perception to be recognized and acknowledged by the greater German society. Third, there is no such group as "the Turks." In spite of discussions in the media that present them as a homogenous Turkish population, the second, third, and fourth generations are developing as heterogeneous groups with relatively few shared characteristics. Such heterogeneity confounds easy statistical analysis (Sinan 2004).

In 2007 a group of Swiss media researchers led by Heinz Bonfadelli conducted surveys of media usage by Turkish and Turkish Kurdish youth in Switzerland (Bonfadelli et al. 2008). Although a Swiss study, the research can be used to extend the conclusions of the Lab One study. Cinema played a very minor role in the discussion; the people surveyed tended not to go to the movies. The lack of engagement with cinema continues from *Migrant Media: Turkish Broadcasting and Multicultural Politics in Berlin* up to the mammoth study *Einwanderungsgesellschaft 2010 (Immigration Society 2010)* (Kosnick 2007; Bade and Fincke 2010). These excellent studies provide discussions of broadcast, print, and new media but not cinema.

The dominant approach is thus to connect media to private consumption and ethnic identification rather than public participation in new interzonal production. Nevertheless there are a few important observations in the Bonfadelli survey vis-à-vis cinema: when the respondents went to the movies, they were attracted to Turkish-language films and then typically chose to go to the cinema as a family. A generational divide is clear among moviegoers in that second and third generation; youth tend to go in groups and then not necessarily to Turkish films. Indeed, this study highlights that the space of the multiplex and the mall allows Turkish German youth to engage in the typical subcultural behavior of their peers. Members of their parent generation express their willingness to organize visits to the cinema for their children and convey a positive attitude about German-language films to them when engaged with the content. They are not rejecting local culture, rather they want family-oriented programming that pleases their children, sometimes even at the expense of their own linguistic accessibility.

A further study of interest here is Nevim Çil's recent documentation of Turkish German experiences of German unification, *Topographie des Außenseiters: Türkische Generationen und der deutsch-deutsche Wiedervereinigungsprozess* (*Topography of Outsiders: Turkish Generations and the German-German Unification Process*). This study offers a corrective to the understanding of the Turkish population as heterogeneous. In her research, Çil explores how 1989 was perceived as a caesura by her interviewees. The process of unification was experienced largely as a process of ethnicization and nationalization of the term "German." After German unification the language of "guestworker" gave way to a discourse of foreigner (*Ausländer*). Key here for the experiences of her interviewees were the xenophobic attacks on foreigners that began in this period, most notably the fire bombings in Hoyerswerda, Rostock, Solingen, and Mölln and that mar the early history of the new republic.

Çil notes that the younger generations that had little or no direct experience of living in Turkey responded by asserting a Turkish identity. Çil sees the responses not as an assertion of a separate ethnicity, noting that Kurdish interviewees also adopted the designation "Turk" during this period. Rather Turk and Turkish for these generations was an expression of pride in response to the experience of exclusion. Many interviewees, who before unification understood themselves as Germans, remarked that for the first time in their lives they began to refer to themselves as Turks. Çil discusses how for this population of German Turks and subsequent generations, Turkey could not be a place to which one could return; at most one could emigrate from Germany, or take up a more dynamic transnational relationship to Turkey and Germany.

As a point of significance for understanding the conflictual and dialogic nature of the interzone, we must underscore that this assertion of Turkishness among Turkish Germans is thus not a long historic identification with a homeland, a commitment to a core ethnicity, but a dynamic shift in identification that developed in response to the Germanification of the dominant population and the great increase of cultural opportunities for and by Turkish Germans. It also paralleled a dramatic expansion of Turkish German entrepreneurial activity in Germany. Indeed, many of the new business initiatives developed out of entertainment and leisure activities.

Slowly in the 1990s, alongside the high-cultural contacts fostered through organizations such as EUROMED and Eurimages, a few people in the German and the Turkish film industry began to consider the populations of German and European Turks in general as a group with interests that go beyond the private sphere. They recognized that Turkish households throughout Europe might have inhabitants who are actually in search of new types of entertainment venues—cinemas for example. This recognition was part of a larger trend. The Essen-based Zentrum für Türkeistudien (The Center for Turkey Studies) noted that, at this time, the general orientation away from questions of return resulted in an intensified engagement with the German labor market. Taking an explicitly ethnic approach, Martina Sauer and Faruk Şen, leading researchers at the center, identified that in 1985 there were 22,000 Turkish businesses in Germany; by 2000, there were 59,500; and by 2003 there were 61,000 (2005: 5–6). Media researchers such as Kutay Erdem, Ruth Schmidt, and Ayşe Çağlar have discussed how the 1990s also began with a series of marketing surveys that first came to recognize Turkish Germans as a recognizable consumer group with niche market potential (Erdem and Schmidt 2008; Çağlar 2004). This coincided with a number of new media developments in Turkey that addressed the larger Turkish diasporic community. The state-run media, Turkish Radio and Television (TRT), began international programming. TRT INT was oriented to people living outside of Turkey, especially in Europe, providing both news and entertainment.

Returning to the specific area of cinema, Maxximum Distribution and Kinostar are leading companies in these developments. Kinostar began in 1997 with an initial orientation toward popular film distribution, mainly Hollywood. Maxximum Distribution was founded in 2001 by Nermin Tutal and A. Anil Sahin, and their marketing strategy began with the plan to bring Turkish mainstream productions to Western Europe. Sahin had left a position at the multiplex corporation CineStar and brought that knowledge of multiplex programming to his own distribution company. It quickly became one of the most successful distributors in Germany, winning the Box Office Germany Award six times for creative programming. Part of the success has been precisely the dearth of venues offering Turkish-language programming along with the presence of a postunification audience interested in maintaining connections to their Turkish heritage. The untapped market allowed Maxximum to arrive at extremely high spectator-per-copy ratios, an important factor of success in the distribution and exhibition branches (Buder 2008, 2009; Harders 2004). In the first two years Maxximum was able to bring thirteen films successfully into German cinemas.

However, as interzonal activity, this distribution has not remained one of simple import across national borders. Maxximum has also turned increasingly to funding production in Turkey, developing films that specifically appeal to diasporic Turks living in Western Europe. Maxximum learned from the business model developed by Hollywood studios such as Warner Brothers in the 1990s and became a producer-distributor unit, but specialized in films with more moderate budgets. Increasingly today the company is also working to develop German productions that can be distributed in Turkey. Cofounder Sahin sees this development of popular film as necessary as he is particularly critical of German Turkish film, including the work of Fatih Akın (Harders 2004: 130). Sahin expresses his interest in overcoming maudlin tales of immigration and suffering that, in his view, still dominate Turkish German productions. In German Turkish coproductions he seeks to offer a form of "normalized" entertainment, not a recollection of Turkish tragedy in Germany. Sahin's interests result in the funding of urban action and comedy films that capture a positive quality of life in Istanbul and Germany. Sahin wants to portray an urbane young successful lifestyle and not clichés of headscarves and honor killings like the ones found in the works of Züli and Feo Aladağ.

Certainly on the Bosphorus, Turkish productions are not infused with a minoritizing gaze, being produced in a different context in which ethnic Turks are in the majority. However, it is clear that this film production is now orienting itself to diasporic Turks as well as those living as minorities outside of Turkey. Cem Yilmaz, a Turkish comedian and star of some of the biggest successes of the last decade, did a special German-language commercial for his star vehicle *Yahşi Batı* (*The Ottoman Cowboys*, 2010). The humor of the commercial is that he does not speak German and advertised his film in a heavy accent reading phonetically. Yilmaz's films are popular enough that they do not need this extended audience, but clearly the film market has learned to consider the particular niche market for Turkish Germans.

In conjunction with the new and reliable distribution of films, Karli Kino in Berlin-Neukölln started in 2003 to present regularly Turkish and Turkish German films in Turkish with German subtitles. Karli Kino is part of the Cineplex group, a cooperative organization of mostly midsized to small cinemas throughout Germany. These cinemas are privately owned or run by groups on a smaller scale than UCI or CinemaxX. This cooperative model allows for a bundling of resources in film rental and distribution. However, it also introduces a greater degree of programming flexibility than found in the more centralized competitors, which allows theaters in the Cineplex group to orient the film offerings more strongly to individual cities and neighborhoods and their specific demographics.

The Turkish programming has developed largely through experimentation. For instance, it is now offered continually from October to April after the management recognized that in the summer months the potential audience tends to travel to Turkey for vacation and during that time often sees many of the latest releases. Thus, the films chosen tend to be drawn from current releases and not a larger repertoire of successful Turkish films. It is important to the management that the films are shown with German subtitles. There is no intention to screen solely Turkish-language original versions. Part of the rationale is that this policy extends the accessibility of the films to second, third, and fourth generation Turkish Germans whose Turkish is not necessarily fluent. They benefit from the German subtitles. Of course, it also opens the films to a German-speaking audience.

The Survey

To consider then who the spectators are for these films and how they understand the functioning of the interzone, I developed a brief survey. I administered it on a regular basis during the October 2009–April 2010 season, at different times and on different days in order to reach different audiences. I passed it out before the film began and remained for the film, collecting it afterward. The survey is in German and Turkish. It first

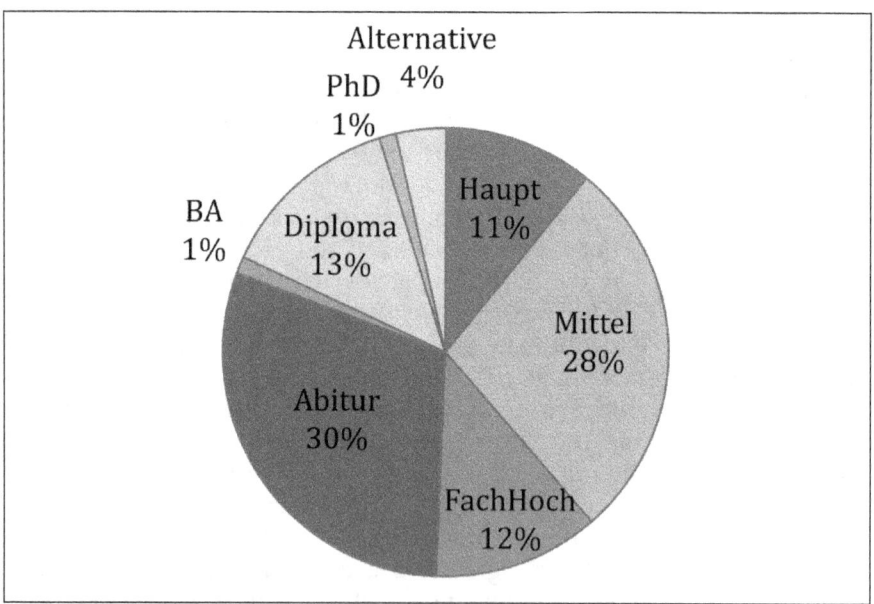

Figure 9.1 Education Level of the Participants
(Haupt: Hauptschule=Secondary General School;
Mittel: Mittelschule=Intermediate Secondary School; FachHoch: Fachhochschule=Technical School; Abitur=Highschool diploma; Diploma=State Examination Masters Level)

asks questions about general film spectatorship and then addresses Karli Kino specifically, e.g., the audience members' views of the ambiance and their motivation for coming to that theater. Furthermore, it inquires about the relationship to the films in subtitled form and the background of the respondent.

I administered one hundred questionnaires out of which eighty-seven were completed, almost quadruple that of Bonfadelli's survey. The gender distribution was balanced in that 56 percent of the respondents were female and 44 percent were male. The average age group was thirty to thirty-five years old. Of the eighty-seven respondents, eighty-three reported their education level. The distribution suggests that those interviewed were a highly educated group.

Other studies have suggested that cinema is not a specific form of entertainment for German Turks, but those studies have neglected to note that they do not differ greatly from the German majority population among which attendance frequency is 1.6 visits to the cinema per year (Filmförderungsanstalt 2009). We can say that regardless of ethnic background, residents of Germany in general prefer to stay home and watch television and DVDs. However, the audience at Karli Kino is by comparison an avid film audience. The majority of the respondents were frequent moviegoers in that 25 percent saw movies six to twelve times a year, followed by the group seeing one to two movies a month. Those who saw as little as a couple of movies a year or as much as one to two times a week were a small minority.

To be sure, very few people who identified as ethnic Germans attended screenings. However, the audience replicates Çil's understanding of

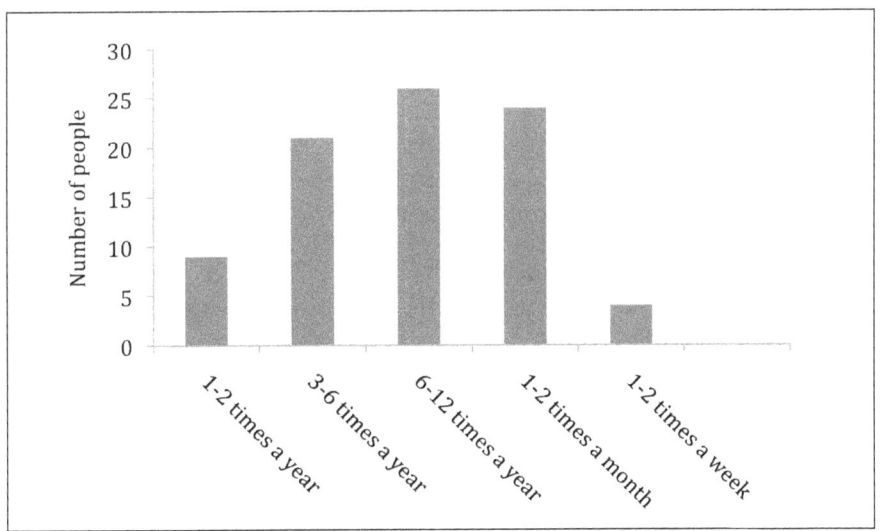

Figure 9.2 How Frequently Do You Go to the Movie Theater?

the Turkish community in that Kurds and Alevites also constitute a significant number of spectators. In part this may have to do with the fact that Turkish popular cinema has begun to include positive images of Kurds, even in nationalist productions such as *Günesi Gördüm* (*I Saw the Sun*, 2009) or *Nefes: Vatan Sağolsun* (*The Breath*, 2009). The Turkish program is popular with a younger crowd, and it is likely that the cinema is functioning for youth especially as a collective gathering place. The cinema offers an alternative to other types of entertainment such as music venues, café culture, youth centers, sports, and so on. Certainly it seems that there is among the respondents a preference for Turkish films but also an ambivalence vis-à-vis German and preference for Hollywood films. And again in this regard the German Turkish audience seems to differ little from all spectators in Germany, where overall the general population attends Hollywood films in greater numbers than German films. Rather than understand this preference for Hollywood among German Turks as a special rejection of a dominant German society, we can understand it as a sign of integration. The choice to attend Turkish films is typical subcultural activity defined by mass media and group taste. In this regard, it remains to be seen how much Turkish film attendance serves simultaneously as a form of distinction and integration into typical behaviors of youth in general. Clearly cinema becomes a choice within larger cultural parameters.

Further analysis of the data will add to the complexity of understanding the audience. It is important to underscore here that the question of ethnicity should not be taken as a homogenizing form of identification. Certainly from the start of this essay, with the framing attention to German Turks and their audiovisual preferences, the discussion runs the risk of developing an ethnically essentializing approach. However, the results reveal indeed the flexibility of identification described by Çil. To view Turkish-language programming does not directly mean one is a "Turk"; rather, various forms of ethnicity as well as other factors come into play. Attendance at the program offered by Maxximum and Kinostar at venues such as Karli Kino can be motivated by factors of age, gender, genre interest, linguistic training, family and/or age cohort interests, and so on. Indeed, rather than reveal a particularizing interest in the Turkish German population, the statistics reveal certain similarities with the overall viewing practices of the entire population in Germany. If we recognize the cinema and its larger apparatus described here as giving structure and support to an interzone, then attendance at Turkish-language programming can be understood as a form of integration into the general popular culture industry.

While we might anticipate that the difference between a film from Turkey and a Turkish German film is that the Turkish films are largely outside of the discourses that operate in the German public sphere, such an approach does not contend with the very real complexities of production that have arisen in the European film industry. The Turkish film industry does not operate distinctly from other national film industries, especially the German one. Nor does the hidden corollary mean that in Germany to watch Turkish film is a sign of a disinterest in German society, even a turning away from that society. Cinema rather becomes an interzonal space in which a new form of culture arises, defined more by market and social interests than by expressly political ones.

Importantly these films do not represent a presence of foreign moving images flickering across the screens of German cinemas. Rather they represent a fundamental cultural transformation that cuts across noncontiguous borders, bringing into proximity places that were once distant, and constructing new ideational spaces or interzones. For those who express an anxiety about the future of Germany, we can underscore that the German nation has become a member state along with twenty-seven others. And for those who resist understanding Turkey as a potential member state in the European Union, the dynamic cinematic apparatus of production, distribution, and exhibition derives as much from German and European presence in Turkey as it does from Turkey's presence in Germany. The transformation taking place is not a union among equals but, as noted throughout this essay, one of conflict and a certain polyphonic dialogism. The cinema of the interzone offers a fundamentally important place for the experience of new imaginative communities.

Note

In preparing the survey I received advice and support from Mohammed Bamyeh, Suzanna Crage, Derya Özkan, Kristin Dickinson, and Ceyda Kirci, and would like to thank them for their assistance. Başak Yavçan-Ural was instrumental in dealing with the data, and is an equal partner in the analysis of the survey. I am very grateful for the privilege of working with her.

Chapter 10

MEHMET KURTULUŞ AND BIROL ÜNEL: SEXUALIZED MASCULINITIES, NORMALIZED ETHNICITIES

Berna Gueneli

Filmic images of people naked in the shower, whether men or women, play pivotal roles in films such as Alfred Hitchcock's *Psycho* (1960), Robert Altman's *M.A.S.H.* (1970), and John Hughes's *Ferris Bueller's Day Off* (1986). Shower scenes "can be the focal point for horror, comedy or intimacy" (Telegraph 2009; cf. French 2010). However, such scenes can also entail exoticizing and eroticizing moments of scopophilia—the pleasure of looking—directed at the ethnic Other. An iconic scene in Rainer Werner Fassbinder's 1974 *Angst essen Seele auf* (*Ali: Fear Eats the Soul*) begins as follows: A medium shot shows Emmi—a German widow in her late fifties—entering a bathroom. Her longing gaze is directed at the naked, dark-skinned body of a man in his late thirties. The counter shot shows a mirror depicting Ali—a Moroccan guestworker—taking a shower and facing the mirror. Framed by the mirror, Ali is completely naked and visible as such for Emmi, the camera, and, the spectator. The scene ends with Emmi's phrase: "You are very handsome, Ali."

Thirty-four years later, a similarly revealing moment in the 2008 *Tatort* (*Crime Scene*) episode *Auf der Sonnenseite* (*On the Sunny Side*) depicts the following: A low angle shot shows a running shower, which is followed by a medium shot depicting a glass wall separating camera and spectator from the shower. Behind that shower glass is Cenk Batu, a Turkish German undercover detective. He turns in the shower revealing different perspectives of his naked body. More so than Fassbinder's film—in which the sexualization of the protagonist is part of the narrative—these images in *On the Sunny Side* are gratuitous to plot development, but in both cases the camera captures the protagonist as a man of color, whose nakedness presents both vulnerability and attractiveness.

Fassbinder's socially critical and didactic film *Ali: Fear Eats the Soul* tried to raise awareness of existing xenophobia in the context of postwar West Germany and its historical continuities. The more recent *Tatort* with Cenk Batu is the first episode in a critically acclaimed entertainment television series to incorporate a Turkish German protagonist as detective. Given that up to this point in time the series had only depicted ethnic Germans from different German cities, the introduction of Cenk Batu as a member of the guild, whether robed or disrobed, represents a move beyond ethnic stereotypes. His presence thus serves as a sign that German society has become multiethnic and that members of different ethnicities are not typecast. But with their firm, naked bodies of color, these men share strikingly similar visual imageries, even though they appear in films from different historical contexts and with different sociopolitical contents.

This essay focuses on the persisting fantasies of ethnic masculinities in contemporary (Turkish) German films and episodes of television series.[1] Although the victimized foreign worker of New German Cinema, represented by Fassbinder's Ali, has, by 2008, become a subject with agency, a detective in contemporary film, namely Cenk Batu, I argue that both characters remain problematically linked to images of ethnicized and sexualized bodies. The plethora of such depictions implies a fascination with these Othered bodies in contemporary films, regardless of whether or not these characters have successfully "integrated" into contemporary German culture. Discussing classical Hollywood cinema and scopophilia, Laura Mulvey exposed the "determining male gaze," which "projects its fantasy on to the female figure" (Mulvey 1988: 62), a gaze that turns the spectator and the male characters in the film into voyeurs, who take sexual pleasure in looking at the "female, eroticized image" (Mulvey 1993: 16).

In this essay, I am interested in the voyeuristic gaze that is directed at the sexualized male characters/actors on which the spectators, male and female, seem to project both fear and desire.[2] In the tradition of star studies, I will draw on the careers, star personae and film roles of Turkish German actors Mehmet Kurtuluş and, to a lesser extent, of Birol Ünel in order to explore the iconic function of sexualized ethnic masculinities in contemporary German film and television.[3] The essay's first section discusses Kurtuluş's sexualization in *Nackt* (*Naked*, 2002) and *On the Sunny Side* against the backdrop of Fassbinder's staging of El Hedi ben Salem in *Ali: Fear Eats the Soul*. The second part considers Ünel's eccentricity in relation to Klaus Kinski's star persona. These comparisons provide insights into the continuities and discontinuities from New German Cinema to contemporary (Turkish) German film via male actors and characters.

My analysis relates the evolving representation of ethnic characters to continuities in images of ethnic masculinities. Two of the most publically visible Turkish German actors, Kurtuluş and Ünel, started their careers in acting schools and worked in German theater, television, and the film industry. The star personae signal a new iconography of sexualized ethnic masculinities developed during the last decade.[4] The past four decades of Turkish German cinema have seen a shift from films depicting marginalized and victimized minorities to poster-children of contemporary youth culture, which is central to the image of Germany as a multicultural European nation. The shift can be mapped from Fassbinder's 1969 film *Katzelmacher*, which brought fame to the director and the pitiful figure of the Mediterranean *Gastarbeiter* (guestworker) onto the cinema screen, to Fatih Akın's 2007 film *Auf der anderen Seite* (*The Edge of Heaven*), in which Akın portrays cosmopolitan characters in the transnational settings of Germany and Turkey. In Turkish German cinema, the mute, victimized guestworker who lived in enclosed, marginal spaces in 1970s Germany has transformed into the multilingual, mobile subject of the twenty-first century who has agency and access to the wide, transnational spaces of Europe and beyond (see, for example, Halle 2008: 141–68).

Akın's films have been instrumental in this change in filmmaking and its discussion in film studies (see Ezli 2010; Göktürk 2010a; Gueneli 2011; Kosta 2010; Mennel 2010). Akın significantly boosted the careers of Kurtuluş through *Kurz und schmerzlos* (*Short Sharp Shock*, 1998) and Ünel through *Gegen die Wand* (*Head-On*, 2004), two films that provided both actors with critical acclaim and recognition for their performances of contemporary Turkish Germans. Kurtuluş and Ünel became visible to other directors and producers by playing ethnic characters, widening their professional repertoire to subsequent roles with non-Turkish directors.

To be sure, current German viewers can see diverse representations of Turkish German masculinities on the screen. Some of these representations might even give the impression of ethnic blindness by ignoring possible ethnic conflicts in the plot. Rob Burns, for example, criticizes *Short Sharp Shock* for its "post-ethnic" way of portraying the friendship between a Croat, a Greek, and a Turk (2006: 141–43). However, I argue that in the cases of Kurtuluş and Ünel, contemporary depictions of ethnic masculinities continue to resemble images of the Other in older films. The images of disrobed or otherwise erotically revealed bodies not only recall Fassbinder's films, but also evoke images from earlier periods. The fascination with the ethnically Other can already be seen in the cinema of the Weimar Republic or the Third Reich.[5] Weimar films such as *Der Student von Prag* (*The Student of Prague*, 1926) or *Das Cabinet des Dr. Caligari* (*The Cabinet of Dr. Caligari*, 1920) eroticize Othered male bodies that are either marked as Jewish, Slavic, pathological, or effeminate. During the Third Reich, the eroticization of ethnically Othered male bodies became more problematic as they were functionalized to promote the Nazis' ethnic and racial stereotypes, while at the same time inviting the audience to fantasize about transgressing ostensible "racial boundaries." In the antisemitic and xenophobic films *Jud Süß* (*Jew Süss*, 1940) and *La Habanera* (1937) sexualized Jewish or other "non-Aryan" characters seduce German women. Klaus Theweleit argues that the Jewish Other has been fantasized as a sexual threat, which finds its extreme expression in fears of miscegenation between Jewish men and German women (1989: 7–12).

A distinction needs to be made here between the style of visual imagery and the intentionality motivating those images during the period of National Socialism and in the contemporary context of globalization and current sexual norms. The intentional denigration of the Other in films such as *Jud Süss* differs from the attraction created by the camera's attention to a masculinity marked by ethnic difference. Undoubtedly, in contemporary films, many actors of Turkish heritage no longer portray stereotypes. They have become integral to the German film landscape, displaying various characters ranging from alcoholic loafers and petty criminals to law-abiding citizens. In films such as *Naked* or *Die Unerzogenen* (*The Unpolished*, 2007), Turkish German ethnicity is neither thematized directly nor presented as a social problem.

As actors in such films, Kurtuluş and Ünel have become stars. The former displays various general star characteristics—celebrity status, participant in award ceremonies, subject of gossip news, sex symbol status—whereas the latter is associated with the specific characteristics of an eccentric star persona similar to the controversial Kinski (*Corriere della Sera* 2011). This comparison links Ünel to a legend of New German Cinema with the effect that his reception focuses on the actor and his personality, beyond ethnic stereotypes. But even though these two actors have each achieved star status, directors and scripts continue to stage them in ways that lead them to display sexualized ethnic masculinities. These two case studies thus demonstrate that the current normalization of ethnicity in contemporary German films, which suggests an enlightened, cosmopolitan society, can also function as a disguise for the exoticizing strategy of presenting ethnic actors as sexualized characters.

Instead of enabling the two actors to leave behind the essential link to ethnicity, the star personae of Kurtuluş and Ünel produce an ethnic coding that inflects their roles. A star, according to Richard Dyer, is a "complex configuration of visual, verbal and aural signs ... It is manifest not only in films but in all kinds of media texts" (1998: 34). A "star image is made out of media texts that can be grouped together as *promotion*, *publicity*, *films*, and *criticism* and *commentaries*" (1998: 60). In the case of Kurtuluş, these texts include educational texts by the Goethe Institute, interviews in newspapers, and promotional texts on television or professional websites (ARD 2011a and c; Berger 2009). While these texts often reference the Turkish German background of the actor and/or character, they also highlight the irrelevance of the ethnic background to the identity of the character, indicating a normalization of ethnicity in a German society presumably free from ethnic stereotypes. Yet stars often bring their image to the filmic characters they play. Dyer mentions Marlene Dietrich as a prominent example. He explains, "[h]er face, her name even, carries the 'mystique,' no matter what films she makes or what she says" (1998: 126). Similarly Kurtuluş's and Ünel's star personae function as subtexts in the construction of their sexualized filmic characters (for a discussion of the relationship between star persona and filmic narrative, see David Gramling's contribution to this volume). Through their casting, they add their Turkish German "'mystique,' no matter what films [they make]..." and help embed long-existing, exoticizing fantasies in the new ethnic masculinities on contemporary German screens.

Normalized Ethnicity—Sexualized Body: Mehmet Kurtuluş

Kurtuluş received formal acting training in Hamburg, followed by theater roles at the Hamburger Kammerspiele and the Theater am Kurfürstendamm in Berlin. He worked as an assistant on the set of the television series *Adelheid und ihre Mörder* (*Adelheid and Her Murderers*, 1993–2007) when he received his first supporting role as Hassan in the 1994 episode *Tod in der Geisterbahn* (*Death in the Haunted House*). Other small parts in television series followed in which Kurtuluş played mainly Turkish characters.

It was his critically acclaimed role as Gabriel, a Turkish German petty criminal, in *Short Sharp Shock* that made him famous. Aspects of this role impacted his casting in two later Akın films as the Turkish German traveler Isa in *Im Juli* (*In July*, 2000), whose attitude and aggressive behavior initially suggest a stereotypical gangster, and the sexually aggressive Turkish bartender in *Head-On*, a shady character of the drug milieus of Istanbul. His reputation with directors and producers thus enhanced, Kurtuluş has since been cast to play either a Turk or Turkish German character. While he has also embodied other ethnicities, such as a Vietnamese-American, Robin, in the Sat.1 television production *Eine Liebe in Saigon* (*A Love in Saigon*, 2005) or an Italian, Vittorio "Vic" Castanza, in the acclaimed SWR television film *Der Tunnel* (*The Tunnel*, 2001), these roles invariably marked him as ethnically Other. It was not until Doris Dörrie's *Naked* that Kurtuluş received a film role that seemed ethnically unmarked. The popular press called *Naked* the first film to feature a Turkish German actor without explicit references to his ethnic background (Berger 2009). Indeed, there are no references in the dialogue or in the character's name—Dylan—to a possible ethnic background.

However, one aspect in the film indicates Dylan's ethnicity in a scene featuring a dinner party with diegetic Turkish music. The six protagonists are dancing to the song *"Düğün"* (wedding) by popular Turkish musician Sezen Aksu. A closeup shows Dylan singing along to the song. By doing so, Dylan, who earlier in the film's narrative sang a French song, suggests his familiarity with the Turkish lyrics. While the knowledge of French seems to be less surprising for an educated German citizen, the knowledge of Turkish presupposes a Turkish background. The subsequent scene combines Dylan's implied ethnic Otherness with overt sexual references through various closeups of protagonists stripping off their clothes. This scene leads to the erotic climax in the film's narrative in which four of the characters (including Dylan and his wife), now blindfolded, have to recognize each other by touching their naked bodies. Multiple closeups of nude body parts—fetishizing particularly breasts, chests, and buttocks—are accompanied by the diegetic sound of smooth jazz.

Although Kurtuluş's character lacks direct references to a particular Turkish ethnicity, the implied ethnic ambiguity of his character reflects fantasies of power and sexuality characteristic of a stereotypical understanding of ethnic masculinities. An early scene in the film foreshadows the overt sexualization of Dylan: His wife Charlotte argues with Dylan in front of a revealing photograph that features prominently on their bedroom wall. This image epitomizes Dylan's sexualized body in the film. The photograph in question replicates the famous Annie Leibovitz photograph of Yoko Ono and John Lennon that appeared on the *Rolling Stone* cover on 22 January 1981 (Holden 2010). The original photo depicts a nude, vulnerable John Lennon curled up in fetal position next to his completely dressed wife. The poster-size photograph in *Naked* features an almost identical pose with the only difference that a nude Dylan looks straight into the camera and covers half of Charlotte's face (in the original, Lennon's face is turned toward Ono, his eyes are closed, while Ono's face is visible). Through this minute difference in pose, the replica does not depict a vulnerable Dylan, but rather seems to prove his vanity and sexual dominance. The photo captures and aestheticizes Dylan's naked body that is doubled in the shot when we see Dylan with a naked torso in the back and Charlotte dressed in the front. The self-confident display of the poster in his own bedroom indicates an active sex life.

In the aforementioned striptease scene Dylan brings this image of the sexualized masculinity to life. Dylan strips off his shirt, shows his tanned,

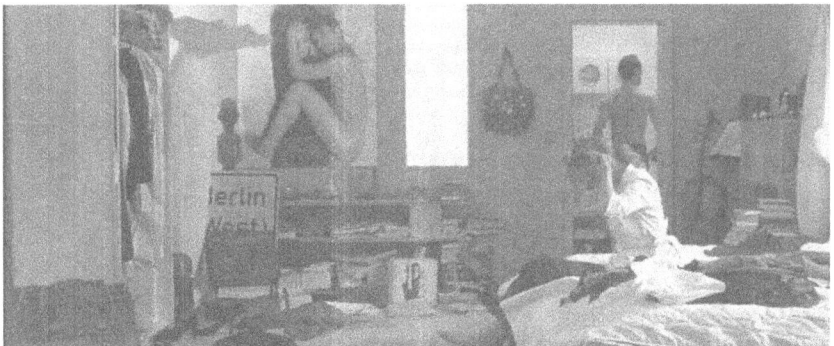

Figure 10.1 Dylan (Mehmet Kurtuluş) and Charlotte (Nina Hoss) in *Naked*, DVD capture

muscular body, dances and playfully flirts with the female guests in the scene, with one of whom Dylan is exposed to have had an affair. By not leaving him, Dylan's wife—betrayed, hysteric, childless, and aging (she has undergone plastic surgery to stay attractive for her husband)—ultimately succumbs to his threatening and ostensibly promiscuous, ethnically Other sexuality.

This image of sexualized ethnic masculinity recasts fears expressed thematically in Fassbinder's socially critical *Katzelmacher* and physically in *Ali: Fear Eats the Soul*. In *Katzelmacher* the character of a Greek guestworker Jorgos, played by Fassbinder himself, introduces the theme of the exoticized male body attractive to German women and as such a potential threat to German masculinity. Fassbinder's white body, filmed as if it were an exotic body, functions as a distancing effect for spectators to reflect on underlying stereotypes of exotic sexuality. In *Ali: Fear Eats the Soul*, this reflection on exotic sexuality is played out more explicitly (via the character's body) and didactically (through dialogue, mise en scène, and stylization). For example, Ali's middle-aged companion and later wife Emmi shows Ali's "clean" and "muscular" body to her colleagues. Throughout the entire scene, Ali stands silently in the background, while the women gaze at him and finally touch his body. The dialogue verbalizes their gaze:

> Colleague: "He really looks very good, Emmi, really, and [he is] so clean."
> Colleague: "I always thought they don't wash."
> Emmi: "He does. He washes himself. He even showers, every day."
> Colleague: "And look at his muscles. And his skin is so soft."

Judith Mayne states that Ali becomes an outsider, somebody who is looked at through objectifying gazes (1977: 65 and 72). The middle-aged women lust after Ali, as does the younger bartender Barbara. A key scene depicts the naked Ali in Barbara's bedroom. In Emmi's quaint apartment Ali appears mainly in the kitchen or living room, whereas in Barbara's modern apartment he is most often seen in long shots in the bedroom framed by the bedroom door. Here Barbara strips off his shirt, touches and caresses his chest before they begin having sex.

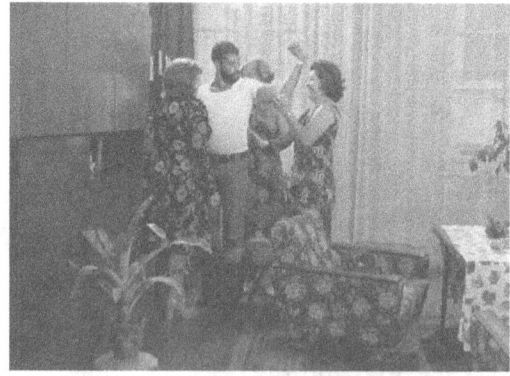

Figure 10.2 Ali (El Hedi ben Salem) in *Ali: Fear Eats the Soul*, DVD capture

Ali is reduced to his sexualized body, either as an object to be looked at and timidly touched, or as a body being undressed and physically experienced (see also LaValley 1994; Mayne 1977; Mennel 2000; Silverman 1992; von Moltke 1994). As Al LaValley observes, El Hedi ben Salem represents the "ideal erotic body type," an "exotic other" for Fassbinder (LaValley 1994: 118). LaValley stresses that Ali is a sexualized and eroticized ideal who explicitly showcases his genitals and sexual power; in so doing, he becomes more than merely a victimized Other for the (homo)sexual gaze (1994: 116–17, 122). However, while Ali's body has entered the private sphere, he has not been accepted into society. This is thematized at the end of the film's narrative, which shows Ali's hospitalization, or the "radical excision" through death or departure of the protagonist, as Randall Halle calls the early depiction of foreigners in German cinema (2008: 141–42).

Three decades later, in a multicultural Germany, *Naked* features Dylan as an active member of German society, who has reached an elevated socioeconomic position as symbolized by his blonde wife and their exorbitantly luxurious house. Yet, despite their different situations, both characters remain sexualized objects whose promiscuous sexuality is linked to betrayal and disloyalty. For instance, we learn that Dylan cannot be trusted sexually. This knowledge creates anxiety and jealousy in his wife, as well as in Emilia's ex-boyfriend Felix. By portraying Dylan in terms of promiscuous masculinity, a hypersexualized body, and acts of betrayal, all of which elicit both fear and temptation in the other filmic characters, *Naked* relates Kurtuluş to long-existing iconographies of exoticized and ethnicized masculinities.

Similar sexualizations are associated with Kurtuluş in his performances in *Tatort*. Since 2008, Kurtuluş has appeared in this quintessential German detective series, which has exerted considerable sociopolitical influence from the 1970s to the present (Brück et al. 2000: 11, 33).[6] By becoming a *Tatort* detective, the actor has brought ethnic normalization onto German screens; this is particularly emphasized through the awarding of Kurtuluş with the *Polizeistern* (police star), a media award by the Hamburg police (ARD 2011b). According to the *Tatort* website, Batu, an undercover detective, is born to Turkish parents in Hamburg. Although the site emphasizes that the Turkish decent is irrelevant to Batu—he positions himself beyond ethnicity—it still remains a constant theme in the series (ARD 2011c). In his debut *Tatort*, Batu's Turkish background becomes an important part of the film's narrative as he takes on the identity of a Turkish German petty criminal in an undercover case.

Apart from these thematic references to Batu's ethnicity, the series makes extensive use of his ethnicized and eroticized body by emphasizing physical features. He is more frequently depicted shirtless or naked than any other German detective, with the exception of *Tatort*'s Duisburg's cult detective Horst Schimanski (1981–91) played by Götz George, a sex symbol of German cinema since the 1960s. In *On the Sunny Side*, Batu displays his body in at least six scenes, either shirtless or naked. These scenes include two shower scenes, four bathing or swimming scenes, and several closeups of his wet face or other body parts.

Batu is first introduced in a closeup in front of a computer. He is wearing a dark grey suit, a black shirt, and fashionable looking glasses. A few minutes into the series we see the detective wearing casual jeans and a T-shirt in his contemporary furnished apartment. Changing outfits and presenting the audience a variety of looks, Batu/Kurtuluş resembles a fashion model, largely defined by his physical features. Consequently, by its sixth minute, the episode takes us to a pool, a shower, and the first nude scenes.

The first shower scene begins with a closeup of Batu's profile and upper torso in the shower. His detective partner enters the frame, displaying a white, ethnically unmarked body that remains in the background. A later scene similarly emphasizes Batu's body through camerawork, frame composition, and choice of costume. Batu and his partner meet undercover in a changing room to discuss an active case. While Batu stays in his tight swim shorts and leaves his torso and legs exposed for the entire conversation, his partner only takes off his shirt. By the time the partner undresses, the scene ends with a cut, implying that it is not worth seeing the other detective's exposed (white) body.

Although the function of *Tatort* detective Batu seems to be a normalizing of ethnic backgrounds on German screens, these examples show that the series still adheres to established sexualized fantasies of ethnic masculinities. Batu might embody the shift from a criminal to a non-criminal figure, but a considerable part of *Tatort* capitalizes on Kurtuluş's presentation as a sexualized, ethnic character who exposes his body of color for an implied (ethnic) German audience. It looks as if the price paid for ethnic normalization of filmic characters is the continuation of overt physical sexualization. How influential Kurtuluş's portrayal of Cenk Batu will be on future *Tatort* detectives after his resignation from the series in 2011 remains to be seen.[7]

Ethnic Body—Eccentric Physicality: Birol Ünel

In terms of acting, star persona, and film roles, Birol Ünel differs from Mehmet Kurtuluş, yet also shares similarities. Ünel began his career in acting school at the Academy of Music and Theater in Hanover. Early on he worked with directors Thomas Brasch and Andy Bausch who were impressed with his personality, especially his face and facial expressions (Hillenkamp 2005). However, in the midst of filming, both directors cut Ünel's parts due to constant conflicts with the actor. Ultimately Ünel's temper, eccentric personality, and altercations with crew members on the set precluded him from future work with these directors. Thereafter

Ünel—who played the quintessential German part of Siegfried in the theater—appeared in minor roles, mainly types without much character development such as a barman, a criminal, or an insane person, and once in a while a Turkish or non-German figure in German film.

With his critically acclaimed role in *Head-On*, Ünel became known to larger audiences. In Germany, he received the German Film Award for Best Actor; in Barcelona he was nominated as Best Actor at the European Film Awards; Turkish newspapers celebrated him as a Turkish star; and the readers of one Turkish magazine even declared him to be the most "erotic man of the year" (Hillenkamp 2005). Ever since Ünel has been cast not only in various roles in Turkish and German film productions but also in French films such as the 2011 *Nuit Blanche* (*Sleepless Night*) or the 2006 *Transylvania*. In his German roles after *Head-On*, Ünel has been cast as an irresponsible parent in *The Unpolished*, a street vendor and lover in *Der Mond und andere Liebhaber* (*The Moon and Other Lovers*, 2008), an eccentric chef in *Soul Kitchen* (2009), and an unconventional theater director in *Method* (2011). While Ünel's new film roles do not always imply a Turkish German background, they often refer to his eccentricity, as well as to his manic and at times erratic behaviors. These characteristics led journalists to compare him to Klaus Kinski, which in turn continues to inform Ünel's public persona and image (*Corriere della Sera* 2011; Kino.de 2011).

Kinski's difficult relationship with Werner Herzog is well known, particularly through the documentary *Mein liebster Feind* (*My Best Fiend*, 1999) based on material from the filming of *Aguirre, der Zorn Gottes* (*Aguirre: The Wrath of God*, 1972). At the same time, Kinski was also a sex symbol, a quality Kinski himself promoted in his autobiographies *Ich bin so wild nach deinem Erdbeermund* (*I Am So Crazy about Your Strawberry Mouth*, 1975) and *Ich brauche Liebe* (*All I Need Is Love*, 1988; *Kinski Uncut: The Autobiography of Klaus Kinski*, 1997). The comparison to the sexualized, eccentric, ill-tempered star certainly gave Ünel an edge, connecting him to an actor who represents New German Cinema and German culture with an ethnically ambivalent body, since Kinski had a Polish father.

Discussing stars acting in films, Dyer states that a film "may bring out certain features of a star's image and ignore others" (1998: 127). In Ünel's

Figure 10.3 Fitzcarraldo (Klaus Kinski) and Molly (Claudia Cardinale) in *Fitzcarraldo*, DVD capture

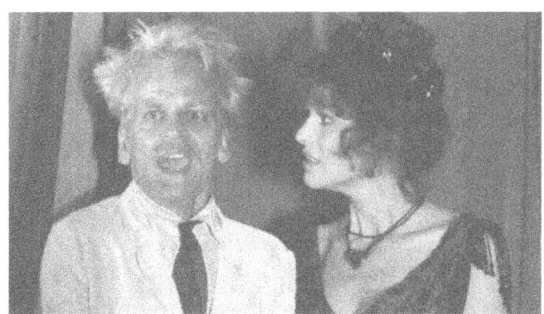

case his Kinskiesque chaotic, unreliable, and eccentric personality features predominantly in the discourse that surrounds him: "Birol Ünel, Traveler and Impostor: Star and Alcoholic" are the concluding words of journalist Sven Hillenkamp in his article about the actor (2005). An analysis of Ünel's roles suggests that these predicates seem to be the central features that Ünel brings to his film roles. Although Ünel's main filmic character is associated with high alcohol consumption, a lower class milieu, or a vagabond lifestyle, he nonetheless performs a complex sexuality tied to ethnic masculinity. This can be seen in his role as Cahit in *Head-On*, which has influenced his subsequent casting in films. Throughout *Head-On*, Cahit, an alcoholic and drug user in his forties, is repeatedly depicted nude and in sexual scenes with two women, Maren and Sibel, who fall in love with him. Furthermore, multiple closeups in the second half of the film emphasize his facial features.

Cahit is shown twice in explicit sex scenes with his long-term sex partner Maren, each of which lasts two minutes. Both scenes take place in Maren's apartment. The camera shows a high angle medium long shot of a dark room, which features a large bed in the center of the room. The sheets have leopard patterns, suggesting an unrestrained sexuality. Both sex scenes expose Cahit's completely nude body. Closeups of lines of cocaine being snorted precede the first sex scene and a medium shot of the naked couple playing *tavla* (Turkish version of backgammon) in the kitchen succeeds it, framing their sex life as intoxicated and intoxicating.

Cahit's nude body and its (sexual) presentation complicate notions of Turkishness in German popular culture, which stereotypically imply (female) modesty and veiled bodies. While the unveiling of the exotic body can please an Orientalist gaze, it can also complicate views about ethnic bodies. Cahit's nudity in the film, for example, is not always displayed erotically. In the beginning of the film we see him intoxicated and partially nude in a chaotic apartment. His middle-aged torso and the mise en scène of his small apartment (music posters, dirty dishes, cigarette butts) expose a certain lifestyle reminiscent of the punk-rock attitude of the 1980s generation. In the following sequences,

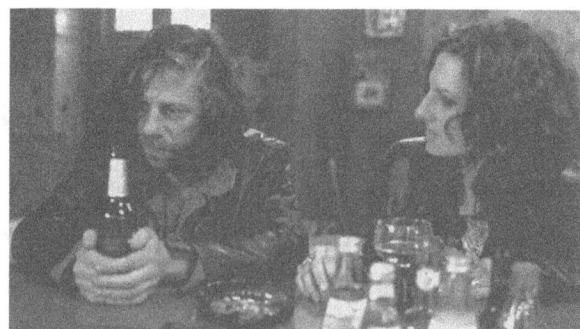

Figure 10.4 Cahit (Birol Ünel) and Maren (Catrin Striebeck) in *Head-On*, DVD capture

however, when Cahit experiences his growing affection for Sibel, his body becomes increasingly eroticized. The aggressive sexual encounter between Maren and Cahit is opposed to the more tender, romanticized depictions of Cahit and Sibel. This tenderness is achieved through closeups of Cahit gazing at Sibel, smelling or touching her softly on various occasions, accompanied on the soundtrack by the couple's breathing. Correspondingly the lighting captures Cahit's body and face as appealing through the natural light in Istanbul, or by means of closeups of his sunlit, now shaven face.

Ultimately the sexualized and ethnicized figure of Akın's Cahit is reincarnated in Ünel's future parts: the drug dealer Axel in *The Unpolished* engages in explicit sex scenes; Gansar in *The Moon and Other Lovers* plays the object of desire for the middle-aged Hanna; Tchangalo in *Transylvania* is a Romanian vagabond and love interest of the French Romanian traveler Zingarina. Just as in *Head-On*, these roles romanticize, eroticize, or sexualize Ünel's body and its filmic presentation. It seems that Ünel's Cahit, the groundbreaking role as a Turkish German that finally brought the actor artistic recognition, has become a blueprint for all subsequent roles. Remembering his collaboration with Ünel in the making of *Head-On*—during which Ünel's alcohol consumption and unreliability caused problems on the set—Akın claims that everything in the script about Cahit goes back to Ünel himself (Hillenkamp 2005). Similarly Kinski—equally famous for his violent outbreaks toward directors and journalists—played characters that dovetailed with his erratic and eccentric personality such as Aquirre, Woyzeck, and Fitzcarraldo.

Conclusion

Contemporary films indicate a normalization of ethnicity by reflecting the multiethnicity of German society in their casting. However, I suggest that while Kurtuluş's and Ünel's new roles often suggest a move beyond stereotypical ethnic categorization, the problem of sexualized or eroticized ethnicization remains. Even though their characters have achieved agency, they often remain subject to the long tradition of fantasies of ethnic masculinities as sexual or sexually threatening Others. This might explain why Batu/Kurtuluş needs to take endless showers and Cahit/Ünel needs to walk naked across the room or have unrestrained sex with his filmic partners. Ultimately, in most of their roles, Ünel and Kurtuluş continue being cast as sexual objects, either as abjects or objects of desire, representing a wild, exoticized, romanticized, or threatening sexuality. Thus contemporary casting of ethnic minorities remains trapped in long-existing fantasies of ethnic masculinities in film.

Notes

I would like to extend my thanks to Janet Swaffar for discussing ideas for this essay. Furthermore, I thank the editors of this volume and the two anonymous reviewers for their comments.

1. Here I use Turkish German film in the broadest sense, including films that feature Turkish German characters and/or actors.
2. For masculinity studies and a general discussion of "new man" imageries in the visual culture of the 1980s and 1990s see Nixon (1997).
3. Star studies rely on a range of methodologies from close textual readings to sociological approaches based on audience studies, or analyses of fan magazines or the popular press. For examples see Fischer and Landy (2004) and Soila (2009).
4. For a discussion of image, iconology, and iconography see Mitchell (1987).
5. Fantasies of sexualized ethnic bodies can be traced back to colonial times: "Africa and the Americas had become what can be called a porno-topics for the European imagination—a fantastic magic lantern of the mind onto which Europe projected its forbidden sexual desires and fears" (McClintock 1995: 22).
6. Kurtuluş's last *Tatort* episode was filmed in December 2011. In 2012 Til Schweiger succeeds him as *Tatort* detective (*Spiegel Online* 2011).
7. Although the series was critically acclaimed while Kurtuluş starred in it, the general ratings of the show dropped (*Spiegel Online* 2011). After Kurtuluş chose to end his contract with the ARD in order to pursue his film career, Til Schweiger, one of Germany's few international stars, is becoming the figurehead for the *Tatort* Hamburg, a decision that will most likely boost ratings. How will Kurtuluş's successor Til Schweiger be depicted as the new *Tatort* detective when he takes over in 2012? While a considerable number of *Tatort* fans opposed Kurtuluş's replacement (Heidböhmer 2011), the ARD's decision to cast Schweiger seems to suggest a demand for a new, eroticized, ethnic German detective in the role. This would allow for a renaissance of a more traditional, "German," sexualized masculinity, a notion that was introduced to the *Tatort* series in 1981 by its most famous detective, Horst Schimanski. While the male eroticized body of color seems to have been a successful plot device as viewer reactions have shown (Beier 2011), the decision to go back to a sexualized German body might be a result of economic considerations.

Chapter 11

THE PERCEPTION AND MARKETING OF FATIH AKIN IN THE GERMAN PRESS

Karolin Machtans

Much has been said and written about Fatih Akın's alleged Turkish German identity. Unlike in academic film studies, where a number of scholars have changed the paradigm from one of cultural in-betweenness to one that stresses the cultural hybridity and transnationalism of Akın's films instead (Ezli 2010; Göktürk 2002a; Kosta 2010; Mennel 2010), in the media, the trope of in-betweenness is still widely prevalent.

In this essay, I focus on the perception and marketing of Akın in the German press and on the ways in which film journalists have applied cultural stereotypes to him. While transnational modes of production make it increasingly problematic to define German film (Halle 2008), in the German media, Akın has nonetheless become the "ambassador" of contemporary German cinema. Unlike the Turkish press, which highlights Akın's "Turkishness" and regards him as "Turkey's political ambassador" (see Ayça Tunç Cox's essay in this volume), German newspapers portray Akın as an ambassador of a different kind. Marketing Akın as the new cultural representative of Germany not only helps to promote German cinema, but also bolsters the image of an open-minded German nation at home and abroad. In the essay's first part, I provide an overview of the German press reaction to Akın's films since the end of the 1990s, which changes in the response from the reviews of his early films to the most recent discussions of *Soul Kitchen* (2009). In the second part, I contrast perceptions of Akın in the German press with his self-stylization in the media.

My focus on the perception of Akın in the German press reflects the fact that despite the rise of the Internet with its plethora of information, German newspapers, including their online editions, now enjoy the widest circulation they have ever had. According to the Federation of

German Newspaper Publishers, seven out of ten Germans over fourteen read a daily newspaper regularly, making Germany's newspaper market the largest in Europe (Pasquay 2010). As a result of the increasing range of choices available to readers, newspapers are under greater pressure to make every effort to maintain their readership and cater to their readers' tastes. It is therefore critical that they provide the information their customers demand and reflect the public sentiments of their particular readership. This often manifests itself in the use of cultural stereotypes, particularly in the tabloid press and in newspapers with a conservative political orientation. Furthermore, with their focus on the public personae of filmmakers as auteurs, newspapers are a particularly illuminating object of investigation.

The changing perception of Fatih Akın in the German newspapers must be seen against the backdrop of the changing political and cultural landscape in the Berlin Republic and especially the significance of film in the promotion of a new, more "normal" and open-minded Germany. Hence, I will begin my discussion with a brief overview of the discourses on normalization and migration in the Berlin Republic.

Turkish German Film and the "Normalization" of the Berlin Republic

Although in the early 1990s the discourses of German normality and *Leitkultur* (dominant culture) were still primarily associated with conservative politicians and intellectuals and their call for a historicization of the German past, by the beginning of the new millennium, the call for a more "normal" Germany—one that is more at ease with its past and presents itself as a more self-confident nation—has become "a mainstay of Germany's social and political consensus" (Taberner and Cooke 2006: 8). The change of government in 1998 played a crucial role on this road to normalization. One of the explicit goals of Germany under Social Democratic Chancellor Schröder was to redefine Germany's identity in the global arena. The hope was that this normalization in the political realm would have a positive impact on international attitudes toward Germany and thereby improve the marketability of its cultural products overseas.

The 1990s saw a renewal of German cinema, with German filmmakers of Turkish origin being perceived as the new auteurs. Young filmmakers are celebrated as stars (Hake 2008: 199), put in the spotlight by the media that shape consumer expectations. Authorial self-reflection—interviews, appearances in talk shows—is a vital part of the marketing process. This cult of personality coincides with a global (auto)biographical turn, mirroring an ever-growing desire for insights into the "personal" life of the author/auteur.

On the one hand, the presence of migrants in the media and literary culture of Germany highlights the fact that Germany has become a multiethnic society. On the other hand, the "striking and sudden visibility of 'minority' personalities in the media" (Taberner 2004: 14) points to what Tom Cheesman, in the context of Turkish German literature, has termed the "diversity envy" of the Germans: the fact that in a globalized market "in which the exotic is at a premium," Germany has historically had little to contribute. Commentators are therefore drawn to the "naturally cosmopolitan" migrants in their search for an internationally marketable new product (Cheesman 2002: 182). The celebration of difference thus becomes a marketing strategy, promoted by both migrants and the media "in order to sell more 'product'" (Taberner 2004: 2). Furthermore, migrants symbolize Germany's postunification openness and tolerance (Hake 2008: 200). At the same time, the threat of global terrorism after 11 September 2001 has added authority to the debates about the dangers of Islamic radicalism and questions of European and German identity.

The change of government in 2005 and the rise to power of the Christian Democratic Union (CDU) coalition government under Chancellor Angela Merkel marks another shift in the debate about German normalization. The second half of the new millennium's first decade saw a new sense of pride in Germany, coupled with a relaxed, easy-going self-representation that could be felt, for instance, in the public viewing areas during Germany's hosting of the 2006 World Soccer Cup or, more recently, during the public celebrations of Germany's winning the Eurovision Song Contest in 2010. At the same time, however, the CDU/CSU's emphasis on a German *Leitkultur* and Germany's (and Europe's) occidental, Christian heritage implies that for conservatives, Germany is not a country of immigration, but of *integration*—with assimilation and adaptability (*Anpassungsbereitschaft*) being key goals. The rejection of dual citizenship for migrants as well as newly established institutions such as the Islam Conference, the Integration Summit, and the German Federal Ministry for Migration and Refugees may suffice to illustrate the importance of the National Integration Plan for the CDU coalition government. Consequently there has been a strong emphasis on so-called model migrants (*Vorzeigemigranten*) whose stories serve as examples of successful integration into German society.

The year 2005 was also the year of the formal opening of negotiations about Turkey's membership in the EU, which further revealed that for Europe, "the Turk" not only represents an internal Other, but also, as an external, oriental Other, challenges the validity of the (Christian) borders of Europe (Halle 2008: 142). Germany's Christian Democrats argue that Turkey should be offered a privileged partnership rather than full membership. Thus, in the debates about a normalization of Germany, the more liberal stance of the progressive politicians and intellectuals toward migrants is confronted with a more conservative position which demands a version of integration marked by cultural assimilation (Hake 2008:

191). These contrasting ideas about what signifies German normality are reflected in the more liberal newspapers *Die Zeit, Spiegel,* and *Süddeutsche Zeitung,* as compared to the more conservative *Welt* and *Bild.*

As B. Venkat Mani and others have argued, the construction of hyphenated German identities allows for a concentration on certain aspects of those hyphenated identities (Mani 2007: 124). In Akın's case, which part of his identity is emphasized in the press—Turkish, German, or the hyphen itself—depends to a large extent on newspapers' stances on issues of migration and is deeply connected to the shifting self-image of the Berlin Republic, as the following overview of the reactions to Akın's films in the German press will show.

Early Films: *Kurz und schmerzlos* (*Short Sharp Shock*, 1998), *Im Juli* (*In July*, 2000), and *Solino* (2002)

Short Sharp Shock is Akın's first feature film. Following the xenophobic attacks on migrants in Germany, the 1990s witnessed the emergence of a new self-consciousness among second- and third-generation Turks in Germany (Halle 2008: 156). Turning away from hitherto dominating representations of Turks as guestworkers in the German media, the focus of the young filmmakers shifted to the migrant underworld milieus of the Tarantino-style gangster genre. Critics of Fatih Akın's early films—*Short Sharp Shock, In July,* and *Solino*—all recognized Akın as "türkischstämmig" (of Turkish descent), the son of Turkish immigrants born and raised in Hamburg's working-class district of Altona. As Hans-Jörg Rother puts it in his review of *Short Sharp Shock* in *Frankfurter Allgemeine Zeitung* from 17 October 1998: "Fatih Akin, son of Turkish immigrant workers, is all too familiar with the dark side of the Hamburg scene, and with those left behind by society ... He has, as he confesses, experienced himself more or less what he describes in his films." The emphasis on the autobiographical character of Akın's early films as well as some of Akın's own statements that reinforce and authenticate the autobiographical perception of his films can be found in most reviews of his early films.

Many critics regard *Short Sharp Shock* as a turning point in German cinema because it is among the first films to depict the life of second- and third-generation migrants in Germany. The stylization of *Short Sharp Shock* as a "turning point"—despite its attracting only about 8,000 spectators (Halle 2008: 159)—foreshadows the importance of Turkish German film for the marketing of Germany's new national identity. Furthermore, ignoring the fictional character of *Short Sharp Shock,* the critics focus on the sociological evidence presented in the film, treating it as an authentic milieu study (Halle 2008: 160), thus typecasting Turkish Others in their roles as native informants of "the Turks" in Germany. By emphasizing Akın's Turkish background, the early film reviews tend toward the Turkish side of the hyphen of Akın's cultural otherness, while simultaneously stressing his position between German and Turkish culture. Yet the assumption of a cultural in-betweenness implies a supposed homogeneity of the culture on each side of the "bridge" to which the migrant is relegated and highlights those traits which set him apart from both cultural entities, thus othering him and denying the flexibility of cultural affiliations (Adelson 2005: 152).

Interestingly even though Akın's 2000 road movie *In July* unmistakably deals with European issues, which might—and should—have invited critics to consider his work in a larger, European context of border crossings, migration, and mobility, it is again Akın's Turkish German background that most reviews emphasize. Focusing on the autobiographical character of *In July*, the boundaries between "real life" and filmic fiction once more become blurred. Manfred Müller in *Spiegel Online* (2000) analyzes Akın's sense of humor in terms of national belonging. This is all the more striking because we would typically expect such a line of argument—integration through assimilation—in more conservative newspapers. Müller describes *In July* as a typical German relationship comedy and does not hesitate to add that one might be pleased to note that the integration of a foreign citizen can indeed go so far that he actually assimilates himself into the native [i.e., the German] sense of humor. This dubious line of argument also underlies the subtitle of his article, "Auch Türken haben einen typisch deutschen Humor" (Turks, too, have a typical German sense of humor).

Birgit Galle's article in *Zeit Online* (2000) is one of the more progressive contributions dealing with *In July* as it stresses the film's European dimension. Yet even though Galle explicitly mentions Akın's annoyance at consistently being labeled as Turkish German, she nonetheless does not refrain from the same sort of categorization when she begins her article referring to Akın as "the Turkish Hamburgian." In general, the analyses of *In July* overlook its European dimension as well as the construction of Istanbul as a field of projections where questions of European and Asian belonging are captured in the image of the bridge.

The Breakthrough: *Head-On*

With the release of *Gegen die Wand* (*Head-On*, 2004) Akın achieved his final breakthrough. The media coverage on the occasion of Akın being awarded the Golden Bear for *Head-On* is therefore of particular interest. The attention drawn by the convoys of Turks in their cars in Akın's hometown Hamburg, the debate about a Turkish renewal of German filmmaking as well as Akın's designation as the new ambassador of German cinema may shed light on Akın's cultural categorization between the poles of his proposed ethnic Turkishness and his presumed role in pioneering a new, young German cinema.

In the reviews of *Head-On*, discussion widely focuses on the portrayal of Akın's hometown Hamburg, more specifically the district of Altona. Even though some of the critics explicitly quote Akın's refusal of a cultural categorization, they do this precisely by repeatedly referring to him as Akın, "born and living in Hamburg" and "of Turkish stock" (Mehlig 2004). Holger Mehlig explicitly tells us that the only thing that Akın would like to read about himself in the press is that he strives to be a good filmmaker—that for him, origin and the like are all hollow words. However, statements like these do not seem to impress many critics, who continue to pigeonhole *Head-On* into the genre of "new Turkish German film," thus promoting Akın as the spokesperson for a new, internationally successful German cinema.

Yet there are other, more conservative voices to be heard in the hymns of praise for *Head-On*—voices that represent the exclusionary strategies in the debates about a German *Leitkultur* and remind us of the dangers of Islamist fundamentalism in Germany, subsuming—especially after 11 September 2001—German "Turks" under the broad category of Muslims and warning us about honor killings, forced marriages, and patriarchal oppression. Peter Zander's review in *Welt Online* (2004) provides probably the best example of this attitude, as he declares without hesitation that *Head-On* is an explicit comment on the recent debates about headscarves: "After all, this debate tends to neglect the fact that Turkish women in Germany often do not have a choice; that orthodox Muslims try to prevent their daughters' participating in sex education and swimming lessons at school. Fatih Akin offers in the character of Sibil [sic] a clear and passionate alternative: a young woman who grew up in Germany and wants to live like a German as well." According to Zander, not only Sibel's father but also Cahit represent the "violent Muslim." It is not surprising that Zander's article was published in the conservative newspaper *Die Welt*, which has been at the forefront in recent years when it comes to warning Germans about the dangers of Islam. Articles in the conservative press often mention reservations about Turkey's EU membership and the dangers of Islam for Europe in the same breath.

Other critics explicitly address the question of what Akın's being awarded the Golden Bear for *Head-On* means for the self-definition of German cinema and of Germanness in general—a question that preoccupies Hanns-Georg Rodek in his article "Gegen die Wand ist durch die Wand" (Against the wall is through the wall), also published in *Welt Online* (2004). "We are somebody again," states Rodek—but who are "we," the Germans, if (as Rodek reminds us) the director of the award-winning film (*Siegerfilm*) is called Fatih Akın and his stars Birol Ünel and Sibel Kekilli? Rodek continues in a rather unsettling tone: "We have already become used to Poles (Miroslav Klose), Brazilians (Kevin Kuranyi), and even a black man (Gerald Asamoah) wearing the colors of the German national soccer team—but a Muslim (who completed his compulsory military service in a regiment of German armored infantry) as a representative of German high culture raises this trend to a qualitative level." According to Rodek, the existence of a growing "enclave" of Turkish German film production must be considered against the backdrop of the especially strong clash of cultures that confronts Muslims in Western Europe. "Turkish" and "Muslim"—for Rodek, these labels are interchangeable. This particular clash of cultures, Rodek continues, makes an evaluation of one's own identity (*eigene Standortbestimmung*) even more pressing than, for example, for Italian immigrants in Germany. On the other hand, Rodek stresses that for the sons of Turkish immigrants, there is no return to their parents' country because they have found a new *Heimat*—namely Hamburg, in Akın's case.

Contrary to Rodek, Katja Nicodemus in *Die Zeit* (2004) celebrates *Head-On* as a turning point in Turkish German cinema and in German cinema in general, moving beyond the cliché of the guestworker and the desire for a German *Leitkultur* and stressing the fact that Germany has indeed become a country of immigration. Nicodemus's article therefore provides a good example of a liberal stance toward questions of German identity, migration, and transnationalism. Even though Nicodemus, like many other critics, highlights the impact of Akın's personal background on his films, she clearly distances herself from the sentimental, marginalizing, and patronizing attitude of other critics. Like Rodek, Nicodemus stresses the meaning of Akın's success for a reevaluation of German cinema, yet from an entirely different angle, suggesting a cinema of migration that self-confidently moves between the worlds and finally depicts Germany as the country of immigration it resists becoming. Unlike the *banlieue* films from France, the focus of the young Turkish German filmmakers is, according to Nicodemus, much broader and defined by a focus on pluralism and hybridity which, in a globalized world of migration, has become entirely normal.

Oliver Hüttmann in his article in *Spiegel Online* (2004) goes even further, stressing that despite being a Turkish drama in Germany, *Head-On*—due to its filmic style and topics—could take place in Asia or Latin America. Hüttmann is also the only film critic who explicitly identifies Akın as a European filmmaker. Others, such as Andreas Busche in *Zeit Online* (2004) and Lars-Olav Beier in *Spiegel Online* (2004), also go beyond cultural stereotypes, arguing that *Head-On* deals with general, human questions such as love and self-destruction, which are only catalyzed through the Otherness, i.e., the Turkish heritage of the protagonists.

Hence, contrary to the conservative papers, the liberal press highlights the transnational perspective of *Head-On*, painting a picture of Germany as an open-minded, multicultural society with a global perspective—a picture which, to be sure, corresponds exactly to the image of a "normal," progressive, globally oriented Germany promoted by the Schröder administration. However, such a liberal stance does not overcome identitarian discourses. According special status to a multicultural auteur conforms to readers' expectations and makes him more marketable, as the film critiques of *Crossing the Bridge: The Sound of Istanbul* (2005), *Auf der anderen Seite* (*The Edge of Heaven*, 2007) and *Soul Kitchen* (2009) will show.

Crossing the Bridge: The Sound of Istanbul

The discussion of Akın's 2005 film *Crossing the Bridge: The Sound of Istanbul* revolves around the stereotypical image of Istanbul as the bridge between two cultures or, as Thomas Winkler puts it, between "all cultures, all points of the compass, and influences" (2005), thus highlighting the Western fascination with Asia as the ultimate Other and the perception of Turkey and the Turks as the external Other. Many critics focus on Istanbul's unique location as the "Eurasian frontier post" (Groß 2005), as the "Turkish metropolis at the intersection of Europe and Asia" (Behrens 2005)—a city of border crossings, visions, and new syntheses. Interestingly Akın's "Istanbul self" is less often evoked than one might expect. Yet Christiane Langrock-Kögel and Hans-Jürgen Jakobs in *Süddeutsche Zeitung Online* (2004) explicitly state that with each of his films, Akın has come closer to Turkey and has now embarked on a search for his Turkish self in Istanbul. Others trace Akın's interest in Istanbul explicitly back to his family history (Behrens 2005). In general, however, allusions to Akın's "Turkish German self" are less explicit than before. This probably owes in large part to the fact that, according to Akın's own definition (Dürr and Wellershoff 2005), *Crossing the Bridge* is widely perceived uncritically as a documentary film about the musical culture of Istanbul—a rather problematic simplification that allows for an ethnicization of Istanbul as the "bridge between Orient and Occident."

The Edge of Heaven

The Edge of Heaven is Akın's first film after the change of government in September 2005 and the rise to power of the CDU coalition government under Chancellor Angela Merkel. The CDU/CSU's emphasis on Germany's occidental, Christian heritage, its striving toward a definition of integration in legal terms, and its attention to concepts of *Heimat* and belonging are therefore crucial to understanding the political landscape of Akın's changing media reception.

Although the stereotype of the Turkish German filmmaker remains, *The Edge of Heaven* is portrayed as a "strong plea for a European 'growing together' beyond the Bosphorus" (Borcholte 2007). According to Christian Buß in *Spiegel Online* (2007), with *The Edge of Heaven*, Akın finally moves beyond the genre of the Turkish German migration film and henceforth defines himself as "representative of a globalized cinema" that traverses national borders. It is the question of *Heimat* that preoccupies Buß, who describes Akın's protagonists as commuters between the Bosphorus and the Elbe. *Heimat* in *The Edge of Heaven* is constructed by each individual somewhere on his/her journey between different places. Buß therefore ranks Akın among filmmakers such as Alejandro González Iñárritu, Fernando Mereilles, and Atom Egoyan—filmmakers who highlight and cross the borders of the national and who depict the problems of identity formation in the global age. Akın finally ascends to the inner circle of (European) auteurs. In general, critics of *The Edge of Heaven* stress the greater sophistication and tranquillity of the film and highlight the differences between *Head-On* and *The Edge of Heaven*. The majority focuses more explicitly on Akın's engagement of general human issues such as death, loss, desperation, forgiveness, identity, and parent-child relationships— his alleged Turkish Germanness seems to be of less importance.

It is illuminating to observe the changes in several film critics' categorizations of Akın: Rodek in *Welt Online* (2007), for example, answers his own question of whether Akın can be counted among German filmmakers by explicitly referring to *The Edge of Heaven* as a German film. Even though Rodek again places *The Edge of Heaven* in the Turkish German context, he claims that—unlike in *Head-On*—Akın creates "a rather normal atmosphere," arguing that what had preoccupied the protagonists of *Head-On* on their erratic journeys from the Elbe back to the Bosphorus has finally lost its urgency—a line of argument to which I will return with Rodek's discussion of *Soul Kitchen*.

Soul Kitchen

With *Soul Kitchen*, Akın finally returns to his "true" hometown, namely Hamburg—at least according to those critics who construct either an upward development or a cyclical movement within Akın's filmic oeuvre and his alleged search for identity. Even though for most film critics he remains an "ethnically Turkish" filmmaker, he has now finally come to be regarded as the *German* star director from Hamburg-Altona. Again and again, reviews quote Akın's own designation of *Soul Kitchen* as his first *Heimatfilm* and an "homage to Hamburg." This comes as no surprise at a time when national film funding has shifted to individual states. Hamburg has been at the forefront of the industry, marketing the city as a media center and utilizing film production as a means to promote Hamburg to tourists—a goal certainly supported by Hamburg's numerous local and regional newspapers. Finally the critics seem to agree that attributes such as an either/or Turkish German dichotomy or a cultural in-betweenness are too limited to describe Akın, who depicts the heterogeneity of Hamburg and its people, love, friendships, and good music instead (Steinhoff 2009).

Heimat, according to Christina Tilmann in *Tagesspiegel Online* (2009), is not defined through questions of nationality, but rather through friends and locations. Zander in *Welt Online* (2009) shows a similar leaning when he (perhaps self-critically) argues that, previously, the discussion of Fatih Akın's films was centered too much on questions of multiculturalism (*Multikulti*), integration, and immigrant identity. Zander speculates that perhaps Akın has always made Hamburg films—just as Werner Herzog made Bavarian films—whose concept of life originates from somewhere between Ottensen and Wilhelmsburg. Rodek, however, would likely disagree with this suggestion. Elsewhere (2009), he suggests that before *Soul Kitchen*, Akın's protagonists' travels back and forth between the bridges of the Elbe and the Bosphorus were an indication of Akın's own insecurity about his roots. *Soul Kitchen*, however, represents a change in this sentiment, with Akın finally calling Hamburg his hometown. Thus Rodek paints a picture of the successful integration of a restless wanderer who—overcoming his stigma of not belonging anywhere—finally finds his home in Germany.

To sum up: What Nezih Erdoğan and Tunç Cox have shown for Akın's perception in the Turkish press also holds true for the German media. The German press in general is mostly interested in Akın as a public persona; the aesthetic qualities of his films remain on the periphery. Hence, Akın is read as a symptom of the dominant political, ideological, and national agendas (Erdoğan 2009: 28). The way Akın is portrayed in the German newspapers reflects the contested self-image of the Berlin Republic and the heated discussions about a German *Leitkultur* and its implications for Germany's relations with its migrants. Akın's international success and his alleged cultural in-betweenness are exploited to promote a specific self-image of the Berlin Republic as a progressive and open-minded society or, in the conservative press, as one based on the principles of cultural assimilation. However, the fact that Akın's public persona overshadows his work (Erdoğan 2009: 28) is also largely due to his own self-staging in the media, to which I now turn.

"I Don't Care What People Think of Me": Fatih Akın's Self-staging in the Media

Akın himself consistently highlights the autobiographical nature of his films. At the same time, he reminds us of their fictional character. Even though his personal background is certainly present in his films, Akın states that questions of nationality are less important for him in his work. Instead, priority is given to "archaic" human questions such as love, pain, self-destruction, and self-discovery (Reicher 2005). He argues, for instance, that *Head-On* does not represent the Turkish minority but rather conveys the story of two outsiders in a society of outsiders. And the story of *The Edge of Heaven*, he states elsewhere, could also take place in New York or Berlin (Jähner 2007). Asked why his protagonists always go (back) to Turkey, Akın explains that for him, Turkey is only an image, a symbol of freedom (Herpell 2009)—a place of longing and redemption that the protagonists never find. In *Soul Kitchen*, on the other hand, the protagonists are not in search of identity or belonging anymore; rather, they defend what they already possess: their *Heimat* (Behrens 2009; Borcholte 2009).

According to Akın, it is no longer necessary to discuss the Turkish German relationship in cinema: the emancipation of the young filmmakers of Turkish descent, born and raised in Germany, has already been accomplished (Farzanefar 2003). He sees himself as a German filmmaker (Philipp 2007) and calls his categorization as a Turkish German filmmaker a false perception. He does not make "immigrant films" but personal films about the subjects he knows best (Langrock-Kögel and Jakobs 2004).

Answering the question of whether Istanbul is a place of longing for him, Akın points out that Istanbul represented an entirely foreign world to him as a child but is now no longer so distant and thus no longer a place of longing. Rather, it is a city in which many things are possible and where everything is in a permanent state of flux (Beier and Matussek 2007). Akın describes his view on Istanbul as simultaneously being that of a tourist and of someone for whom it is a second home (Langrock-Kögel and Jakobs 2004). In another interview, Akın explains how Istanbul has taken on an increasingly significant role in his life. Hamburg, on the other hand, Akın calls his hometown (Lau 2004). Elsewhere, Akın states that his ethnic belonging (European or Asian) "is a mixture of contradictions. It is both and neither. It is in the middle" (Bauer 2005). Asked about his role as a mediator between the cultures, Akın replies: "To be honest: I don't care anymore what people think of me. I can't change it anyway" (Dürr and Wellershoff 2005).

Yet how are we to judge Akın's supposed indifference regarding his public image, given that he is very actively engaged in the construction of a highly marketable public persona? Akın certainly knows how to broadcast a certain image of himself (Erdoğan 2009: 27). In interviews and DVD bonus materials, Akın addresses his dual sense of belonging on numerous occasions. He explicitly refuses to be pigeonholed as German, Turkish, or Turkish German. Yet by engaging *ex negativo* with the prevalent identitarian discourses, Akın is able to use them to his own advantage, capturing the fascination of his audience and the media with his bicultural heritage and his transnational identity as a filmmaker. By consistently commenting on the content of his films and on his own identity, Akın maintains control over his work and engages in an act of authorial self-staging. Furthermore, by explicitly linking his films through an authorial signature, Akın encourages us to see each film as part of his oeuvre (Wexman 2003: 45). Highlighting the autobiographical character of his films, Akın himself blurs the boundaries between his films and reality. Presenting himself as a different persona in each DVD interview, Akın provides us with a public self-image of upward social mobility: from the gangster and hip-hop milieu portrayed in the bonus material of *Short Sharp Shock* to an intellectually engaged Akın in *The Edge of Heaven* to the visibly relaxed Akın commenting on *Soul Kitchen* while lying on a kind of deck chair.

The success of Akın's films certainly owes much to their exploration of global questions of mobility, belonging, border crossings, and crosscultural identities. Yet I would argue that beyond the quality of his films, it is Akın's projection of himself as a citizen of the world, while simultaneously upholding his unquestioned local attachments to Hamburg-Altona, that secures his success. In her discussion of Akın's diasporic documentary *Wir haben vergessen zurückzukehren* (*We Forgot to Go Back*, 2001) in this volume, Angelica Fenner utilizes Svetlana Boym's concept of nostalgia in the globalized world—a concept that can be used to describe the success of the "phenomenon Akın" in general: in his longing for a home that has never existed, Akın embodies a universal "longing for continuity in a fragmented world" (Boym 2001: xvi). As a migrant, he can project his nostalgia onto an imagined homeland. At the same time, Akın is a master at finding the balance between nostalgic longing and a reconciliatory, down-to-earth celebration of *Heimat* and belonging. This capturing of the modern nostalgia, coupled with his easy-going and straightforward public persona, for which he repeatedly claims authenticity, accounts for much of the immense media attention Akın manages to draw and retain both in Germany and abroad.

Chapter 12

HYPHENATED IDENTITIES: THE RECEPTION OF TURKISH GERMAN CINEMA IN THE TURKISH DAILY PRESS

Ayça Tunç Cox

The success of Turkish German filmmaker Fatih Akın initiated new debates on the identity of Turkish diasporic filmmakers in Germany. While star director Akın and other Turkish German filmmakers have been celebrated in the German media with the slogan "the new German cinema is Turkish," the Turkish media seems to downplay the German side of their hyphenated identity.[1] Instead, the Turkish press uses the achievements of these Turkish filmmakers in Germany to bolster a positive image for Turkey in an international context.

In this essay, I am particularly concerned with how hyphenated identities, which allow for "simultaneous denial and acceptance of their cultural and ethnic specificities," are reconstructed in Turkey in the context of wider Turkish politics (Mani 2007: 124). Investigating the reception of these filmmakers in the Turkish press sheds light on a number of pertinent issues. First, the Turkish press utilizes the success of the filmmakers in order to make a case about Turkey's accession to the EU. The emotionally charged controversies surrounding Turkish German filmmakers suggest that more is at stake than just the reputation of individual filmmakers. Second, it also endeavors to establish a national sentiment about Turkish identity by making them appear more or even exclusively Turkish. Celebrating the international success of these hyphenated filmmakers seems to be intended to revive Turkish national pride. Particularly prominent in the press are nationalist discourses, which challenge the filmmakers' ambiguous sense of belonging (for a comparative perspective, see Karolin Machtans in this volume).

Focusing on the coverage of Turkish German cinema in newspapers, this essay constitutes only *one* aspect of the overall reception of Turkish

German cinema in Turkey, and does not claim to be exhaustive. Nonetheless I argue that daily newspapers are by far the most important media sector in Turkey. According to a recent report published by the Turkish National Statistics Institution (TÜİK), there are currently 6,073 newspapers and magazines published in Turkey, and the total circulation figure for 2009 was around 2.3 billion, of which newspapers accounted for 94.4 percent (TÜİK 2010).[2] These figures clearly suggest that magazines in general, let alone specialist film publications, are far less influential in terms of shaping public opinion than daily newspapers. Specialist film magazines are more concerned with issues of film aesthetics, genre, narrative, and, in terms of their coverage of Turkish German cinema, comparable to other international film magazines. The study of these specialist publications would therefore have been less revealing than the close reading of news items in the Turkish daily press. This does not mean that reviews in newspapers' art and culture sections do not provide insightful analyses of the films themselves, but when it comes to Turkish German filmmakers, such examples seem to be the exception rather than the rule. This alone is evidence that the discussion of Turkish German films and filmmakers in the Turkish press is a special case worth investigating.

The politics of the Turkish press is crucial to understanding its role in the reproduction of ideologies such as Turkish nationalism.[3] Chart 1 and Chart 2 (see page 163), which are based on my readings of pertinent news items, reviews, and commentaries, are not conclusive, but aim to present a compact yet informative classification of the Turkish press, and are devised to facilitate following the correlations between the papers' ideologies and their particular coverage of Turkish German filmmakers.

Filmmakers or Diplomatic Ambassadors?

It is widely known that migrant-sending peripheral countries hugely benefit from the economic contribution of their populations abroad.[4] Yet Turkey's relation with its diasporic subjects has moved beyond dependence on remittances only. Diasporas across the world have gained ever more significance in international affairs (Davies 2007: 62). Today what matters more is the powerful role they play in terms of the representation of the sending country. "The conditions of the Turks in Germany take on added significance given the relationship of Turkey to the European Union (EU) ... which sensitizes the border between Turkey and the EU, between the Germans and the Turks" (Halle 2008: 142). In this context, Turks in the diaspora, particularly those in one of the most important and powerful countries in the union, become strong political actors. In so far as "Turkey is seen through the prism of experience of Turkish diaspora" in Europe (Giddens et al. 2004: 29), the recent achievements of Turkish German filmmakers, who are simultaneously

Turkish and German, have come into prominence. This is not only because their hyphenated identities provide the means for newspapers to speculate about their national belonging, but also due to the increased recognition they receive in an international context. They are constructed as representatives of the entire Turkish nation in the Turkish press, and are expected to epitomize the concept of Turkishness.

Furthermore, integration into the EU has always had a symbolic meaning for Turkish people as it is regarded as the culmination of

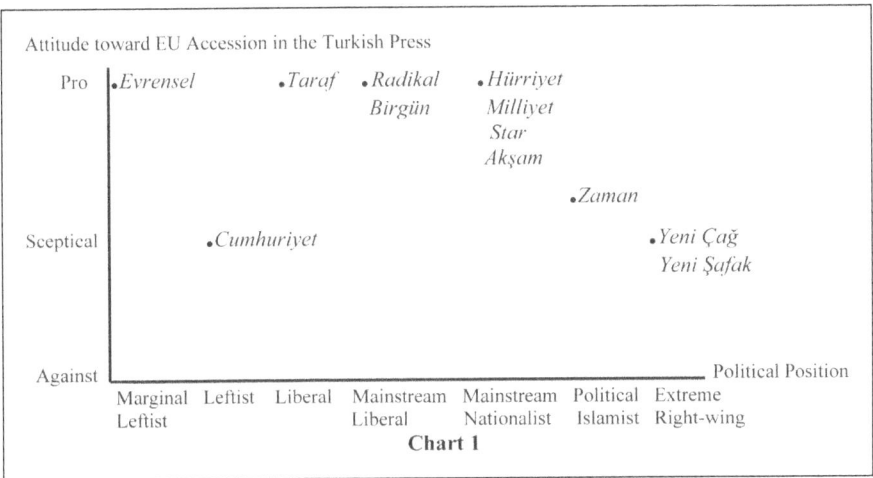

Figure 12.1 Attitude toward EU Accession in the Turkish Press (above) and Nationalist Tone in the Turkish Press (below)

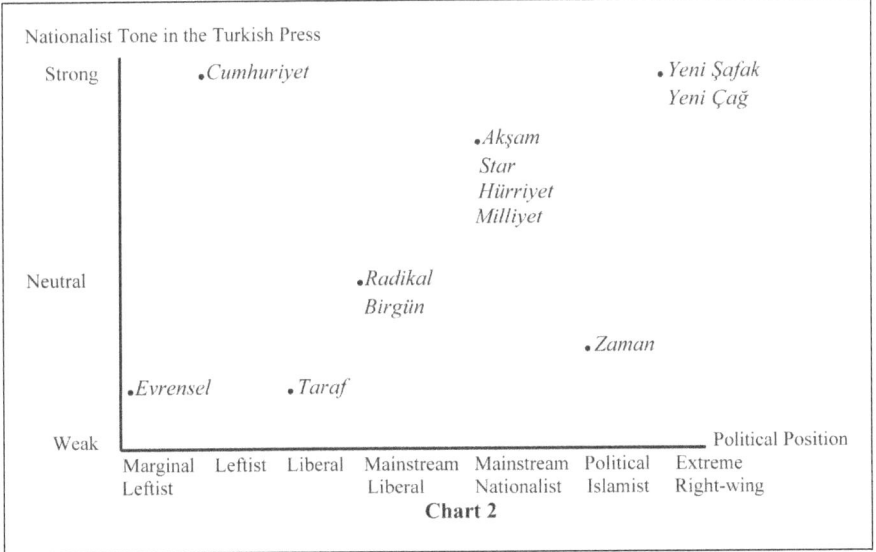

Atatürk's vision to reach the level of contemporary civilizations.[5] The so-called "social engineering project" (Keyder 1997) led by Atatürk in the early years of the Turkish Republic can actually be formulated as "global modernity = European civilization = Westernization" (Kahraman and Keyman 1998: 72), underlining the foundational role the Westernization principle played in the process.[6] Consequently, any incident regarding the relations between Turkey and the EU has occupied a significant place in the political agenda of the Turkish state, and more generally, in the Turkish public sphere; hence the importance and resulting high coverage of this issue in the Turkish press.

With regards to the press coverage of Turkish German filmmakers in general, there were hardly any news items about them until the mid-2000s. This changed in 2004 with Fatih Akın's award-winning film *Gegen die Wand* (*Head-On*, 2004), which can be seen as a turning point for the international recognition of Turkish German cinema.[7] As a result, Akın has indisputably attracted the most extensive attention from the Turkish press. As Erdoğan puts it, "in fact, any mention of Turkish German cinema is more likely to conjure up his name than that of other talented Turkish German auteurs" (2009: 27). However, in the majority of cases, this is not merely due to his directorial merits or the artistic quality of his films, but rather to a combination of diverse factors; namely, his amusing personality, rhetorical skills, and the political messages he embeds in his public speeches and interviews. This, at the same time, indicates that in Turkey, Turkish German filmmakers still do not have enough importance to generate news, and for that reason, they are mostly represented in relation to wider thematic frameworks such as Turkish-EU relations and identity politics.

Upon receiving the Golden Bear for *Head-On*, Akın became the focus of national interest in Turkey for a variety of reasons that had little to do with the film's aesthetic merits. What *Hürriyet*, as a mainstream nationalist paper, was really interested in was Akın's attitude toward Turkey's position within the EU. "If I made a film about Turkey's accession to the EU, it would have a happy ending. There are millions of Turks already living in the EU in general and in Germany in particular. They are part of the society. In practice, Turkey is already in the EU thanks to the existence of these people. Why should we not make Turkey an official member of the EU then?" (*Hürriyet* 2004).[8] By articulating sentiments widespread among the Turkish population, Akın expresses Turkey's demands for a fair and inclusive negotiation process.[9] However, Akın on his own is not responsible for reiterating the subject. It is the persistent questioning and encouraging of journalists that ensures that Akın takes up his presumed role as cultural representative and political ambassador of his country of origin. Hereby a deprived, unwanted, but proud self (Turkey/Turkish) is constructed through and against a privileged and judging Other (Europe/European).

When it comes to the liberal mainstream papers, the subtlety in the nationalist tone is immediately noticeable. As in other Turkish newspapers, the news items in *Radikal* are mainly politicized; references to Turkey's accession to the EU still set the tone of the news items even where films and filmmakers are concerned. However, the majority of the news stories and articles in *Radikal* contain film analysis, bringing the issue of aesthetics into the discussion. In accordance with the stress on the artistic merits of the filmmakers, these journalists generally refrain from resorting to any essentialist definition of national identity. Instead, they underscore the possibility of multiple belongings and hybridity and address the filmmakers carefully as Turkish Germans.

The journalistic portraits of Turkish German filmmakers in leftwing Turkish newspapers differ remarkably from those in mainstream nationalist papers in terms of language and attitude. *Cumhuriyet*, as the nationalist Kemalist representative of the Turkish press, uses the success story of the film *Head-On* to highlight invidious EU policies in connection with Turkey's accession to the EU. The fact that the opera version of the film received a European Tolerance Award in 2009 suggests that not only in Turkey, but also abroad, Turkish German filmmakers are seen as messengers of their country of origin. The fact that the foreign newspapers, too, represent these filmmakers as cultural ambassadors corresponds to the stance of the Turkish press. One particular article about this award emphasizes the comments of Dieter Kopp, the president of the European Cultural Assembly, on Turkish-EU relations (*Cumhuriyet* 2009). Kopp states that the opera contributed remarkably to Turkish German relations, and it is incomprehensible that Turkey, in spite of its enormous potential, is excluded from the EU. Conveying the message by quoting a European representative's declaration that Turkey deserves to become a member of the EU unmistakably presents an unbiased account of the issue. This at the same time befits the paper's tacit Eurosceptic ideological stance.[10]

When considering news coverage in an explicitly Kurdish newspaper such as *Evrensel*, one should bear in mind the enduring Kurdish-Turkish conflict, and the fact that the EU represents the agency that monitors human rights violations. Since Kurdish people in Turkey claim to be subject to discrimination and official oppressive policies, they envisage Turkey's accession to the EU as a progressive move.[11] So does *Evrensel*. These factors influence the paper's approach toward Turkish German filmmakers, interwoven with the process of Turkey's inclusion in the EU. Correspondingly Aydın Yıldırım and Suzan Işık (2007) evaluate Akın's film *Auf der anderen Seite* (*The Edge of Heaven*, 2007) with reference to Turkey's relationship to the EU through a focus on the film's character developments. They argue that Ayten, Lotte, and her mother Susanne, represent different levels of agency and alternative points of view in regard to Turkish-EU relations. Rather than speculating about Akın's hyphenated identity, they focus solely on the film's structure and narrative based on the fact that the film deals explicitly with Turkish-EU relations.

In brief, every newspaper in Turkey seems to attribute significance to Turkey's accession to the EU and to consider the issue as a newsworthy subject matter. The only exceptions to this are papers such as *Zaman*, on the one hand, and *Yeni Şafak* and *Yeni Çağ*, on the other, which can be considered Islamist and extreme rightwing respectively. Their predictable lack of coverage is probably due to their traditionalist and conservative perception of the EU, which, in its current structure, is seen as a Christian Union.[12] Overall, the newspapers exploit Turkish German filmmakers and their success either in order to support their pro-EU perspective or to underline their skepticism of the union based on its presumed insincerity and mistreatment of Turkey.

The Ceaseless Battle of Inclusion and Exclusion

The Turkish press endorses a feeling of identification with Europe while at the same time engendering a sense of hostility. The dominant negative perception of Turkey by Europeans, as a "threat" that would change the union's values and could easily become a burden on its structure and capacity as a "large, poor, Muslim" country (Negrine et al. 2008), enhances the sense of rejection and exclusion among Turkish people. This instigates a strong sense of frustration and resentment caused by being subjected to an incessant process of othering by Europeans who oppose Turkey's membership in the EU; hence the newspapers, especially the nationalist ones, continuously attempt to reinvigorate national pride by reiterating successful stories of individuals in tandem with a reconstructed glorious past.

"Narratives not only endow particular events with meaning, thus helping us understand and make sense of the social world, but also serve as tools of identity construction" (Mihelj et al. 2009: 59). Accordingly news coverage in the Turkish press concerning Turkish German filmmakers constitutes a metanarrative that serves to stimulate national pride. Of all the newspapers examined, the mainstream ones with a populist and nationalist attitude persistently accentuate the Turkishness of the filmmakers in question. In a parallel manner, when a Turkish German filmmaker makes displeasing comments that would hurt this sense of national pride or endanger the reputation of Turkish identity, the overwhelming reaction of the Turkish press is disavowal and exclusion, an emphasis on the other side of the hyphenated identity. Hence the reception continually wavers between ambivalent commentaries about inclusion in and exclusion from the Turkish nation state.

"What makes hybridity dubious is its complete dependence on location and affiliation—be it ethnic, national, religious, gendered, or even linguistic—in order to dislocate and disaffiliate" (Mani 2007: 125–26). Hybridity thereby implies instability and negotiation. It neither provides straightforward lines of affiliation, nor "does it resolve the tension between two cultures" (Bhabha 1994: 113). Turkish German filmmakers can be considered culturally hybrid subjects, but Turkish journalists use the ambiguity of hybridity to reinvigorate national identity.

The recurrent attempts to reassure readers of Turkey's national worthiness imply a widespread lack of self-esteem. But why does Turkishness require such an approval at all? The explanation for this draws on two closely interlinked issues: first, the impact of the totalitarian modernization project introduced by the founders of the republic, which ultimately cut the entire nation's connection with its traditions and history; and second, the resultant identity crisis that the Turkish nation has endured.

Bozkurt Güvenç suggests that a sense of inferiority has shaped the self-perception of the Turkish nation from the beginning, for the term "Turk" is considered to be relatively new and without an efficiently written history (2005: 19–52).[13] Ottoman identity was not simply associated with Turkish identity (Lewis 1988); the theorization of Turkishness was introduced by Turkish politicians and theorists at the beginning of the twentieth century.[14] The construction of an imagined Turkish identity was also shaped by the state-controlled curriculum of modernization that aspired to create a cohesive society based upon values exported from the West. Therefore, the foundation of the Turkish nation state was closely interconnected with the ideal of Westernization while erasing the memories of the Ottoman Empire. Having taken European modernity as a reference point to define and understand its own experiences, the historical, intellectual, and political trajectories of Turkey have been determined by its dependence on Europe (Göle 1998: 58–59). The superior position, however contradictory, willingly ceded to Europe has inevitably brought about a process of self-othering. The result has been a continuous concerted effort to resemble Europeans, to become part of Europe, to be recognized by it. Turkish identity is perpetually imagined and constructed in relation to Europe, leading to an ambivalent sense of self because Turkey has long been denied any proximity by its everlasting object of desire.

Consequently the constant reproduction and reaffirmation of national identity has become necessary in mitigating the concomitant feeling of inferiority toward the idealized European Other. The mundane nature of nationalism epitomized by routine symbols such as national songs, sporting events, and flags requires a special awareness of discourses that reproduce nation and nationhood undetected. "Banal nationalism," as conceptualized by Michael Billig (1995), "covers all those unnoticed, routine practices, ideological habits, beliefs and representations that make the daily reproduction of nations … possible" (Yumul and Özkırımlı 2000: 788). In this context, the press acts as a very efficient apparatus to flag nationhood on a daily basis.[15] There is a discernible continuity concerning this process as the earlier press coverage of Turkish filmmakers in Germany registers similar patterns.

The 1980s were a difficult period for Turkey, marked by political and social turmoil in the aftermath of the third coup d'état in the country's history. Busy with domestic problems, governments could not prioritize Turkish-EU relations; hence the lack of editorial interest in the issue. Instead news stories about neo-Nazi attacks targeting Turks in Germany and the mistreatment of Turkish guestworkers by German authorities and society predominated from the mid-1980s to the early 1990s. Mainstream papers such as *Hürriyet* and *Sabah* reported these events in narratives that constructed a familiar discursive universe of "us" versus "them." Personalized sentimental stories such as "This Baby is Orphaned by Skinheads" (*Hürriyet* 1986a), "Skinhead Violence is Spreading" (*Hürriyet* 1986b) and "Heroic Turk" (*Günaydın* 1986) appeared on the front pages and were used to enhance the impact of comments on the German judiciary system being unjust and discriminatory. While different in content, the discursive strategies of the mainstream newspapers in the past exhibit certain correlations with those of the present: a nationalist political discourse based on binary oppositions frames the circulation of images of Turks as victimized subjects and/or undervalued national heroes.

Despite an intense interest in the sociopolitical situation concerning the Turkish community in Germany, none of the papers, *Cumhuriyet* being the exception, devoted much attention to Tevfik Başer, who happened to represent the Turkish community in his social realistic films at the time. This noticeable neglect can be explained through the political pressures on publishers, namely strict censorship and intimidation policies, broad-spectrum depoliticization of society, and the privatization and tabloidization of the press. More importantly, Başer was seen as a leftist intellectual, employing a critical cinematic language to deal with serious controversial issues such as patriarchal Turkish culture, the resultant oppression of women, and the experience of Turkish political exiles forced to flee the country as a result of the last military coup. All these were subjects the government of Turkey would rather cover up than reveal. Only the Kemalist *Cumhuriyet*, which was associated with the leftist rebellion at the time, put an emphasis on Başer and his films. However critically informed and analytical the reviews were, it is still striking that the interest in the filmmaker increased only during international film festivals when his films were found worthy of nomination.[16] He was continuously addressed as a successful young Turkish filmmaker, and discussed only in terms of his impact on European film critics and audiences.

Newspapers with varied ideological affiliations continue to subscribe to differing interpretations of the hyphenated identities of Turkish German filmmakers today. The case of Sibel Kekilli exemplifies the link between national pride and the achievements of prominent, successful Turks in interesting ways. As soon as the German tabloid *Bild* disclosed the private life of the lead actress in *Head-On*, revealing that she used to work as a porn actress, the Turkish press vacillated in their response. The otherwise proudly patriarchal and traditional Turkish press acted rather unexpectedly on this issue. In his article entitled "Crusades against Kekilli," Yalçın Doğan (2004) condemned the German press for covering the issue in a very derogatory manner. The attacks on Kekilli were treated as if they were a matter of national importance, and consequently, she had to be protected against the evil unleashed by the "other" nation's press. Doğan alleged that the German press did not want to acknowledge the success of a Turkish film and, for that reason, despicably assaulted the actress to undermine the credibility of the film. Likewise, Fatih Altaylı, who is infamous for his sexist as well as nationalist attitude, commented on the same issue by surprisingly taking sides with Kekilli (2004; compare Arslan 2006). This unexpected response is clearly driven by national sensitivities: Kekilli, in her relationship with the critical German press, stands for the entire Turkish nation, and therefore Altaylı readily reframes his presumed ideals and values to save the country's honor.

Liberal mainstream *Radikal* appears to emphasize the issue of national identity and multiple belongings despite readily categorizing Turkish German filmmakers under the umbrella term "Turks" regardless of their ethnic origin or more complicated affiliations. Accordingly journalists often question filmmakers about their sense of belonging in articles investigating their transnational and/or hybrid identities. The second-generation filmmaker Ayşe Polat's response to a question about how she describes her identity underscores the complexity of the issue, for she states that she is simultaneously German, Turkish, and Kurdish. Moreover, being a Shiite, as she stresses, constitutes her sub-identity (Başutçu 2004). Similarly the third-generation Turkish German filmmaker Özgür Yıldırım is sometimes questioned on his identity (Akça 2008). The filmmaker's comments on the issue shed light on the changing self-perception of the Turkish community in Germany inasmuch as he claims not to be interested in the Turkish versus German division at all. Another Turkish German filmmaker who is repeatedly exposed to questions about his "double occupancy" is Thomas Arslan. He, too, insistently refuses to define himself according to national affiliations (Şirin 2008). Unlike Fatih Akın, less popular Turkish German filmmakers, who still seem to be confined to a niche, appear to act much more courageously. As a result, they are neglected by the mainstream populist nationalist or rightwing papers in Turkey.

Leftwing newspapers engage in a discussion more attentive to ethnic identity than the emphasis on the nationality of Turkish German filmmakers. *Evrensel* systematically contests the homogenizing classifications of Turkish German filmmakers merely as Turks. Instead, the paper generally addresses them as filmmakers originating from Turkey, which conclusively puts the emphasis on the country of origin rather than on nationality. In this respect, filmmakers such as Züli Aladağ, Yüksel

Yavuz, and Ayşe Polat are explicitly described as Kurdish. The paper attempts to construct a counternationalist discourse that challenges the attitude of the hegemonic Turkish press. In either way, the newspapers employ Turkish German filmmakers in order to establish their political narratives around national sensitivities.

Turkish German filmmakers attract more attention from the rightwing and political Islamist representatives of the Turkish press when the issue is their identity rather than their role in Turkish-EU relations. The most striking coverage in the far right paper *Yeni Çağ* concerns Akın's declaration about his compulsory military service in Turkey. Akın controversially stated that he was a pacifist and would prefer to renounce his Turkish passport rather than do military service. Abdullah Özdoğan attacks Akın for being a traitor in a nationalist and populist text: "The name destiny gives to people is sometimes a blessing and sometimes a curse. For instance, the biggest enemy of the Turks might have a Turkish name. Or destiny might give the name of a great Turkish soldier to someone who rascally tries to avoid military service" (Özdoğan 2007).[17]

Nezih Erdoğan, elaborating on the same news item, argues that the author "conflates the values associated with national identity with the actual 'piece of paper' that he calls *kimlik* (identity) and states that if Akın were to give up his Turkish identity card, he would be renouncing his Turkish self" (2009: 33). Özdoğan warns Turkish readers about this "deviant traitor" who betrays his Turkish identity. Such a portrayal of Akın reflects a process of othering that ultimately constructs an image of him as a "fixed reality which is at once other and yet entirely knowable and visible" (Bhabha 1983: 21). This underlines Akın's hybridity that makes it possible for others to distil certain specificities of identity out of these hyphenated nationals. They can either be included through praise or excluded through othering.

The majority of the news coverage that prioritizes the national identity of the filmmakers in question serves to build a narrative that glorifies Turkish identity and endorses national pride. A readily available repertoire of discursive strategies has been employed since the early 1980s. Undermining the very components of the "sacred" and "inviolable" Turkish national identity, only the marginal leftist newspaper *Evrensel* and the political Islamist *Zaman* are distinguished from the rest with their challenging interpretation of identity. They highlight the complicated nature of identity and how it is shaped by a variety of factors such as ethnic, cultural, and religious allegiances. In brief, the general tendency in the Turkish press appears to prey on the ambiguous sense of belonging by Turkish German filmmakers.

In conclusion, the Turkish press cannot engage with these filmmakers on their own terms, but seeks to frame them in the context of Turkish concerns, predominantly over the relationship with Europe: firstly, in terms of the political negotiations with the EU, and secondly in terms of Turkish national identity and pride. In fact, both aspects are two sides of the same coin in so far as both are about combating a sense of inferiority with regard to Europe, which epitomizes civilization and modernity. In the 1980s the dominant narrative promulgated by the political classes was that of European discrimination against Turks, whereas now it seems opportune to promote the idea that the relationship between Turkey and Europe is growing stronger. While all newspapers subscribe to this agenda, there are nuanced differences that reflect the papers' political and ideological standpoints. The contestability of the filmmakers' hybrid identities lends itself well to strategic deployment by the press. The press can highlight different aspects selectively for their particular purposes, and most papers prefer to reduce these complex identities to monolithic ones. In a nutshell, the press uses the filmmakers both as supposed ambassadors in the context of EU relations, and as devices for exploring what Turkish identity is supposed to be.

Notes

I gratefully acknowledge the funding I received from the University of London Central Research Fund, which enabled me to conduct archival research in Turkey.

1. See Rendi (2006) and Berghahn (2006) with reference to Kulaoğlu (1999).
2. For further statistics and reviews on the issue, see the webpage of the Press and Publicity Head Office: http://www.bik.gov.tr.
3. For a detailed historical analysis of the Turkish press see Erdoğan (2007), Christensen (2007), Darendeli (2007), Adaklı (2006 and 2003), Bek (2004), Kejanlıoğlu (2004), Tunç (2004 and 2002), and Finkel (2000). The structure of the Turkish press is very dynamic and undergoing rapid change.
4. See Itzigsohn (2000) for a detailed discussion of institutional patterns of transnational politics and economics. He argues that the novelty of contemporary transnationalism resides in the high degree of institutionalization of transnational linkages.
5. Here Atatürk actually refers to Western societies.
6. Also see Keyman (2003), İnaç (2003), Kahraman (2001 and 1999), İnalcık (1998), Göle (1998) and Belge (1983) for comprehensive discussions of the Turkish modernization project.
7. The year 2004 also constitutes a particularly significant date in terms of Turkey's process of accession to the EU. Having applied for full membership in the EU in 1987, Turkey was finally endorsed to begin the negotiation process subsequent to a decision made at the Brussels Summit in 2004 (see Yetkin 2002; Belge 2003; and Erol and Efegil 2007 for detailed analyses of Turkish-EU relations). This meant Turkey got one step closer to its perpetually pursued ideal of becoming an EU country. Consequently the public interest and the resulting press coverage of the issue inevitably escalated and intensified from then on.
8. The abundance of news items without named authors reinforces the argument that these stories actually reflect the papers' editorial and ideological positioning.
9. According to the statistics revealed by Ali Çarkoğlu (2003), the majority of the Turkish population was supportive of the EU at this point.

10. It is widely known that together with the main opposition party CHP, *Cumhuriyet* has a wary attitude concerning Turkey-EU relations, since it does not support Turkey's membership unconditionally.
11. See Türker (2009) for a recent debate on the official, however implicit, state policies over Kurds and their consequences.
12. *Zaman* has mitigated, if not totally surrendered, its negative attitude toward the membership in the EU in line with the incumbent Islamist party AKP's temperate approach. Nonetheless, it still does not cover any news stories about Turkish German filmmakers and the EU.
13. The term "Turk" actually had derogatory connotations during the Ottoman era as it was used to address nomads or illiterate and rude peasants (see Güvenç 2005 for a detailed analysis of the history and etymology of the term).
14. See Gökalp (1923); Gürsoy and Çapcıoğlu (2006).
15. The role of the press in the making of a nation is neither a new phenomenon nor particular to the Turkish press. See Anderson (1983) for instance.
16. For examples, see *Cumhuriyet* news items and reviews: Başutçu (1986a and 1986b), Dorsay (1986, 1989, 1991a, and 1991b), Yüreklik (1989a, 1989b, and 1991), Sayar (1991a and 1991b), and *Cumhuriyet* (1991).
17. Fatih Akın is the namesake of an Ottoman Emperor, Fatih the Conquerer.

IV

THE CINEMA OF FATIH AKIN: AUTHORSHIP, IDENTITY, AND BEYOND

Chapter 13

COSMOPOLITAN FILMMAKING:
FATIH AKIN'S *IN JULY* AND *HEAD-ON*

Mine Eren

A striking sequence in *Gegen die Wand* (*Head-On*, 2004), Fatih Akın's first feature of his "love, death, and devil" film trilogy, sums up the film's theme of love and fate but also devolves into a story about family and roots. Announced by a closeup of a compact disc, this montage sequence follows Akın's female protagonist Sibel from attempting to commit suicide after her husband's imprisonment, while she is home alone, to her escape from her violent brother in a street scene that concludes the sequence. Rapid crosscutting between shots of the heroine and her family draws spectators into Akın's imaginary worlds of disparate identities. The foregrounding of painful details, which capture the characters' experiences of loss, creates a chilling effect. The extreme closeup of Sibel's cut wrist accords an emotional magnitude to the dilemma of belonging and citizenship in the present-day globalized culture, particularly for immigrant populations.

Applauded for taking both a transnational and a humanist approach, Akın's films have evoked strong reactions from many scholars. Stephan K. Schindler and Lutz Koepnick suggest that Akın's characters represent "existential nomads ready to leave a past of stifling conventions behind" (Schindler and Koepnick 2007: 6). Whereas in *Im Juli* (*In July*, 2000) his characters live in an idealized borderless world, transcending cultural differences, *Head-On* offers a grim portrait of family dynamics and his characters struggle to maintain their roots in a specific nation and culture. Both films question the possibility of simultaneous transnationalism and rootedness.

Contemporary theories of cosmopolitanism also represent this tension and therefore offer a productive framework to discuss Akın's comedy and melodrama. With the recent development of globalization, cosmopolitanism has become a key concept to discuss the specificities of globalization, forms of belonging, and cultural difference. Traditional scholars of cosmopolitanism, such as Martha Nussbaum, advocate the universalist idea of a borderless world while claiming that the emphasis on national loyalty is the cause for conflict, clash of ideologies, and territorial struggle (1994; 1996). As other critics have noted, this model of an imaginary community could result in the homogenization of diverse cultures and identities. In his book *Cosmopolitism: Ethics in a World of Strangers* (2006) the philosopher Kwame Anthony Appiah proposes that cosmopolitanism is neither to be conceived as liberal universalism (i.e., the idea of imposing one's values onto others) nor cultural relativism (i.e., the belief that cultural differences cannot be bridged). Our responsibilities for others, as Appiah suggests, extend beyond those that are connected to us through kinship and citizenship. For Appiah cosmopolitanism represents "the name not of the solution but of the challenge" (2006: xv). Practicing cosmopolitanism, on the other hand, as B. Venkat Mani suggests in his reading of Amanda Anderson (2001) and Rebecca Walkowitz (2006), can mean a "disposition" and "an intellectual practice" by which authors "simultaneously attach ... and detach themselves from both the nation and their ethnicities, and, thus, transform themselves" (Mani 2007: 41). While the aspect of "irony ... and negative freedom," to reiterate Mani on Anderson, functions as a preferred mode for detachment, elements such as "triviality," "treason," "mix-up and vertigo"—as discussed by Walkowitz—characterize the "cosmopolitan style" of postmodern authors (Mani 2007: 40).

It is from this perspective that I discuss Akın's *In July* and *Head-On*, two love stories that address questions of mobility, belonging, and cultural difference. First my essay examines the changes in media systems to shed light on the connection between the globalization of culture and Akın's cinematic aesthetic. Then I will discuss how his comedy and melodrama present the particularities of cultural experience. Specifically in my reading of *Head-On* I suggest that the use of music opens up a horizon of references that go beyond the film's narrative time and space (see also the two subsequent essays in this section). In the final part of my discussion I argue that the idea of achieving a "rooted cosmopolitanism," in Appiah's words, drives the narrative of Akın's melodrama.

Media Globalization

In an interview conducted by Hasibe Eren and Orkun Yeşim, published in the Turkish newspaper *Cumhuriyet* in 2001, Akın shares his memories about growing up in Hamburg and Turkish life in pre-1989 Germany:

> During the 1980s, we had only one Turkish newspaper in Germany. There was no Turkish television at all. On Saturdays, a Turkish program of thirty

minutes was broadcasted. During this time only videos existed; they were rented. Acquaintances would visit each other and watch four to five films a day. Everyone cried. We children cried too. Sometimes we visited leftist teachers and their families. Then we would watch Yılmaz Güney films. Why do I make films today? Maybe because of these films.

(Eren and Yeşim 2001)

Akın's personal anecdote about his childhood sounds familiar to many members of his generation as he recounts an era of Turkish videos that were imported and circulated through the Turkish *Gemüseläden* (grocery stores). They became a popular form of entertainment during the 1970s and 1980s when cable television, satellite networks, and "niche" channels for ethnic viewers had not yet entered Turkish German households.

Akın's account also implicitly refers to the videocassette recorder (VCR) that was introduced to consumers worldwide in the late 1970s. "The mantra of the VCR was giving choice back to people," argues Frederick Wasser (2001: 101). Although a greater variety of television programming existed in countries such as the United States and Japan, this was, according to Wasser, different for the rest of the world. While television was an important part of the domestic environment, the video recorder revolutionized lifestyles and changed viewing habits of audiences. According to Wasser, astronomical growth made the video business a $1 billion industry by 1992 (2001: 101). The technology gradually began to change work and family schedules as it offered viewers the option to choose among television shows, recorded programs, and rented movies (2001: 76).

Before privatization and satellite technology, mass media offerings for immigrants were very small in Germany. With limited television and radio airtime, the beginning of foreign-language media was characterized by a broadcasting monopoly that followed a specific agenda. As Kira Kosnick chronicles in *Migrant Media*, the first programs for *Gastarbeiter* (guestworkers) "were initially instituted in West German public service domain of broadcasting in order to facilitate their insertion into the labor market" (2007: 15). The ZDF series *Nachbarn in Europa* (*Neighbors in Europe*) or the ARD program *Ihre Heimat—Unsere Heimat* (*Your Home—Our Home*), which were televised in different languages and existed until the 1990s, provided an "aid to orientation" in the foreign country and information about a migrant's home country but were also meant as a "bridge to home" to ease homesickness (2007: 15 and 32). The second half of the 1980s, however, Kosnick points out, "witnessed not only the crumbling of the public service broadcasting monopoly … but also a shift in political discourse toward the recognition of (West) Germany as a multicultural society" (2007: 15).

The rise of video technology falls into a time period in German history when "the political establishment acknowledged that the labor migrant populations were 'here for good'" (Kosnick 2007: 9). As a consequence, the Turkish video market in West Germany started booming. Small businesses owned and operated by Turkish migrants, according to Kosnick, discovered in the distribution of videos a new venue for ethnic advertising and for reaching out to customers. Soon this concept also extended to the German business community as they "discovered migrant populations as social groups with increased buying power" (2007: 29). Drawing on Ayşe Çağlar's work, Kosnick notes, "[c]orporations like the German Telekom advertise in European editions of Turkish newspapers such as *Hürriyet, Sabah*, and the like and air commercials on television stations such as TRT-International and Kanal D" (2007: 29). With the expansion of media offerings, Turkish immigrants were not only targeted as audiences but also considered as potential consumers (2007: 14). The media landscape has changed considerably since the introduction of cable and satellite television in the 1990s, resulting in a boom of Turkish television channels accessible for the Turkish German population. Together with Turkish language media production in Germany, such as Radio MultiKulti in Berlin, "radio and ... television ... far outrank all other options as the mass media of choice for migrants from Turkey in Germany" (2007: 4). Media practices have become a key phenomenon in generating Turkish transnationality.

The continuous media flow within and beyond the diasporic space constitutes an important dimension for the discussion of minority discourse. In an increasingly globalized world, media production, as film scholar Brian Rice explains, "comes to soothe populations deterritorialized by the shifts and expansions of capital" (2010: 115). More importantly, as social theorist Arjun Appadurai argues, the "new global cultural economy has to be understood as a complex, overlapping, disjunctive order, which cannot be understood in terms of existing center-periphery models" (1996: 32). Appadurai's differentiation of five dimensions of modern "scapes" (*ethnoscapes, mediascapes, technoscapes, financescapes,* and *ideoscapes*) offers a useful framework for thinking through the relation between migration and media. These are, as Appadurai notes, "the building blocks of what (extending Benedict Anderson) I would like to call *imagined worlds*, that is, the multiple worlds which are constituted by the historically situated imaginations of persons and groups spread around the globe" (1996: 33). In other words, not only are media embedded in our lives and have become accessible for individuals from all social classes; the global movement of media also limits its experience no longer to those with privileged access. Global media has become, as Appadurai argues, a resource and a means for empowerment of ordinary people and thus takes on a democratizing effect.

Appadurai's remarks about our globally imagined world and the future of the nation state also imply a shift in the definition of cinema and spectatorship. In our contemporary world the transnational flow of art cinema, as Brian Rice suggests, is obtained by means of film festivals, art house cinemas, and DVD sales (2010: 114). Through watching films we can both partake in world culture and experience cultural plurality. He further notes, "[t]he ubiquity of global art cinema on DVD and the Web ... has made it easier for us to become travelers who never actually leave home" (2010: 115). "We can now see anything," he remarks, "but we are likely to see it alone," and thus he wonders whether the "infinite access to world culture has led us ... to an advanced state of cultural isolationism" (2010: 115). Rice suggests that "cosmopolitanism is ... beginning to re-emerge, for many, as a corrective to the isolating character of globalization," as a new way for characterizing the "immobile consumer, the virtual traveler" (2010: 117).

Concurrently the shift from video rental market to DVD sales and niche television broadcasting has produced a hybrid spectator. The transnational flow of digital images allows for a virtual engagement with one's own (ethnic) group and/or with others. Prior to the expansion of the DVD market, video circulation allowed migrants to stay in touch with a homeland "remembered as more timeless and essential than the actual place that was left behind" (Schein 2002: 231), to cite Louisa Schein on Hmong media practices. In today's world, the commercial DVD gives viewers unprecedented access to cinemas from different parts of the world without going to the movie theater. With its accelerated circulation of cultural texts, this constructs, in Rice's term, an "immobile consumer" (2010: 117).

The change of media landscapes has also transformed domestic or national cinemas. *In July* was produced a decade after the collapse of the Berlin Wall, which had brought rapid and dramatic change for Germany. As Randall Halle remarks, this transformation had also an impact on the German cinema that had so far provided "a set of stories proper to the high cultural interests of a nation" (2010: 303). It was during the 1990s, that a more transnational quality of film production emerged but also when "active efforts began to convene more than 300 Million potential spectators across Europe's regions into a more coherent viewing public" (2010: 303). With the formation of the European Union, Germany presented itself as a cosmopolitan society, declaring its world-openness (*weltoffen*) to other cultures (Mandel 2008: 14). Akın adopts precisely the "cosmopolitan vision" of this era, to use Ulrich Beck's term (2006), for *In July* as I will discuss below.

The Cosmopolitan Europe of *In July*

Akın's romantic comedy, which earned high praise, is a road movie constructed around a developing love relationship that results in a happy ending (Mortimer 2010). "It hinges," Claire Mortimer describes, "around the central couple, who initially are antagonistic towards each other" (2010:

4). Influenced by the work of Shakespeare (*A Midsummer Night's Dream*), Serbian filmmaker Emir Kusturica, and French directors of the 1960s, *In July* is about the mixing up of characters, questions of identity, and the pitfalls of self-discovery. The film's characters have different cultural backgrounds originating from Germany, Hungary, Romania, and Turkey, which explains the multinational cast of the film.

Through the unconventional narrative structure and the use of flashbacks, we witness the adventures of Akın's male protagonist Daniel Barnier, a German math teacher, and Juli, a free-spirited woman who sells him a ring, promising him true love. Daniel finds himself unexpectedly on a journey to the Bosphorus in order to follow Melek, who he believes is his long awaited true love. Cosmic forces, however, intervene, when Daniel, en route to Istanbul, picks up Juli who is hitchhiking. Subsequently they are separated and reunited several times while they travel across Europe. The challenges of travel turn Daniel's journey into an experience of self-discovery. The dilemma of mistaken identities, in a Shakespearean sense, is resolved as all characters find their true partners at the end. Daniel would never have become the man that Juli wanted if he had not crossed countries searching for Melek, the girlfriend of Isa. Conflicts occur due to crosscultural miscommunication. Isa, the Turk who carries a dead body in his trunk, is in fact not a murderer; and Leo, the German truck driver, is not a rapist but helps Juli by goading Daniel to fight for her. As Daniel abandons his preconceived ideas and belief in rationality, he finds both his true love and his true identity. *In July* puts pressure on notions of identity by repeatedly reversing viewers' assumptions about characters.

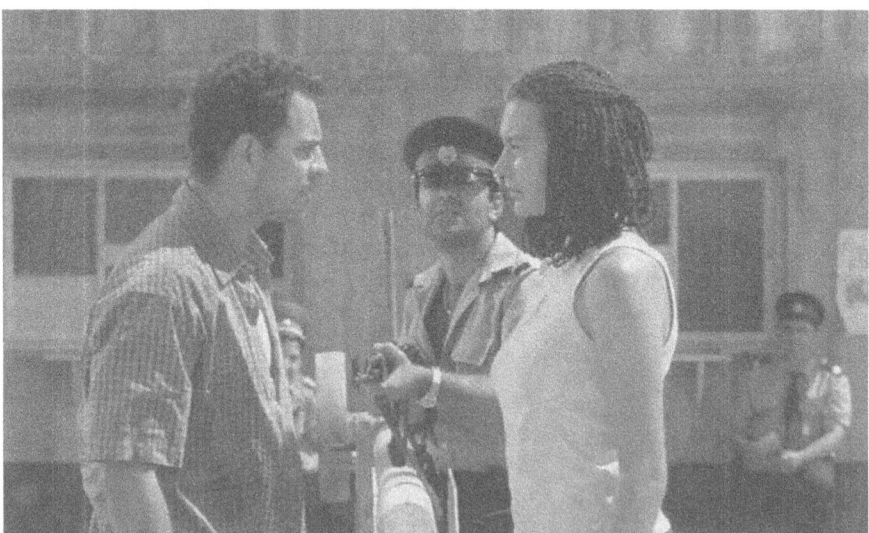

Figure 13.1 Daniel (Moritz Bleibtreu), Juli (Christiane Paul), and Fatih Akın (cameo) in *In July*, DVD capture

Akın's film language is influenced by music, revelry of festivals, wild characters (Luna and Club Doyen), intoxication, ecstasy, or, in one word, irrationality. At the same time, while ordinary boundaries limiting human existence are dismantled, crosscultural alliances are formed and imagined on the screen, all proposing a cosmopolitan existence. This is even more consistently the case in Akın's use of Europe's geography and the way he artificially merges various geopolitical "scapes" of Europe, to construct, as Margit Sinka suggests regarding Tom Tykwer's *Run Lola Run*, "spatial unity where none exists" (2000).

But there is also the aspect of spectator identification, which is, I would argue, a productive reference point that explicitly foregrounds the cosmopolitan idea of *In July*. By identifying with Daniel's character, an audience member can participate in "the ceaseless alteration of [his] environment," and the transformation of his consciousness (Rice 2010: 115). *In July* models that the encounter with the unfamiliar and uncanny (implied in the existence of supernatural forces) can be rewarding. By concentrating the journey's final point in Istanbul and placing the action under the Bosphorus Bridge, a symbol for uniting Occident and Orient, Akın resolves ambivalence toward innovation or accepting different values. The question of Turkey's entry into the European Union also plays an unmistakable role here. Akın's comedy reacts to a political agenda that advances a nationalist culture, as indicated by debates on German *Leitkultur* (dominant culture) and fears over failed integration policies. The film's happy ending, where the four characters travel together for the first time, privileges the notion of a sustained crosscultural exchange in a cosmopolitan sense. The viewer, together with Akın's characters, has come to an understanding of tolerance and the fact that, as Appiah suggests, "our knowledge is imperfect, provisional, subject to revision in the face of new evidence" (qtd. in Rice 2010: 116). In the end Daniel's mobility familiarizes the audience with the idea of "a fluid sense of belonging and invisibility" (2010: 116). In that sense *In July* is "nothing less than a love letter to the notion of a newly unified Europe" (2010: 117).

Central for my discussion, however, is Akın's transition from comedy to melodrama, which, I argue, marks a significant shift in his filmmaking and auteur persona. With *Head-On*, the filmmaker enables us to see a different world as it emerged after the events of 11 September 2001, which triggered the reemergence of hegemonizing nationalist discourse. The inherent darkness and pessimistic mood of *Head-On* reflects the realization that national solidarities are not likely to diminish in the post-9/11 era. This distinction, however, does not imply that the filmmaker's cosmopolitan worldview is less visible in *Head-On*. Instead, reading his comedy and melodrama in conjunction with each other allows the cosmopolitan project to emerge.

"And Yet My Heart is Still Turkish"
– Arabesk in *Head-On*[1]

Melodrama, in the traditional sense, means a drama accompanied by music, which allows an audience to see characters' emotions voiced in their speech or through gestures (Brooks 1995: 4). According to renowned film director Douglas Sirk, melodrama is a powerful expression of the human condition. The genre has received critical attention in film studies because of its appeal to mass audiences (Brooks 1995: ix). At the same time, its ability to provide an audience with a commentary on the world carries significance for this discussion. Various scholars have suggested that the conventional structure of the melodrama requires a reading beneath the surface to unmask the hidden ideological tensions and contradictions in society (Gledhill 1987; Klinger 1994; Sirk and Halliday 1972: 119; Töteberg and Lensing 1992; Willemen 1994: 87–98). Laura Mulvey, for instance, suggests that a slowing down of film speed is necessary for a detailed analysis of a single cinematic image and its hidden denotation (2005: 228–43). Mulvey's argument that "mise-en-scène 'fills in' meaning at the point where speech fails" is significant for this discussion (2005: 231).

In the Sirkian melodrama, emotion remains, according to Mulvey, displaced and inscribed into the cinematic language. Hence objects become metaphors and the dispersed net of signifiers surface in a specific cinematic style. A particular framing, music, and editing represent added meaning, which the spectator becomes aware of and begins to decipher (2005: 232). Mulvey explains the audience's act of decoding as a moment that "marks the gap between the unselfconscious 'I see' and the self-consciousness of '*I see!*'" (2005: 232). The act of including what Mulvey calls a visual trope into the mise en scène asks the viewer to see this image detached from its ordinary place as it preserves an autonomous meaning within the story world. This distinct feature, as proposed by Mulvey, also becomes visible in the particular scene in Akın's melodrama, with which I opened this essay and which I will discuss extensively below. *Head-On* portrays the lives of two marginal characters and is, according to one critic, a "hardcore love story" (Suner 2005: 18). Once again, it is fate that brings Akın's two protagonists together; both have attempted suicide, meet in a psychiatric institution, and belong to the second generation of Turkish immigrants in Germany. Cahit is a middle-aged, disillusioned alcoholic who works collecting empty bottles from the floor of a music club. As the narrative unfolds, we learn that the reason for Cahit's excessive alcohol and drug consumption is his late German wife's death. Sibel, on the other hand, wants to escape from the restraints imposed on her by her conservative Turkish family. By marrying Cahit, she desires to liberate herself from her parents' authority to become promiscuous. Cahit, who initially refuses this marriage proposal, eventually gives in. Ironically this decision forces him to reconnect with his Turkish roots that he had disavowed when assimilating into German culture. The leitmotif in *Head-On* of returning to one's roots leads to Cahit's return to his *Heimat* (homeland) at the film's conclusion but is also key to the sequence that opens with the closeup of the compact disc.

In this scene, the song "Ağla Sevdam" (Cry My Love), written by Turkish lyricist and actress Aysel Gürel and performed by Yusuf Taşkın, becomes part of the narrative space and echoes the heroine's inner world. The lyrics for this song, with its *arabesk* quality (a term to be defined below), emphasize passion but also the tragic fate of two lovers in the image of the imprisoned soul. The words as well as the diegetic sound parallel Sibel's situation, and by presenting her in tears, the film conveys her emotions of separation, powerlessness, pain, and sadness (see image 13.2). Crosscutting adds another dimension to the story by showing Sibel's family members burning photographs, which signals the heroine's permanent separation from her family. The catharsis, which occurs in Sibel's character, is also meant to happen for the viewer.

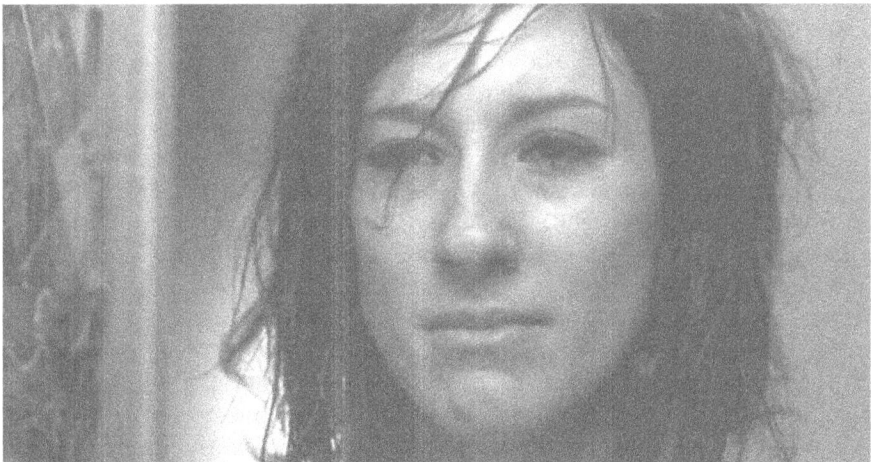

Figure 13.2 Sibel (Sibel Kekilli) in *Head-On*, DVD capture

"Adding emotions to a film," argues Tejaswini Ganti within the context of the Bombay film industry, "involves placing a character in a web of social relations of which kin are the most significant and common in Hindi films" (2002: 291). A lack of kinship-related conflicts in Hollywood films, as Ganti notes, are a reason why Hindi audiences feel distant to these narratives as they interpret American films as less emotional. At the same time, this addition in Hindi films, she further argues, signals a greater concern with morality as "being connected to others means that one's actions have consequences greater than oneself" (2002: 292). In order to "Indianize" a film, in this sense, emotions need to be added.

Head-On reconstructs this kind of emotionally loaded domestic world and questions the social forms and conventions based on kinship. The image of the burning photographs that functions like a flashback allows for a particular mode of self-representation. Moreover, the use of diegetic sound with an *arabesk* quality implies the theme of movement and displacement, and manipulates the text in widening its historical and cultural scope. It also adds emotions to construct a reference to the psychological dimension of the diaspora.

Ganti's argument offers a way to read *Head-On* in terms of its aural intertextualities. The image of the CD references Mustafa Altıoklar's *Ağır Roman* (*Cholera Street*, 1997), a film that alludes to the 1950s and Turkey's transition from a rural to an urban-based economy. Internal population shifts resulted in the formation of *gecekondu* districts or houses "built overnight." In *The Arabesk Debate: Music and Musicians in Modern Turkey* (1992), musicologist and historian Martin Stokes points out that *arabesk* songs gained popularity through the "Dolmuş" (shared taxis) culture. The transportation of laborers from the peripheries to the urban centers contributed to the dissemination of this music among the city population (1992: 126).[2] Labor migrants identified with *arabesk* lyrics because they describe the social reality of the urban experience, a vast fusion of facts and intense emotions. This music, according to Stokes, enabled a mode of self-representation of the marginalized subject similar to other popular music forms, such as *rebetika*, *flamenco*, *tango*, or *rai*. This language of emotions, or, as Stokes puts it, "discourse of sentiment," also found its way into film (1992: 12). In the *arabesk* image, the protagonists struggle against social boundaries. Themes such as loneliness, sadness, oppression, and fate and questions regarding gender, masculinity, and sexuality surface in these low-budget films that began to emerge in the 1970s and 1980s in Turkey. The stories present a portrayal of life as is, in which non-professional actors used their real names and performed roles that were closely related to their own biographies. Turkish sociologists have regarded *arabesk* as a counterculture that maps not only social change but, in Stokes's words, also "an aura of chaos and confusion surrounding every aspect of urban existence, from traffic to language, from politics to kitsch" (1992: 1; see also Göle 1996).

In *Head-On* the prop of the CD surfaces in a scene that takes place in Germany. Through visual and aural presentation it not only dramatizes the story of the heroine and her family but also alludes to a particular historic precondition that shapes the characters' collective identity and individual subjectivities. When Akın contrasts the closeup shots of Sibel with the image of the mass-manufactured CD, this not only claims belonging (expressed in the Turkish song) but also implies how the digital era requires a new understanding of deterritorialized populations. The CD signifies the dissemination of digital media and the role this new media form plays in the expansion of identities beyond national borders. The act of playing the disc demonstrates the easy access to global culture and the transformation of national subjects into "hyperlinked" individuals.

Through global communication "invisible" relationships are formed simultaneously in transnational networks, while digital media satisfies individuals' changing needs and pleasures. Read in this context, *Head-On* is more than a response to the dominant paradigm of "failed" ethnic integration. Instead the film calls for a new understanding of transnational migrant identities to overcome the politicized discussion of minority-majority relations. Akın leaves it up to viewers to answer the question of how we should perceive the self, others, time, and space in our technology-saturated world.

Conclusion

The new concept of freedom suggested by the European community with the formation of the European Union, the intensification of parliamentary and public debates about Europe's Muslim population, and the dramatic changes in immigration policies since 9/11 have affected the experience of ethnic subjects. Both *In July* and *Head-On* mirror this idea, but in different ways. *In July* celebrates the cosmopolitan idea, which it recognizes in the newly unified Europe but also proposes as "a solution," to borrow Appiah's term, for the rest of the world. The aspects of uninterrupted mobility and ease regarding border-crossings visualize this very idea. *Head-On*, however, reacts to the changing face of the post-9/11 world that I have also discussed elsewhere (Eren forthcoming 2013). Borders and frontiers exist but are imaginative and invisible, and establish the discords of identity politics against which Akın's characters struggle.

While *In July* represents a celebration of the New Europe, *Head-On* unmasks the political limits of hybridity discourses in the face of the events of 9/11. In his depiction of Turkish diasporic identity, Akın's melodrama presents us with taboo subjects such as alcoholism, sexuality, drugs, and fatalism. The visible presence of emotions in Akın's film language (expressed in the subversive *arabesk* discourse) references the repression of emotions during the labor migration of the 1960/70s. In today's culture where emotions are commodified by mass media, *Head-On* creates a cinematic counter-discourse to express the emotional dimension of alienation in migration. While *In July* celebrates cosmopolitanism, *Head-On* reminds us that the cosmopolitan project is not completed but rather exists as a process.

Notes

1. I borrow this title from Tejaswini Ganti's essay "'And Yet My Heart Is Still Indian': The Bombay Film Industry and the (H)Indianization of Hollywood" (2002).
2. According to Stokes, by 1988 the Turkish recording company produced a total of 200 million cassettes, of which 150 million were *arabesk* music (1992: 126).

Chapter 14

REMIXING HAMBURG: TRANSNATIONALISM IN FATIH AKIN'S *SOUL KITCHEN*

Roger Hillman and Vivien Silvey

Just for Starters

Within about a year of the release of Fatih Akın's film *Soul Kitchen* (2009), in October 2010, German Chancellor Angela Merkel declared Germany's multiculturalism policy a failure. After the official stance had long been that Germany was not a country of immigration, she now concluded that migrants were reluctant to assimilate into German society. *Soul Kitchen* creates a world that presents a rebuttal of this political verdict, offering a positive vision of transnationalism in Hamburg wherein people and food from multiple European backgrounds mix with verve. The film localizes music with a broad geographical scope and references cinematic titles from various periods of film history. In postwar Germany food was often associated with regionalism. New German Cinema, the film movement that reestablished (West) German films globally, came with a name that announces its defining characteristic as a national cinema. Yet the presence of occupying troops of the victor nations transmitted global notions of popular culture, especially of popular music. *Soul Kitchen* makes food, film, and music the ingredients of a big city comedy. It depicts a new Germany in the new millennium that relies on a transnationalism that is already taken for granted.

Soul Kitchen establishes links that effectively invert Chancellor Merkel's claims, as the film's German community (of European background) is integrated into a cosmopolitan, transnational mix of citizenry. Once the gateway to the world in a maritime context, the Hamburg portrayed here thrives on its openness to the world and transcends monocultural national models steeped in classical European notions. Akın's musical utopia and cinematic intertextuality converge in the space of a restaurant in order to celebrate Hamburg's openness. Our chapter traces the archaeology of these crosscultural links and the artistic cartography of contemporary Hamburg.

Soul Kitchen takes its name from a decrepit Hamburg building that comes to house a cult restaurant whose daring food is complemented by pulsating music. Its plot reads like a multicultural fantasy: Zinos, the restaurant owner, decides to follow his girlfriend Nadine to China and enlists his paroled brother Illias to cover during his planned absence. But Illias gambles away the restaurant to Zinos's German school "friend" Neumann, until Zinos wins it back at an auction. The outcome guarantees ongoing changes to the menu as the new cook Shayn leaves his indelible imprint on the hitherto stodgy German food. Two other important figures add to the romance of cosmopolitanism. The waitress Lucia lends Zinos much-needed support and becomes Illias's lover. And Zinos's neighbor Sokrates, a crusty old sailor only in appearance, spars with Zinos until the auction, at which point he becomes his strongest ally.

Beyond the character constellations, the real hero of the film is Hamburg, though shots of the city show neither a tourist panorama nor guestworkers in ghettos. Any sense of a diaspora has receded, and instead the passing parade of characters consists of world citizens based on transnational flows of people detectable in the figures' appearances, accents, or other external markers. An ongoing motif across Akın's body of films is the two-way travel between a German city and Istanbul. In *Im Juli* (*In July*, 2000) and *Gegen die Wand* (*Head-On*, 2004) the German city is Hamburg, while *Auf der anderen Seite* (*The Edge of Heaven*, 2007) features Bremen.

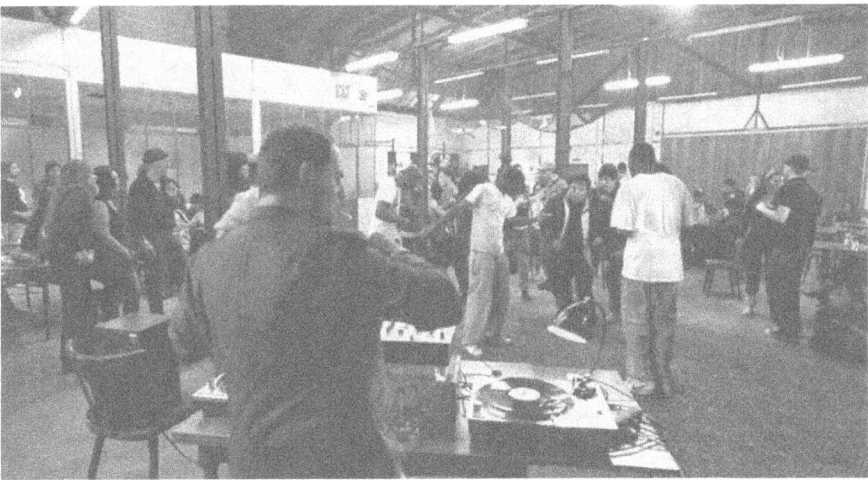

Figure 14.1 Illias (Moritz Bleibtreu) in *Soul Kitchen*, DVD capture

In *Soul Kitchen* nomadic mobility is counterbalanced by satisfaction with a rootedness no longer seen as provincial. Two-way travel is observed only with Nadine's return from China when her grandmother dies, and by shots of trains traveling across the screen in both directions, the pendulum of the city's rhythm. Hamburg, renowned gateway to the world via the sea, and thereby the launching pad for German emigration to the United States in particular, is transformed into a dry dock harbor. Sokrates becomes the true incarnation of this Hamburg, a local with an evocative Greek name whose Odyssey remains landlocked in *the* German city of emigration (the boat he occupies right next to the restaurant is never launched). Like Sokrates, Zinos never forsakes Hamburg, so that despite the evocation of his brother Illias's name, no epic Odyssey eventuates, for all the multiple references to both Homeric titles. In contrast, Shayn's final message, knifed to the door of the restaurant, claims that his journey is not over, in keeping with the fleeting reference to him as a gypsy.

Soul Kitchen's treatment of this corner of Hamburg suggests the microcosm of a chaotic but desirable community. "Transnationalism offers new imaginings of community ... primarily through the mediation of audiovisual culture" (Halle 2008: 28). To that smorgasbord, supplemented by the musical and cinematic intertextuality discussed later in this essay, *Soul Kitchen* adds the culture and cultivation of food. The materiality of food and music consumption provides a concrete grounding. While the film's fictional world must seem utopian if judged by Chancellor Merkel's pronouncement, it is not a nowhere (utopia) but very much a somewhere, a hidden gem in Germany's second largest city.

The playful treatment of the crosscultural and intracultural mixes is familiar from Akın's other films. Its closest correlate is Anno Saul's *Kebab Connection* (2004), coscripted by Akın, with Adam Bousdoukos

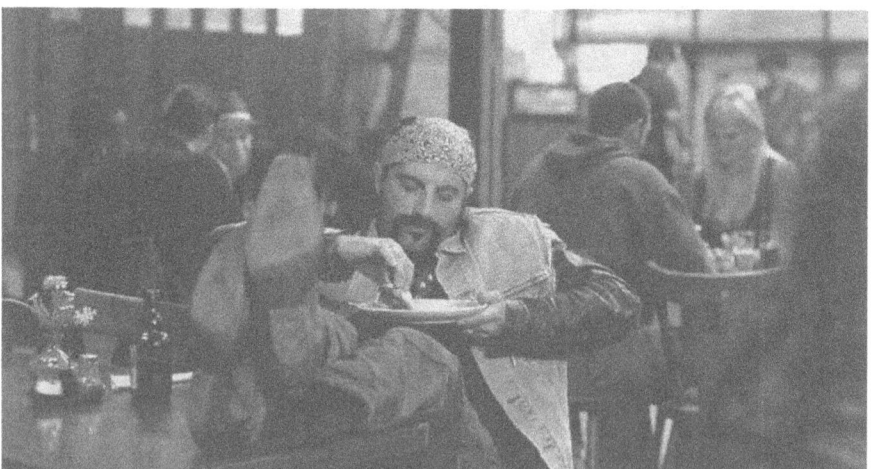

Figure 14.2 Ali Davidson (Bülent Celebi) in *Soul Kitchen*, DVD capture

(Zinos here) taking a major role. Both films build on gastronomy as an identity marker beyond national roots. *Kebab Connection* focuses on two restaurants on opposite sides of a street, with the Greek restaurant no match for the slick advertising of its Turkish competitor, as both contend for German customers (a kind of mirror image of EU realities). Such rivalry is an internal affair in *Soul Kitchen*, with the parody of a German menu supplanted by the daring nouvelle cuisine of the outsider cook Shayn. This combination yields a Turkish-German-Greek triangulation, presented with a light touch, that offers a variation on the Turkish-Jewish-German triangulation in *The Edge of Heaven* (Silvey and Hillman 2010: 101–2).

Conceived as a detour from the trilogy *Liebe, Tod und Teufel* (*Love, Death, and the Devil*), *Soul Kitchen* is a fusion of motifs, casting, and music familiar from other Akın films, though with none of the edginess of his *Kurz und schmerzlos* (*Short Sharp Shock*, 1998) or the visceral confrontation of *Head-On*. It is a relaxed film by a director assured of his own place within Hamburg, to the point where he can unearth and transform local treasures. The comedic vein of *In July* is recognizable, but whereas that film was largely set in the geographical spaces between Hamburg and Istanbul, Akın (continuing from *Head-On*) styles Hamburg itself as a transnational metropolis. Without the central love stories of *In July*, and with a more self-conscious brand of humor, *Soul Kitchen* successfully aspires to be more chaotic, even random, its narrative emerging from Skype connections and aphrodisiac substances. And the more contemplative, lyrical tones of *The Edge of Heaven* represent another world. The closest parallel to *Soul Kitchen* might be *Solino* (2002) where a pizzeria is established in Duisburg and where Moritz Bleibtreu plays the unreliable brother in a different historical period when the first-wave Italian guestworkers catered to their fellow expatriates and only gradually made inroads into their host country. *Soul Kitchen* does not focus on one national cuisine but shows the more adventurous culinary directions embraced by its German clientele.

Soul Searching: Transnational Musical Markers

Global influences are absorbed into the soul of Hamburg through *Soul Kitchen's* soundtrack. The synthesis of African American 1960s, 1970s, and 1980s soul music and various transnationally inflected types of music anchors the film. *Soul Kitchen* realigns identities in Hamburg so that globalization appears as a liberating rather than a colonizing force. The film embraces minority standpoints, using music from a mix of cultures to articulate the characters' multiple identities.

Soundtracks attuned to transnationalism accompany each of Akın's filmic cultural crossings. *Crossing the Bridge* documents music and musicians of various backgrounds and influences in Turkey, and questions Turkey's Eastern and Western *"in-betweenism"* (Halle 2008: 8). *In July, Solino, Head-On*, and *The Edge of Heaven* echo exchanges between different cultures via music (Göktürk 2010b: 223; Petek 2007: 182-84, Siewert 2008: 198–208). Whereas these films featured visible border crisscrossings (Mennel 2010), *Soul Kitchen* gravitates around Hamburg as a cultural (re) mix. Deniz Göktürk's essay in this collection discusses the globalization of the local in *The Edge of Heaven*'s soundtrack. *Soul Kitchen* presents the inverse: a localization of global music. Based on musical selections by Akın and his musical director (Pride 2010), *Soul Kitchen* uses a wide variety of music such as American rhythm and blues, funk and soul, reggae, German electronica, hip hop, punk rock, popular song, Greek contemporary dance music, and multiple versions of "La Paloma."

Soul Kitchen harnesses the effects of globalization upon musical exchange, influence, and authorship in order to portray and reposition minority groups in Akın's hometown of Hamburg. In an interview given in the United States Akın states:

> If you wanted to go out to soul music in Germany, you must go to Hamburg. If this is a movie about the city, soul music must be dominating. I don't mean this politically, but there is a strange identification for people with Greek, Italian, and Spanish backgrounds to identify with African-Americans. They are a minority in Europe, and African Americans are a minority here so it's not the same history, but there is an adoption of certain cultural things. So it made sense to use the R and B tracks of the '60s and '70s and even the '80s.

(Slifkin 2010)

American music has a significant place in German films, notably in Wim Wenders's films from the 1970s such as *Im Laufe der Zeit* (*Kings of the Road*, 1976), *Alice in den Städten* (*Alice in the Cities*, 1974), and more recently *Viel passiert—Der BAP-Film* (*Ode to Cologne: A Rock 'n' Roll Film*, 2002). In these films rock music reverberates as a key instrument in America's colonization of German culture. At the same time, characters' adoption of this culture also offers them a mode of expression that rejects German traditions associated with Nazi cultural politics. Wenders uses popular music to articulate a break from the past and a sense of uncertainty about Germany's contemporaneous place in the world (Gemünden 2004: 188–89).

Soul Kitchen, however, uses primarily African American music that adds a further dimension to the marking of cultural identities within Germany, specifically minority communities. Unlike Wenders's ambivalence about American "colonization," Akın uses music that arose from the history of slavery and came to a crescendo in the civil rights movement of the 1960s and 1970s, itself a symbol of a minority culture's resistance. This protest era is concurrent with the flows into Germany of migrants and guestworkers from countries such as Turkey and Greece, the protagonists' parents and grandparents. The presence of black characters in the orgy scene further visualizes this particular aspect of transnationalism, perhaps referring to Germany's former African colonies. Favoring trendy alternative standpoints, the film musically shapes the German waitress Lucia as transnational in addition to her gypsy lifestyle as a squatter. Complementing her leather jacket, heavy drinking, and bold haircut, her musical motifs consist of a wide range of alternative influences. She dances to local Hamburg techno artists at clubs, and at the bars she frequents we hear reggae, rock, and German hip hop, German R&B, and female rock vocalists. The German adoption of these styles, along with Lucia's free-spirited personality and romance with Zinos's brother Illias, reinforce the notion of Hamburg as a transcultural and soulful city.

Music articulates class and cultural differences but also blurs these dividing lines in *Soul Kitchen*. Two different restaurant scenes align African American music with minority communities and associate dominant Hamburg society with hegemonic oppression, an opposition that is musically negotiated. The film opens with Zinos arriving at Soul Kitchen and preparing a slapdash dinner for his customers using mismatching crockery and reheated supermarket food. Played nondiegetically, Kool & the Gang's cheeky funk song "Rated X" endears us to the restaurant and Zinos. Its funk rhythms, laidback synthesizer, lively brass syncopations, and wah-wah pedal poke fun at Zinos's haphazard attempts to set up the restaurant. Quincy Jones's "Hicky Burr," the theme song from the early 1970s African American sitcom *The Bill Cosby Show*, teasingly accompanies shots of the customers who happily consume generic defrosted foods (schnitzels, pizza, hamburgers) in lieu of restaurant-worthy cuisine. Hicky Burr's comedic associations, nonsense lyrics, and zany tongue rolls complement the farce and again associate Zinos with African American music and what was once a minority standpoint within a dominant culture. The fact that *The Bill Cosby Show* became popular with white audiences underscores *Soul Kitchen*'s ultimate repositioning and popularization of marginal voices and cuisines within Hamburg.

Akın states that he used soul music in the film because: "We felt like they speak about us, people with backgrounds. We have more soul than the white Germans have" (Qureshi 2010: 1). This partly explains why the villainous white German property developer Neumann lacks musical motifs save monotonous techno in one scene. However, the film's musical and cultural modulations move beyond Akın's own binary claim of immigrants vs. non-immigrant "white" Germans. In a scene at the prestigious restaurant Papillon tensions simmer between Hamburg's entrenched upper class and minority immigrant groupings. Nadine's wealthy German family shares a birthday celebration to which Zinos arrives late, inappropriately dressed and smelly. Reminiscent of parental attitudes to intercultural couples in *Solino*, *Kebab Connection*, and *Head-On*, Nadine's parents greet Zinos disapprovingly. Artie Shaw's jazz rendition of "La Paloma" accompanies this scene. Symbolic of conflicts as well as cultural bridges between white and black Americans, jazz evokes cultural identifications other than the African American grooves at Zinos's restaurant. Similar to Artie Shaw's music in America the tensions between Zinos, Nadine, and her family, and with other restaurant clients recall conflicts between majority and minority cultures in Germany over dominant cultures' homogenization and distortion of Others' traditions. During the scene arguments break out between a German patron who orders his gazpacho hot and Shayn, the gypsy chef who furiously insists that the traditional Spanish soup be served cold, and between Zinos and Nadine about her attitudes toward his career. However, the music's connotation of cultural mediations also mirrors the narrative's suggestion that these tensions are resolvable. Although controversial, Artie Shaw's employment of musicians such as Billie Holiday helped to influence the civil rights movement (Purnell 2002: 453). Likewise Nadine's grandmother demands a peace treaty, directing Zinos, Nadine, and her parents to abandon personal and cultural differences. *Soul Kitchen* thus uses music to connote cultural mediations, not simply oppositions.

Two appropriations of Anglophone rock music spark Soul Kitchen's successful nights when the bartender Lutz's band performs German punk rock songs and later when they cover the American soul song "Ain't That Good News" in a rock style. In this latter scene the band members dress to resemble Angus Young from the Australian band AC/DC and Bono from the Irish band U2, the latter indelibly associated with Wenders since they provided music for his films *In weiter Ferne, so nah!* (*Faraway, So Close!*, 1993) and *Bis ans Ende der Welt* (*Until the End of the World*, 1991). A Union Jack singlet points to British bands such as The Who and the Sex Pistols (conversely, The Beatles found fame in Hamburg). These outfits, the punk rock associations with England and the voices from its colonies, again signal counterpositions to dominant powers, illustrating global dialogues resistant to cultural imperialism. Unlike New German Cinema, German characters here localize international influences and convert them through performance to articulate their own social positions, thereby placing themselves within a global exchange rather than under a perceived colonization.

The characters of Greek origins, Zinos, his brother Illias, and the restaurant's boarder Sokrates are associated with a mixture of Greek and international musical styles, which illustrates their elastic identities. Sokrates is Zorba-like, and Illias is a soft-hearted criminal. However, their musical tastes update these stereotypes. Sokrates stays to the end of the orgy, dancing and listening to different types of music (although he wears ear muffs for the rock music). Illias is awkward in a nightclub where techno music and blue lights render the dancers a cool, exclusive group. Instead, at the culturally eclectic Soul Kitchen, Illias masters the (stolen) DJ equipment and gets into the groove when he selects the German Romanian DJ Shantel's remix of the Greek Zaharias Kasimatis's 1929 recording of "Manolis Hasiklis."

In relation to *The Edge of Heaven*, Göktürk in this volume discusses Shantel as an artist who westernizes East European music. In *Soul Kitchen* Shantel's music reflects back upon the local community, articulating the global within the local. The influence of Balkan and gypsy sounds on Shantel's music also gestures to the gypsy character Shayn. Shayn is otherwise acoustically associated with the barman Lutz's band's punk rock song "Moon Shayn" and the restaurant's soul music rather than any musical "gypsy" marker. As Illias and Zinos dance in a traditional Greek style to Shantel's remix, this re-envisioning and updating of a Greek song through transnational ears inflects the brothers' Greek roots with contemporary transnational identifications. Greek music infused with other styles such as reggae and blues characterizes other scenes in which Sokrates, Illias, and Zinos appear. These acoustic border crossings mix with evocations of stereotypes to position these identities as flexible and multifaceted.

The international popularity of the Spanish song "La Paloma" and its connotations of exoticism position both the film's settings and the characters as palimpsests of multiple identities, origins, translations, and global radiations. "La Paloma" elegizes divided foreign lovers, has been translated into many languages, and draws connections between Europe and the Americas. Through an extended bridging sequence the song mourns Nadine's and Zinos's imminent parting of ways. Four versions of the song blend smoothly into each other in the sequence tracking Nadine's departure to Shanghai. While this might recall the bridges between Europe and the East explored in *Crossing the Bridge*, in this film China is not linked to a particular musical theme. The bridges in this motif remain in Europe, keeping Zinos's and Nadine's relationship within a transnational European and Western orbit.

After leaving the Papillon where we hear an American version of "La Paloma," Gabriella Ferri's recording plays diegetically and then crescendos nondiegetically while Zinos and Nadine drive home in his van. They are tense about Nadine's imminent departure and other relationship frictions, but the music emphasizes their lingering bond as they tenderly embrace. Zinos's continuation of the tune as he sings in the shower actualizes his associations with the song, steeping him in European traditions. Another almost seamless sonic transition connects Zinos's rendition to Natalino Otto's diegetic recording as Nadine unsuccessfully tries to teach Zinos how to use Skype. "La Paloma" nondiegetically bridges their farewell at the airport and fades out as Nadine's plane disappears into the clouds. Otto's old recorded version has pops and crackles, implying that their relationship will soon be an artifact, too. Although Ferri sings the song in Spanish, both Ferri and

Otto are Italian singers, deepening the film's blurring of identities. Renditions after Nadine's departure (on the music box, whistled, and as harmonica and guitar versions at the restaurant) voice Zinos's conscious and unconscious recollections of Nadine and his reluctance to leave his restaurant. These and the remarkably protracted sound bridge of "La Paloma" embed the inter-European romance within the context of European transnationalism and global export, balancing the film's portrait of European and Western global musical exchange.

During Zinos and Nadine's final breakup at a diner, a nondiegetic German song acoustically docks their exhausted relationship in Hamburg. Hans Albers's "Das letzte Hemd hat leider keine Taschen" (The last shirt unfortunately has no pockets) is from the 1957 Hamburg film *Das Herz von St. Pauli* (*The Heart of St. Pauli*). This humorous popular song about poverty mirrors Zinos's situation for he has lost everything: his restaurant, his apartment, his reimprisoned brother, and his girlfriend. The scene and the music locate Nadine and Zinos's relationship in Hamburg, which is underscored by the fact that Zinos munches on chips and chicken, the type of generic food he used to serve his customers. Without any hint of soul music or other foreign influences, the German song accompanies their final breakup, connecting Zinos with the heart of Hamburg, while Nadine is soon to depart.

Soul Kitchen's wide-ranging music identifies its protagonists as trendily transnational globalized citizens, while Hamburg locates the heart and soul of these multifaceted identities. Akın's film inextricably intertwines its Greek German, gypsy, and German protagonists. At the end Zinos gives up on his German girlfriend and instead has an intimate dinner with his nurse who introduced him to the "bone cruncher," a Turkish chiropractor. The soundtrack, which includes Louis Armstrong's "The Creator has a Master Plan," self-referentially points to Akın as the film's creator. Moving away from essentialist musical portraits that presume a "European *intactness*" and countering notions of cultural imperialism via voices of resistance and mediation, *Soul Kitchen* presents a transnational soundscape of cultural exchanges, parallels, and adoptions within Hamburg (Halle 2008: 8). Music is central to Akın's depiction of the city, and an integral transnational marker alongside the film's cinematic intertextuality, particularly its comedic dimension.

Ingredients of Comedy

From the farcical funeral scene via the mass orgy under the influence of an aphrodisiac, this film situates itself as comedy, a dominant genre in German cinema of the mid-1990s. We do well however to observe the following context: "the German Comedy Wave of the 1990s, often credited with revitalizing the German national film industry, making

German film popular again for Germans, actually was not a specifically German phenomenon but part of a European trend" (Halle 2008: 27). In that sense Akın yet again seizes on the European possibilities of German culture. But he also returns us to the mayhem of the silent era, where Chaplinesque comedy had translated across cultures as visual Esperanto. Roughly a century later, Akın combines comedic elements emerging within a transnational community.

Soul Kitchen's approach to satire is typified by its approach to food; with a keen eye for the ridiculous, it nonetheless tracks foibles lovingly. Food had played an important role in crucial scenes of *Head-On* and *The Edge of Heaven*, not to mention the establishment of the Ruhr pizzeria in *Solino*. The closeups, vibrant colors, and accelerated footage of the first two examples are signatures of mediated cooking instruction, and typify what Shayn has to impart to Zinos. Cookbooks by icons in the English-speaking world such as Jamie Oliver and Nigella Lawson adorn German bookshop windows too.

In *Kebab Connection*, harmony across the fraught historical interactions of the Mediterranean neighbors Greece and Turkey is forged through food. The same happens here with a broadened sense of neighbors—Sokrates is no longer the cranky man next door when consuming Shayn's new dishes. The challenge provided by those dishes is mirrored by new and unforeseeable transnational combinations. The fact that "La Paloma" accompanies the farewell from Nadine shows that China is not on Zinos's radar. Not China itself, but global commerce takes Nadine away from Hamburg and Zinos, and ultimately to her Chinese lover. Altogether Akın revels in puns that are a further product of transnationalism and that slide with relish across stereotypes and languages. A classic example is the restaurant client Ali Davidson, beyond the cultural blend of his name. Just as Sokrates is a beached mariner, this indelible secondary figure is a domesticated Easy Rider minus his Harley Davidson. Hamburg, this film proclaims, makes such blends possible.

Cinematic Intertextuality

Associations with Hamburg yield a kind of cultural archaeology of this city as *Heimat*, bearing in mind that Germany had defined itself according to *jus sanguinis* (right of blood), yielding to *jus soli* ([birth-]right of place). As one might expect with Akın, film culture is central to his archive of this city, complementing the film's sound archive. Toward the end of the film, when Zinos goes to Kemal the bone cruncher for chiropractic treatment, the contraption attached to the floor-bound patient is visually reminiscent of a scene in Luis Buñuel's *Un chien andalou* (1929), which links a donkey to a piano. The graveyard obituary for Nadine's grandmother is laced with film titles, such as the biblically based *Through a Glass Darkly*, Ingmar

Bergman's film of 1961. The biblical tone accords with the funeral oration (the phrase comes from Corinthians 1:13), but the resonance is decidedly with cinephilia, not religious ritual. The death of cinema is not on the horizon, even in the digital age that in this film is held effectively at bay. The only death is that of Nadine's grandmother; the only potentially waning force is the original biblical resonance. Still more joyfully iconoclastic is the sermon's incorporation of the phrase *Face to Face*, a further Bergman title (1976), but also of an Italo-Western of 1967 by Sergio Sollima. This constellation, on the one hand a Nordic model, on the other a generic interloper fusing backgrounds, embodies the very alternatives into which Akın refuses to be pigeonholed.

Ahead of these Bergman references, the script of this mock sermon varies the recurring refrain "when the child was a child" that permeates Wenders's *Der Himmel über Berlin* (*Wings of Desire*, 1987). New German Cinema yet again provides the most fertile reference point for Akın's film in its tacit repositioning of territory marked by Rainer Werner Fassbinder and Wenders. While its mood rules out Fassbinder references such as those crucial to *Head-On* (Fachinger 2007; Hillman 2010), *Soul Kitchen*'s relaxed dénouement contrasts to the Otherness of the outsider through the ostracization or sentimentalization found in Fassbinder's *Katzelmacher* (1969). Fassbinder's Jorgos the Greek, originally mistaken for an Italian, was lost in Germany and seemingly unable to return home. Akın's Zinos would be lost without Germany, specifically Hamburg.

The Wenders film most relevant to Hamburg is *The American Friend* (1977). In a scene toward the end of *Soul Kitchen* the dastardly Neumann's representative holds sway until the last moment at the auction that will seal the fate of the restaurant. This undoubtedly draws on the early scene in Wenders's film where a fake masterpiece is on offer, a transaction seen through solely by the German Jonathan. With Akın, Zinos is really the one to salvage culinary culture from the clutches of Neumann and his henchmen, on behalf of his clientele of mixed, but predominantly German background. Neumann remains a Teutonic variant of capitalistic excess, a generic villain who happens to be German. Where the clash of transatlantic cultures remains an important subtext in Wenders's film, the merry melting pot in *Soul Kitchen* is unproblematic, and largely matches the way in which the United States had always styled itself. The old motif of Hollywood images vis-à-vis German images had preoccupied the New German Cinema, and Wenders in particular. Such a tension is superseded by the transnationalism of Akın's films. This new paradigm would have been deemed a most unlikely achievement of a (Euro-)German director or indeed any director before the new millennium.

Wenders's soundtracks in films after *The American Friend* lend themselves to closer comparison with Akın's roving musical choices, a parallel pursued above. But one detail further links the two directors, the tiny music box-like machine with its rotating lever that Zinos plays with fascination in an early scene at the restaurant. The viewer has seen one of these before, somewhere in a shelved memory. It belonged to none other than the Homer figure in *Wings of Desire*. His face expressed similar delight, and via this visual allusion reinforces the film's countless references to the Iliad and Odyssey. Where Homer in *Wings of Desire* preserved the narrative of history midst the disorientation of postwar Potsdamer Platz, Akın's Sokrates preserves a myth of Hamburg with his boat that is never launched, and is housed in the same derelict building. That he is the resident *spiritus locus* emerges with his spirited defense of Zinos's bidding at the auction, when any historical continuity is threatened by the schemes of Neumann. Thus even ancient and modern Greek literary references are harmonized, given that the restaurateur's surname is Kazantzakis, author of *Zorba the Greek* and revered by Thomas Mann.

As elsewhere in his oeuvre, Akın's allusions proliferate, redirecting another New German Cinema notion, namely Alexander Kluge's wish to activate the film in the spectator's head. Where Kluge had implied a cerebral creative process, catalyzed by a nonlinear narrative, Akın activates films in the cinephile's head, a process complementing an almost independent narrative. It is also a process pointing to a quality of open-endedness in watching an Akın film, but in a different sense compared to European cinema's frequent counterpointing itself against the seamless and rounded narrative ideals of classical Hollywood. While the setting of *Soul Kitchen* never leaves Hamburg, the narrative ranges across ancient European culture and history, New German Cinema, Turkish German Greek triangulations, Anglo American, African American, and German music, and the very notion of *Heimat*. While conceived as a light break from Akın's trilogy, it is also a film that mixes rich ingredients for audiences far beyond Hamburg.

Chapter 15

WORLD CINEMA GOES DIGITAL:
LOOKING AT EUROPE FROM THE OTHER SHORE

Deniz Göktürk

How do we know where we are when we watch a film? What kinds of topographical hints do traveling directors and producers give their audience—in feature films and in bonus materials? How do viewers orient themselves in relation to varying locations, especially when they are watching cinema in digital format? In the DVD presentation of films, extra features invite viewers to perform combinatory tasks. Paratexts such as commentary, fragments cut from the main film, or footage documenting the process of location hunting, rehearsal, and shooting allow spectators to glimpse behind the scenes. Furthermore, they can follow cues to find further supplemental material on Google, YouTube, or other DVDs. A focus on such "digitextual convergence" and "click pleasure" that opens up an infinite number of windows is bound to complicate linear readings of the narrative (Everett 2003: 3–28). Digital spectators participate interactively in the imagination of topographies.

Taking Fatih Akın's film *Auf der anderen Seite* (*The Edge of Heaven/Yaşamın Kıyısında*, 2007) as an example, my following analysis addresses tensions between mobility and immobility in contemporary European cinema and, more broadly speaking, world cinema. As a mobile player in the international film festival circuit, Akın joined the Filmmakers Board of the World Cinema Foundation launched by Martin Scorsese in 2007.[1] In his films and commentaries he is known to draw on a range of international cinematic references. Hence critics ought to rethink his ready subsumption under the flags of German, Turkish German, or Turkish cinema. The characters in Akın's films, just as the filmmaker himself, travel mostly along an axis connecting spaces in Germany and Turkey, and the actors speak German and Turkish. However, English also enters these conversations, rendering the films increasingly trilingual. As a viewer who works in these three languages, my aim is not to substitute national identifications by another value-adding marketing label, but rather follow Martin Roberts's definition of "world cinema," as films that are "about something called 'the world' itself" (Roberts 1998: 62). I propose that *The Edge of Heaven* might satisfy that requirement, as it hints at a locally specific but nonetheless planetary consciousness with subtle allusion to environmental concerns. Speaking with cultural geographer Doreen Massey (1994; compare Cresswell 2004), we could say that the film's universalizing structure of address encourages spectators to acquire "a global sense of place," or, as I would like to call it, a grasp of *situated transit*: an awareness of the infrastructures that enable or hinder mobility (Sassen 1998: 176–94; Urry 2007) and "friction" on the ground (Tsing 2005).

Our sense of place is never given, but always assembled from sensual and mediated experiences. Possibilities of topographic orientation and contextualization through proliferating links and supplementary fragments complement the pleasure of watching a story unfold. Film does not offer unequivocal meaning; it is up to the viewer to make connections and fill "gaps" (Iser 1984: 267–355). While such participatory activity on part of the viewer is in line with the reader-focus of reception aesthetics, digital media further open up the text to associative linkages. Combinatory reading and viewing practices necessitate that we rethink the structuralist conception of an implied reader (Iser 1984: 50–67) in an expanded and dynamic horizon. World cinema's producers and spectators might be in transit, but they are still situated. As we shall see in *The Edge of Heaven*, for viewers willing to dig deeper, music plays a central role in the layered production of atmosphere with local bearings and translocal resonances, just as in Akın's earlier films *Gegen die Wand* (*Head-On/Duvara Karşı*, 2004) and *Crossing the Bridge: The Sound of Istanbul* (2005), a point already examined in an earlier piece (Göktürk 2010b: 153–71). This time, tracing the musical journey will lead us to the shores of the Black Sea. In this layered viewing experience, regional identification appears as an infinite process of mediation, never a return to stable grounds and roots.

The Sound of Nuclear Disaster

The film begins with a quiet tableau. A little white hut in the sun, behind it a wall, trees and electricity poles, a bench in front, a dog sniffing at a bowl. The camera slowly tracks right. In the background, a man is busy changing a tire on a bus. Red and white gas pumps appear in the frame—initially three in the background, then two in the middle and two more in the foreground. The staggered positioning of the pumps lends the image a tripartite depth of field, visually anticipating the three-part structure of the film. The sleepy gas station with the inscription "Petrol" and the inoperative bus in the background is a transfer site of energy, albeit lacking traffic. Initially only the camera moves. Then a white car enters the frame from left, heading in the opposite direction to the camera. In a carefully composed shot, the car stops in the middle, framed by the two pumps in the foreground. The tension between mobility and stillness, which defines the entire film, is already established in this first shot. An attendant greets the driver in Turkish: "Bayramınız mübarek olsun!" (Happy Bayram!) After a short dialogue, the driver goes to the store in the back where another man welcomes him with festive wishes.

The camera films the traveler's entrance into the store from inside. The music, which was quietly audible in the background, now becomes louder, reveals itself as diegetic, originating from a source within the scene, and even becomes a topic of conversation. The traveler—sweating, shirt open over a white undershirt—regards the display absentmindedly.

He inquires: "Bu şarkı nedir?" (What is this song?)

The shopkeeper answers: "Kazım Koyuncu. Hiç duymadınız mı?" (Kazım Koyuncu. Have you never heard him before?)

Traveler: "Hayır." (No.)

Shopkeeper: "Burada Karadeniz'de çok tutulur." (He is very popular here at the Black Sea.)

Traveler: "Tanımıyorum." (I don't know him.)

Shopkeeper: "Artvin'li. İki sene önce kanserden öldü. Çok gençti. Sizin yaşınızda." (He came from Artvin. Two years ago, he died of cancer. He was very young. Your age.)

The traveler concerns himself with bags of chips on the shelf, briefly raising his eyebrows. His facial expression shows him taking the comparison into consideration with a distanced nonchalance.

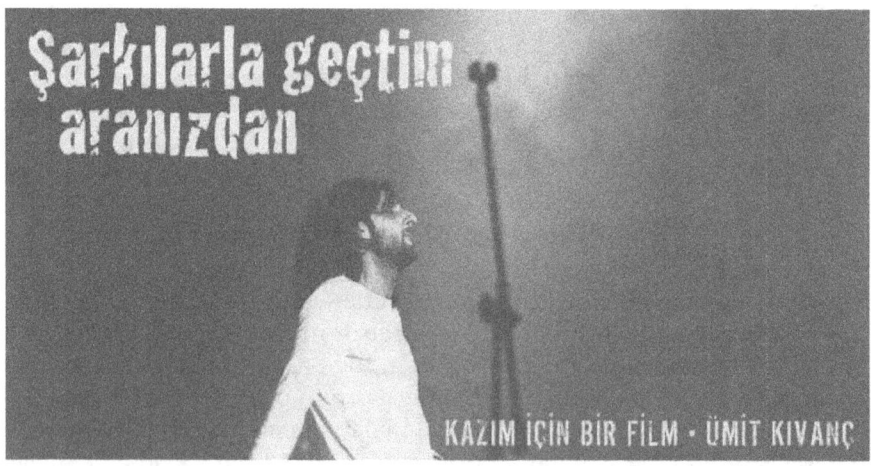

Figure 15.1 *I Passed Through with Songs: A Film for Kazım*, courtesy Kalan Müzik

The shopkeeper explains further: "Hep Çernobil'den. Bunların hepsi yeni yeni ortaya çıkıyor!" (All because of Chernobyl. Everything is now coming to light!)

The traveler pays without a word. The Turkish-language dialogue makes it clear that we are in Turkey. The deictic use of "here" further locates the setting in the Black Sea region. The camera's distance from the figures positions the viewer as a detached observer.

As a prologue, the gas station scene suggestively anticipates themes and structures of *The Edge of Heaven*. The traveler speaks the language and is familiar with holiday greetings, but does not understand all of the signs. The music is foreign to him. With his hesitant interest he can be read as a stand-in not only for the director Akın, who experienced a similar encounter on his trip to filming locations (as he elucidates in bonus materials on the German DVD edition), but also for the spectator, who watches the scene at an international film festival or on a screen somewhere on another continent and brings no knowledge of language or place. Empathy for an unknown singer who died early of cancer arises with reserve; the "tourist gaze" (Urry 1990) can identify with vernacular stories only selectively. Meanwhile the gas station attendant articulates the presence of the global in the local. The reference to the nuclear accident at Chernobyl in the Ukraine on 26 April 1986 as the cause of an increase in cancer cases suggests the connection of destinies across the sea and national borders. Indeed the extent of the long-term effects of the radioactive contamination twenty years after the biggest nuclear catastrophe in the history of atomic energy (meanwhile equaled by Fukushima) is difficult to measure. Decisive is the interdependence between the mediatized incident and lesser-known fates, which the resident explains to the traveler. Directly at the outset, the film thus unsettles a critique that thumps clear affiliations and propagates a strict differentiation between an internal and external perspective on a national culture.[2]

For Ulrich Beck, the nuclear disaster of Chernobyl presents an anthropological shock, the epitome of what he calls risk society:

> A fate of endangerment has arisen in modernity, a sort of counter-modernity, which transcends all our concepts of space, time, and social differentiation. What yesterday was still far away will be found today and in the future at the front door. Chernobyl, for instance. Causality can extend over decades. The effects manifest themselves globally, but delayed in time—indeed, only in the struggle over statistical significance or behind the smokescreen of isolation.

(Beck 1995: 69)

While Beck's account of the disaster emphasizes the homogenizing impact of the cloud that renders national sovereignty obsolete, I would like to propose that the opening scene of *The Edge of Heaven* (and, more broadly speaking, film as a medium) allows for a more exemplary and evocative staging of lasting long-distance effects and echoes.[3] The emotive significance of Chernobyl twenty years later at this sleepy gas station near the Turkish shore of the Black Sea can only be teased out by listening closely to undertones of conversations and traveling songs.

Looking Outside the Frame

As DVD spectators, we can watch the beginning of the film repeatedly and even turn on another audio track. The director's commentary begins with the warning that audio commentaries contribute to demystification and are therefore only suited for film students.[4] Akın's commentary on the opening scene (on the German edition of the DVD) culminates in his assertion that *The Edge of Heaven* is a film suited for the cinema:

> These images are all intended for the movie screen. When I now watch it, I think that viewing habits have indeed changed. With DVDs and watching films on the computer—soon we will be watching films on cell phones—, there's not much sense anymore to shooting films with gigantic long shots, when one only sees tiny pixels on a monitor. This film is meant for the movie screen. Accordingly we dealt expansively with the spaces.

However, we do not hear this commentary in a dark cinema, but rather in front of the television or computer screen in our living room, with the remote control in hand (on home viewing practices, see Klinger 2006). Ironically the emphatic assertion of the traditional, big-screen cinema with its collective mode of viewing is first made possible through the new, digital format of presentation, which attaches an additional layer to the film in simultaneous exhibition and gives the viewer the choice of watching the film multiple times or in fragments, with the original audio track or with voice-over commentary. As is so often the case in media history, the new medium does not simply replace the old one; rather, both emerge in a complementary relation to each other.

Akın's elucidation of the long take with which *The Edge of Heaven* opens as a shot in the cinematic style of Michelangelo Antonioni situates the film in the great tradition of European auteur cinema, underscoring its pitch to the Cannes Film Festival. The commentary's authorial performance of creative control and quality cinema partly confirms Jonathan Gray's argument that paratexts on DVDs tend to be employed for marketing purposes to reanimate the aura of the work of art and the myth of original creativity on part of the auteur in the era of digital reproduction (Gray 2010: 81–115; see also Kreimeier et al. 2004). However, the disclosure of models and aspirations can also arouse the viewer's curiosity to find other DVDs, view image composition in a comparative light, and perceive of places as constructed in a layered topography of correspondences and superimpositions.

In her book *Death 24x a Second*, Laura Mulvey describes the experience of viewing a film on DVD:

> [E]xtra-diegetic elements have broken through the barrier that has traditionally protected the diegetic world of narrative film and its linear structure. Furthermore, as a DVD indexes a film into chapters, the heterogeneity of add-ons is taken a step further by non-linear access to the story. ... Once the consumption of movies is detached from the absolute isolation of absorbed viewing (in the dark, at 24 frames a second, in narrative order and without exterior intrusions), the cohesion of narrative order comes under pressure from external discourses, that is, production context, anecdote, history. But digital spectatorship also affects the internal pattern of narrative: sequences can be easily skipped or repeated, overturning hierarchies of privilege, and setting up unexpected links that displace the chain of meaning invested in cause and effect.
>
> (Mulvey 2006: 27)

Altered viewing habits impact the structure of visual narration even when it claims to adhere to the classical cinema tradition. One important effect of extradiegetic features and nonlinear forms of reception might be the viewer's stimulation to look both inside and outside the frame, or consider multiple frames. In this open-ended, ramified reception, narrative cinema potentially follows documentary and experimental film in the direction of an "expanded cinema" (Marchessault and Lord 2007; Youngblood 1970).

Journey to the Black Sea

In "Tagebuch eines Filmreisenden" (Diary of a Film Traveler), an interview conducted by his wife Monique Akın that is contained on the bonus disc of the German DVD release, as well as the American DVD edition as "The Making of *The Edge of Heaven*," Akın comments on the choice of filming locations, especially the gas station in the opening sequence:

> For me, Turkey is still virgin soil that can be discovered and understood. A good example for this is the first motif of the film, the gas station on the Black Sea. I still remember how Andreas [Thiel] found the place too special, too sought-out, too romantic, not realistic enough. Later he changed his mind. Sırma, our Turkish set designer, made the setting of the gas station believable.

This disclosure that the setting was an old gas station no longer in operation is intriguing. The filmmakers did not shoot at one of the modern gas stations along the new main traffic artery of the Black Sea region where the big trucks stop, as is briefly visible in one of the road movie interludes in *The Edge of Heaven*. Instead an abandoned gas station was reanimated from the past—one that was left by the wayside off the new street. The patina contributes to the atmosphere of melancholic stagnation that hangs over this scene and is also addressed by the gas station attendant when he brings the music of Kazım Koyuncu in connection with long-term radioactive contamination and lingering death. As Akın reports in his commentary, this place—and the hut in the opening image of the film in particular—symbolized "the South" for the cameraman Rainer Klausmann. The glimpse behind the scenes in the bonus material on the DVD allows the viewer to partake in the process of location scouting, designing, and staging, and deters from reading this scene as a mimetic copy. This gas station, as depicted here, does not exist in reality. The scene is therefore a good example of the mediated and affective production of place in the interplay of image and sound.

The melancholy grounding of the scene at the gas station is achieved not least through music. *Diary of a Film Traveler* includes a comment by Akın on the music of Koyuncu:

> During our closing trip on the Black Sea, I fell in love with the music of Kazım Koyuncu. I was in an Internet café right when his song "Ben Seni Sevdugumi" played from the speakers. I asked the store attendant who it was. And what then followed was pretty much one-to-one like the dialogue at the beginning of the film. Kazım Koyuncu comes from the Black Sea coast and is held in high esteem by the people there. His early death from cancer called many people into action. ... The song by Kazım Koyuncu is the leitmotiv for the entire soundtrack. With it, I hope that I have given necessary tribute to his life's work.

This comment in *Diary of a Film Traveler* is synchronized with documentary shots of Koyuncu's concert appearances and his funeral. Kazım Koyuncu (1971–2005) was indeed an important role model in the eastern Black Sea region. In his folk rock concerts with the group Zuğaşi Berepe from the early 1990s onwards, he brought the Laz language (related to the Georgian) on the stage and made it attractive for a supraregional young audience. During the advanced stage of his illness, he still appeared before thousands of spectators with Lazian songs such as "Ella Ella" or "Didou Nana."[5] Koyuncu died from lung cancer at the age of thirty-three. On YouTube one finds innumerable clips of his concerts and television appearances as well as his funeral, which resembled a large demonstration, and adulatory clips by fans who have matched his songs with souvenir photos.[6] His life story is told in Ümit Kıvanç's documentary *Şarkılarla Geçtim Aranızdan: Kazım İçin Bir Film* (*I Passed Through with Songs: A Film for Kazım*, 2008). There, one can see scenes from his childhood village, the long walk to school through the forests, his development as a guitar-playing singer, and concerts in Istanbul and other cities in Holland, Germany, or England. The skinny, longhaired singer with a lively stage presence was also vocal as an environmental activist. In interviews he articulates his active involvement against the transformation of the landscape through the coastal highway, where the sand beaches often had to give way to artificial mounts with boulders so that children could no longer play "viya" in the waves—what in Laz means body surfing without a board, a word that Koyuncu uses as the title for a CD.[7] The radioactively contaminated tea, which the government declared nonhazardous, also comes up. Shocking images show the extent of the region's pollution, for which Koyuncu criticized both the government and the populace's lack of environmental consciousness and responsibility. Through such intertexts evoked by the music in *The Edge of Heaven* spectators can get a sense of frictions underlying life and artistic expression in the region.

Kazım Koyuncu does not personally appear in *The Edge of Heaven*, but his spirit is nonetheless omnipresent—he is the absent hero of the film. The film's musical leitmotiv, introduced in the prologue, is a love song full of longing in the dialect of the Turkish Black Sea region: "Ben Seni Sevduğumi Dünyalara Bildirdum" ("I Told the World(s) that I Love You"). The inclusion of "the world" in the song's structure of address places the local in a global horizon. As the leitmotif of the film, this song is repeated many times with variations. Shantel (Stefan Hantel), a DJ from Frankfurt who, according to Akın's commentary, specializes in "making ethnic music appealing to Western ears," is responsible for the electronic remix. Shantel is primarily known for his work with Balkan sounds and wind orchestras in a remix style, which he calls "Bukowina Dub." The sound concept for *The Edge of Heaven* involved the sparse use of music and the deployment of classical instruments from the Black Sea region, the bagpipe and *kemenche*. Akın comments: "That sounds very strenuous. He [Shantel] translated it, so to speak, electronically, so that it sounds attractive." Like Akın himself, or Alexander Hacke and Brenna MacCrimmon in his previous films *Head-On* and *Crossing the Bridge*, Stefan Hantel is also a mediator who translates local specifics for an international world music and cinema audience.[8]

The prologue scene at the gas station is repeated near the end of the film. All shots are identical (though embedded in a different context), the same song is playing, but this time a different female voice is singing, even though the gas station attendant again refers to the singer as Kazım Koyuncu. It is indeed his arrangement of the song. The singer in the reiteration, however, is Şevval Sam, who sang the song together with Koyuncu on television. The video recording of this duet (from the television series *Gülbeyaz*) is found in the documentary *I Passed Through with Songs: A Film for Kazım*, as well as on YouTube.[9] It stages the encounter of Şevval Sam and Koyuncu as a meeting of two people from the Black Sea coast, who recognize each other by their dialect, on a bustling street in the big city of Istanbul. The revaluation of regional folklore takes place in an urban context, mediated through music companies like Kalan Müzik, appearances in clubs and at European festivals, as well as on television. The television series *Gülbeyaz* (produced on the private channel Kanal D under the direction of Özer Kızıltan and first aired in 2002), for which Koyuncu arranged the music and in which he also appeared as an actor, contributed greatly to the singer's popularity and made characters from the Black Sea region, as well as their dialect, songs, and customs, familiar to the mainstream audience in Turkey, generating a different kind of empathy than the widespread jokes poking fun at the Laz. As in other countries in Turkey, too, the EU accession process has strengthened interest in regional cultures, which also manifests itself in the growing tourism sector.

Unexpected Kinships

Another extra on the bonus disc of the German-edition DVD is a fragment that was cut out of the main film "for dramaturgical reasons," as Akın explains to us in his commentary, but is nonetheless accessible to the viewer at home on the DVD as the short film *Das Schwarze Meer* (The Black Sea). The song "I Told the World(s) that I Love You," sung by Şevval Sam, plays in an Internet café that Nejat enters. A further version of the musical leitmotif is later heard at night, as he stands alone on a deserted street in the coastal city of Trabzon. Lured by the music, he goes into a bar on the upper level of a building. There Şevval Sam sits on stage with a musician and sings once again the same song, "I Told the World(s) that I Love You." Other than the waiter, no one is in the room. When the song comes to an end, Nejat claps and praises the song as beautiful and "hüzünlü" (sad, melancholy). The singer puts on a jacket with the inscription "Mexico 70" and explains: "Buranın insanı acıyı sever." (People around here love to suffer.) On the way out, she says: "Mesela Bob Dylan. Anneannesinin Trabzon'lu olduğunu biliyor muydun?" (Bob Dylan, for example. Did you know that his maternal grandmother came from Trabzon?) Indeed, one finds the following passage in Bob Dylan's autobiography:

> [My grandmother] lived back in Duluth on the top floor of a duplex on 5th Street. ... She was a dark lady, smoked a pipe. The other side of my family was more light-skinned and fair. My grandmother's voice possessed a haunting accent—face always set in a half-despairing expression. Life for her hadn't been easy. She'd come to America from Odessa, a seaport town in southern Russia. It was a town not unlike Duluth, the same kind of temperament, climate and landscape and right on the edge of a big body of water. Originally, she'd come from Turkey, sailed from Trabzon, a port town, across the Black Sea—the sea that the ancient Greeks called the Euxine—the one that Lord Byron wrote about in *Don Juan*. Her family was from Kagizman, a town in Turkey near the Armenian border, and the family name had been Kirghiz.

(Dylan 2005: 92–93)

The reference to Bob Dylan, and his unexpected connection to the Black Sea, is significant in many regards. For one, it suggestively places the region in a further geographic and historical context and links it to supraregional stories of emigration that lead to the American Midwest. On the other hand, Bob Dylan serves as an internationally known parallel figure for Koyuncu, as both musicians discovered, translated, and arranged regional folk music for the rock stage. This fragment, detached from the feature film, is only found on the bonus disc of the German and Turkish editions of the DVD. In the transfer to the English-language market, the fragment—and with it, an impression of the local specificity—is sacrificed for the sake of universal comprehensibility. The resemblance with Bob Dylan might have been appealing to an American audience, so it is surprising that the American distributor Strand Releasing considered the sequence too insignificant to include on the DVD. In worldwide circulation translatability runs up against its limits (Apter 2006).

The Black Sea, with its six neighboring countries (Turkey, Georgia, Russia, Ukraine, Romania, and Bulgaria), is an important energy transit corridor of strategic significance. The eastern Black Sea was historically the border region to "the Barbarians"; Colchis, the modern-day Georgia, was the homeland of Medea where Jason and the Argonauts seized the Golden Fleece (King 2004; Stephan 2006). During the Cold War, the fronts extended here between the USA in NATO alliance and the Soviet Union. With the admission of Romania and Bulgaria into the European Union at the beginning of 2007, the EU has established a presence on the Black Sea and is attempting to expand its influence in this post-Cold War border and buffer zone. The region is a major hub for the transport of petroleum and natural gas with big pipeline projects in order to reduce shipping congestion on the Bosphorus. In consequence, massive transformations of the landscape and living conditions in the region are in progress (Bellér-Hann and Hann 2001; Hamilton and Mangott 2008). Ursula Biemann's synchronized two-channel video essay *Black Sea Files* (2005), shown as an installation as part of the collaborative visual research project *B-Zone: Becoming Europe and Beyond* at Kunstwerke Berlin in 2005 and, among other places, at the Istanbul Biennial in 2007, strikingly captures life and friction along the Baku-Tbilisi-Ceyhan oil pipeline in scenes featuring workers, engineers, farmers, politicians, and prostitutes. The multi-screen installation staged these "geobodies" along with the transnational infrastructure in the gallery space, inviting viewers to become part of the spatial arrangement.[10]

The closing image of *The Edge of Heaven* depicts Nejat—the professor of German literature from Hamburg, turned bookseller in Istanbul—on the seashore, an image that is echoed in the film's Turkish title *Yaşamın Kıyısında* (literally, "On the Shore of Life").[11] Nejat has been underway in his father's homeland, just as the director Akın himself. The final take where Nejat is seen from behind looking out at the sea, waiting

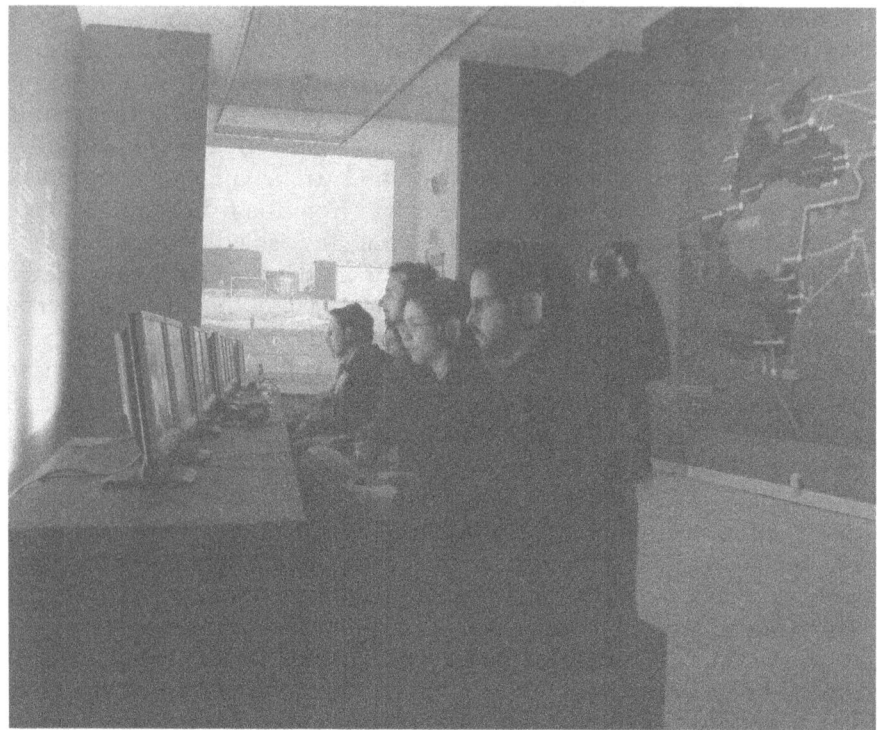

Figure 15.2 Black Sea Files, 2007 installation, Peacock Visual Arts, Aberdeen, courtesy Ursula Biemann

for his father Ali who is out fishing, can be read on the background of the geopolitics around the Black Sea as an ironically distanced gaze at Europe from "the other shore."

The location of the final scene, the village with the green hills of tea plantations and the beach, where Nejat looks at the sea and waits for his father Ali (who is out fishing), resonates with family history for Akın, whose grandparents hailed from this village, Çamburnu. Akın's engagement led him to join the village residents' struggle against a landfill site planned by the government that would be set up in an inoperative copper mine above the village, designed to store the entire trash of the eastern Black Sea region. Akın is said to be working on a documentary film *Der Müll im Garten Eden* (*Garbage in the Garden of Eden*) about the village Çamburnu.[12] The film might translate regional concerns that are also voiced in the filmic portrayal of Koyuncu, *I Passed Through with Songs: A Film for Kazım*, for an international audience. As the documentary *Crossing the Bridge* complements *Head-On*, this documentary on garbage also promises to stand in an intertextual relation to *The Edge of Heaven*, opening up spaces behind the diegetic containment of the film. The ongoing cinematic discovery of the Black Sea region in feature

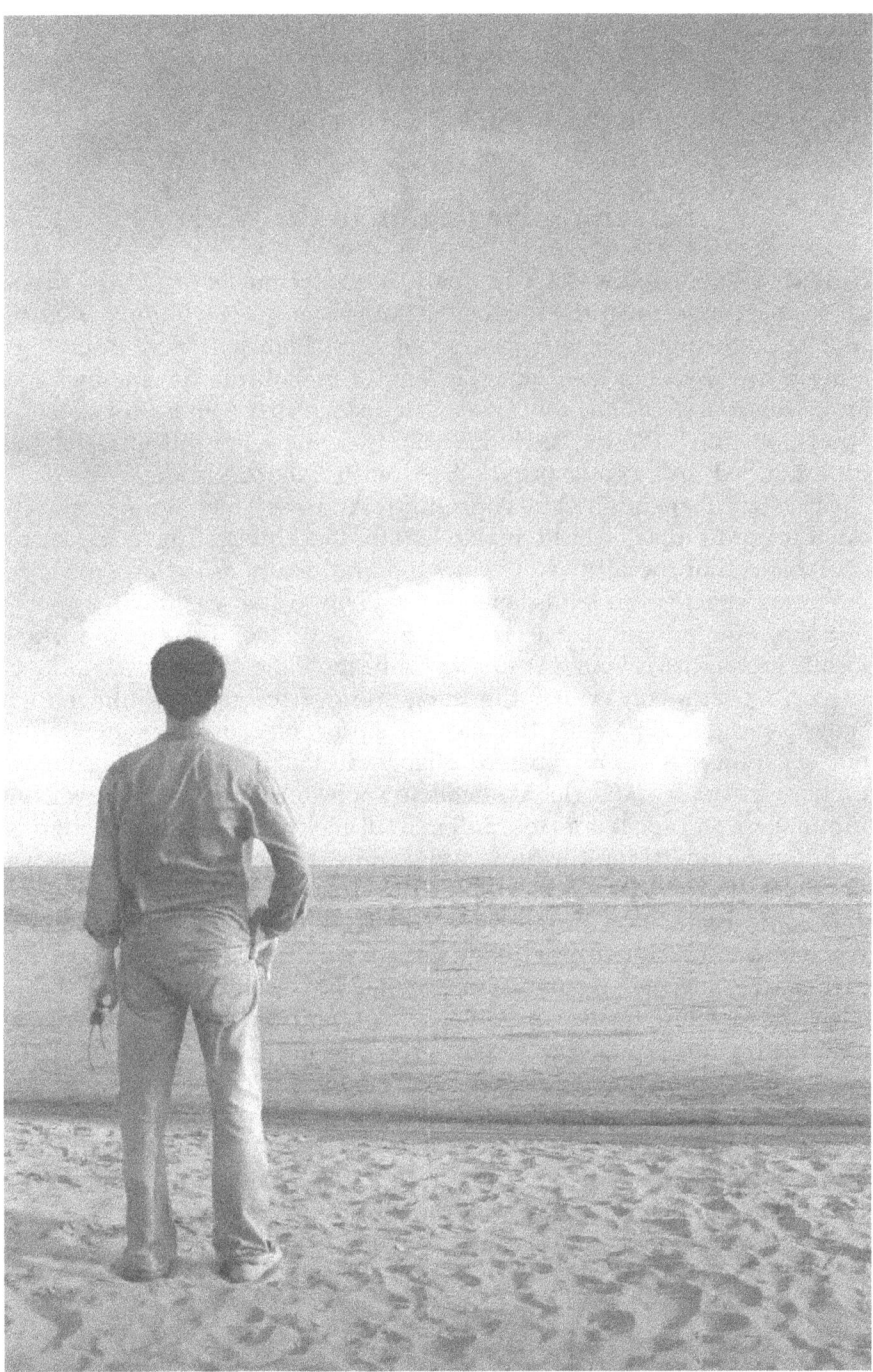

Figure 15.3 Nejat (Baki Davrak) in *The Edge of Heaven*, courtesy corazón international

films such as *Trilogia: To livadi pou dakryzei* (*Trilogy: The Weeping Meadow*, 2004), *Bulutları Beklerken* (*Waiting for the Clouds*, 2003), *Pandora'nın Kutusu* (*Pandora's Box*, 2008), *Sonbahar* (*Autumn*, 2008), *Vavien* (2009), and *Bal* (*Honey*, 2010) adds further texture to such interlaced readings.

Screening the Region in the World

Unlike Alejandro González Iñárritu's melodrama *Babel* (2006), where all stories converge in the fate of the American nuclear family in crisis (not least through the star-casting of Cate Blanchett and Brad Pitt), aiming to raise emotive understanding of global interdependencies in an US audience, *The Edge of Heaven* is a decentralized, more consistently "polyglot film" (Wahl 2005: 139–82) in which not all threads are disentangled and neatly bundled. Alfonso Cuarón's film *Y Tu Mamá También* (2002), mentioned by coproducer Andreas Thiel in his interview on the bonus disc, would make for another interesting comparison on the basis of the attitude toward life and death, as well as the road movie perspective on landscape and the trip to the seaside. In a global horizon, new proximities arise, which extend beyond German Turkish localizations that remain confined within the logic of bounded national spaces. Debates concerning the integration of migrants within nation states or the EU pale in the face of disasters caused by exploding nuclear power stations, uncontrollable destruction, and neocolonial economic exploits. The global effects in such constellations require both filmmakers and spectators to think in multiple frames and new horizons. In order to understand the films and acquire a "sense of place and sense of planet" (Heise 2008), we will need to draw on both textual analysis and contextualization through extradiegetic materials. As multimedia resonances underscore our readings, we might begin to imagine life in border zones or around transnational infrastructures of mobility such as coastal highways and oil pipelines, and thus develop a sense of situated transit. *The Edge of Heaven* promotes not least a meta-reflection on the status of national cinema in a digital age, where localization and delocalization, place-bound specificity and universal comprehensibility overlap in ever varying configurations. Spectators engage in affective affinities and emplacements, and, through the expanded lens of cinema, are able to adopt a fresh look at Europe from the other shore. Indeed, we never know *per se* where we are.

Notes

Earlier versions of this paper were presented at the following conferences: "Film Transnational: Europäische und amerikanische Perspektiven," Universität Göttingen (18–

19 July 2008); "Evenementalisierung der Kultur," Universität Konstanz (10–11 December 2008); "Culture, Politics and Performativity: Cinemas of the Middle East and South Asia," University of California Davis, Middle East/South Asia Studies Program and Film Studies Program (15–16 March 2009), and as an invited lecture at the Center for European Studies of the University of Florida, Gainesville (11 September 2009). I am grateful to the organizers and participants of these events for inspiring discussions. In particular, I would like to thank Nilgün Bayraktar, Peter Krämer, Andreas Langenohl, and Barbara Mennel for reading and commenting on earlier versions of this text. For the published German version, see Ezli (2010). Nicholas Baer helped with translation into English and with good suggestions.

1. See http://worldcinemafoundation.net/filmmakers-board.
2. In his critique of the film in the Turkish daily paper *Cumhuriyet*, Vecdi Sayar writes that Akın views Turkey "from the other side" (play on the German title *Auf der anderen Seite*) and appeals to the bad conscience of Western intellectuals. See Vecdi Sayar, "Cannes'ın Kıyısında," *Cumhuriyet* (25 May 2007), quoted in Dönmez-Colin (2008: 78).
3. *The Edge of Heaven* thus presents a take on Chernobyl as a key reference in our comprehension of the fateful entanglements of globalization. However, rather than confirming Ulrich Beck's theory of globalization as an overbearing force of homogenization, the film compares better to Christa Wolf's narrative *Störfall: Nachrichten eines Tages* (*Accident: A Day's News: A Novel*, 1987), which, like the first version of Beck's essay, was also published shortly after the event. Wolf resists and complicates the homogenizing perception of the overbearing cloud with place-bound experiences, fragmentary personal memories, and intertextual resonances. Life in the modern world thus appears inextricably entangled with news from elsewhere and long-distance communications, despite practical, sensory, and ideational moorings in one place. On Chernobyl and Wolf's book see also Heise (2008: 178–203).
4. Translations from the bonus materials in the following are Nicholas Baer's.
5. http://www.youtube.com/watch?v=dWOjNcDioH0. Ironically, the video sharing site YouTube has been closed in Turkey by a court ruling since 7 March 2007. However, users are finding ways of circumventing the ban.
6. Some of these clips have found over a million viewers on YouTube: http://www.youtube.com/watch?v=5yYx0k08_q0.
7. Kazım Koyuncu. *Viya!* CD. Istanbul: Metropol Müzik, 2001.
8. Stefan Hantel took a liking to Istanbul and shot a music video there, "Disco Partizani," a wild vision of Eastern European presence, migration, and fantastic mobility, which culminates on a flying carpet that sails by a luxury cruise ship: http://www.youtube.com/watch?v=gViaOYgV8yI and http://www.bucovina.de.
9. See http://www.youtube.com/watch?v=Vst61GIt11A.
10. See http://geobodies.org/01_art_and_videos/2005_black_sea_files/.
11. *Yaşamın Kıyısında* also is the Turkish release title for Martin Scorsese's film *Bringing out the Dead* (1999). Fatih Akın emphasized repeatedly that Scorsese has been a role model for him as a filmmaker (Ranze 2002).
12. *Garbage in the Garden of Eden* according to the Internet Movie Database is currently in postproduction: http://www.imdb.com/title/tt1205487 and http://www.fatih4cam burnu.com. See also Seibert (2007) and Brodde and Rigos (2007).

Notes on Contributors

Marco Abel is Associate Professor of English and Film Studies at the University of Nebraska. He is the author of *Violent Affect: Literature, Cinema, and Critique after Representation* (2007), and his publications on contemporary German cinema have appeared or are forthcoming in various anthologies as well as *Quarterly Review of Film and Video*, *New German Critique*, *Cineaste*, and *Senses of Cinema*. He is currently writing a book on the Berlin School (under contract with Camden House), tentatively entitled *The Counter-Cinema of the Berlin School: Redistributing the Sensible*.

Nilgün Bayraktar is an actor, director, and James R. Gray Lecturer at the University of California, Berkeley. She received her PhD in Performance Studies with a Designated Emphasis in Film Studies from UC Berkeley in 2011. In her dissertation "Moving Images Against the Current: The Aesthetics and Geopolitics of (Im)mobility in Contemporary Europe," she studied critical cinematic representations of migration, (im)mobility, and the new border regime in Europe. Bayraktar has been teaching classes on migrant and diasporic cinema, European cinema, Iranian cinema, Turkish cinema, road movies, and aesthetics of mobility at UC Berkeley since 2007. Her academic publications include articles on coup d'état novels, migrant cinema, and contemporary art. In 2010, she was the recipient of a *European Union Center of Excellence Research Grant*.

Daniela Berghahn is Professor in Film Studies in the Media Arts Department at Royal Holloway, University of London. She is the author of *Raumdarstellung im englischen Roman der Moderne* (1989) and *Hollywood Behind the Wall: The Cinema of East Germany* (2005). Her coedited books include *Unity and Diversity in the New Europe* (2000) and *Millennial Essays on Film and Other German Studies* (2002). She led an AHRC-funded international Research Network on "Migrant and Diasporic Cinema in Contemporary Europe" (www.migrantcinema.net), the findings of which were published in the anthology *European Cinema in Motion: Migrant and Diasporic Film in Contemporary Europe* (with Claudia Sternberg, 2010) and in a special issue of *New Cinemas*, "Turkish German Dialogues on Screen" (2009). She subsequently held an AHRC Research Fellowship for a project on The Diasporic Family in Cinema (www.farflungfamilies.net) and is currently completing a monograph entitled *Far-flung Families in Film: The Diasporic Family in Contemporary European Cinema* (forthcoming with Edinburgh University Press).

Mine Eren received a MA in *Deutsch als Fremdsprache* from the Ludwig Maximilian University and her MA and PhD in German Studies from Brown University. She is Associate Professor of German and Director of the Film Studies Program at Randolph-Macon College in Ashland, Virginia. She has organized film festivals to introduce the work by Turkish German and other ethnic film directors to an American audience. She has essays included in the collection *Moving Pictures, Traveling Identities: Migration, Exile, and Border Crossings* (2003) and in the *Biographical Encyclopedia of the Modern Middle East* (2007), of which she is also the associate editor. Her current book project examines the impact of the 1960s on Turkish German culture and cinema.

Angelica Fenner is Associate Professor of German and Cinema Studies at the University of Toronto. She is author of *Race under Reconstruction in German Cinema: Robert Stemmle's* Toxi (2011), coeditor of *Fascism and Neofascism: Critical Writings on the Radical Right in Europe* (2004), and currently coediting the anthology *The Autobiographical Turn in German Documentary and Experimental Film*. She has also published on the representational politics of transnational migration and cultural displacement in the journals *Camera Obscura, Cine-Action, Feminist Media Studies*, and *Women in German*, and in the anthologies *Moving Pictures, Traveling Identities: Migration, Exile, and Border Crossings* (2003), *Fascism and Neofascism* (2004) and *The Cinema of Me: Self and Subjectivity in First-Person Documentary Film* (2012).

Deniz Göktürk is Associate Professor in the Departments of German and Film & Media at the University of California, Berkeley. Publications include a book on literary and cinematic imaginations of America in early twentieth-century German culture. She is coeditor of *The German Cinema Book* (2002, with Tim Bergfelder and Erica Carter), *Germany in Transit: Nation and Migration, 1955–2005* (2007, with David Gramling and Anton Kaes, updated German edition in 2011 as *Transit Deutschland: Debatten zu Nation und Migration*), and *Orienting Istanbul: Cultural Capital of Europe?* (2010, with Levent Soysal and Ipek Türeli). Her work on Turkish German cinema has been trend-setting in unsettling framings of minority cinema and introducing a focus on staging, performance, and transnational mobility. She also published translations from Turkish literature. Her current book projects are: "Transient Archives: A Short History of Migration in the Digital Age" and "Uniformed Identity: Transnational Perspectives on Comedy and Community."

David Gramling is Assistant Professor and ACLS New Faculty Fellow in the Department of German Studies at the University of Arizona in Tucson. He received his PhD in German Literature and Culture from the University of California, Berkeley in 2008. With publications on Primo Levi, Fatih Akın, Emine Sevgi Özdamar, and Orhan Pamuk, his recent work highlights the productive conflict of interest between monolingual textuality and a multilingual world. His current book project, *The Invention of Monolingualism*, proposes new theoretical approaches to literary monolingualism, as it developed from the Enlightenment period to twenty-first century migration fiction and film.

Berna Gueneli is Assistant Professor of German Studies at Grinnell College. She received her PhD in Germanic Studies at the University of Texas at Austin (2011) with a dissertation on Fatih Akın's cinema and his aesthetics of heterogeneity in the spatial, aural, and visual construction of Europe. Her research interests comprise contemporary transnational cinema in a European context, German film history, Weimar and German exile cinema, film sound, as well as Turkish German studies.

Sabine Hake is the Texas Chair of German Literature and Culture at the University of Texas at Austin. She is the author of six books, including *German National Cinema* (2008, second revised edition), *Topographies of Class: Modern Architecture and Mass Society in Weimar Berlin* (2008), and *Screen Nazis: Cinema, History, and Democracy* (2012) and has published numerous articles and edited volumes on German film and Weimar culture. Her new book project is tentatively titled "Fragments of a Cultural History of the German Proletariat."

Randall Halle is the Klaus W. Jonas Professor of German Film and Cultural Studies at the University of Pittsburgh. He is the author of numerous essays and is the coeditor of *After the Avant-Garde* (2008), *Light Motives: German Popular Film in Perspective* (2003), and the double special issue of *Camera Obscura* on "Marginality and Alterity in Contemporary European Cinema" (44 and 46). His most recent book is *German Film after Germany: Toward a Transnational Aesthetic* (2008). Professor Halle is currently working on a project tentatively entitled *Interzone Europe: Social Philosophy and the Transnational Imagination*.

Roger Hillman is Associate Professor of Film Studies and German Studies at the Australian National University, Canberra. Book publications include *Unsettling Scores: German Film, Music, and Ideology* (2005) and (coauthored) *Transkulturalität: Türkisch-deutsche Konstellationen in Literatur und Film* (2007). Other research interests include European cinema, and film and music more generally.

Karolin Machtans is Assistant Professor of German Studies at Connecticut College in New London. Her main interests are post-1945 German literature and film. Her first book, *Zwischen Wissenschaft und autobiographischem Text: Saul Friedländer und Ruth Klüger*, was published by Niemeyer (Conditio Judaica) in 2009. She is the coeditor of a volume on *Hitler in German Film* (2012) and is currently working on a book-length study on the representation of Istanbul in German-language literature and film.

Ingeborg Majer-O'Sickey is Associate Professor of German, Comparative Literature, and Women's Studies at the State University of New York at Binghamton. Publications include *Triangulated Visions: Women in Recent German Cinema* (1998, with Ingeborg von Zadow), *Riefenstahl Screened: An Anthology of New Criticism* (2008, with Neil Christian Pages and Mary Rhiel), and articles on contemporary German film. Her current work deals with issues of gender and *Heimat* in postwar German cinema.

Barbara Mennel is Associate Professor of German Studies and Film and Media Studies at the University of Florida, Gainesville. She is author of *The Representation of Masochism and Queer Desire in Film and Literature* (2007), *Cities and Cinema* (2008), and *Queer Cinema: Schoolgirls, Vampires, and Gay Cowboys* (2012). She coedited S*patial Turns: Space, Place, and Mobility in German Literature and Visual Culture* with Jaimey Fisher (2010). Her current book project, tentatively titled "Reproducing Europe," addresses women, labor, and migration in the films of the New Europe.

Brent Peterson is Professor of German and Chair of the German Department at Lawrence University. Numerous articles and his two books, *Popular Narratives and Ethnic Identity* (1991) and *History, Fiction and Germany* (2005), deal with the construction and consumption of identity myths, and he has recently turned his attention to minorities in Germany. In the summers of 2010 and 2012, he codirected a NEH Summer Seminar in Berlin entitled "Germany's Cosmopolitan Capital: Berlin and the Myth of German Monoculturalism."

Brad Prager is Associate Professor of German and a member of the Program in Film Studies at the University of Missouri. He is the author of *The Cinema of Werner Herzog: Aesthetic Ecstasy and Truth* (2007) and *Aesthetic Vision and German Romanticism: Writing Images* (2007). He is the editor of *A Companion to Werner Herzog* (2012) and the coeditor of a volume on Visual Studies and the Holocaust entitled *Visualizing the Holocaust: Documents, Aesthetics, Memory* (2008), as well as of a volume on contemporary German cinema entitled *The Collapse of the Conventional: German Cinema and its Politics at the Turn of the Twenty-First Century* (2010).

Vivien Silvey is a PhD candidate at the Australian National University. Her research focus is on network narratives and comparative studies in world cinema. In 2010 she presented papers on this topic at conferences in Cork and Stirling and at the NECS conference held in Istanbul. *GFL* published the article "Akin's *Auf der anderen Seite* (*The Edge of Heaven*) and the Widening Periphery" in 2011, which she coauthored with Roger Hillman.

Ayça Tunç Cox is an Assistant Professor of Film Studies in the Industrial Design Department, Faculty of Architecture at the İzmir Institute of Technology. She completed her fully funded PhD at Royal Holloway, University of London with a dissertation entitled *Diasporic Cinema: Turkish-German Filmmakers with Particular Emphasis on Generational Differences*. She received her MA from Ege University with a thesis on *Independent Cinema: Alternative Tendencies in Turkish Cinema in the 1990s*. She worked as a Research Assistant at Ege University for ten years and as a visiting member of the teaching staff in the Media Arts Department at Royal Holloway between 2008 and 2010. Among her research interests are transnational cinema, diasporic cinema, national cinemas, European cinema, independent and alternative cinema, and new Turkish cinema. She has published several articles and two book chapters on cinema, and has made many short films.

Works Cited

Abu-Lughod, Lila. 2002. "Do Muslim Women Really Need Saving?" *American Anthropologist* 1043: 783–90.
Ackermann, Irmgard and Harald Weinrich, eds. 1986. *Eine nicht nur deutsche Literatur: Zur Standortbestimmung der "Ausländerliteratur."* Munich: Piper.
Adaklı, Gülseren. 2003. "Türk Basınından Türk Medyasına: Hakim Medya Gruplarının Kısa Tarihi." http://www.barikat-lar.de/gorusler/medya20.htm.
Adaklı, Gülseren. 2006. "Yeni Hegemonya Köşe Yazarlarına Çok Şey Borçlu." *Sol Dergisi*. 25 June. http://arsiv.sol.org.tr/?yazino=884.
Adelson, Leslie A. 2001. "Against Between: A Manifesto." In *Unpacking Europe: Towards a Critical Reading*, ed. by Salah Hassan and Iftikhar Dadi, 244–55. Rotterdam: NAi Publishers.
Adelson, Leslie A. 2005. *The Turkish Turn in Contemporary German Literature: Toward a New Critical Grammar of Migration*. New York: Palgrave.
Adorjan, Johanna. 2004. "Es ist mein Leben: Sibel Kekilli im Interview." *Frankfurter Allgemeine Zeitung Online*. http://www.faz.net/s/Rub8A25A66CA9514B9892E0074EDE4E5AFA/Doc~E6C3D32F5ED9D4A4CB29E01DC0E61F072~ATpl~Ecommon~Scontent.html.
Akça, Kerem. 2008. "Fatih Akın'la Çalışmak Özgürlük." *Radikal*. http://www.radikal.com.tr/Radikal.aspx?aType=RadikalHaberDetay&ArticleID=881134&Date=2.6.2008&CategoryID=113.
Alanyali, Iris. 2004. "Jetzt bloß nicht romantisch werden: Fatih Akin lässt seine Helden *Gegen die Wand* fahren. Und damit beginnt für sie das Leben." *Welt Online*. 10 March. http://www.welt.de/print-welt/article298924/Jetzt_bloss_nicht_romantisch_werden.html.
Allan, Seán. 1997. "'Der Herr aber, dessen Leib du begehrst, vergab seinem Feind': The Problem of Revenge in Kleist's *Michael Kohlhaas*." *Modern Language Review* 92.3: 630–42.
Altaylı, Fatih. 2004. "Pornocu Pornocu mu Kalmalı." *Hürriyet*. http://arama.hurriyet.com.tr/arsivnews.aspx?id=207979.
Alter, Nora. 2002. *Projecting History: German Nonfiction Cinema 1967–2000*. Ann Arbor: University of Michigan Press.
Anderson, Amanda. 2001. *The Powers of Distance: Cosmopolitanism and the Cultivation of Detachment*. Princeton, NJ: Princeton University Press.

Anderson, Benedict. 1983. *Imagined Communities: Reflections on the Origin and Spread of Nationalism*. London: Verso.
Appadurai, Arjun. 1996. *Modernity at Large: Cultural Dimensions of Globalization*. Minneapolis: University of Minnesota Press.
Appiah, Kwame Anthony. 2006. *Cosmopolitanism: Ethics in a World of Strangers*. New York: W. W. Norton.
Apter, Emily. 2006. *The Translation Zone: A New Comparative Literature*. Princeton, NJ: Princeton University Press.
ARD 2011a. "Abschied von Cenk Batu." *DasErste*. http://www.daserste.de/tatort/beitrag_dyn~uid,njh6dw1q4m9awz8h~cm.asp.
ARD 2011b. "Ein Stern für den Hamburger NDR-Tatort." *DasErste*. http://www.daserste.de/tatort/beitrag.asp?uid=drkpc5s1jah0wo3v.
ARD 2011c. "Verdeckter Ermittler in Hamburg (NDR): Mehmet Kurtuluş als Hauptkommissar Cenk Batu." *DasErste*. http://www.daserste.de/tatort/teams.asp?iid=7.
Arslan, Savaş. 2006. "Head-on Head-off: How the Media Covered a Former Porn Actress's Rise to Stardom." *Film International* 36.6: 62–71.
Arslan, Thomas. 2004. "Löcher." *Film-Dienst* 23: 16.
Ascherson, Neal. 1995. *Black Sea*. New York: Hill and Wang.
Aust, Michael. 2006. "Wie tolerant bist du? Regisseur Züli Aladag über seinen provozierenden Fernsehfilm." *Kölner Stadt-Anzeiger*. 26 September. http://www.ksta.de/html/artikel/1157542205925.shtml.
Bade, Klaus and Gunilla Fincke, eds. 2010. *Einwanderungsgesellschaft 2010: Jahresgutachten 2010 mit Integrationsbarometer*. Berlin: Sachverständigenrat deutscher Stiftungen für Integration und Migration.
Baer, Nicholas. 2008. "Points of Entanglement: The Overdetermination of German Space and Identity in *Lola + Bilidikid* and *Walk on Water*." *Transit: A Journal of Travel, Migration and Multiculturalism in the German-speaking World*. http://german.berkeley.edu/transit/2008/articles/baer.htm.
Barthes, Roland. 1973. *Mythologies*. Trans. Annette Lavers. New York: Hill and Wang.
Başutçu, Mesut. 1986a. "Tevfik Başer Altın Kamera'ya Aday." *Cumhuriyet*. 16 May.
Başutçu, Mesut. 1986b. "Tevfik Başer Ödülü Kıl Payı Kaçırdı." *Cumhuriyet*. 31 May.
Başutçu, Mesut. 2004. "Sıradan İnsanlar Önemli." *Radikal*. http://www.radikal.com.tr/Radikal.aspx?aType=RadikalHaberDetay&ArticleID=719599&Date=16.8.2004&CategoryID=113.
Bauer, Edda. 2005. "Mischung aus Zufall und Instinkt." *Kölner Stadt-Anzeiger Online*. 10 June. http://www.ksta.de/html/artikel/1118069710765.shtml.
Baykal, Emre. 2008. *Kutluğ Ataman Sen Zaten Kendini Anlat/ You Tell Me About Yourself Anyway!* Istanbul: Yapı Kredi Yayınları.
Beck, Ulrich. 1986. *Risikogesellschaft: Auf dem Weg in eine andere Moderne*. Frankfurt am Main: Suhrkamp Verlag.

Beck, Ulrich. 1995. "Anthropological Shock: Chernobyl and the Contours of the Risk Society." In *Ecological Enlightenment: Essays on the Politics of the Risk Society*, 63–76. Trans. John Torpey. Atlantic Highlands, NJ: Humanities Press.
Beck, Ulrich. 2006. *The Cosmopolitan Vision*. Cambridge: Polity.
Behn, Manfred, ed. 1994. *Schwarzer Traum und weiße Sklavin: Deutschdänische Filmbeziehungen 1910–1930*. Munich: edition text + kritik.
Behrens, Volker. 2005. "Soundtrack einer Stadt: *Crossing the Bridge*, Akins Liebeserklärung an 'sein' Istanbul." *Hamburger Abendblatt Online*. 9 June. http://www.abendblatt.de/kultur-live/kino/article746936/Soundtrack-einer-Stadt.html.
Behrens, Volker. 2009. "Filmregisseur Fatih Akin über *Soul Kitchen*: Helden verteidigen ihre Heimat." *Kieler Nachrichten Online*. 22 September. http://www.kn-online.de/schleswig_holstein/kultur/114413-Filmregisseur-Fatih-Akin-ueber-Soul-Kitchen-Helden-verteidigen-ihre-Heimat.html.
Beier, Lars-Olav. 2004. "Berlinale-Tagebuch: Gehört Plappern zum Handwerk?" *Spiegel Online*. 12 February. http://www.spiegel.de/kultur/kino/0,1518,286103,00.html.
Beier, Lars-Olav. 2011. "Mach uns den Schimanski, Til!" *Spiegel Online*. http://www.spiegel.de/kultur/tv/0,1518,798614,00.html.
Beier, Lars-Olav and Matthias Matussek. 2007. "'Erst mit zwei Frauen wurde die Geschichte sexy.'" *Spiegel Online*. 26 September. http://www.spiegel.de/kultur/kino/0,1518,507996,00.html.
Bek, Mine Gencel. 2009. "The Effects of the Membership Processes of the European Union on Media Policies in Turkey." In *Media, Democracy and European Culture*, ed. by Ib Bondebjerg and Peter Madsen, 325–38. Lanham, MD: Intellect Books.
Bek, Müge G. 2004. "Research Note: Tabloidization of News Media." *European Journal of Communication* 19.3: 371–86.
Belge, Murat. 1983. "Cumhuriyet Döneminde Batılılaşma." *Cumhuriyet Dönemi Türkiye Ansiklopedisi*. Volume 1. Istanbul: İletişim Yayınları.
Belge, Murat. 2003. *Yaklaştıkça Uzaklaşıyor mu? Avrupa Birliği ve Türkiye*. Istanbul: Birikim Yayınları.
Bellér-Hann, Ildikó and Chris Hann. 2001. *Turkish Region: State, Market, and Social Identities on the East Black Sea Coast*. Santa Fe, NM: School for American Research Press.
Berger, Christopher. 2009. "A Reluctant Figure of Integration: *Tatort*-Inspector Mehmet Kurtulus." Radio and TV–Formats–Goethe Institute. http://www.goethe.de/wis/med/rtv/for/en4176359.htm.
Bergfelder, Tim. 2005. "National, Transnational or Supranational Cinema? Rethinking European Film Studies." *Media, Culture & Society* 27.3: 315–31.
Bergfelder, Tim, Erica Carter, and Deniz Göktürk, eds. 2008. *The German Cinema Book*. London: British Film Institute.

Berghahn, Daniela. 2006. "No Place Like Home? Or Impossible Homecomings in the Films of Fatih Akin." *New Cinemas* 4.3: 141–58.
Berghahn, Daniela. 2009. "From Turkish Greengrocer to Drag Queen: Reassessing Patriarchy in Recent Turkish–German Coming-of-Age Films." *New Cinemas: Journal of Contemporary Film* 7.1: 55–69.
Berghahn, Daniela and Claudia Sternberg, eds. 2010. *European Cinema in Motion: Migrant and Diasporic Film in Contemporary Europe*. New York: Palgrave.
Berliner Kurier. 2005. "Musste Hatun sterben, weil sie ihren Mann verlassen hatte?" 9 February.
Berliner Zeitung. 2005. "Hinrichtung auf offener Straße." 9 February.
Beyer, Tom. 1998. "*Kurz und schmerzlos.*" *Schnitt Online*. April. http://www.schnitt.de/202,1970,01.
Bhabha, Homi K. 1983. "The Other Question." *Screen* 24.6: 18–36.
Bhabha, Homi K. 1990. "DissemiNation: Time, Narrative, and the Margins of the Modern Nation." In *Nation and Narration*, ed. by Homi K. Bhabha, 291–322. London: Routledge.
Bhabha, Homi K. 1994. *The Location of Culture*. London: Routledge.
Billig, Michael. 1995. *Banal Nationalism*. London: Sage Publications.
Blieswood, David. 2007. "Oscar für den Hamburger Fatih Akin?" *Bild Online*. 25 September. http://www.bild.de/BTO/leute/kino-tv/kinoprogramm/2007/09/27/auf-der-anderen-seite,geo=2554936.html.
Bogle, Donald. 1989. *Toms, Coons, Mulatos, Mammies, and Bucks: An Interpretive History of Blacks in American Films*. New York: Continuum.
Bonfadelli, Heinz et al., eds. 2008. *Jugend, Medien und Migration empirische Ergebnisse und Perspektiven*. Wiesbaden: VS Verlag für Sozialwissenschaft.
Boran, Erol. 2005. "Faces of Contemporary Turkish-German Kabarett—Probing the New Millennium." *Text & Presentation: Journal of the Comparative Drama Conference* 25: 172–86.
Borcholte, Andreas. 2007. "Fatih Fassbinder." *Spiegel Online*. 23 May. http://www.spiegel.de/kultur/kino/0,1518,484552,00.html.
Borcholte, Andreas. 2009. "Ich hatte Bock zu lachen." *Spiegel Online*. 23 December. http://www.spiegel.de/kultur/kino/0,1518,668682,00.html.
Bordwell, David. 2003. "Authorship and Narration in Art Cinema." In *Film and Authorship*, ed. by Virginia Wright Wexman, 42–49. New Brunswick, NJ: Rutgers University Press.
Bordwell, David, Janet Staiger, and Kristin Thompson. 1985. *The Classical Hollywood Cinema: Film Style & Mode of Production to 1960*. New York: Columbia University Press.
Boym, Svetlana. 2001. *The Future of Nostalgia*. New York: Basic Books.
Braziel, Jana Evans and Anita Mannur. 2003. *Theorizing Diaspora: A Reader*. Malden, MA: Blackwell Publishers.
Brockmann, Stephen. 2010. *A Critical History of German Film*. Rochester, NY: Camden House.

Brodde, Kirsten and Alexandra Rigos. 2007. "Die Türkei ist so liberal wie nie." Interview with Fatih Akın. *greenpeace magazin*. 5.07. http://www.greenpeace-magazin.de/index.php?id=2559&no_cache=1&sword_list[]=akin.
Brooks, Peter. 1995. *The Melodramatic Imagination: Balzac, Henry James, Melodrama, and the Mode of Excess*. New Haven, CT: Yale University Press.
Brück, Ingrid, Andrea Guder, Reinhold Viehoff, and Karin When. 2000. "Abschlußbericht: Das Kriminalsujet im ost-, west- und gesamtdeutschen Fernsehen: Die Programmgeschichte des deutschen Fernsehkrimis." http://server4.medienkomm.uni-halle.de/krimi/theorie/forschungsprojekt/abschlussbericht-krimiprojekt.pdf.
Buder, Bernd. 2008. "Turkish Flavour: Bewegung in Deutschlands 'türkischer' Blockbuster-Verleiherszene." *Film-Dienst* 4: 11.
Buder, Bernd. 2009. "Süper Agent K 9." *Der Freitag*. 20 January. http://www.freitag.de/kultur/0913-tuerkei-film-kommerzkino.
Buhre, Jakob. 2002. "Ich könnte gar keine Filme machen, die keinen persönlichen Bezug zu mir haben." Interview with Fatih Akın. *Planet Interview*. 16 October. http://www.planet-interview.de/fatih-akin-16102002.html.
Burns, Rob. 2006. "Turkish-German Cinema: From Cultural Resistance to Transnational Cinema?" In *German Cinema Since Unification*, ed. by David Clarke, 127–50. London and New York: Continuum.
Burns, Rob. 2007a. "The Politics of Cultural Representation: Turkish-German Encounters." *German Politics* 16.3: 358–78.
Burns, Rob. 2007b. "Towards a Cinema of Cultural Hybridity: Turkish-German Filmmakers and the Representation of Alterity." *Debatte* 15.1: 3–24.
Busche, Andreas. 2004. "Punk oder türkische Folklore? Fatih Akins Film *Gegen die Wand* rockt gegen alle kulturellen Zuschreibungen an." *Zeit Online*. 11 March. http://www.zeit.de/2004/12/Gegen_die_Wand.
Buß, Christian. 2007. "Jedem seine eigene Heimat." *Spiegel Online*. 25 September. http://www.spiegel.de/kultur/kino/0,1518,507815,00.html.
Buß, Christian. 2010. "Schrecken, ganz ohne Schleier." *Spiegel Online*. 10 March. http://www.spiegel.de/kultur/kino/0,1518,682504,00.html.
Butler, Judith. 1990. *Gender Trouble: Feminism and the Subversion of Identity*. London: Routledge.
Butterwegge, Christoph. 2006. *Massenmedien, Migration und Integration: Herausforderungen für Journalismus und politische Bildung*. Wiesbaden: VS Verlag für Sozialwissenschaft.
Çağlar, Ayşe. 2004. "Mediascapes, Advertisement Industries and Cosmopolitan Transformations: German Turks in Germany." *New German Critique* 92: 39–61.
Çarkoğlu, Ali. 2003. "Who Wants Full Membership? Characteristics of Turkish Public Support for EU Membership." *Turkish Studies* 4.1: 171–94.

Casarino, Cesare and Antonio Negri. 2008. *In Praise of the Common: A Conversation on Philosophy and Politics*. Minneapolis: University of Minnesota Press.
Cheesman, Tom. 2002. "Akçam—Zaimoğlu—'Kanak Attak': Turkish Lives and Letters in German." *German Life and Letters* 55.2: 180–95.
Cheesman, Tom. 2007. *Novels of Turkish German Settlement: Cosmopolite Fictions*. Rochester, NY: Camden House.
Chiellino, Carmine. 2007. *Interkulturelle Literatur in Deutschland: Ein Handbuch*. Stuttgart: Metzler.
Chin, Rita. 2007. *The Guestworker Question in Postwar Germany*. Cambridge: Cambridge University Press.
Christensen, Christian. 2007. "Concentration of Ownership, the Fall of Unions and Government Legislation in Turkey." *Global Media and Communication* 3.2: 179–99.
Çil, Nevim. 2007. *Topographie des Außenseiters: Türkische Generationen und der deutsch-deutsche Wiedervereinigungsprozess*. Berlin: Verlag Hans Schiler.
Clark, Christopher. 2006. "Transculturation, Transe Sexuality, and Turkish Germany: Kutluğ Ataman's *Lola und Bilidikid*." *German Life & Letters* 59: 555–72.
Conquergood, Dwight. 2002. "Performance Studies: Interventions and Radical Research." *TDR / The Drama Review* 46.2: 145–53.
Corriere della Sera. 2011. "Birol Ünel: Il Kinski turco." http://cinema-tv.corriere.it/personaggi/birol-220-nel/04_03_93.shtml.
Cowie, Elizabeth. 2009. "On Documentary Sounds and Images in the Gallery." *Screen* 50.1: 124–34.
Crary, Jonathan. 2003. "Foreword." In *Installation Art in the New Millennium: The Empire of the Senses*, ed. by Nicolas De Oliveira, Nicola Oxley, and Michael Perry, 4–9. New York: Thames & Hudson.
Cresswell, Tim. 2004. *Place: A Short Introduction*. Oxford: Blackwell.
Cumhuriyet. 1991. "Tevfik Başer Cannes'da." 20 March.
Cumhuriyet. 2009. "Duvara Karşıya Avrupa'dan Ödül." http://www.cumhuriyet.com.tr/?im=yhs&hn=37168.
Curtis, Robin. 2006. *Conscientious Viscerality: The Autobiographical Stance in German Film and Video*. Berlin: Edition Imorde.
Darendeli, Vahap. 2007. "Medya, Yoğunlaşması Tekelleşmenin Denetimi ve Çoğulculuğun Kurulması." *Türkiye Barolar Birliği Dergisi* 68. http://www.rtuk.org.tr/sayfalar/IcerikGoster.aspx?icerik_id=0977101d-4e81-4e87-a3bb-6f2e10388fd5.
Davies, Rebecca. 2007. "Reconceptualising the Migration-Development Nexus: Diasporas, Globalization and the Politics of Exclusion." *Third World Quarterly* 28.1: 59–76.
De Certeau, Michel. 1984. *The Practice of Everyday Life*. Trans. Steven Rendall. Berkeley: University of California Press.
De Lauretis, Teresa. 1984. *Alice Doesn't: Feminism, Semiotics, Cinema*. Bloomington: Indiana University Press.

De Lauretis, Teresa. 1987. *Technologies of Gender*. Bloomington: Indiana University Press.
Deleuze, Gilles. 1978. "Deleuze/Spinoza: Cours Vincennes 24/01/1978." Trans. Timothy S. Murphy. http://www.webdeleuze.com/php/texte.php?cle=14&groupe=Spinoza&langue=2.
Deleuze, Gilles. 1989. *Cinema 2: The Time-Image*. Trans. Hugh Tomlinson. Minneapolis: University of Minnesota Press.
Deleuze, Gilles and Félix Guattari. 2007. *A Thousand Plateaus: Capitalism and Schizophrenia*. Vol. 2. Trans. Brian Massumi. Minneapolis: University of Minnesota Press.
Demirhan, Mehmet. 2008. "The Eurimages Experience: Case Study of a Turkish Co-production Supported by Eurimages." *Euromed Audiovisual*. http://www.euromedaudiovisuel.net/Files/2008/07/10/1215713135121.pdf.
Derin, Seyhan. 2010. "No Money, No Movie." *Studies in European Cinema* 7.1: 25–27.
Desai, Jigna. 2004. *Beyond Bollywood: The Cultural Politics of South Asian Diasporic Film*. London: Routledge.
Deshpande, Shekhar. 2010. "Anthology Films in European Cinema: New Frontiers of Collective Identities." *Studies in European Cinema* 7.1: 77–88.
Distelmeyer, Jan, ed. 2006. *Spaß beiseite, Film ab: Jüdischer Humor und verdrängendes Lachen in der Filmkomödie bis 1945*. Munich: edition text + kritik.
Doane, Mary Ann. 1986. "The Voice in the Cinema: The Articulation of Body and Space." In *Narrative, Apparatus, Ideology*, ed. by Philip Rosen, 335–48. New York: Columbia University Press.
Doane, Mary Ann. 2000. "Film and the Masquerade: Theorizing the Female Spectator." In *Feminism and Film*, ed. by E. Ann Kaplan, 418–36. Oxford: Oxford University Press.
Doane, Mary Ann, Patricia Mellencamp, and Linda Williams, eds. 1984. *Re-vision: Essays in Feminist Film Criticism*. Frederick, MD: University Publications of America and the American Film Institute.
Doğan, Yalçın. 2004. "Kekilli'ye Haçlı Seferi." *Hürriyet*. http://arama.hurriyet.com.tr/arsivnews.aspx?id=207560.
Dönmez-Colin, Gönül. 2008. *Turkish Cinema: Identity, Distance and Belonging*. London: Reaktion.
Dorsay, Atilla. 1986. "Türklerin Sorunlarını İki Odalı Bir Evde Anlattım." *Cumhuriyet*. 25 May.
Dorsay, Atilla. 1989. "Şenlikte Türkler Var mı Yok mu?" *Cumhuriyet*. 17 February.
Dorsay, Atilla. 1991a. "Berlin'de Kadın Yüzleri." *Cumhuriyet*. 17 May.
Dorsay, Atilla. 1991b. "Alkışlar Yuhlara Karıştı." *Cumhuriyet*. 24 May.
Dürr, Anke and Marianne Wellershoff. 2005. "Unsere Zeit ist zu unpolitisch." *Spiegel Online*. 6 June. http://www.spiegel.de/spiegel/print/d-40630230.html.

Dyer, Richard. 1998. *Stars*. London: BFI Publishing.
Dylan, Bob. 2005. *Chronicles*. Vol. 1. New York: Simon & Schuster.
Eakin, Paul John. 1999. *How Our Lives Becomes Stories: Making Selves*. Ithaca, NY: Cornell University Press.
Early, Gerald. 1998. "Pulp and Circumstance: The Story of Jazz in High Places." In *The Jazz Cadence of American Culture*, ed. by Robert G. O'Meally, 393–430. New York: Columbia University Press.
Eken, Ali Nihat. 2009. *Representations of Turkish Immigrants in Turkish-German Cinema: Tevfik Başer's "40 Square Meters of Germany" and Fatih Akın's "Head-On."* Saarbrücken: Verlag Dr. Müller.
Elsaesser, Thomas. 2005. "Double Occupancy and Small Adjustments: Space, Place and Policy in the New European Cinema since the 1990s." In *European Cinema: Face to Face with Hollywood*, ed. by Thomas Elsaesser, 108–30. Amsterdam: Amsterdam University Press.
Erdem, Kutay and Ruth Ä. Schmidt. 2008. "Ethnic Marketing for Turks in Germany." *International Journal of Retail & Distribution Management* 36.3: 212–23.
Erdoğan, İrfan. 2007. *Türkiye'de Gazetecilik ve Bilim İletişimi*. Ankara: Pozitif Matbaacılık.
Erdoğan, Nezih. 2009. "Star Director as Symptom: Reflections on the Reception of Fatih Akın in the Turkish Media." *New Cinemas: Journal of Contemporary Film* 7.1: 27–38.
Eren, Hasibe and Orkun Yeşim. 2001. "Gercek Evi Türk" (His Real Home is Turkish). *Cumhuriyet*: 7. 22 April.
Eren, Mine. 2003. "Traveling Pictures from a Turkish Daughter: Seyhan Derin's *Ben annemin kızıyım–I'm My Mother's Daughter*." In *Moving Pictures, Migrating Identities*, ed. by Eva Rueschmann, 39–54. Jackson: University Press of Mississippi.
Eren, Mine. 2013. "Breaking the Stigma? The Anti-heroine in Fatih Akın's *Head On*." In *Contested Imaginaries: Reading Muslim Women and Muslim Women Reading Back: Transnational Feminist Reading Practices, Pedagogy and Ethical Concerns*, ed. by Lisa Taylor and Jasmin Zine. New York: Palgrave. (forthcoming)
Erol, Mehmet S. and Ertan Efegil. 2007. *Türkiye AB İlişkileri: Dış Politika ve İç Yapı Sorunsalları*. Ankara: Alp Yayınları.
Everett, Anna. 2003. "Digitextuality and Click Theory: Theses on Convergence Media in the Digital Age." In *New Media: Theories and Practices of Digitextuality*, ed. by Anna Everett and John T. Caldwell, 3–28. London: Routledge.
Ewing, Katherine Pratt. "Between Cinema and Social Work: Diasporic Turkish Women and the (Dis)Pleasures of Hybridity." *Cultural Anthropology* 21.2: 265–294.
Ezli, Özkan. 2009. "Von der interkulturellen zur kulturellen Kompetenz. Fatih Akıns globalisiertes Kino." *Wider dem Kulturenzwang: Migration,*

Kulturalisierung und Weltliteratur, ed. by Özkan Ezli, Dorothee Kimmich, and Annette Werberger, 207–30. Bielefeld: Transcript.

Ezli, Özkan, ed. 2010. *Kultur als Ereignis: Fatih Akıns Film "Auf der anderen Seite" als transkulturelle Narration*. Bielefeld: Transcript.

Faas, Ania. 2000. "Papa Courage: Mit *Im Juli* bringt der deutsch-türkische Regisseur Fatih Akin seinen zweiten Spielfilm ins Kino: ein Roadmovie durchs wilde Niemandsland." *Spiegel Online*. 31 July. http://www.spiegel.de/spiegel/kulturspiegel/d-17071461.html.

Fachinger, Petra. 2001. *Rewriting Germany from the Margins: "Other" German Literature of the 1980s and 1990s*. Montreal: McGill-Queens University Press.

Fachinger, Petra. 2007. "A New Kind of Creative Energy: Yadé Kara's *Selam Berlin* and Fatih Akın's *Kurz und schmerzlos* and *Gegen die Wand*." *German Life and Letters* 60.2: 243–60.

Fanon, Frantz. 2003. "Algeria Unveiled." Trans. Haakon Chevalier. *Decolonization: Perspectives from Now and Then*, ed. by Prasenjit Duara. London: Routledge.

Farzanefar, Amin. 2003. "Migrantenkino heißt jetzt Mittelmeerkino: Der Filmregisseur Fatih Akin sieht die ethnische Emanzipation der Einwandererkinder vollendet." *Berliner Zeitung Online*. 9 August. http://www.berlinonline.de/berliner-zeitung/archiv/.bin/dump.fcgi/2003/0809/feuilleton/0006/index.html.

Fassbinder, Rainer Werner. 1992. "Imitation of Life: On the Films of Douglas Sirk." In *The Anarchy of the Imagination: Interviews, Essays, Notes*, ed. by Michael Töteberg and Leo A. Lensing, 77–89. Baltimore, MD: Johns Hopkins University Press.

faz.net. 2006. "Fritz Pleitgen: 'Ich bin zornig.'" 24 September. http://www.faz.net/s/Rub475F682E3FC24868A8A5276D4FB916D7/Doc~E3E9A12DEA52D40F393E88A72648FA115~ATpl~Ecommon~Scontent.html.

Fenner, Angelica. 2003. "Traversing the Screen Politics of Migration: Xavier Koller's *Journey of Hope*." *Moving Pictures, Migrating Identities*, ed. by Eva Rueschmann, 18–38. Jackson: University Press of Mississippi.

Festenberg, Nikolaus von. 2006. "Türkischer Teufel." *Spiegel Online* 38. 18 September. http://www.spiegel.de/spiegel/0,1518,437978,00.html.

Filmförderungsanstalt. 2009. *Besucher-, Umsatz- und Eintrittspreisentwicklung der deutschen Filmtheater 2005 bis 2009*. http://www.ffa.de/downloads/marktdaten/3_Besucher_Umsatz_Preise/3.2_bundesw_alteundneue_BL/2005_bis_2009.pdf.

Finkel, Andrew. 2000. "Who Guards the Turkish Press? A Perspective on Press Corruption in Turkey." *Journal of International Affairs* 54.1: 147–66.

Fischer, Lucy and Marcia Landy, eds. 2004. *Stars: The Film Reader*. London: Routledge.

Foster, Hal. 1996. "The Artist as Ethnographer." In *The Return of the Real: The Avant-garde at the End of the Century*, ed. by Hal Foster, 171–204. Cambridge, MA: MIT Press.

Fowler, Catherine. 2004. "Room for Experiment: Gallery Films and Vertical Time from Maya Deren to Eija Liisa Ahtila." *Screen* 45.4: 324–43.
French, Philip. 2010. "The Greatest Film Scenes Ever Shot." *Guardian*. 14 March. http://www.guardian.co.uk./film/2010/mar/14/greatest-movie-scenes-psycho.
Freud, Sigmund. 1959. "On Narcissism." *Collected Papers*. Vol. 4. Trans. Joan Rivière, 30–59. New York: Basic Books.
Freud, Sigmund. 1975. *The Standard Edition of the Complete Psychological Works of Sigmund Freud*. Ed. and trans. by James Strachey. London: The Hogarth Press and the Institute of Psycho-Analysis.
Gaines, Jane. 1988. "White Privilege and Looking Relations: Race and Gender in Feminist Film Theory." *Screen* 29.4: 12–27.
Gallagher, Jessica. 2006. "The Limitations of Urban Space in Thomas Arslan's *Berlin Trilogy*." *Seminar* 42.3: 337–52.
Galle, Birgit. 2000. "Der Sonnenstich: Fatih Akins romantisches Road-Movie *Im Juli* schickt einen Spießer in den Abenteuerpark Südeuropa." *Zeit Online*. 24 August. http://www.zeit.de/2000/35/Der_Sonnenstich.
Galt, Rosalind and Karl Schoonover, eds. 2010. *Global Art Cinema: New Theories and Histories*. Oxford: Oxford University Press.
Gansera, Rainer. 2005. "Ich rocke, also bin ich: Fatih Akin macht sich in 'Crossing the Bridge' auf die Suche nach dem 'Sound of Istanbul'." *Süddeutsche Zeitung Online*. 9 June. http://www.sueddeutsche.de/kultur/fatih-akins-film-crossing-the-bridge-ich-rocke-also-bin-ich-1.413744.
Gansera, Rainer. 2007. "Fatih Akin arbeitet sich in den inneren Zirkel der europäischen Autorenfilmer vor." *Epd Film Online*. http://www.epd-film.de/33178_51923.php.
Ganti, Tejaswini. 2002. "'And Yet My Heart Is Still Indian': The Bombay Film Industry and the (H)Indianization of Hollywood." In *Media Worlds*, ed. by Faye D. Ginsburg, Lila Abu-Lughod, and Brian Larkin, 281–300. Berkeley: University of California Press.
Gemünden, Gerd. 2004. "Hollywood in Altona: Minority Cinema and the Transnational Imagination." In *German Pop Culture: How "American" Is It?*, ed. by Agnes C. Mueller, 180–90. Michigan: University of Michigan Press.
Giddens, Anthony, Marcelino O. Aguirre, Michel Rocard and Albert Rohan. 2004. "Turkey in Europe: More than a Promise?" Report of the Independent Commission on Turkey. Brussels: British Council and the Open Society Institute.
Ginsburg, Faye D., Lila Abu-Lughod, and Brian Larkin, eds. 2002. *Media Worlds: Anthropology on New Terrain*. Berkeley: University of California Press.
Gledhill, Christine, ed. 1987. *Home Is Where the Heart Is: Studies in Melodrama and the Woman's Film*. London: British Film Institute.

Glombitzka, Birgit. 2007. "'Ich wollte die Frauen entdecken.'" Interview with Fatih Akın. *Taz Online.* http://www.taz.de/1/archiv/archiv/?dig=2007/09/26/a009525.
Gökalp, Ziya. 1923. *Türkçülüğün Esasları.* www.iskenderiyekutuphanesi.com.
Göktürk, Deniz. 1994. "Multikulturelle Zungenbrecher: Literatürken aus Deutschlands Nischen." *Sirene: Zeitschrift für Literatur* 12–13: 77–93.
Göktürk, Deniz. 1999. "Turkish Delight-German Fright: Migrant Identities in Transnational Cinema." *Transnational Communities Working Paper Series,* 1–14.
Göktürk, Deniz. 2000. "Turkish Women on German Streets: Closure and Exposure in Transnational Cinema." In *Spaces in European Cinema,* ed. by Myrto Konstantarakos, 64–76. Exeter: Intellect.
Göktürk, Deniz. 2001. "Turkish Delight—German Fright: Migrant Identities in Transnational Cinema." In *Mediated Identities,* ed. by Deniz Derman, Karen Ross, and Nevena Dakovic, 131–49. Istanbul: Bilgi University Press.
Göktürk, Deniz. 2002a. "Beyond Paternalism: Turkish German Traffic in Cinema." In *The German Cinema Book,* ed. by Tim Bergfelder, Erica Carter, and Deniz Göktürk, 248–56. London: British Film Institute.
Göktürk, Deniz. 2002b. "Introduction." In *The German Cinema Book,* ed. by Tim Bergfelder, Erica Carter, and Deniz Göktürk, 213–16. London: British Film Institute.
Göktürk, Deniz. 2010a. "Mobilität und Stillstand im Weltkino digital." In *Kultur als Ereignis,* ed. by Özkan Ezli, 15–46. Bielefeld: Transcript.
Göktürk, Deniz. 2010b. "Sound Bridges: Transnational Mobiliy as Ironic Melodrama." In *European Cinema in Motion,* ed. by Daniela Berghahn and Claudia Sternberg, 215–34. New York: Palgrave.
Göktürk, Deniz, David Gramling, and Anton Kaes, eds. 2007. *Germany in Transit: Nation and Migration, 1955–2005.* Berkeley: University of California Press.
Göktürk, Deniz, David Gramling, Anton Kaes, and Andreas Langenohl, eds. 2011. *Transit Deutschland: Debatten zu Nation und Migration.* Constance: University of Constance Press.
Göle, Nilüfer. 1996. *The Forbidden Modern: Civilization and Veiling.* Ann Arbor: University of Michigan Press.
Göle, Nilüfer. 1998. "Batı-dışı Modernlik Üzerine Bir İlk Desen." *Doğu Batı* 1.2: 57–64.
Gramling, David. 2010. "On the Other Side of Monolingualism: Fatih Akın's Linguistic Turn(s)." *German Quarterly* 83.3: 353–72.
Gray, Jonathan. 2010. *Show Sold Separately: Promos, Spoilers, and other Media Paratexts.* New York: New York University Press.
Grimme-Preis. 2007. "Adolf-Grimme-Preis, 2007, Wettbewerb Unterhaltung, Begründung der Jury." http://www.grimme-institut.de/html/index.php?id=498.

Groß, Thomas. 2005. "Das Beste aus zwei Welten." *Zeit Online.* 17 February. http://www.zeit.de/2005/08/Istanbul-Musik.
Günaydın. 1986. "Kahraman Türk." 11 May.
Gueneli, Berna. 2011. "Crossing European Borders: Fatih Akın's Filmic Visions of Europe." PhD diss. University of Texas at Austin.
Gürsoy, Şahin and İhsan Çapcioğlu. 2006. "Bir Türk Düşünürü Olarak Ziya Gökalp: Hayatı, Kişiliği ve Düşünce Yapısı." *AÜIFD* 47.2: 89–98.
Gusner, Iris and Helke Sander. 2009. *Fantasie und Arbeit: Biografische Zwiesprache.* Marburg: Schüren.
Güvenç, Bozkurt. 2005. *Türk Kimliği.* Istanbul: Remzi Kitabevi.
Hagemann, Martin. 1999. "Extrem. Radikal. International." In *Szenenwechsel: Momentaufnahmen des jungen deutschen Films,* ed. by Michael Töteberg, 219–29. Reinbek: Rowohlt.
Hake, Sabine. 2008. *German National Cinema.* Sec. enlarged and rev. ed. London: Routledge.
Halle, Randall. 2008. *German Film after Germany: Toward a Transnational Aesthetic.* Urbana: University of Illinois Press.
Halle, Randall. 2009. "Experiments in Turkish-German Filmmaking: Ayşe Polat, Kutluğ Ataman, Neco Çelik, Aysun Bademsoy and Kanak Attak." *New Cinemas: Journal of Contemporary Film* 7.1: 39–53.
Halle, Randall. 2010. "Offering Tales They Want to Hear: Transnational European Film Funding as Neo-Orientalism." In *Global Art Cinema: New Theories and Histories,* ed. by Rosalind Galt and Karl Schoonover, 303–19. Oxford: Oxford University Press.
Hamilton, Daniel and Gerhard Mangott, eds. 2008. *The Wider Black Sea Region in the 21st Century: Strategic, Economic and Energy Perspectives.* Washington, DC: Center for Transatlantic Relations.
Hannam, Kevin, Mimi Sheller, and John Urry. 2006. "Editorial: Mobilities, Immobilities and Moorings." *Mobilities* 1.1: 1–22.
Harders, Antje. 2004. "Jugendkultur: Sehnsucht nach Istanbul." *Der Spiegel* 36: 130.
Heidböhmer, Carsten. 2011. "Cenk Batu darf nicht sterben!" *stern.de.* http://www.stern.de/kultur/tv/zuschauer-feiern-tatort-mit-mehmet-kurtulus-cenk-batu-darf-nicht-sterben-1764470.html.
Heise, Ursula K. 2008. *Sense of Place and Sense of Planet: The Environmental Imagination of the Global.* Oxford: Oxford University Press.
Helmcke, Cornelia. 2010 "Sibel Kekilli will auch Muslime kritisieren dürfen." *Welt Online.* 11 March. http://www.welt.de/kultur/article6726835/Sibel-Kekilli-will-auch-Muslime-kritisieren-duerfen.html.
Herpell, Gabriela. 2009. "Verdummungsfernsehen ist politisch: Erfolgsregisseur Fatih Akin spricht über seinen neuen Film mit Moritz Bleibtreu und über Quotenfilme für Europa." *Süddeutsche Zeitung Online.* 18 December. http://www.sueddeutsche.de/kultur/fatih-akin-verdummungsfernsehen-ist-politisch-1.146834.

Hess, Jonathan M. 2010. *Middlebrow Literature and the Making of German-Jewish Identity*. Stanford, CA: Stanford University Press.
Higson, Andrew. 2000. "The Limiting Imagination of National Cinema." In *Cinema and Nation*, ed. by Mette Hjort and Scott Mckensie, 63–74. London: Routledge.
Hillenkamp, Sven. 2005. "Der Heftige." *Zeit Online*. 10 February. http://www.zeit.de/2005/07/Birol__86nel_07.
Hillman, Roger. 2010. "Transnationalism in the Films of Fatih Akın." In *Europe and its Others: Essays on Interperception and Identity*, ed. by Paul Gifford and Tessa Hausdewell, 263–76. Oxford: Peter Lang.
Hjort, Mette. 2009. "On the Plurality of Cinematic Transnationalism." In *World Cinemas, Transnational Perspectives*, ed. by Kathleen Newman and Natasha Durovicova, 12–33. London: Routledge.
Höbel, Wolfgang. 2010. "Sonne im Herzen, Sommer im Hirn." *Spiegel Online*. 21 August. http://www.spiegel.de/spiegel/print/d-17167273.html.
Holden, Stephen. 2010. "Lennon's Music: A Range of Genius." *Rolling Stone*. http://www.rollingstone.com/music/news/lennons-music-a-range-of-genius-20101207.
Holst-Warhaft, Gail. 1983. *Road to Rembetika: Music of a Greek Sub-Culture, Songs of Love, Sorrow and Hashish*. Athens: Denise Harvey & Company.
hooks, bell. 1992. *Black Looks: Race and Representation*. Boston: South End Press.
Horrigan, Bill. 2003. "All Talk." In *Image Stream*, ed. by Helen A. Molesworth, 22–29. Columbus: Wexner Center for the Arts.
Horrigan, Bill. 2004. "Küba, Si!" In *Küba*, ed. by Kutluğ Ataman and Bill Horrigan. London: Artangel.
Huntington, Samuel P. 1996. *The Clash of Civilizations and the Remaking of World Order*. New York: Simon & Schuster.
Hürriyet. 1986a. "Bu Bebeği Dazlaklar Öksüz Bıraktı." 15 January.
Hürriyet. 1986b. "Dazlak Dehşet Büyüyor." 12 June.
Hürriyet. 2004. "Türkiye-AB Filmini Mutlu Sonla Bitirirdim." http://arama.hurriyet.com.tr/arsivnews.aspx?id=204674.
Hürriyet. 2010. "Sibel Kekilli Türbana girdi! 'Ayrılık' filmi 21 Mayıs'ta Türkiye'de!" http://www.hurriyetport.com/kultur-sanat/sibel-kekilli-turbana-girdi-ayrilik-filmi-21-mayis-ta-turkiye-de-foto-galeri.
Hüttmann, Oliver. 2002. "Fatih Akins *Solino*: Italienisch für Anfänger." *Spiegel Online*. 8 November. http://www.spiegel.de/kultur/kino/0,1518,221981,00.html.
Hüttmann, Oliver. 2004. "Fatih Akins *Gegen die Wand*: Atemloses Ohnmachtsdrama." *Spiegel Online*. 12 March. http://www.spiegel.de/kultur/kino/0,1518,290229,00.html.
İnaç, Hüsamettin. 2003. "Avrupa Birliği Entegrasyon Sürecinde Türkiye'nin Kimlik Problemleri." *Doğu Batı* 23:6: 185–208.
İnalcık, Halil. 1998. "Türkiye ve Avrupa: Dün Bugün." *Doğu Batı* 1.2: 11–30.

Ingraham, Chrys. 1999. *White Weddings: Romancing Heterosexuality in Popular Culture*. London: Routledge.
Iser, Wolfgang. 1984. *Der Akt des Lesens*. Munich: Fink.
Itzigsohn, José. 2000. "Immigration and the Boundaries of Citizenship: The Institutions of Immigrants' Political Transnationalism." *International Migration Review* 34.4: 1126–54.
Jähner, Harald. 2007. "Bildung macht sexy." *Berliner Zeitung Online*. 27 September. http://www.berlinonline.de/berliner-zeitung/archiv/.bin/dump.fcgi/2007/0927/kulturkalender/0007/index.html.
Jameson, Fredric. 2000. "Reification and Utopia in Mass Culture." In *The Jameson Reader*, ed. by Michael Hardt and Kathi Weeks, 123–48. Malden, MA: Blackwell.
Jenkins, Mark. 2011. "Feo Aladağ: Exploring Honor Crimes Close To Home." National Public Radio. http://www.npr.org/2011/01/28/133247303/feo-aladag-exploring-honor-crimes-close-to-home.
Jenny, Urs. 2002. "Heimweh nach gestern: Fatih Akins italienisch-deutsche Familiensaga *Solino*: Nichts Halbes, aber auch nichts Ganzes." *Spiegel Online*. 4 November. http://www.spiegel.de/spiegel/print/d-25604167.html.
Junghänel, Frank. 2004. "Identitätsfragen." *Berliner Zeitung Online*. 13 February. http://www.berlinonline.de/berliner-zeitung/archiv/.bin/dump.fcgi/2004/0213/feuilleton/0033/index.html.
Kahraman, Hasan B. 1999. "Türkiye'de Kültürel Söylem Kurguları: Kopuştan Eklemlenmeye ve Geleneksizliğin Geleneği." *Doğu Batı* 3.9: 125–41.
Kahraman, Hasan B. 2001. "Türk Modernleşmesinin Xanadu'su: Türk Modernleşmesi Kurucu İradesinde Yeni Bir Bakış Denemesi." *Doğu Batı* 4.14: 8–27.
Kahraman, Hasan B. and Emin F. Keyman. 1998. "Kemalizm, Oryantalizm ve Modernite." *Doğu Batı* 1.2: 65–77.
Kanak Attak. 1998. "Manifest." http://www.kanak-attack.de.
Kanak TV. 2002. "Weißes Ghetto." http://www.kanak-tv.de/volume_1.shtml.
Kaplan, E. Ann. 1997. *Looking for the Other: Feminism, Film and the Imperial Gaze*. London: Routledge.
Kappert, Ines. 2010. "Der Türke als Zeitbombe." *taz.de*. 11 March. http://www.taz.de/!49519/.
Karpf, Ernst, Doron Kiesel, and Karsten Visarius, eds. 1995. *"Getürkte Bilder": Zur Inszenierung von Fremden im Film*. Marburg: Schüren.
Kaya, Ayhan. 2007. "German-Turkish Transnational Space." *German Studies Review* 30.3: 483–502.
Kaye, Nick. 2000. *Site-specific Art: Performance, Place, and Documentation*. London: Routledge.
Kejanlıoğlu, Beybin. 2004. *Türkiye'de Medyanın Dönüşümü*. Ankara: İmge Kitabevi.

Kelek, Necla. 2005. *Die fremde Braut: Ein Bericht aus dem Inneren des türkischen Lebens in Deutschland*. Cologne: Kiepenheuer & Witsch.
Kelek, Necla. 2010. *Himmelsreise: Mein Streit mit den Wächtern des Islam*. Cologne: Kiepenheuer & Witsch.
Keyder, Çağlar. 1997. "Whither the Project of Modernity." In *Rethinking Modernity and National Identity in Turkey*, ed. by Sibel Bozdoğan and Reşat Kasaba, 37–51. Seattle: University of Washington Press.
Keyman, Emin Fuat. 2003. "Türkiye'de Laiklik Sorunu'nu Düşünmek: Modernite, Sekülerleşme, Demokratikleşme." *Doğu Batı* 23.6: 113–30.
Kilb, Andreas and Peter Körte. 2007. "Keine Angst vor Islamismus in der Türkei." Interview with Fatih Akın. *Frankfurter Allgemeine Zeitung Online*. 3 September. http://www.faz.net/s/Rub8A25A66CA9514B9892E0074EDE4E5AFA/Doc~EAF2656812E1C41DEA18144FCF5C25FD0~ATpl~Ecommon~Scontent.html.
King, Charles. 2004. *The Black Sea: A History*. Oxford: Oxford University Press.
King, Susan. 2011. "Feo Aladağ Focuses her Camera on Honor Killings." *The Los Angeles Times*. 28 January.
Kino.de. 2011. "Star: Birol Ünel." http://www.kino.de/star/biroluenel/104069.html.
Kinski, Klaus. 1975. *Ich bin so wild nach deinem Erdbeermund*. Munich: Rogner und Bernhard.
Kinski, Klaus. 1988. *All I Need Is Love*. New York: Random House.
Kinski, Klaus. 1997. *Kinski Uncut: The Autobiography of Klaus Kinski*. New York: Penguin.
Kılıçbay, Barış. 2006. "Impossible Crossings: Gender Melancholy in *Lola + Bilidikid* and *Auslandstournee*." *New Cinemas: Journal of Contemporary Film* 4.2: 105–15.
Klinger, Barbara. 1994. *Melodrama and Meaning: History, Culture, and the Films of Douglas Sirk*. Bloomington: Indiana University Press.
Klinger, Barbara. 2006. *Beyond the Multiplex: Cinema, New Technologies, and the Home*. Berkeley: University of California Press.
Kosnick, Kira. 2007. *Migrant Media: Turkish Broadcasting and Multicultural Politics in Berlin*. Bloomington: Indiana University Press.
Kosta, Barbara. 2010. "Transcultural Space and Music: Fatih Akın's *Crossing the Bridge: The Sound of Istanbul* (2005)." In *Spatial Turns: Space, Place, and Mobility in German Literary and Visual Culture*, ed. by Jaimey Fisher and Barbara Mennel, 343–60. Amsterdam: Rodopi.
Kraenzle, Christina. 2009. "At Home in the New Germany? Local Stories and Global Concerns in Yüksel Yavuz's *Aprilkinder* and *Kleine Freiheit*." *German Quarterly* 82.1: 90–108.
Kreimeier, Klaus, Georg Stanitzek, and Natalie Binczek, eds. 2004. *Paratexte in Literatur, Film, Fernsehen*. Berlin: Akademie Verlag.
Krutnik, Frank. 1998. "Love Lies: Romantic Fabrication in Contemporary Romantic Comedy." In *Terms of Endearment: Hollywood Romantic Comedy*

of the 1980s and 1990s, ed. by Peter William Evans and Celestino Deleyto, 15–36. Edinburgh: Edinburgh University Press.
Kulaoğlu, Tunçay. 1999. "Der neue 'deutsche' Film ist 'türkisch'?: Eine neue Generation bringt Leben in die Filmlandschaft." *Film Forum* 16 (February/March): 8–11.
Kwon, Miwon. 1997. "One Place after Another: Notes on Site Specificity." *October* 80: 85–110.
Lacan, Jacques. 1981. *The Four Fundamental Concepts of Psycho-Analysis*. Trans. Jacques-Alain Miller. New York: Norton.
Lackey, Kris. 1997. *Roadframes: The American Highway Narrative*. Lincoln: University of Nebraska Press.
Lambert, Greg. 2005. "Expression." In *Gilles Deleuze: Key Concepts*, ed. by Charles J. Stivale, 31–41. Montreal: McGill-Queen's University Press.
Lane, Jim. 2002. *The Autobiographical Documentary in America*. Madison: University of Wisconsin Press.
Langrock-Kögel, Christiane and Hans-Jürgen Jakobs. 2004. "'Ich hab' die deutschen Türken nicht ins Kino bewegt—das bricht mir das Herz.'" *Süddeutsche Zeitung Online*. 5 November. http://www.sueddeutsche.de/kultur/regisseur-ich-hab-die-deutschen-tuerken-nicht-ins-kino-bewegt-das-bricht-mir-das-herz-1.894423.
Lau, Jörg. 2004. "Die Türken sind da." *Zeit Online*. 26 February. http://www.zeit.de/2004/10/T_9frken.
LaValley, Al. 1994. "The Gay Liberation of Rainer Werner Fassbinder: Male Subjectivity, Male Bodies, Male Lovers." *New German Critique* 63: 109–39.
Lebow, Alisa. 2007–8. "Worldwide Wigs: Kutluğ Ataman and the Globalized Art Documentary." *Journal of Arab Studies* 15.2 & 16.1: 57–82.
Lejeune, Philippe. 1989. "The Autobiographical Pact." In *On Autobiography*, ed. by Paul John Eakin, trans. Katherine Leary, 3–30. Minneapolis: University of Minnesota Press.
Levin, G. Roy. 1971. Interview with Jean Rouch. In *Documentary Explorations: Fifteen Interviews with Filmmakers*, ed. by G. Roy Levin, 131–45. New York: Doubleday.
Levin, Richard A. 1985. *Love and Society in Shakespearean Comedy: A Study of Dramatic Form and Content*. Newark: University of Delaware Press.
Lewis, Bernard. 1988. *Modern Türkiye'nin Doğuşu*. Ankara: TTK.
Malik, Sarita. 1996. "Beyond 'the Cinema of Duty'? The Pleasures of Hybridity: Black British Film of the 1980s and 1990s." In *Dissolving Views: New Writings on British Cinema*, ed. by Andrew Higson, 202–15. London: Cassell.
Mandel, Ruth. 2008. *Cosmopolitan Anxieties: Turkish Challenges to Citizenship and Belonging in Germany*. Durham, NC: Duke University Press.
Mani, B. Venkat. 2007. *Cosmopolitical Claims: Turkish-German Literatures from Nadolny to Pamuk*. Iowa City: University of Iowa Press.
Marchessault, Janine and Susan Lord, eds. 2007. *Fluid Screens, Expanded Cinema*. Toronto: University of Toronto Press.

Massey, Doreen. 1994. *Space, Place, and Gender*. Minneapolis: University of Minnesota Press.
Mather, Nigel. 2006. *Tears of Laughter: Comedy Drama in 1990s British Cinema*. Manchester: Manchester University Press.
Mayne, Judith. 1977. "Fassbinder and Spectatorship." *New German Critique* 12: 61–74.
McClintock, Anne. 1995. *Imperial Leather: Race, Gender, and Sexuality in the Colonial Contest*. London: Routledge.
Mehlig, Holger. 2004. "'So sehen Gewinner aus'." *Spiegel Online*. 15 February. http://www.spiegel.de/kultur/kino/0,1518,286519,00.html.
Mehlig, Holger. 2005. "*Crossing the Bridge*: Ein Hauch von Rebellion." *stern.de* 9 June. http://www.stern.de/kultur/film/crossing-the-bridge-ein-hauch-von-rebellion-541512.html.
Mennel, Barbara. 2000. "Masochistic Fantasy and Racialized Fetish in Fassbinder." In *One Hundred Years of Masochism: Literary Texts, Social and Cultural Contexts*, ed. by Michael C. Finke and Carl Nieberk, 191–205. Amsterdam: Rodopi.
Mennel, Barbara. 2002a. "Bruce Lee in Kreuzberg and Scarface in Altona: Transnational Auteurism and Ghettocentrism in Thomas Arslan's *Brothers and Sisters* and Fatih Akin's *Short Sharp Shock*." *New German Critique* 87: 133–56.
Mennel, Barbara. 2002b. "Local Funding and Global Movement: Minority Women's Filmmaking and the German Film Landscape of the Late 1990s." *Women in German Yearbook* 18: 45–66.
Mennel, Barbara. 2004. "Masochism, Marginality, and the Metropolis: Kutluğ Ataman's *Lola and Billy the Kid*." *Studies in Twentieth Century Literature* 28: 286–315.
Mennel, Barbara. 2010. "Criss-Crossing in Global Space and Time: Fatih Akın's *The Edge of Heaven* (2007)." *Transit* 5.1. http://escholarship.org/uc/item/28x3x9r0.
Mercer, Kobena. 1990. "Black Art and the Burden of Representation." *Third Text* 4.10: 61–78.
Merleau-Ponty, Maurice. 1989. *Phenomenology of Perception*. Trans. Colin Smith. London: Routledge.
Mielke, Michael. 2010. "Warum Hatun Sürücü sterben musste." *Berliner Morgenpost*. 7 February.
Mihelj, Sabina, Veronika Bajt, and Miloś Pankov. 2009. "Television News, Narrative Conventions and National Imagination." *Discourse and Communication* 3.1: 57–78.
Mitchell, Katheryne. 1997. "Different Diasporas and the Hype of Hybridity." *Environment and Planning: Society and Space* 15.5: 533–53.
Mitchell, William J. T. 1987. *Iconology: Image, Text, Ideology*. Chicago: University of Chicago Press.

Moorti, Sujata. 2003. "Desperately Seeking an Identity: Diasporic Cinema and the Articulation of Transnational Kinship." *International Journal of Cultural Studies* 6.3: 355–76.
Mortimer, Claire. 2010. *Romantic Comedy*. London: Routledge.
Moulakis, Athanasios. 2005. "The Mediterranean Region: Reality, Delusion, or Euro-Mediterranean Project?" *Mediterranean Quarterly* 16.2: 11–38.
Müller, Manfred. 2000. "*Im Juli*: Romantisches Roadmovie mit Physiklehrer." *Spiegel Online*. 21 August. http://www.stern.de/kultur/film/crossing-the-bridge-ein-hauch-von-rebellion-541512.html.
Mulvey, Laura. 1988. "Visual Pleasure and Narrative Cinema." In *Feminism and Film Theory*, ed. by Constance Penley, 57–68. London: Routledge.
Mulvey, Laura. 1993. "Some Thoughts on Theories of Fetishism in the Context of Contemporary Culture." *October* 65: 3–20.
Mulvey, Laura. 2005. "Repetition and Return: Textual Analysis and Douglas Sirk in the Twenty-First Century." In *Style and Meaning: Studies in the Detailed Analysis of Film*, ed. by John Gibbs and Douglas Pye, 228–43. Manchester: Manchester University Press.
Mulvey, Laura. 2006. *Death 24x a Second: Stillness and the Moving Image*. London: Reaktion Books.
Naficy, Hamid. 2001. *An Accented Cinema: Exilic and Diasporic Filmmaking*. Princeton, NJ: Princeton University Press.
Naiboğlu, Gözde. 2010. "'Sameness' in Disguise of 'Difference'? Gender and National Identity in Fatih Akın's *Gegen die Wand* and *Auf der anderen Seite*." *German as a Foreign Language* 3: 75–98.
Neale, Steve and Frank Krutnik. 1990. *Popular Film and Television Comedy*. London: Routledge.
Negrine, Ralph, Beybin Kejanlioğlu, Rabah Aissaoui, and Stylianos Papathanassopoulos. 2008. "Turkey and the European Union: An Analysis of How the Press in Four Countries Covered Turkey's Bid for Accession in 2004." *European Journal of Communication* 23.1: 47–68.
Nichols, Bill. 2010. *Introduction to Documentary*. Bloomington: Indiana University Press.
Nicodemus, Katja. 2004. "Ankunft in der Wirklichkeit: Mit Fatih Akins *Gegen die Wand* siegt das deutsche Kino über die deutschen Träume von einer Leitkultur." *Zeit Online*. 19 February. http://www.zeit.de/2004/09/Berlinale-Abschluss.
Nietzsche, Friedrich Wilhelm. 1956. *The Birth of Tragedy and the Genealogy of Morals*. Garden City, NJ: Doubleday.
Nixon, Sean. 1997. "Exhibiting Masculinity." In *Representation: Cultural Representations and Signifying Practices*, ed. Stuart Hall, 291–330. London: Sage.
Nussbaum, Martha. 1994. "Patriotism and Cosmopolitanism." *The Boston Review* 19.5: 1–7.
Nussbaum, Martha. 1996. *For Love of Country?* Boston: Beacon Press.

Osteen, Mark. 2008. "Noir's Cars: Automobility and Amoral Space in American Film Noir." *Journal of Popular Film and Television* 35.4: 183–92.

Özdoğan, Abdullah. 2007. "Vatan Bir Parça Kağıtsa." *Yeni Çağ*. http://www.tumgazeteler.com/?a=2377446.

Pasquay, Anja. 2010. "Zur wirtschaftlichen Lage der Zeitungen in Deutschland 2010." 24 April. http://www.bdzv.de/wirtschaftliche_lage+M5650c2f558e.html.

Perren, Alisa. 2004. "A Big Fat Indie Success Story? Press Discourses Surrounding the Making and Marketing of a 'Hollywood' Movie." *Journal of Film and Video* 56.2: 18–31.

Petek, Polona. 2007. "Enabling Collisions: Re-thinking Multiculturalism through Fatih Akın's *Gegen die Wand/Head On*." *Studies in European Cinema* 4.3: 177–86.

Peterson, Brent O. 2005. *History, Fiction, and Germany: Writing the Nineteenth-Century Nation*. Detroit: Wayne State University Press.

Philipp, Claus. 2007. "Fremde Zärtlichkeit zwischen zwei Kulturen: *Auf der anderen Seite*." *Standard Online*. 6 November. http://derstandard.at/3061506/Fremde-Zaertlichkeit-zwischen-zwei-Kulturen-Auf-der-anderen-Seite?_lexikaGroup=2.

Pride, Ray. 2010. "Interview: The Savory Sound of Fatih Akın's *Soul Kitchen*." *Movie City News*. http://moviecitynews.com/2010/09/the-savory-sound-of-fatih-akins-soul-kitchen/.

Purnell, Kim L. 2002. "Listening to Lady Day: An Exploration of the Creative (Re)negotiation of Identity Revealed in the Life Narratives and Music Lyrics of Billie Holiday." *Communication Quarterly* 50.3: 444–66.

Qureshi, Bilal. 2010. "A German *Soul Kitchen* That's More Than A Restaurant." *NPR Music*. http://www.npr.org/templates/story/story.php?storyId=129706282.

Radway, Janice A. 1984. *Reading the Romance: Women, Patriarchy, and Popular Literature*. Chapel Hill: University of North Carolina Press.

Radway, Janice A. 1997. *A Feeling for Books: The Book-of-the-Month Club, Literary Taste, and Middle-Class Desire*. Chapel Hill: University of North Carolina Press.

Rancière, Jacques. 1999. *Disagreement: Politics and Philosophy*. Trans. Julie Rose. Minneapolis: University of Minnesota Pres.

Rancière, Jacques. 2004. *The Politics of Aesthetics: The Distribution of the Sensible*. Trans. Gabriel Rockhill. New York: Continuum.

Rancière, Jacques. 2009. "The Aesthetic Dimension: Aesthetics, Politics, Knowledge." *Critical Inquiry* 36: 1–19.

Ranze, Michael. 2002. "'Heimat ist ein mentaler Zustand: *Solino*, Scorsese und die Globalisierung: Fatih Akin im Gespräch." *epd Film* 11. http://www.filmportal.de/material/interview-mit-fatih-akin-2002.

Reicher, Isabelle. 2005. "Die subtile Form von Politik." *Der Standard*. 26 March. http://www.derstandard.at/1620546/Die-subtile-Form-von-Politik?_lexikaGroup=8.

Rendi, Giovannella. 2006. "Kanaka Sprak? German-Turkish Women Filmmakers." *German as a Foreign Language* 3. http://www.gfl-journal.de/3-2006/rendi.pdf: 78–93.
Rice, Brian. 2010. "Art/Cinema and Cosmopolitanism Today." In *Global Art Cinema: New Theories and Histories*, ed. Rosalind Galt and Karl Schoonover, 109–24. Oxford: Oxford University Press.
Roberts, Martin. 1998. "*Baraka*: World Cinema and the Global Culture Industry." *Cinema Journal* 37.3: 62–68.
Rodek, Hanns-Georg. 2004. "Gegen die Wand ist durch die Wand." *Welt Online*. 16 February. http://www.welt.de/print-welt/article293530/Gegen_die_Wand_ist_durch_die_Wand.html.
Rodek, Hanns-Georg. 2007. "Sein Film hat das Zeug zum Sieger." *Welt Online*. 23 May. http://www.welt.de/kultur/article891469/Sein_Film_hat_das_Zeug_zum_Sieger.html.
Rodek, Hanns-Georg. 2009. "Heimatfilm *Soul Kitchen*: Fatih Akins letzte Party vor der Yuppie-Invasion." *Welt Online*. 22 December. http://www.welt.de/kultur/article5613359/Fatih-Akins-letzte-Party-vor-der-Yuppie-Invasion.html.
Rogoff, Irit. 2006. "'I Was Happy When I was a Virgin.' On Being Puzzled." In *Küba: Journey Against the Current*, ed. by Gabrielle Cram and Daniela Zyman, 34–37. Vienna: Springer.
Rogoff, Irit. 2009. "De-regulation: With the Work of Kutluğ Ataman." *Third Text* 23.2: 165–79.
Rother, Hans-Jörg. 1998. "Not lehrt beten: Fatih Akins Kinodebüt *Kurz und schmerzlos*." *Frankfurter Allgemeine Zeitung*. 17 October.
Rowe, Kathleen. 1995. *The Unruly Woman: Gender and the Genres of Laughter*. Austin: University of Texas Press.
Safranski, Rüdiger. 2005. *How Much Globalization Can We Bear?* Trans. Patrick Camiller. Cambridge: Polity Press.
Sarrazin, Thilo. 2010. *Deutschland schafft sich ab: Wie wir unser Land aufs Spiel setzen*. Munich: Deutsche Verlags-Anstalt.
Sassen, Saskia. 1998. *Globalization and Its Discontents: Essays on the New Mobility of People and Money*. New York: New Press.
Sauer, Martina and Faruk Şen. 2005. *Türkische Unternehmer in Berlin: Struktur – Wirtschaftskraft – Problemlagen. Eine Analyse der Stiftung Zentrum für Türkeistudien im Auftrag des Beauftragten des Senats von Berlin für Integration und Migration*. Berlin: Der Beauftragte des Senats von Berlin für Integration und Migration.
Sayar, Vecdi. 1991a. "Cannes'da Amerika'yla Dans." *Cumhuriyet*. 20 April.
Sayar, Vecdi. 1991b. "Başer'in Filmi Yarışacak." *Cumhuriyet*. 8 May.
Sayar, Vecdi. 2007. "Cannes'ın. Kıyısında." *Cumhuriyet*. 25 May.
Schatz, Heribert, ed. 2000. *Migranten und Medien: Neue Herausforderungen an die Integrationsfunktion von Presse und Rundfunk*. Wiesbaden: Westdeutscher Verlag.

Schatz, Thomas. 1981. *Hollywood Genres: Formulas, Filmmaking, and the Studio System*. Boston: McGraw Hill.
Schein, Louisa. 2002. "Mapping Hmong Media in Diasporic Space." In *Media Worlds: Anthropology on New Terrain*, ed. Faye D. Ginsburg, Lila Abu-Lughold, and Brian Larkin, 229–44. Berkeley: University of California Press.
Schindler, Stephan K. and Lutz Koepnick, eds. 2007. *The Cosmopolitan Screen: German Cinema and the Global Imaginary, 1945 to the Present*. Ann Arbor: University of Michigan Press.
Schmidt, Matthias. 2007. "Cannes-Tagebuch. Wir fordern: Goldene Palme für Fatih." *stern.de*. 24 May. http://www.stern.de/kultur/film/cannes-tagebuch-wir-fordern-goldene-palme-fuer-fatih-589617.html.
Schmitt, Carl. 2007. *The Concept of the Political*. Trans. George Schwab. Chicago: University of Chicago Press.
Schöning, Jörg, ed. 1995. *Fantaisies russes: Russische Filmmacher in Berlin und Paris 1920–1930*. Munich: edition text + kritik.
Schöning, Jörg, ed. 2005. *Film Europa—Babylon: Mehrsprachenversionen der 1930er Jahre in Europa*. Munich: text + kritik.
Seeßlen, Georg. 2000. "Das Kino der doppelten Kulturen/Le Cinema du métissage/The Cinema of inbetween: Erster Streifzug durch ein unbekanntes Kino-Terrain." *epd Film* 12: 22–29.
Seibert, Thomas. 2007. "Mülldeponie an der Teeplantage." *Der Tagesspiegel*. 3 September. http://www.tagesspiegel.de/weltspiegel/Tuerkei;art111 7,2372134.
Şenocak, Zafer. 2011. *Deutschsein: Eine Aufklärungsschrift*. Hamburg: Edition Körber-Stiftung.
Serrao, Marc Felix. 2006. "Diese Wut ist echt: Berliner Hauptschüler loben das deutsch-türkische Drama, das die ARD ins Spätprogramm verschoben hat." *Der Tagesspiegel*. 29 September. www.tagesspiegel.de/medien/diese-wut-ist-echt/757442.html.
Seyhan, Azade. 2001. *Writing Outside the Nation*. Princeton, NJ: Princeton University Press.
Sezgin, Hilal, ed. 2011. *Manifest der Vielen: Deutschland erfindet sich neu*. Berlin: Blumenbar Verlag.
Shohat, Ella and Robert Stam. 1994. *Unthinking Eurocentrism: Multiculturalism and the Media*. London: Routledge.
Shumway, David R. 2003. "Screwball Comedies: Constructing Romance, Mystifying Marriage." In *Film Genre Reader*, ed. by Barry Keith Grant, 396–416. Austin: University of Texas Press.
Sieg, Katrin. 2002. *Ethnic Drag: Performing Race, Nation, Sexuality in West Germany*. Ann Arbor: Michigan University Press.
Siewert, Senta. 2008. "Soundtracks of Double Occupancy: Sampling Sounds and Cultures in Fatih Akın's *Head On*." In *Mind the Screen: Media Concepts According to Thomas Elsaesser*, ed. by Jaap Kooijman and Patricia Pisters, 198–208. Amsterdam: Amsterdam University Press.

Silberman, Marc. 1996. "What is German in the German Cinema?" *Film History* 8: 297–315.
Silverman, Kaja. 1992. *Male Subjectivity at the Margins*. London: Routledge.
Silvey, Vivien and Roger Hillman. 2010. "Akin's *Auf der anderen Seite* (*The Edge of Heaven*) and the Widening Periphery." *German as a Foreign Language* 3: 99–116.
Sinan, Ozan. 2004. "Berliner Gespräche zur digitalen Integration: Lebenswelten Deutschtürken." http://www.digitale-chancen.de/transfer/assets/575.pdf.
Sinka, Margit. 2000. "Tom Tykwer's *Lola rennt:* A Blueprint of Millennial Berlin." *Glossen* 11. http://www2.dickinson.edu/glossen/heft11/lola.html.
Şirin, Dinçer. 2008. "Kimlik Problemi Abartılıyor." *Radikal*. http://www.radikal.com.tr/Radikal.aspx?aType=RadikalEklerDetay&ArticleID=867870&Date=15.3.2008&CategoryID=41.
Sirk, Douglas and Jon Halliday. 1972. *Sirk on Sirk: Interviews with Jon Halliday*. New York: Viking Press.
Slifkin, Irv. 2010. "Director Fatih Akın and his Movie *Soul Kitchen*: An Interview." *MovieFanFare*. 27 August. http://www.moviefanfare.com/movie-buzz/director-fatih-akin-and-his-movie-soul-kitchen-an-interview.
Soila, Tytti, ed. 2009. *Stellar Encounters: Stardom in Popular European Cinema*. New Barnet: John Libbey Publishing.
Spiegel Online. 2006. "Stoiber kritisiert Verschiebung als 'fatales Signal.'" 28 September. http://www.spiegel.de/kultur/gesellschaft/0,1518,439789,00.html.
Spiegel Online. 2011. "Til Schweiger ermittelt als Kommissar." 3 December. http://www.spiegel.de/kultur/tv/0,1518,druck-801539,00.html.
Stam, Robert and Louise Spence. 1983. "Colonialism, Racism and Representation." *Screen* 24.2: 2–20.
Steinhoff, Marieke. 2009. "Liebe! Sex! Die Seele!" *Schnitt Online*. 20 December. http://www.schnitt.de/202,5875,01.
Stephan, Inge. 2006. *Medea: Multimediale Karriere einer mythologischen Figur*. Cologne: Böhlau.
Stokes, Martin. 1992. *The Arabesk Debate: Music and Musicians in Modern Turkey*. Oxford: Oxford University Press.
Suner, Asuman. 2005. "Dark Passion." *Sight & Sound* 15:3: 18–21.
Taberner, Stuart. 2004. "Introduction: German Literature in the Age of Globalisation." In *German Literature in the Age of Globalisation*, ed. by Stuart Taberner, 1–24. Birmingham: University of Birmingham Press.
Taberner, Stuart and Paul Cooke. 2006. "Introduction." In *German Culture, Politics, and Literature into the Twenty-First Century: Beyond Normalization*, ed. by Stuart Taberner and Paul Cooke, 1–15. Rochester, NY: Camden House.

Taylor, Ella. 1989. "From the Nelsons to the Huxtables: Genre and Family Imagery in American Network Television." *Qualitative Sociology* 12.1: 13–28.
Telegraph. 2009. *"Psycho* Tops Poll of Greatest Movie Shower Scenes." *Telegraph.* http://www.telegraph.co.uk/culture/film/film-news/6021124/Psycho-tops-poll-of-greatest-movie-shower-scenes.html.
Teraoka, Arlene A. 1996. *EAST, WEST, and Others: The Third World in Postwar German Literature.* Lincoln: University of Nebraska.
Terkessidis, Mark. 2010. *Interkultur.* Berlin: Suhrkamp Verlag.
Terkessidis, Mark and Tom Holert. 1996. *Mainstream der Minderheiten: Pop in der Kontrollgesellschaft.* Berlin: ID Verlag.
Theweleit, Klaus. 1989. *Male Fantasies: Volume 2: Male Bodies, Psychoanalyzing the White Terror.* Trans. Erica Carter and Chris Turner. Minneapolis: University of Minnesota Press.
Thompson, David, Janet Staiger, and Kristin Thompson. 1985. *The Classical Hollywood Cinema: Film Style and Mode of Production to 1960.* London: Routledge.
Tibi, Bassam. 2008. "Die deutsche verordnete Fremdenliebe." In *Die Gotteskrieger und die falsche Toleranz,* ed. by Alice Schwarzer, 105–20. Cologne: Kiepenheuer & Witsch.
Tilmann, Christina. 2009. "Fatih Akins *Soul Kitchen* in Venedig." *Tagesspiegel Online.* 11 September. http://www.tagesspiegel.de/kultur/kino/fatih-akins-soul-kitchen-in-venedig/v_default,1597860.html.
Toprak, Ahmet. 2010. *Integrationsunwillige Muslime? Ein Milieubericht.* Freiburg im Breisgau: Lambertus.
Töteberg, Michael and Leo A. Lensing, eds. 1992. *Rainer Werner Fassbinder: The Anarchy of Imagination.* Baltimore, MD: Johns Hopkins University Press.
Tsing, Anna Lowenhaupt. 2005. *Friction: An Ethnography of Global Connection.* Princeton, NJ: Princeton University Press.
TÜİK. 2010. http://www.tuik.gov.tr/PreTablo.do?alt_id=15
Tunç, Aslı. 2002. "Pushing the Limits of Tolerance. Functions of Political Cartoonists in the Democratization Process: The Case of Turkey." *Gazette: The International Journal for Communication Studies* 64.1: 47–62.
Tunç, Aslı. 2004. "Faustian Acts in Turkish Style: Structural Change in National Newspapers as an Obstacle to Quality Journalism in 1990–2003." *Quality Press in Southeastern Europe,* ed. by Orlin Spassov, 306–323. SOEM2: Sofia.
Türeli, Ipek. 2010. "Istanbul through Migrants' Eyes." In *Orienting Istanbul: Cultural Capital of Europe?,* ed. by Deniz Göktürk, Levent Soysal, and Ipek Türeli, 144–64. London: Routledge.
Türker, Yıldırım. 2009. "CHP'nin onuru, evlâdı Kerbela'ya karşı." *Radikal.* http://www.radikal.com.tr/Default.aspx?aType=RadikalYazarYazisi&ArticleID=964590&Yazar=YILDIRIM%20TÜRKER&Date=16.11.2009&CategoryID=97.

Urry, John. 1990. *The Tourist Gaze: Leisure and Travel in Contemporary Societies.* London: Sage.
Urry, John. 2007. *Mobilities.* Cambridge: Polity.
Vahabzadeh, Susan. 2007. "Im Migrationskarussell." *Süddeutsche Zeitung Online.* 26 September. http://www.sueddeutsche.de/kultur/artikel/67/134809/.
Voigt, Claudia. 2009. "Die Traumfabrik." *Spiegel Online.* 7 December. http://www.spiegel.de/spiegel/0,1518,665406,00.html.
von Moltke, Johannes. 1994. "Camp in the Art Closet: The Politics of Camp and Nation in German Film." *New German Critique* 63: 77–109.
Wahl, Chris. 2005. *Das Sprechen des Spielfilms: Über die Auswirkungen von hörbaren Dialogen auf Produktion, Rezeption, Ästhetik und Internationalität der siebten Kunst.* Trier: Wissenschaftlicher Verlag.
Waldman, Diane and Janet Walker, eds. 1999. *Feminism and Documentary.* Minneapolis: University of Minnesota Press.
Walkowitz, Rebecca. 2006. *Cosmopolitan Style: Modernism beyond the Nation.* New York: Columbia University Press.
Wartenberg, Thomas E. 1999. *Unlikely Couples: Movie Romances as Social Criticism.* Boulder, CO: Westview Press.
Wasser, Frederick. 2001. *Veni, Vidi, Video: The Hollywood Empire and the VCR.* Austin: University of Texas Press.
WDR. 2006. "NRW-Integrationsminister Laschet nennt Diskussion um WDR-Film *WUT* 'unverständlich.'" 28 September. http://www.presseportal.de/pm/7899/879453/wdr_westdeutscher_rundfunk.
Wexman, Virginia Wright. 2003. *Film and Authorship.* New Brunswick, NJ: Rutgers University Press.
Willemen, Paul, ed. 1994. "The Sirkian System." In *Looks and Frictions: Essays in Cultural Studies and Film Theory*, 87–98. Bloomington: Indiana University Press.
Winkler, Thomas. 2005. "*Crossing the Bridge: The Sound of Istanbul.*" *Fluter Online.* 8 June. http://film.fluter.de/de/110/kino/3999/.
Winston, Brian. 1995. *Claiming the Real: The Documentary Film Revisited.* London: BFI Publishing.
Wohlrab-Sahr, Monika and Levent Tezcan, eds. 2007. *Konfliktfeld Islam in Europa.* Baden-Baden: Nomos.
Wolf, Christa. 1987. *Störfall: Nachrichten eines Tages.* Berlin: Aufbau Verlag.
Yetkin, Murat. 2002. *Avrupa Birliği Bekleme Odasında Türkiye.* Ankara: İmge Kitabevi.
Yıldırım, Aydın and Suzan Işık. 2007. "Bir Fatih Akın Filmi: Yaşamın Kıyısında." *Evrensel.* www.genchayat.evrensel.net/kultur.php?txt_arsiv_tarihi.
Yıldız, Kerim. 2005. *The Kurds in Turkey: EU Accession and Human Rights.* London: Pluto Press.
Youngblood, Gene. 1970. *Expanded Cinema.* New York: E. P. Dutton.

Yumul, Arus and Umut Özkırımlı. 2000. "Reproducing the Nation: Banal Nationalism in the Turkish Press." *Media, Culture & Society* 22: 787–804.
Yüreklik, Güner. 1989a. "Hapishanede Özgürlük." *Cumhuriyet*. 21 January.
Yüreklik, Güner. 1989b. "Aman Schönhuber Duymasın." *Cumhuriyet*. 19 February.
Yüreklik, Güner. 1991. "Sürgünde Bir Türk Yazarı." *Cumhuriyet*. 7 March.
Zaimoglu, Feridun. 2004a. "Ein Gespräch mit Feridun Zaimoglu." Interview with Fatih Akın. In *Gegen die Wand: Das Buch zum Film. Drehbuch, Materialien, Interviews*, ed. by Helge Malchow, 233–37. Cologne: Kiepenheuer & Witsch.
Zaimoglu, Feridun. 2004b. "Lebenswut, Herzhitze: Der Berlinale-Überraschungssieger kommt ins Kino. Fatih Akins herrlich maßloses Liebesdrama *Gegen die Wand*." *Tagesspiegel Online*. 10 March. http://www.tagesspiegel.de/kultur/lebenswut-herzhitze/497810.html.
Zander, Peter. 2004. "Not der Zweisamkeit: Die deutschen Beiträge II. Fatih Akins Ehe-Anfangsdrama *Gegen die Wand*." *Welt Online*. 12 February. http://www.welt.de/print-welt/article292580/Not_der_Zweisamkeit_Die_deutschen_Beitraege_II.html.
Zander, Peter. 2009. "Schmutziger Heimatfilm. Genuss mit Ironie: Fatih Akins *Soul Kitchen*." *Welt Online*. 10 September. http://www.welt.de/kultur/article4506128/Genuss-mit-Ironie-Fatih-Akins-Soul-Kitchen.html.
Zaptcioglu, Dilek. 2004. "Seltsame Welt der Deutschländer." *taz.de*. 22 March. http://www.taz.de/1/archiv/archiv/?dig=2004/03/22/a0209.
Ziegler, Helmut. 2004. "Ich will kein Sonntagskind sein!" Interview mit dem Filmregisseur Fatih Akin, 17 February. http://www.presseportal.de/pm/2790/528586/der-tagesspiegel-ich-will-kein-sonntagskind-sein-interview-mit-dem-filmregisseur-fatih-akin.

Index of Names

A., Aziza 83
Adelson, Leslie 8–9, 60, 61, 98–99, 153
Akın, Fatih 6, 7, 9–15, 21, 36, 37, 40, 42, 45, 59, 61–71, 75, 95, 124, 131, 138, 140, 147, 149–160, 161, 164, 165, 169, 170, 172, 175–185, 186–191, 194–197, 198–206, 208, 211
Akın, Monique 203
Akkus, Sinan 20, 24
Aksu, Sezen 140
Alabora, Derya 41
Aladağ, Feo 7, 13, 21, 22, 34–35, 39, 40, 42, 43
Aladağ, Züli 40, 109, 111, 113, 115, 117–120, 169
Aladağ, Züli and Feo 131
Alakuş, Buket 7, 14, 72–73, 75–78, 81
Albers, Hans 194
Althusser, Louis 82
Altıoklar, Mustafa 184
Altman, Robert 136
Anderson, Amanda 177
Anderson, Benedict 172, 179
Appadurai, Arjun 8, 14, 65, 67, 69, 125, 179
Appiah, Kwame Anthony 176–177, 181, 185
Armstrong, Louis 194
Arslan, Thomas 6, 7, 13, 44–50, 52–55, 60, 75, 95, 169
Assmann, David 82
Ataman, Kutluğ 6, 12, 14, 39, 42, 75, 84–95
Atatürk, Mustafa Kemal 164, 171

Austen, Jane 30

Bademsoy, Aysun 6, 14, 72–77, 79–82, 95
Balanovsky, Gabriel 82
Barthes, Roland 13, 32–34, 39,
Başer, Tevfik 5, 46
Bausch, Andy 144
Beck, Ulrich 125, 180, 201, 211
Belmondo, Jean-Paul 67
Berger, John 77, 139, 140
Berghahn, Daniela 7, 10, 13, 21, 43, 99, 112, 119, 120, 171
Bergman, Ingmar 195–196
Berksoy, Semiha 85
Bhabha, Homi 8, 20, 60, 167, 170
Biemann, Ursula 207, 208
Bleibtreu, Moritz 175, 187, 189
Bogle, Donald 83
Bohm, Hark 5, 19, 21, 112
Bonfadelli, Heinz 128, 133
Bono 192
Bousdoukos, Adam 40, 188
Boym, Svetlana 69–71, 160
Brasch, Thomas 144
Broder, Henryk 33
Buck, Detlev 111
Buñuel, Luis 195
Burns, Rob 21–22, 45, 50, 138
Burton, Julianne 79
Butler, Judith 82
Byron, Lord 206

Çağlar, Ayşe 130, 178
Certeau, Michel de 61

Ceylan, Nuri Bilge 95, 126
Chadha, Gurinder 30, 73
Chin, Rita 2–3, 102
Çil, Nevim 129, 133–134
Cosby, Bill 43, 191
Coutard, Raoul 67
Crary, Jonathan 89
Cuarón, Alfonso 210

Dagetin, Bora 106
De Lauretis, Teresa 82
De Niro, Robert 114
Deleuze, Gilles 47–48, 52, 54
Derin, Seyhan 6, 12, 61–62, 65, 75–76, 95
Desai, Jigna 20
Dietrich, Marlene 139
Dörrie, Doris 63, 140
Dresen, Andreas 63
Drew, Robert 67
Dyer, Richard 139, 145
Dylan, Bob 206, 207

Egoyan, Atom 157
Eipp, Max 112, 117, 119
El-Tayeb, Fatima 75
Elçi, Ismet 21–22
Elsaesser, Thomas 46
Erdem, Kutay 130
Erkmen, Emre 8
Ewing, Katherine Pratt 42, 43, 80
Ezli, Özkan 8, 10, 138, 149, 211

Fassbinder, Rainer Werner 6, 112, 136–138, 142–143, 196
Ferri, Gabriella 193
Foster, Hal 89
Fowler, Catherine 88
Freud, Sigmund 64, 66, 68
  Freudian 65, 67, 78

Gaines, Jane 83
Galt, Rosalind 14
Ganti, Tejaswini 183–185
Gemünden, Gerd 63, 190

Gentile, Ginger 82
George, Götz 143
Godard, Jean-Luc 67
Göktürk, Deniz 2, 5, 8, 10, 15, 21, 33, 43, 45–46, 60, 84, 95, 112, 138, 149, 190, 193, 199
Gray, Jonathan 202
Grierson, John 79
Guattari, Felix 52
Güney, Yılmaz 6, 177
Gürel, Aysel 183
Gusner, Iris 76

Hacke, Alexander 205
Hagemann, Martin 123
Halle, Randall 8, 9, 14, 87–88, 138, 143, 149, 151–152, 162, 180, 188, 190, 194–195
Haneke, Michael 43, 110
  Hanekesque 119
Hantel, Stefan (see also Shantel) 205, 211
Harfouch, Corinna 110
Hepp, Anna 7
Herzog, Werner 145, 148
Hillenkamp, Sven 144–147
Hitchcock, Alfred 136
Holiday, Billie 192
hooks, bell 83
Horrigan, Bill 86, 91, 94
Hosseini, Bahareh 82
Hughes, John 136
Huntington, Samuel 27

Iñárritu, Alejandro González 157, 210

Jameson, Fredric 63
Jones, Quincy 191

Kaplan, E. Ann 83
Karpf, Ernst 8
Kasimatis, Zaharias 193
Kaye, Nick 88
Kazantzakis, Nikos 197

Kelek, Necla 33
Kekilli, Sibel 37, 40–43, 154, 168–169, 176
Kinski, Klaus 137, 139, 145, 147
Kinskiesque 146
Kıvanç, Ümit 204
Kızıltan, Özer 206
Klausmann, Rainer 204
Kleinert, Andreas 63
Kleist, Heinrich von 113, 116–117
Kluge, Alexander 197
Köse, Nursel 40–41
Kosnick, Kira 128, 178
Koyuncu, Kazım 15, 200, 204–208, 211
Kusturica, Emir 180
Kurtuluş, Mehmet 14, 136–148
Kutlucan, Hussi 6, 42
Kwon, Miwon 89

Lacan, Jacques 66
Laschet, Armin 109–110, 112
LaValley, Al 143
Lawson, Nigella 195
Leacock, Richard 67
Lebow, Alisa 88–90, 95
Leibovitz, Annie 141
Lennon, John 141
Lewis, Juliette 114
Lilienthal, Peter 12, 63

Maccarone, Angelina 75
MacCrimmon, Brenna 205
Mackenzie, Jenny 82
Malik, Sarita 5, 43
Mandel, Ruth 9, 99, 124, 180
Mani, B. Venkat 9, 99, 152, 161, 167, 177
Mann, Thomas 197
Maron, Monika 33
Massey, Doreen 29, 199
Mayne, Judith 142, 143
Mennel, Barbara 8, 45, 75–76, 84, 95, 110, 138, 143, 149, 190, 210
Mereilles, Fernando 157

Merkel, Angela 151, 156, 186, 188
Merleau-Ponty, Maurice 61
Moorti, Sujata 29
Mortimer, Claire 180
Mulvey, Laura 75, 77–78, 82, 137, 182–183, 203

Naficy, Hamid 8, 46
Najafi, Ayat 82
Nichols, Bill 79
Nolte, Nick 114

Ono, Yoko 141
Oliver, Jamie 195
Otto, Natalino 193–194
Özdemir, Oktay 110–111, 117
Özdoğan, Abdullah 170
Özge, Asli 7–8

Panahi, Jafar 82
Pennebaker, D. A. 67
Perisemboğlu, Tayfun 126
Pleitgen, Fritz 109
Polat, Ayşe 6, 7, 12, 95, 169–170
Priessner, Martina 7

Rancière, Jacques 13, 45, 48–49
Refig, Halit 95
Rice, Brian 179–181
Riemann, Katja 63
Rich, B. Ruby 75
Roberts, Martin 199
Rogoff, Irit 91
Rouch, Jean 67
Rowe, Kathleen 31

Safranski, Rüdiger 116–118
Sahin, A. Anil 130–131
Salem, El Hedi ben 137, 142, 143
Sam, Şevval 205, 206
Samdereli, Yasemin 1
Sander, Helke 76
Sanders-Brahms, Helma 5, 33, 46
Sarrazin, Thilo 33, 97
Saul, Anno 7, 188

Sauer, Martina 130
Sayar, Vecdi 172, 211
Schein, Louisa 180
Schmidt, Ruth 130
Schoonover, Karl 15
Schröder, Gerhard 150, 155
Scorsese, Martin 62–63, 66, 120, 198, 211
Şen, Faruk 130
Seyhan, Azade 8–9
Shantel (*see also* Hantel, Stefan) 193, 205
Shaw, Artie 191, 192
Shaw, George Bernard 31
Shohat, Ella 29
Sieg, Katrin 9, 16
Silverman, Kaja 143
Sinka, Margit 181
Sirk, Douglas 182
Sollima, Sergio 196
Spinoza, Baruch de 54
Stam, Robert 29, 83
Sternberg, Claudia 10, 213
Stoiber, Edmund 109, 112
Stokes, Martin 184, 185
Strempel, Gesine 76

Tanrıöğen, Settar 41
Taşkın, Yusuf 183

Tessnow, Gregor 111
Theweleit, Klaus 139
Thiel, Andreas 203, 210
Trotta, Margarete von 110
Türeli, Ipek 92, 95
Tutal, Nermin 130
Tykwer, Tom 181

Ünel, Birol 14, 136–140, 144–147, 154
Üner, Idil 50
Ustaoğlu, Yeşim 126

Walkowitz, Rebecca 177
Wartenberg, Thomas E. 23
Wasser, Frederick 178
Waugh, Thomas 79
Wenders, Wim 190, 192, 196
Wolf, Christa 211

Yavuz, Yüksel 6, 22, 62, 75, 95, 169–170
Yigit, Tamer 49, 51
Yilmaz, Cem 131
Yıldırım, Özgür 169
Young, Angus 192

Zirner, August 110, 114
Zwick, Joel 24

Index of Films

2 Girls (*İki Genç Kız*, Kutluğ Ataman, 2005) 95
A Love in Saigon (*Eine Liebe in Saigon*, Uwe Janson, 2005) 140
Adelheid and Her Murderers (*Adelheid und ihre Mörder*, Stefan Bartmann et al., 1993–2007) 140
Ae Fond Kiss... (Ken Loach, 2004) 24
Afghan Girls Can Kick (Bahareh Hosseini, 2008) 82
After the Game (*Nach dem Spiel*, Aysun Bademsoy, 1997) 6, 72, 74
Aguirre: The Wrath of God (*Aguirre, der Zorn Gottes*, Werner Herzog, 1972) 145
Ali: Fear Eats the Soul (*Angst essen Seele auf*, Rainer Werner Fassbinder, 1974) 6, 24, 136–137, 142
Alice in the Cities (*Alice in den Städten*, Wim Wenders, 1974) 190
Almanya: Welcome in Germany (*Almanya-Willkommen in Deutschland*, Yasemin Samdereli, 2011) 1, 7
American Friend, The (*Der amerikanische Freund*, Wim Wenders, 1977) 196
April Children (*Aprilkinder*, Yüksel Yavuz, 1998) 6, 19, 21–22
Autumn (*Sonbahar*, Özcan Alper, 2008) 208

Babel (Alejandro González Iñárritu, 2006) 210

Bend It Like Beckham (Gurinder Chadha, 2002) 73
Bill Cosby Show, The (Bill Cosby, Edwin Weinberger, Michael Zagor, 1969–71) 191
Birds of Exile (*Gurbet Kuşları*, Halit Refig, 1964) 95
Black Sea Files (Ursula Biemann, 2005) 207, 208, 211
Boxing Girl (*Ein Mädchen im Ring*, Aysun Bademsoy, 1996) 82
Breath, The (*Nefes: Vatan Sağolsun*, Levent Semerci, 2009) 134
Breathless (*À bout de souffle*, Jean-Luc Godard, 1960) 67
Bride & Prejudice (Gurinder Chadha, 2004) 20, 30
Brothers and Sisters (*Geschwister—Kardeşler*, Thomas Arslan, 1997) 6, 44, 45, 110

Cabinet of Dr. Caligari, The (*Das Cabinet des Dr. Caligari*, Robert Wiene, 1920) 138
Cape Fear (Martin Scorsese, 1991) 114, 120
Chiko (Özgür Yildirim, 2008) 110
Cholera Street (*Ağir Roman*, Mustafa Altıoklar, 1997) 184
Chronicle of a Summer (*Chronique d'un été*, Jean Rouch, 1960) 67–68
Cosby Show, The (Jay Sandrich et al., 1984–92) 43

Crossing the Bridge: The Sound of Istanbul (Fatih Akın, 2005) 156, 189, 193, 199, 205, 208

Dare to Dream: The Story of the US Women's Soccer Team (Ouisie Shapiro, 2005) 82
Dealer (Thomas Arslan, 1999) 44–45, 49–51
Death in the Haunted House (*Tod in der Geisterbahn*, Ulrich Stark, 1994) 140
Distant (*Uzak*, Nuri Bilge Ceylan, 2002) 95
During Summertime—the Visible World (*Im Sommer—Die sichtbare Welt*, Thomas Arslan, 1992) 46–48, 50
Düğün – The Wedding (*Düğün – Die Heirat*, Ismet Elçi, 1991) 19, 21–22

East is East (Damien O'Donnell, 1999) 31
Edge of Heaven, The (*Auf der anderen Seite*, Fatih Akın, 2007) 10, 15, 36, 39, 41, 138, 156–157, 160, 165, 187, 189–190, 193, 195, 198–205, 208–210
Educating Rita (Lewis Gilbert, 1983) 31
English for Beginners (*Englisch für Anfänger*, Hannelore Gottschalk, 1982) 96
Everything Will Be Fine (*Alles wird gut*, Angelina Maccarone and Fatima El-Tayeb, 1997) 75
Evet, I Do! (*Evet, ich will!*, Sinan Akkus, 2009) 19, 20, 23–30

Face to Face (*Ansikte mot ansikte*, Ingmar Bergman, 1976) 196
Face to Face (*Faccia a faccia*, Sergio Sollima, 1967) 196
Faraway, So Close! (*In weiter Ferne, so nah!*, Wim Wenders, 1993) 192

Father, The (*Baba*, Yılmaz Güney, 1971) 6
Ferris Bueller's Day Off (John Hughes, 1986) 136
Finnish Tango (*Finnischer Tango*, Buket Alakuş, 2008) 7
Fitzcarraldo (Werner Herzog, 1982) 145
Football Under Cover (*Anstoß in Teheran*, David Assmann and Ayat Najafi, 2008) 82
Forty Square Meters of Germany (*40 qm Deutschland*, Tevfik Başer, 1986) 5, 46
Four Weddings and a Funeral (Mike Newell, 1994) 20, 23, 24, 31
From Far Away (*Aus der Ferne*, Thomas Arslan, 2006) 45, 60
Funny Games (Michael Haneke, 1997) 110, 120

German Police (*Deutsche Polizisten*, Aysun Bademsoy, 1999) 82
Girls of Summer, The (Max Tash, 2008) 82
Girls on the Pitch (*Mädchen am Ball*, Aysun Bademsoy, 1995) 72, 74, 79, 80
Goals for Girls (Ginger Gentile and Gabriel Balanovsky, 2010) 82
Guess Who's Coming to Dinner (Stanley Kramer, 1967) 24

Head-On (*Gegen die Wand*, Fatih Akın, 2004) 15, 21, 37, 40–41, 75, 124, 138, 140, 145–147, 153–155, 157, 158, 164, 165, 169, 175–177, 182–185, 187, 189–191, 195, 196, 199, 205, 208
Heart of St. Pauli, The (*Das Herz von St. Pauli*, Eugen York, 1957) 194
Honey (*Bal*, Semih Kaplanoğlu, 2010) 208

I Am My Mother's Daughter (*Ben Annemin Kızıyım-Ich bin die*

Tochter meiner Mutter, Seyhan Derin, 1996) 6, 61, 75
I Passed Through with Songs: A Film for Kazım (*Şarkılarla Geçtim Aranızdan: Kazım İçin Bir Film*, Ümit Kıvanç, 2008) 200, 204–205, 208
I Saw the Sun (*Günesi Gördüm*, Mahsun Kırmızıgül, 2009) 134
In July (*Im Juli*, Fatih Akın, 2000) 15, 42, 62, 140, 152–153, 175–177, 180–182, 185, 187, 189–190
In the Game (*Ich gehe jetzt rein*, Aysun Bademsoy, 2008) 72, 74–75
In the Shadows (*Im Schatten*, Thomas Arslan, 2010) 7, 45
Infidel, The (Josh Appignanesi, 2010) 31
It Happened One Night (Frank Capra, 1934) 23, 25
Italianamerican (Martin Scorsese, 1974) 62

Jew Süß (*Jud Süss*, Veit Harlan, 1940) 138
Jungle Fever (Spike Lee, 1991) 24

Katzelmacher (Rainer Werner Fassbinder, 1969) 138, 142, 196
Kebab Connection (Anno Saul, 2004) 7, 188–189, 191, 195
Kick like a Girl (Jenny Mackenzie, 2008) 82
Kings of the Road (*Im Lauf der Zeit*, Wim Wenders, 1976) 190
Küba (Kutluğ Ataman, 2004) 14, 84–95

La Habanera (Detlef Sierck, 1937) 138
Lola and Billy the Kid (*Lola + Bilidikid*, Kutluğ Ataman, 1999) 6, 40, 42, 84–85, 95
Luk's Luck (*Luks Glück*, Ayşe Polat, 2010) 7

M.A.S.H. (Robert Altman, 1970) 136
Me Boss, You Sneakers! (*Ich Chef, Du Turnschuh*, Hussi Kutlucan, 1998) 6, 42
Mean Streets (Martin Scorsese, 1973) 62
Men on the Bridge–Köprüdekiler (Asli Özge, 2009) 7
Method (Ulaş Inan Inaç, 2011) 145
Mississippi Masala (Mira Nair, 1991) 24
Monsoon Wedding (Mira Nair, 2001) 20
Moon and Other Lovers, The (*Der Mond und andere Liebhaber*, Bernd Böhlich, 2008) 145, 147
Moonstruck (Norman Jewison, 1987) 31
My Best Fiend (*Mein liebster Feind*, Werner Herzog, 1999) 145
My Best Friend's Wedding (Paul John Hogan, 1997) 20
My Big Fat Greek Wedding (Joel Zwick, 2002) 20, 23, 24, 27, 30
My Crazy Turkish Wedding (*Meine verrückte türkische Hochzeit*, Stefan Holtz, 2006) 19–20, 26, 31
My Fair Lady (George Cukor, 1964) 31
My Father, the Guestworker (*Mein Vater, der Gastarbeiter*, Yüksel Yavuz, 1995) 62
My Mother (*Anam*, Buket Alakuş, 2000) 75

Naked (*Nackt*, Doris Dörrie, 2002) 137, 139–141, 143
Neighbors in Europe (*Nachbarn in Europa*) 178

Ode to Cologne: A Rock 'n' Roll Film (*Viel passiert—Der BAP-Film*, Wim Wenders, 2002) 190
Offside (*Eine andere Liga*, Buket Alakuş, 2005) 72–73, 75–78

Offside (Jafar Panahi, 2006) 82
On the Edge of the Cities (*Am Rande der Städte*, Aysun Bademsoy, 2006) 82
On the Sunny Side (*Auf der Sonnenseite*, Richard Huber, 2008) 136–137, 143
One Fine Day (*Der schöne Tag*, Thomas Arslan, 2001) 44
Ottoman Cowboys, The (*Yahşi Batı*, Ömer Faruk Sorak, 2010) 131

Pandora's Box (*Pandora'nın Kutusu*, Yeşim Ustaoğlu, 2008) 208
Paradise (Kutluğ Ataman, 2006) 86
Pretty Woman (Garry Marshall, 1990) 23, 31
Promise, The (*Das Versprechen*, Margarethe von Trotta, 1994) 110
Psycho (Alfred Hitchcock, 1960) 136

Rage (*Wut*, Züli Aladağ, 2006) 14, 109–120
Run Lola Run (*Lola rennt*, Tom Tykwer, 1998) 181

semiha b. unplugged (Kutluğ Ataman, 1997) 85, 95
Serpent's Tale (*Karanlık Sular*, Kutluğ Ataman, 1993) 95
Shirin's Wedding (*Shirins Hochzeit*, Helma Sanders-Brahms, 1976) 5, 19, 33, 46
Short Sharp Shock (*Kurz und schmerzlos*, Fatih Akın, 1998) 6, 40, 45, 62, 68, 110, 138, 140, 152, 160, 189
Sleepless Night (*Nuit Blanche*, Frédéric Jardin, 2011) 145
Solino (Fatih Akın, 2002) 152, 189–191, 195
Soul Kitchen (Fatih Akın, 2009) 7, 15, 40, 42, 145, 149, 156–160, 186–197
Student of Prague, The (*Der Student von Prag*, Henrik Galeen, 1926) 138

Through a Glass Darkly (*Såsom i en spegel*, Ingmar Bergman, 1961) 195
Tough Enough (*Knallhart*, Detlev Buck, 2006) 102, 110–111, 120
Tour Abroad (*Auslandstournee*, Ayşe Polat, 2000) 6
Transylvania (Tony Gatlif, 2006) 145, 147
Trilogy: The Weeping Meadow (*Trilogia: To livadi pou darkyzei*, Theodoros Angelopoulus, 2004) 208
Tunnel, The (*Der Tunnel*, Roland Suso Richter, 2001) 140
Turkish for Beginners (*Türkisch für Anfänger*, Oliver Schmitz et al., 2006–8) 14, 96–108, 111, 120
Turn Down the Music (*Mach die Musik leiser*, Thomas Arslan, 1994) 44
Turkish Kraut (*Rotkohl und Blaukraut*, Anna Hepp, 2011) 7

Un chien andalou (Luis Buñuel, 1929) 195
Unpolished, The (*Die Unerzogenen*, Pia Marais, 2007) 139, 145, 147
Until the End of the World (*Bis ans Ende der Welt*, Wim Wenders, 1991) 192

Vacation (*Ferien*, Thomas Arslan, 2007) 7, 44
Vavien (Yağmur and Durul Taylan, 2009) 208

Waiting for the Clouds (*Bulutları Beklerken*, Yeşim Ustaoğlu, 2003) 208
We Are Based Down South (*Wir sitzen im Süden*, Martina Priessner, 2010) 7
We Forgot to Go Back (*Wir haben vergessen zurückzukehren*, Fatih Akın, 2001) 14, 59, 61, 63–71, 160

Wedding Planner, The (Adam Shankman, 2001) 20
Wedding Singer, The (Frank Coraci, 1998) 20
When We Leave (*Die Fremde*, Feo Aladağ, 2010) 7, 13, 21, 22, 32–43, 64
Wings of Desire (*Der Himmel über Berlin*, Wim Wenders, 1987) 196–197

Women Who Wear Wigs (Kutluğ Ataman, 1999) 85–86

Y Tu Mamá También (Alfonso Cuarón, 2002) 210
Yasemin (Hark Bohm, 1988) 5, 19, 21
Your Home—Our Home (*Ihre Heimat—Unsere Heimat*) 178

www.ingramcontent.com/pod-product-compliance
Lightning Source LLC
Chambersburg PA
CBHW072149100526
44589CB00015B/2156